Excellence in Reporting

Excellence in Reporting

Edward Jay Friedlander
University of Arkansas at Little Rock

Harry Marsh
Kansas State University

Mike Masterson
The Arizona Republic

West Publishing Company

St. Paul * New York * Los Angeles * San Francisco

Cover photo: Misti Snow, Mindworks editor, and Neal St. Anthony, business reporter, Minneapolis Star-Tribune.
Cover/Interior Design: Adrianne Onderdonk Dudden
Copyediting: Jan Richardson
Interior Art: Alice Thiede/Carto-Graphics
Indexing: Virginia Hobbs

COPYRIGHT © 1987 By WEST PUBLISHING COMPANY
50 W. Kellogg Boulevard
P.O. Box 64526
St. Paul, MN 55164–1003

All rights reserved

Printed in the United States of America

Library of Congress Cataloging in
 Publication Data

ISBN: 0–314–29523–2

PORTRAIT PHOTOS

Page 105 Jon Franklin, photo courtesy of The Baltimore Sun; **page 112** William K. Marimow, photo courtesy of The Philadelphia Inquirer; **page 113** David Zucchino, photo courtesy of The Philadelphia Inquirer; **pages 158 and 159** Peter Rinearson, photo by Christopher Johns; **page 179** David Hacker, photo courtesy of the Wichita Eagle-Beacon; **page 173** Robert C. Trussell, staff photo by Gary Dunkin, Kansas City Star; **page 196** Richard Johnson, photo courtesy of the Kansas City Star; **page 196** David Hayes, staff photo by Gary Dunkin, the Kansas City Times; **page 214** Nancy Weaver photo by Morgan Ono; **page 240** Rick Alm, staff photo by Gary Dunkin, the Kansas City Star; **page 249** Roger Linscott, photo by Joel Librizzi; **pages 272 and 273** Lucy Morgan, photo courtesy of the St. Petersburg Times; **pages 271 and 273** Jack Reed, photo by Robin Donina, St. Petersburg Times.

To Roberta, Ellie and Kathleen
and to the Pulitzer Prize winners,
past, present and future

About the Authors

Edward Jay Friedlander has reported for the Northern Wyoming Daily News in Worland, the Delaware County Daily Times in Chester, Pa., the Longmont Daily Times-Call in Longmont, Colo. and The Denver Post. He has written free-lance stories for 50 other newspapers and magazines. He also edited the 43rd, 44th and 45th annual reports of the Federal Communications Commission. Friedlander has a bachelor's degree from the University of Wyoming, a master's from the University of Denver and a doctorate from the University of Northern Colorado. He is a professor of journalism at the University of Arkansas at Little Rock.

Harry Marsh has worked for nine newspapers, ranging from the Hillsboro, Texas, Evening Mirror to the New York Daily News. Marsh has a bachelor's degree from Baylor University, a master's from Columbia University and a doctorate from the University of Texas. He has taught at Baylor and the University of Arkansas at Fayetteville and is currently a professor of journalism at Kansas State University.

Mike Masterson is editor of the investigative team at The Arizona Republic in Phoenix. Prior to joining that newspaper, Masterson was editorial projects director for six Arkansas dailies. He also has been editor of two Arkansas daily newspapers and a reporter for the Los Angeles Times and the Chicago Sun-Times. He is a member of the board of directors of the Investigative Reporters and Editors group. Masterson, the winner of two dozen national journalism prizes, has twice won the IRE national award honoring the best investigative reporter in America and is the only four-time winner of the Robert F. Kennedy journalism award. He also was one of 40 national finalists for the Journalist in Space program. He holds a bachelor's degree in journalism.

Contents

Preface	xiii
To The Student	xix

PART ONE: Remembering the Basics

Chapter 1 NEWS BASICS — 2

A Definition of News	4
Elements of News	5
NO NEWS HERE	6
MAKING THE WRONG DECISION?	8
Deciding What to Exclude	10
FOUR HUNDRED MILE-PER-HOUR CHICKENS	11
Accuracy	13
Objectivity	15
Completeness, Fairness and Balance	16
Consequences of Stories	17
The Public	18
Complaints	21
HOW TO IMPROVE THE CREDIBILITY OF AMERICA'S NEWSPAPERS	21

Chapter 2 NEWSROOM BASICS — 26

The Reporter	28
Newsroom Organization and the Role of the Editor	29
More About the Copy Desk	32
How a Reporter Functions in an Electronic Newsroom	33
The Traditional Newsroom	35
Dealing with Deadlines	36
The Changing Newspaper	39
ANOTHER ANSWER: THE "TAILORED" NEWSPAPER	40

Broadcast News ... 41
   The Reporter ... 41
   Newsroom Organization and the Role of the Editor ... 42
   How a Reporter Functions in a Broadcast Newsroom ... 43

Chapter 3 NEWSWRITING BASICS ... 46

The Summary News Lead: Who, What, When, Where, Why and How ... 48
Varying the Lead ... 49
The Inverted Pyramid ... 50
Electronic and Traditional Copy Preparation ... 52
Writing Obituaries ... 54
An Overview of Wire Service Style ... 57
Rewriting the Press Release ... 59
Writing the Simple News Story ... 60
Attribution ... 62
Writing the Multiple Incident Story ... 63
Copy Editing for Clarity and Conciseness ... 64
Radio Newswriting ... 65
   Radio Newswriting Style ... 66
   Types of Radio Stories ... 67

PART TWO: Reporting News

Chapter 4 GENERAL ASSIGNMENT REPORTING ... 70

The General Assignment ... 72
The Advance Speech Story ... 73
Covering the Speech ... 74
SPEECH COVERAGE TIPS ... 74
Note-Taking Techniques ... 75
   Writing the Story ... 77
The Advance Meeting Story ... 79
Covering the Meeting ... 81
MEETING COVERAGE TIPS ... 81
Covering the Press Conference ... 83
PRESS CONFERENCE TIPS ... 83
Writing Under Deadline ... 87
Winning A Pulitzer Prize Under Deadline ... 88
"Toutle School Turns Rescue Site" ... 90
SOME CHARACTERISTICS OF EXCELLENCE ... 92

Chapter 5 INTERVIEWING ... 95

A Documented Conversation ... 96
Preparing for the Interview ... 96

The Effective Interview	98
Further Attribution Guidelines	101
PROTECTING YOUR SOURCES	102
Using Recording Devices	103
SECRET TAPING OF TELEPHONE INTERVIEWS	104
Advice from Pulitzer Prize-Winning Reporters	104
"Chemical Workings of the Brain Herald Psychiatry's New Frontier"	105
THE ART OF INTERVIEWING	108
Putting it all Together	110
Organizing the Interview Story	110
Writing the Story	111
"The K-9 Cases"	112
"Yasir Arafat Tries to Dodge the Bullet"	113
Keeping an Open Mind	114

Chapter 6 USING DOCUMENTS EFFECTIVELY   116

The Paper Trail	118
Practice Makes Perfect	119
Sources for Documents	120
YOUR COMMUNITY'S VITAL STATISTICS	122
Using Data Bases and Libraries	123
Keeping an Eye on Public Officials	126
Pursuits of the Paper Trail	128
RESEARCHING GAIL SMITH	129
Using Freedom of Information Acts	136
USING POLICE RECORDS	136

PART THREE: Beat and Specialized Reporting

Chapter 7 BEAT REPORTING TECHNIQUES   142

The Beat	144
Making Friends and Influencing People	145
Transforming the Press Release	148
Mastering Five Tricks of the Trade	152
SEEKING THE TRUTH	153
Covering Southern Illinois	154
A Pulitzer Prize-Winning Beat Series	157
"Making It Fly"	158
"The Delivery: It Was Two Weeks Late and Eastern Was Impatient"	159

Chapter 8 THE BASICS: FIRE, POLICE AND COURT REPORTING 168

Covering Fires 170
    Using Fire Department Records 172
"By the Minute, Dispatchers Hear Tragedy Unfold" 173
Covering the Police Beat 175
    Police Department Organization 175
A DAY IN A POLICE BEAT REPORTER'S LIFE 177
    Interviewing Witnesses and Victims 178
"The Day the Music Stopped" 179
Covering the Courts 182
    Types of Court Systems 183
HINTS FROM A VETERAN COURT REPORTER 184
    A Criminal Case Step by Step 186

Chapter 9 GOVERNMENT REPORTING 190

Local Government 192
    Municipal Board, Commission or Council 193
    Other Boards and Commissions 194
    Mayor or City Manager 194
    City Attorney 194
    Other City Officials 195
"City's Inspectors Lie, Cheat on Jobs" 196
State Government 198
    Governor 198
A DAY ON THE STATE CAPITOL BEAT 199
    Legislature 200
    Attorney General 201
    Secretary of State 201
    Boards and Commissions 201
    Lobbyists 201
Excellence in State Government Reporting 202
"Conferees Reach Tentative Accord on Education" 202
National Government 204
Government Reporting Tips 205

Chapter 10 SPECIALIZED REPORTING 208

Education Reporting 210
HINTS FROM A YOUNG EDUCATION REPORTER 211
"Desegregation in Mississippi Leaves Public Schools Wanting" 214
Business and Economic Reporting 216
Agricultural Reporting 221
Consumer Reporting 222
Science and Medical Reporting 223

Arts, Entertainment and Sports Reporting   225
Finding a Specialty   227

PART FOUR: Presenting the News in Special Ways

Chapter 11 INTERPRETIVE STORIES   230

A New Kind of Reporting   232
Interpreting the News   233
In-Depth Interpretive Stories: Interpreting a Disaster   236
INTERPRETIVE TECHNIQUES   238
"Critical Design Change is Linked to Collapse of Hyatt's
   Sky Walks"   240
News Analyses   244
Columns and Editorials   245
"Our $213 Million Gift Horse"   249
Using Sources   250
   Types of Sources   251
   Interpretive Techniques   254
A Pitfall   255

Chapter 12 INVESTIGATIVE STORIES   258

Uncovering the Covered   260
Practicing First Amendment Journalism   261
The Investigative Reporter   263
How to Begin   264
Interviewing Hostile Sources   265
Unnamed Sources   266
Using Records   267
Blending People and Paper   268
ADVICE FROM A PROFESSIONAL INVESTIGATIVE REPORTER 269
Anatomy of a Pulitzer Prize Investigative Story 269
"Inside the Pasco County Sheriff's Department"   271
"Pasco Deputy Did Not Reveal Arrest Record"   272
"Doing Business With the Boss in Pasco"   273

Chapter 13 SERIES   276

Why the Series?"   278
Types of Series   279
Reprints: Creating a Series After the Fact   280
Advantages of Series   281
Disadvantages of Series   282
Thinking Through the Traditional Series   284
Organizing and Writing the Series   285

THE SERIES: LIKE PUTTING SHOES IN A BOX	287
Tantalizing the Reader	287
Using Photos in a Series	289
Examining a Pulitzer Prize-Winning Series	290
"A Story of Dust, Delays—and Death"	293
"A Living Death: A Worker Waits for Company's Help"	294
"States Let Violators' Cases Gather Dust"	295

PART FIVE: Responsibility

Chapter 14 LAW, ETHICS AND TASTE — 298

The First Amendment	300
Libel: A Type of Defamation	302
An Overview of Defamation Defenses	305
Truth	305
Privilege	305
Fair Comment and Criticism	306
Consent	306
Public Officials, Public Persons and Private Figures	306
THE COST OF LIBEL	307
Invasion of Privacy	308
Intrusion	309
Publicity	309
False Light	309
Appropriation	310
An Overview of Invasion of Privacy Defenses	310
Obscenity	311
National Security	311
Fair Trial and Free Press	313
Reporters' Ethics	315
The Public	316
Those You Identify	316
Sources	317
Other News People	318
Credibility and Good Taste	319
CREDIBILITY: TWO EXAMPLES	320
A Pulitzer Hoax	324
Appendix A: Wire Service Style Guide	327
Appendix B: America's Open Records Laws	337
Index	369

Preface

Focus of the Book

Journalism graduates who seek newspaper employment frequently first work for weekly newspapers or dailies of moderate circulation. While this textbook will serve students skilled or lucky enough to find their first job with one of America's biggest newspapers, the book is primarily designed for students who will become reporters for smaller publications. Although reporting techniques are essentially similar at all newspapers, reporters who work for smaller newspapers are more likely to be given significant responsibility quickly. They may find challenges in general assignment and beat reporting, interpretive, investigative and series stories all within the first year or two of employment. These challenges must be met skillfully, lest the reporter, his or her publication, journalism at large and the community suffer.

Thus, many examples in this textbook are drawn from award-winning newspapers with a circulation of less than 100,000. In studying stories from publications like The Daily News in Longview, Wash., The Clarion-Ledger in Jackson, Miss., and The Berkshire Eagle in Pittsfield, Mass., students should be able to more readily identify with the work environment they will soon encounter. Larger newspapers are not ignored, though. Readers will also find stories from The Baltimore Evening Sun, The Philadelphia Inquirer, The Seattle Times, the Kansas City Star and the Kansas City Times, the St. Petersburg Times and The Charlotte Observer. Each of these publications has won the newspaper field's most coveted award, the Pulitzer Prize.

Pulitzer Prize-Winning Examples

The title of this textbook, "Excellence in Reporting," reflects our premise that journalistic excellence—high quality work accompanied by enthusiasm, courage and integrity—is rewarded by professional success in this increasingly competitive field.

Of course, excellence is difficult to define. We have used newspaper journalism's best known award, the Pulitzer Prize, as a convenient yardstick. Much of the advice in this book comes from Pulitzer Prize winners. The book also offers more than a dozen Pulitzer Prize-winning stories or excerpts for reinforcement and discussion.

In all, nearly 40 experienced journalists of national stature contributed to this book either by their example or through interviews. The interviews and examples provide a blend of realism and idealism—the journalists tell it "like it is," and where necessary, like it should be.

Other Features of the Book

Accompanying boxed articles provide reinforcement of points made in the body of each chapter. An entire chapter is devoted to series, a form rarely addressed in reporting texts but one becoming increasingly important for in-depth reporting. Special attention is given to women newspaper journalists, a group that now accounts for nearly 40 percent of America's weekly and daily newspaper reporters (and more than 60 percent of U.S. college journalism students). Finally, the book follows the style guidelines of The Associated Press (with a few minor exceptions). This should help students master the style used by many U.S. newspapers.

The book is also up-to-date (virtually all of the examples in the text were published after 1980) and authoritative (the authors have a combined total of 75 years practicing and teaching journalism, and one of the authors has earned more than 20 national journalism awards).

Organization of the Book

This book is designed for use in a reporting course. Because reporting students typically will have taken a prerequisite newswriting course, Part One is provided only for review and reinforcement. Parts Two, Three and Five provide the essentials covered in most reporting courses and Part Four provides material for those courses that cover interpretive, investigative and series reporting.

Appendices

Appendix A is a quick reference guide to spelling and the appropriate use of proper names, as determined by The Associated Press and United Press International. Students will be able to use the appendix as a supplement to the AP and UPI stylebooks.

Appendix B provides a basic listing of open records laws for each state. This material is excerpted from a study done by The Society of Professional Journalists, Sigma Delta Chi, in the mid-1980s. The state-by-state listing will permit students to compare open records laws in the state in which they are attending college with the laws in other states.

Instructor's Manual

The instructor's manual contains suggestions for structuring the course, classroom exercises and projects, audio-visual suggestions and examination questions for each chapter. The manual is available to adopters of the text.

Acknowledgements

The authors wish to thank the following individuals for their contributions to this book: W. Wat Hopkins, Jeanne Norton, Manny Paraschos and Luther W. "Sonny" Sanders of the University of Arkansas at Little Rock Department of Journalism faculty; Carol Oukrop and Roberta Applegate of the Kansas State University Department of Journalism and Mass Communication faculty; Geoffrey S. George, Maxine "Max" Parker and Walter Hussman Jr. of WEHCO Media; and Nancy Crochiere and Jean Cook of West Publishing; and the reviewers of the manuscript:

> Maria Braden Clark, University of Kentucky
> George Flynn, California State University-Fresno
> Roy Halverson, University of Oregon
> Ivan Innerst, University of New Mexico
> Richard Lentz, Arizona State University
> Jeff Smith University of Iowa
> Richard Streckfuss, University of Nebraska-Lincoln
> Carl Stepp, University of Maryland
> Leonard Teel, Georgia State University

Credits

The authors also wish to thank the following journalists, publications and organizations for their assistance and for generously granting permission to reprint material in this book:

Excerpts of editorial material about news coverage of the Ponce disaster, Oct. 7, 1985, El Diario-La Prensa, New York, N.Y. Courtesy/El Diario-La Prensa. Reprinted by permission.

Excerpts from "Public Perception of Newspapers: Credibility," September, 1984, by the American Press Institute, Reston, Va. Reprinted by permission.

Excerpts from "Why We Do What We Do," by Dave Ranney, former editor of The Hillsboro Star-Journal, Hillsboro, Kan. Reprinted by permission.

Excerpts from "Plans We'd Rather Not Make," by Mike Moore, The Quill, November, 1985, The Society of Professional Journalists, Sigma Delta Chi, Chicago, Ill. Reprinted by permission.

Information about journalism placement and salaries, from 1985 and 1986 Dow Jones Newspaper Fund news releases, The Dow Jones Newspaper Fund, Princeton, N.J. Reprinted by permission.

Excerpts from "'Tailored' Newspaper to Answer Dreams," a 1983 report by Clark Hoyt and Trueman Farris for The Associated Press Managing Editors Association Writing and Editing Committee. Reprinted by permission of Trueman Farris, managing editor, the Milwaukee Sentinel, Milwaukee, Wis.

"Toutle School Turns Rescue Site," by Linda Wilson and Tom Paulu, May 19, 1980, The Daily News, Longview, Wash. Reprinted by permission.

Excerpts from "The Mind Fixers," by Jon Franklin, July 23–31, 1984, The Baltimore Evening Sun, Baltimore, Md. Reprinted by permission of The Baltimore Evening Sun.

"Sourcery," by James Polk, David Hayes and Steve Weinberg for the Investigative Reporters and Editors association, Columbia, Mo. Reprinted by permission.

Excerpts from the "K–9" series, by William K. Marimow, The Philadelphia Inquirer, Philadelphia, Pa. Reprinted by permission of The Philadelphia Inquirer, April 15–Aug. 3, 1984.

Excerpts from "Yasir Arafat Tries to Dodge the Bullet," by David Zucchino, The Philadelphia Inquirer, Philadelphia, Pa. Reprinted by permission of The Philadelphia Inquirer.

Excerpts from "The Paper Trail: How To Dig Into Documents," by Steve Weinberg, August, 1985, the Washington Journalism Review, Washington, D.C. Reprinted by permission from the Washington Journalism Review.

Sample FOI request letter from "How to Use the Federal FOI Act," Fifth Edition, edited by Elaine P. English, Esq., Director, FOI Service Center, a project of the Reporters Committee for Freedom of the Press, Washington, D.C. Reprinted by permission.

Excerpts from "Gaining Access '84," by Rick Dent, David Freedman and Ben Ginsberg for The Society of Professional Journalists, Sigma Delta Chi, Chicago, Ill. Reprinted by permission.

"The Truth," by James Polk, David Hayes and Steve Weinberg for the Investigative Reporters and Editors association, Columbia, Mo. Reprinted by permission.

Excerpts from "Making It Fly," by Peter Rinearson, The Seattle Times, June 19–26, 1983. Reprinted by permission.

"By the Minute, Dispatchers Hear Tragedy Unfold," by Robert C. Trussell, July 19, 1981, the Kansas City Star, Kansas City, Mo. Reprinted by permission of The Kansas City Star Company, copyright 1981. Excerpts from "The Day the Music Stopped," by David Hacker, July 25, 1981, the Kansas City Times. Reprinted by permission of The Kansas City Star Company, copyright 1981. "City's Inspectors Lie, Cheat On Jobs," by Richard M. Johnson and David Hayes, Jan. 30, 1983, the Kansas City Star. Reprinted by permisson of The Kansas City Star Company, copyright 1983.

"Conferees Reach Tentative Accord on Education," by Fred Anklam Jr., Dec. 20, 1982, The Clarion-Ledger. Reprinted from The Clarion-Ledger, Jackson, Miss. "Desegregation in Mississippi Leaves Public Schools Wanting," by Nancy Weaver, Nov. 29, 1982, The Clarion-Ledger. Reprinted from The Clarion-Ledger, Jackson, Miss.

"Critical Design Change is Linked to Collapse of Hyatt's Sky Walks," by Rick Alm and Thomas G. Watts, July 21, 1981, the Kansas City Star, Kansas City, Mo. Reprinted by permission of The Kansas City Star Company, copyright 1981.

"Our $213 Million Dollar Gift Horse," by Roger B. Linscott, March 17, 1972, The Berkshire Eagle, Pittsfield, Mass. Reprinted by permission.

Excerpts from "Inside the Pasco County Sheriff's Department" series, including "Pasco Deputy Did Not Reveal Arrest Record," by Lucy Morgan, and "Doing Business with the Boss in Pasco," by Lucy Morgan and Jack Reed, February, 1984, St. Petersburg Times, St. Petersburg, Fla. St. Petersburg Times, reprinted with permission.

Excerpts from "A Story of Dust, Delays—and Death," by Bob Drogin; excerpts from "A Living Death," by Howard Covington and Marion A. Ellis; and excerpts from "States Let Violators' Cases Gather Dust," by Howard Covington and Bob Dennis, Feb. 3–10, 1980, The Charlotte Observer. © 1980 The Charlotte Observer. Reprinted with permission.

Excerpts from "Oral Roberts, The Man, The Mystique, The Money," by Mary Hargrove, Grant Williams and Pam Infield, Feb. 3–12, 1986, The Tulsa Tribune, Tulsa, Okla. The Tulsa Tribune, reprinted by permission.

Adaption of The Associated Press Stylebook, The Associated Press, New York, N.Y. Used by Permission of The Associated Press.

To The Student

In an era when communication technology is expanding so rapidly that computer systems are outmoded by the time they are installed in newsrooms, one aspect of journalism fortunately never changes, namely, the dedication to excellence, the driving internal force that motivates young men and women to become the very best reporters and editors possible.

As in any other profession in America today, journalism is replete with mediocrity, with those content with simply drawing paychecks and fulfilling the minimum expected of them; by and large, they view journalism as a job rather than as a calling. The ordinary are quickly identified, however, because this is a profession where one cannot hide. A reporter's productivity and the quality of his or her work is regularly bared not only to the public but also to colleagues.

This book is devoted to those students who seek to achieve far beyond the minimum expected of them; to the ones whose driving fires, fanned by enthusiasm and dedication, run deep in their quests for excellence.

Edward Jay Friedlander
Harry Marsh
Mike Masterson

**Excellence
in Reporting**

PART 1
Remembering The Basics

CHAPTER 1

News Basics

A Definition of News
Elements of News
Deciding What to Exclude
Accuracy
Objectivity
Completeness, Fairness and Balance
Consequences of Stories
The Public
Complaints

A Definition of News

You have a good sense of what news is even if you haven't studied journalism. News is what you should know that you don't know. News is what has happened recently that is important to you in your daily life. News is what fascinates you, what excites you enough to say to a friend, "Hey, did you hear about . . . ?" News is what local, national and international shakers and movers are doing to affect your life. News is the unexpected event that, fortunately or unfortunately, did happen.

News is also what editors say it is. Ask a newspaper reporter if anything is ever in the paper that did not deserve to be and the reporter will probably say yes. Ask that same reporter if anything should have been in the newspaper that was not, and the answer will probably be yes again. Ask a broadcast reporter the same questions and you'll get an even louder yes because of the large number of stories competing for limited air time.

In other words, reporters and editors sometimes do not agree on what is news and often do not agree on what to emphasize in a particular news story. Reporters are the ground troops, however, and editors are the generals—and generals usually tell the troops where the war is and precisely how to fight it.

Ultimately, then, news is all of these things—what you feel is news, what you know is news, and most importantly, what the editor says is news.

News is culturally, politically and geographically defined as well. Journalists in different places see news in different ways.

German journalists provide a good example of differing cultural and geopolitical views of news because of the two decidedly different Germanys. After the defeat of Hitler in 1945, the country was partitioned into two states. The western two-thirds of Germany—commonly known today as West Germany—is governed under a constitution drawn up with the help of the United States, Great Britain and France. The eastern one-third of Germany—East Germany—was nurtured by the Soviet Union.

The West Germans developed print news media much like that of the Americans and the British. The primary role of their newspapers is to inform. West German newspapers are privately owned, timely, generally serious, accurate, largely objective and somewhat similar in appearance to American and British newspapers.

The East German newspapers, however, developed differently after the war, and 40 years later, are still different. Their role, in general, is to encourage the stability of the country and to report information that will enhance that stability. Most East German newspapers, in fact, are tied to or subsidized by national or quasi-national political organizations. As a result, many stories are delayed while numerous policy decisions are made. For example, if an airplane operated by Interflug, the state airline, crashed, the accident might not be reported. The rea-

Chapter opening photo: President Ronald Reagan holds a press conference. (AP/Wide World Photos)

son is obvious to an East German journalist. Interflug is a state airline. Reporting a crash might cause a drop in passenger boardings or at least a lapse in consumer confidence. The state and the passengers own the airline. To report a crash would be like deliberately shooting yourself in the foot, an East German journalist would reason.

Let's meet an East German editor. Between puffs on an unfiltered cigarette, she defines news: "News is the same everywhere. We define it the same as you would."

Are her stories censored?

"No, of course not," she says. "There is certainly no one standing over me saying, 'You will print this and you will not print that.'"

Would she report an airplane crash or crop failure?

"Who knows?" says the journalist. "There is an old German saying. It translates, 'The scissors are in your head.' Of course, it means that you decide what you will report and what you will not report."

Could she criticize the leader of East Germany in a story?

"Of course," the East German journalist answers. "But why would I want to? The people elected him."

You can see by the editor's answers that what is obviously news in the United States and Western Europe may or may not be news in other parts of the world. A major epidemic in Mexico is clearly news in the United States. The epidemic is probably even news in East Germany. If an epidemic occurs in East Germany, however, the story may be ignored there. (The epidemic would be news in the West, if Western journalists, in fact, learn about it.)

News is also geographically defined by the audience. For example, a major news story in Canada may be virtually unreported in the United States. Similarly, a major story in California may receive little coverage in Tennessee.

In a sense, then, every reporter and editor in the world operates with a different definition of what makes news. That definition takes national, regional, state and local interests into consideration. Strangely, a ferryboat disaster in China may be ignored by the Chinese media, prominently covered by major American news organizations, and as in China, ignored by small town U.S. media.

Elements of News

Despite the relativity of news, American reporters need a working definition of news just like a cook needs a basic recipe. Reporters, in fact, do have such a definition.

News has seven characteristics, or elements. For news to be news, it *must* have some of these elements, and in general, the more elements a particular event has, the more news value it has.

Perhaps the most important news element is *timeliness*. The more recent an event is, the more news value it has. Newspapers have time

> **NO NEWS HERE**
>
> At 1:23 a.m. local time, Saturday, April 26, 1986, an accident occurred at the Chernobyl nuclear power station 600 miles southwest of Moscow in the Soviet Union.
>
> The accident led to the evacuation of nearly 100,000 people, seriously injured hundreds and killed dozens. Yet Soviet citizens heard nothing about the accident until a Monday evening Moscow television newscaster read the following announcement: "An accident has taken place at the Chernobyl nuclear power station, and one of the reactors was damaged. Measures are being taken to eliminate the consequences of the accident. Those affected by it are being given assistance. A government commission has been set up." Period.
>
> As radiation spilled over the Soviet Union and Europe, Soviet media largely ignored the story. A week after the accident Soviet officials began to provide detailed information.
>
> The delay infuriated Western governments and even annoyed Soviet readers of Pravda, the Communist Party newspaper, according to United Press International. UPI quoted one Pravda reader who wrote: "There are many evacuees in our town but one can hear about all this only from a neighbor, not from the local newspaper. Our local radio station tells us nothing." Another reader wrote: "One hears all kinds of things—at bus stops. It seems the local mass media should use the services of specialists who would give competent recommendations and tell about the state of affairs in the region. The activities of the mass media should contribute to a great extent to the solution of the problems of those affected."

cycles. A newspaper editor is primarily interested in covering what has happened during the previous 24 hours. In a small city, a minor crime that happened the night before would be reported. If the crime occurred two nights before, however, and for some reason had not been reported in the newspaper, the likelihood of it being covered is diminished. Similarly, if a crime had happened the previous week and for some reason had gone unreported, the newspaper probably would not do a story.

Although this book deals primarily with newspaper reporting, we should mention that news elements also apply to broadcast journalism. For example, timeliness is crucial for a broadcast reporter. Radio and television reporters are accustomed to covering events as they happen, and even news as recent as a few hours old may be discarded in favor of a fresher story.

A second element is *conflict*. (The elements other than timeliness are presented in alphabetical order, rather than by order of importance.) Some sociologists have noted that war or conflict over issues such as territoriality is part of the human condition. In fact, however, most of us—if we're lucky—go through our lives without experiencing serious physical conflict such as war or even fist fights. We are intrigued and sometimes fascinated, though, when conflict does occur. Events that intrigue us are newsworthy. It is not news when the mayor and the city attorney have a meeting about a minor item, but it is news when that meeting results in the mayor punching the city attorney in the nose. Conflict can be psychological, too. Do not overlook the conflict when two politicians lambast each other verbally. That's news, too.

Human interest is a catchall category for those things in our world that intrigue people. The definition of human interest tends to change from editor to editor and from time to time. Two types of human interest stories, though—articles about children and animals—have stood the test of time, and at most times and in most places, you can count on articles about these topics to be well received. The ultimate human interest article may be a story about a child searching for a lost puppy. Of course, other types of human interest stories may also be newsworthy. For example, in the 1980s, Americans, who are aging as a total population, seem to be especially interested in health matters such as cancer cures and new diets.

Another element of news is *importance*, or impact, which is an essential part of every major news story. Simply put, the number of people affected by an event determines its relative importance. For example, if 1,000 people are evacuated from their homes in Institute, W. Va., because of an accidental release of toxic fumes from a chemical plant, you have big news. On the other hand, if your neighbor has to leave her

Two passengers look down from the deck of the Italian liner Achille Lauro, where American tourist Leon Klinghoffer was murdered by terrorists. (AP/Wide World Photos)

house for the night because her plumbing broke, that is probably not news (unless your neighbor happens to be the mayor or the manager of the city water plant). Importance does not have to be tied to disasters. School lunch menus printed in small town newspapers are widely read because many people are affected.

Prominence is another element. Names make news. If you fall down in front of your house and twist your ankle, that's probably not news. If the president of the United States trips, as did President Gerald Ford while descending the steps of Air Force One, the stumble is news. A little name makes a little news; a big name makes bigger news.

Proximity, or the nearness of the news event to your primary readers, also determines newsworthiness. If a Norwegian fishing boat overturns in the North Atlantic and two crewmen drown, that is only nominal news to the residents of Longmont, Colo. On the other hand, if two high school students from Longmont are killed on nearby Interstate 25, that's big news, and probably will be news for days, as the accident investigation is conducted and the funerals are held. Psychological proximity can be equally important. Even though the space shuttle Challenger exploded over Florida in 1986, people from Rhode Island to Alaska devoured information about the disaster because many felt psychologically close to school teacher Christa McAuliffe, who was killed in the explosion with six other astronauts.

Let's not forget *unusualness*. We expect that commercial airliners will take off and land safely each day at Washington's National Airport. When an airliner does not take off safely—when one crashes into a District of Columbia highway bridge packed with cars, for instance—that event is newsworthy. As another example, armed robberies of all-night gas stations are fairly common in the nation's 10 largest cities. A

MAKING THE WRONG DECISION?

On the first Monday of October in 1985, Palestinian terrorists hijacked an Italian cruise ship named the Achille Lauro in the Mediterranean. American tourists were among the 400 passengers aboard. A few days later, one American was murdered. On the same day, The Associated Press and United Press International reported that at least 55 people died in a mud slide in Puerto Rico, a commonwealth of the United States. A few days later, the toll of dead and missing persons had risen to more than 100 people.

The New York Times positioned both stories on the front page, but other major U.S. newspapers such as The Washington Post and The Miami Herald initially published the ship hijacking on page one and the Puerto Rico story on inside pages. By Thursday, the mud slide story moved to the front page of the Post and other major newspapers, but some Puerto Rican leaders were outraged at the delayed news judgment. One Puerto Rican official was quoted by The New York Times as saying, "I don't want to sound critical, but there's a lack of sensitivity [in the coverage]." El Diario-La Prensa, a New York City Spanish language daily, editorialized, "We find it painfully hard to believe that our colleagues in the wide world of media—with the single exception of The New York Times—seemed to give so little importance to the life of our Puerto Rican brothers and sisters who died this week."

Was the hijacking bigger news than the mud slide disaster? Both stories had timeliness. Both were important. Both had human interest. Both were unusual. The mud slide story had more proximity value than the ship hijacking, but the ship story had more inherent conflict. Even if both stories were featured on the front page, one would have to be displayed more prominently than the other. Which one do you think had the most news value?

daring robbery of a downtown bank in broad daylight is more unusual. In a large city newspaper, the service station robbery probably would not be covered at all (unless someone was injured), but the bank robbery would, indeed, be reported.

Weighing the importance of these seven elements of news can be tricky when you must decide which one of two stories should go on the front page. Suppose, for instance, that you live in a city of 100,000 and are a reporter for the daily newspaper there. You write a story about a new business, a Japanese owned auto assembly plant that will employ 2,000 people. The business is important to the economy of the town, because it will mean additional direct and indirect jobs in the community. On the other hand, you also have written a story about teachers who are planning to strike the public schools. Which story is the more newsworthy? Which story do you think should be more prominently displayed, and why?

Both stories are newsworthy, but let's look at each story in terms of the *number* and *quality* of news elements each possesses. Let's look at the business story first. We will assume it has *timeliness*. (You wouldn't be interested in yesterday's news.)

What else? Is there *conflict*? Probably not. Everyone is happy to see a new industry coming to town, unless the business happens to be extremely controversial, such as a rendering plant or a pornographic publishing company.

Is there *human interest*? No, unless the business is an adoption agency or a kennel.

Does the story have *importance*? Yes, because 2,000 men and women will have jobs in the community. If they are being transferred from another city, 2,000 new homes or apartments will be occupied, 2,000 new bank accounts will be opened, and every business in town will have 2,000 more potential customers. If the assembly plant hires locally, 2,000 unemployed or underemployed people will have jobs, with new income.

Is there *prominence*? No, unless some prominent person has invested in the business.

Is there *proximity*? Of course, because the new plant is in your city.

Is there *unusualness*? That depends. Is the opening of a new business in your city a rare event? Have companies been closing with every toll of the church bells and is unemployment soaring? If so, the opening is unusual. Or, on the other hand, is the business itself unusual? A breeding facility mating male lions and female tigers in order to produce ligers would be unusual. An assembly plant is fairly commonplace. The story, then, has only timeliness, importance and proximity. We can give the new business story three points.

Now, let's look at the impending teacher strike. It has *timeliness* just like the business story.

Does it have *conflict*? Imagine teachers walking picket lines, angry parents at school board meetings, heated negotiation sessions between the school board and the teachers' group. Picture press conferences with calculated name-calling. Picture perhaps even a little violence, with an arrest here and there. The story undoubtedly has conflict.

Does it have *human interest*? Imagine parents trying to figure out how to keep their restless offspring occupied during the teacher strike.

Does it have *importance*? Yes, because thousands of children who would otherwise be in school will find themselves unsupervised. Parents will have to hire baby-sitters or stay home from work to take care of their children. The economic impact alone is important, aside from the human impact.

Does the story have *prominence*? Yes, in the sense that leaders of the school board and teachers' group probably will gain prominence as negotiations proceed.

How about *proximity*? Yes, it's a local event.

And *unusualness*? Again, that depends on the circumstances in your city. If teachers strike every year in your city, it's obviously not an unusual event. Let's assume strikes do not happen every year. The school strike story, then, has *all* seven elements, or seven points. The new business story had only three points, so the school strike story is the choice for the most prominent display.

What if you were reporting for a newspaper in a town of 25,000 with huge unemployment? The new business story might be as important as the strike story because of its overall impact on the life of the town. New jobs might be as important as teachers who want better jobs. The impending school strike would still be a strong story, but calling the play would be tougher in this situation.

When determining whether a story is newsworthy, you have to take into consideration not only whether the story has a large number of elements that would tend to make it newsworthy, but also how important those elements are to your readers. You must always remember that you are not reporting in a vacuum; you are writing for readers who have needs, who pay for your product, and who will not buy it any more if those needs are not met. One way to do this is to imagine a typical reader. Picture an aunt or an uncle, a brother or a sister, and write for that person. If your story doesn't interest your aunt, it may bore most of your readers.

Deciding What to Exclude

Judging newsworthiness is only the first step in a four-part editorial process. As you know, *determination* comes first. The editor usually determines what will be covered, but the reporter determines how it will be covered because he handles the second stage, the *gathering* of the news. After the news is gathered, it is *written* and *edited*, the third and fourth stages of the process. In essence, the decision about what to include (and more importantly, what to exclude) from a story rests with several people: the editor who assigns the story, the reporter who gathers the news and reports it, and other editors who try to improve the story. All of these journalists use their judgment of news elements to determine what stays in a story and what winds up, as they say in Hollywood, on the cutting room floor. Each excludes material at different points in the process.

Let's briefly follow a newspaper story through this process and see how the elements of news influence what gets removed from a story. The place is Laramie, Wyo., a railroad center and university town of about 25,000, nestled on a high desert between two mountain ranges. The city editor of Laramie's daily newspaper receives dozens of news tips every day. Some arrive as written press releases and others come in over the telephone. On this day, the city editor receives a call from Alice Parker, the president of the Garden Club at the nearby University of Wyoming. Parker tells the editor the club is having an important meeting at 2 p.m., a meeting that she says is so significant the newspaper should cover it.

The editor asks what the meeting is about and decides to assign Wally Nelson, a new reporter, to cover it. Nelson goes to the meeting in the

---

FOUR HUNDRED MILE-PER-HOUR CHICKENS

Deciding what to exclude—or to include—can be difficult. Ask Peter Rinearson.

Rinearson, an aerospace reporter for The Seattle Times, won a Pulitzer Prize in 1984 for a seven-part series about the birth of a Boeing 757 jetliner. (The Pulitzer is perhaps print journalism's highest honor; the prize is synonymous with excellence and many consider the winners America's best newspaper journalists.) Rinearson was faced with many decisions regarding what to leave out in his long series. One special dilemma was whether to include information about Boeing's doomed chickens.

Boeing officials, who had been cooperating with Rinearson on the story, were not ecstatic when they learned that the reporter was going to tell the world that Boeing used compressed air guns to fire live (but anesthetized) four-pound chickens into airliner windows at 400 mph. (The Federal Aviation Administration required the safety test.)

Rinearson says Boeing "had a fair amount of apprehension" about the series in general. "It was sort of overwhelming how much time I was spending down there. My [working] regime was from the time I got up in the morning until I couldn't stay up any later at night. [Boeing] became aware of it. They couldn't help but become aware of it because of the amount of time going into the thing."

Boeing officials' apprehension grew when they learned Rinearson was going to write specifically about the "chicken tests." According to Rinearson, Boeing officially said "We can't control what you write, but we're not going to help you. In fact we are going to hinder you in any way we can in the pursuit of that [part of the] story, because the public's not going to understand. There'll be a certain segment of the public that says we're abusing animals. Birds hit planes all the time, and if we don't know that our planes stand up to that, we're going to lose a lot of human lives. So there are going to be some birds that die in testing."

"It didn't stop me at all from telling the story," Rinearson says. "[But] I told the story in context. I didn't do a story that said, 'Four hundred and thirteen live birds were smashed to death by Boeing last year against the windshields of airliners.' You could write a lead like that and it's accurate, but ... what I did in telling the story was [present] the story in a context. It was a very matter-of-fact thing. [Boeing] never complained. They never said a word about that because of the way it was presented was in context. All of the information they didn't want used was in [the story], but I tried to be very responsible about how to use it—not looking out after their interests, but trying to portray reality accurately."

Rinearson says Boeing's reaction is common: Subjects of news stories may have nothing to hide but may be concerned about whether the truth is portrayed within an appropriate context.

Student Union, introduces himself to Parker and watches the session unfold. Twenty-five people attend, including the group's faculty adviser, Luther Norton, who is a professor of biology at the university. First, the minutes from the past meeting are read. A treasurer's report follows. The group's secretary has quit school, so Parker asks for nominations from the floor. A student named Cliff Hopkins is nominated, and he wins the secretary's office by acclamation. There is no old business, so the group moves directly to new business. Someone moves that dues be raised from $10 a year to $20 a year. The motion is seconded and wins 17 votes to 6, with Parker and Norton abstaining.

At 2:30 p.m., the group begins discussing the major issue, a scientific garden called an arboretum. By 3 p.m., a vote is taken. The group unanimously votes to build an arboretum the next spring on a two-acre plot at one end of campus. The group will ask for donations of flowers from all over the state and will plant and label the specimens. They will ask the university administration for permission to use the land the next morning.

Nelson hurries back to the office, working the story over in his mind as he drives from campus to downtown. At his video display terminal—which resembles a typewriter connected to a television set—he types the following story:

A scientific garden will be planted next spring on a two-acre plot on the University of Wyoming campus, if plans made Tuesday by the UW Garden Club are approved by the UW administration.

Club members discussed the plans at a meeting yesterday afternoon in the UW Student Union. The club will ask UW officials for their permission to use the land today, according to Alice Parker, club president.

The proposed plot will be at the southwest corner of the university, club members decided. The flowers will be collected by donation from interested individuals around the state, Miss Parker said.

"There isn't anything like this anywhere in the state," Miss Parker said. "We need it. It will be our gift to the university and to the people of the state."

Nelson leaves out a great deal of information, based on his news judgment. He omits the reading of the minutes and the treasurer's report because they are not of interest to most readers. He also leaves out the number of people attending the meeting, the increase in dues and the election of the new secretary. If Nelson had been writing for the campus newspaper, he might have included the election of the secretary because it would have some interest for the smaller, more specific university audience.

News judgment first dictated that the meeting should be covered, then dictated what would not be covered in the meeting. Nelson's judgment is not altogether satisfactory, however. His editor tells him to add another paragraph summing up any early reaction he can get from university officials. The final story includes this new third paragraph:

Jay Edwards, UW's vice president for educational services, said, "It's the first we've heard of this. We'll have to look at their plans very carefully."

Reporters are under pressure to exclude extraneous material from stories while, at the same time, they must provide readers with a well-rounded story. The new paragraph fills the story out a little. We'll come back to completeness later.

Accuracy

Deciding what to report is only part of the journalist's responsibility. Accuracy is another part of the job.

First, here's a sobering statistic. A 1981 Public Agenda Foundation study showed that 52 percent of Americans surveyed believe that newspapers usually are not accurate. That figure would greatly displease Joseph Pulitzer. Pulitzer is remembered for the famous annual Pulitzer Prizes, as well as for waging a newspaper war against rival William Randolph Hearst. But perhaps he should be remembered most for saying, and demanding, "Accuracy! Accuracy!! Accuracy!!!" News judgment is critical, but a reporter with good news judgment and no respect for accuracy is a reporter who is destined for the unemployment line, or worse. What's worse than being fired for incompetence? How about being sued for libel, losing a million-dollar jury verdict, and *then* being fired?

Accuracy means being careful: double-checking names, numbers, quotations and other facts. Being careful might not sound difficult; you just proceed with caution and report like you might drive your car, at a safe, deliberate 55 mph rather than at a dangerous 100 mph. Unfortunately, little in a newsroom proceeds at the equivalent of 55 mph. Journalism has been likened to writing history in a hurry. The newsroom is usually the scene of absolutely frenetic activity as reporters work against deadlines to write their stories. Speed is the enemy of accuracy, yet speed is required in reporting. Reporters are condemned to write accurately in a hurry, to drive safely at 100 mph.

How do they do it? America's best reporters, such as Rinearson, say they report quickly and accurately by cultivating key skills. Reporters who strive for excellence and reporters who work for the country's best news organizations explain that they have learned to listen carefully and to take accurate notes.

Furthermore, they do not make assumptions. They ask questions—lots of questions. They check and double-check everything. Some inaccuracies creep into stories just because reporters make assumptions. Assumptions are usually based on some kind of observation. You look at your car's gasoline gauge and it says "full"—you assume you have gasoline. Generally, there is no great harm in making certain assumptions in daily living. If you make an assumption about your car's fuel and err, you may be stranded. If you make a false assumption as a reporter, however, the results can be legally and professionally devastating.

Let's look at assumptions another way. If you assume the speaker at a meeting you are covering is, in fact, the person billed as the speaker, you may find, after your story is printed, that a last minute substitution was made. Similarly, if you assume that Smith is always spelled S-M-I-T-H, you're destined to stumble into the pit of inaccuracy as soon as you meet your first S-M-Y-T-H-E. If you assume that the Ralph Peters arrested for assault is the gentleman who owns Ralph Peters Chevrolet—and you publish it and you're wrong—you also can assume you'll find a termination slip in your pay envelope with your check.

Worse yet, some inaccuracies occur because of traps set for reporters. Why? Somebody out there may not like you or your news organization. Let's take a classroom example. Suppose a university journalism teacher brings what appears to be a can of beans into the classroom.

"Tell me three things you know to be absolutely true about this can," the teacher says. The teacher holds the can in his palm. The can appears to be sealed and has a label on it that says "beans."

"The can is made of metal," a student offers. "And it's full of edible legumelike material. It also has a label on it."

"The contents are brown or green. The can weighs at least 16 ounces because that's a 16-ounce size can," another student says.

A third student says, "The can has beans in it because that's what the label says."

Then the teacher turns over the can to reveal that the bottom of the can has been removed and nothing is inside. Only two of the six "absolutely true" statements the students made about the can are accurate. The can is made of metal, and it does have a label on it. The rest of the statements were made based on faulty assumptions, which were caused by an intention to deceive.

Journalists can be trapped into reporting inaccuracies by sources such as politicians who tell half-truths, police officers who lie on reports and interviewees who exaggerate. One solution to this problem is double-checking. The other is simple attribution—the inimitable *he said* or *she said*.

In sum, accuracy is the goal. The stumbling blocks are carelessness, inadequate observations that lead to false assumptions, and false assumptions created by sources who do not have your best interests at heart.

Accuracy is not enough, though. Accuracy with speed is the real goal. Excellent reporters have learned to organize and write their material quickly. Practically all news stories have a deadline. If reporters take a long time verifying material, they must make up that time by putting the story together in a hurry. Reporters seldom succeed in journalism if they make mistakes, but reporters who never make mistakes but who miss deadlines also seldom succeed.

Rinearson says that as a beginning reporter he concluded that he had to master speed and accuracy before he could improve his writing style. Rinearson explains: "For my first couple of years, I was very much production oriented. This was a conscious campaign to improve [speed and accuracy skills]. I remember one year I had over 450 bylines. That was very much my emphasis. Then, after I felt like I had that skill down, I said ... 'Now I really want to write.' [Then] I tried to focus on the writing quality. I think that's a pretty good strategy."

All of these skills—listening, questioning, taking notes, organizing material and writing—might be summed up in two words: precision and speed. Precise and fast reporters are usually excellent reporters.

Objectivity

Through all of this struggle for precision and speed, the reporter must also struggle to be objective.

Some published and broadcast material is not intended to be objective, of course. Editorial writing is persuasive writing; objectivity is not required. Columns and commentary are also meant to be persuasive in many cases, and objectivity may fall by the wayside. Investigative and interpretive reporting should be objective, but may also have a point of view. Features usually have a point of view, too. News stories, however, should be neutral, objective and dispassionate.

Some journalists maintain that objectivity, while worthy as a goal, is nonsense. Objectivity cannot be obtained, they argue, because no one can divorce oneself from one's education, upbringing and view of the world. Thus, they say, everything you report is colored by what you are. For example, some critics of the goal of objectivity would say that if you are a product of a typical middle-class upbringing, you would be hard-pressed to be objective when doing a story about foreign terrorists who hijack a plane loaded with American tourists. Your stories, they would say, would not convey a truly objective view of the incident; they would, instead, be tilted toward the view of the U.S. government and the families of the passengers.

That is perhaps true, but truly excellent reporters pride themselves on their ability to write so neutrally that the reader does not have the slightest hint of where the reporter stands on the issue being covered. That is what we call objectivity. Here's an example. A young general assignment reporter for a 10,000 circulation daily newspaper in a rural Southern state was assigned to cover the leader of the state's Moral Majority group, a religious organization with a decidedly conservative tilt. The reporter disagreed with everything the organization stood for and disliked the local leader. At the same time, however, the reporter knew he had to cover the organization's meetings and press conferences objectively, because the community demanded coverage and the newspaper staff was too small for another reporter to replace him. After the reporter had covered the group for two years, the Moral Majority leader pulled the reporter aside one day and said: "You're doing a good job. Keep it up." The reporter took the compliment as proof of how well he had been able to bury his own feelings in covering the group.

This is not uncommon. Reporters generally agree that when people they dislike congratulate them on accurate and objective coverage, they are being paid one of journalism's highest compliments. Total objectivity is probably difficult if not impossible to attain, but it is a desirable goal.

Completeness, Fairness and Balance

Though reporters will always need to struggle to meet the demands of objectivity, they should have no difficulty achieving completeness, fairness and balance. Unfortunately, at least one Public Agenda Foundation survey indicates that they fail at the task, or at least that there is a problem with public perception of newspaper completeness, fairness and balance. The 1981 study reported that 54 percent of Americans surveyed thought that newspapers are usually not fair. In addition, a vast majority of those interviewed in the study favored laws requiring newspapers to give major party candidates an identical amount of coverage. A majority of those interviewed also favored laws giving opponents of an issue as much coverage as proponents, a concept the U.S. Supreme Court has thus far not applied to the print media.

Completeness, fairness and balance have no mystical qualities nor do they require any complicated explanation. The terms simply mean that the story should present an honest picture. For example, if a highly controversial speaker is given two rousing rounds of applause after a speech, that applause should be mentioned in the story. On the other hand, if the speaker is constantly interrupted by heckling, and half of the audience walks out before the speech is completed, that information should be included in the story as well. In short, completeness, fairness and balance mean that if there are two sides to a situation, both sides should be represented in the story.

In covering the University of Wyoming Garden Club plans for the campus arboretum, reporter Wally Nelson initially did not contact university officials for their reaction. If he had written the story without any university comment, the article would have been incomplete, because it would have suggested that the arboretum would be built without difficulty. As it turned out, the club had neglected to sound out the university administration about the idea, and consequently, the idea may have been doomed to failure. When the editor required Nelson to insert the paragraph describing the university's initial reaction, the story became more complete—and the story provided a service to both the readers and the club members.

The additional paragraph also balanced the story and made it more fair. Fairness and balance are typically thought of in conjunction with balancing two controversial views. Not too long ago in a rural Southwestern state, a sheriff, angry at a prominent politician, called the man "no better than a pimp." The media duly reported the sheriff's attack, but also gave the politician a chance to respond in the next paragraph.

Occasionally, reporters have to go to great lengths to get subjects to respond to charges. Pulitzer winner William K. Marimow of The Philadelphia Inquirer, investigating a deadly 1985 police bombing of a residential neighborhood, went to the home of the police bomb squad commander twice in order to get the officer's side of the story. A Chicago investigative reporter, faced with a subject who would not answer the telephone, first hand-delivered a set of questions to the subject's office, then sent a telegram to the subject and finally confronted the man on the street with the questions. Only when the subject refused all comment did the reporter write the story.

The rules are simple. When a proposal is made, contact the affected party. When a charge is made, call the person who is being attacked. If you can't reach the other side, tell the reader that you tried but that the other party could not be reached before deadline.

Consequences of Stories

Almost all local news stories have consequences of some kind. For example, suppose you write a story about a university professor who is arrested for shoplifting or a story about a local author who makes a provocative speech before a civic organization. You must expect those stories to have human consequences. Writing a story is like firing a bullet into the air—it *will* come down, although it may not injure anyone. Similarly, the story about the university professor may not injure him, but it probably will, bringing him humiliation and perhaps censure from his employer. Even coverage of the provocative speech will have consequences, though perhaps they will be positive. A news story is like a fired bullet in that it always comes down somewhere.

There can be personal consequences for reporters as well. In large cities, reporters are often unaware of the consequences because they are insulated through anonymity. Journalists at metropolitan newspapers seldom face story subjects in social settings, and in addition, newspapers often have security officers at the front door to prevent readers from wreaking violence in the newsroom. Still, there are consequences. For example, Don Bolles, a reporter for The Arizona Republic, was murdered in 1976 after investigations of organized crime. Recently, and much less seriously, an angry reader tried to cram a crumpled column into the mouth of the managing editor of the Arkansas Democrat in Little Rock, roughing the journalist up in the process.

In smaller towns, reporters often cross paths with their subjects and in the process, get feedback in the most direct kind of way—a figurative or literal punch in the nose. In Kentucky, for instance, when the Lexington Herald-Leader reported financial irregularities involving players on University of Kentucky basketball teams, the newspaper received a bomb threat, subscription cancellations and more than a few nasty letters. One letter writer summed up her feelings by saying: "May the sprays from a million polecats fall inside your pressroom and linger on through eternity." Despite the negative reactions, however, the newspaper later won a Pulitzer Prize for its work.

Like the Kentucky example, essentially negative stories often eventually yield positive results. For example, Arthur Howe of The Philadelphia Inquirer wrote a series of Pulitzer Prize-winning stories in 1985 about deficiencies in the Internal Revenue Service's processing of tax returns. The stories put pressure on the IRS and eventually inspired major changes in agency procedures as well as a public apology to U.S. taxpayers. In 1981, Paul Henderson of The Seattle Times won a Pulitzer Prize for a series examining how an innocent man was convicted of rape.

In general, editors tell reporters not to worry about the consequences of their stories. In practice, reporters often do. A staff attorney of a state utility commission in a Southern state, in an interview with a reporter, candidly attacked the judgment of his supervisor. Later, he asked the reporter not to use those remarks. The reporter considered the request, talked about the problem with his editors and ultimately decided not to use the comments because they were not essential to the story but would have caused great professional damage to the attorney.

In another instance in the same state, a reporter and editor decided to report a story knowing it would have negative consequences. An official in charge of suspending operator's licenses of motorists convicted of driving while under the influence of alcohol was himself convicted of a DWI. The paper printed a prominent story of the sentencing of the official. For the official, the consequences of coverage were significant. In both instances, reporters and editors had to make decisions and live with those decisions.

The Public

Defining news, deciding what to exclude, maintaining accuracy under deadline, being objective, writing complete, fair and balanced stories and handling the consequences all may seem to add up to an impossible task for the reporter. The reporter's responsibilities and problems are, indeed, serious. In fact, the reporter has the additional formidable hurdle of communicating with the reader.

First, the very nature of the mass communicative process is flawed by "noise." Noise, or interference, also is found in most other forms of communication. (Other common communicative varieties include *intrapersonal* communication—thinking is an example—and *interpersonal*, or one-on-one communication. Most authorities agree that mass communication is a variety of *organizational* communication, which also includes public speaking and group communication.)

Damaging noise in most other communicative modes can be identified by immediate feedback—messages from the audience, for example—and eliminated by modifying the message. For example, if you speak to a group and you see that you're putting audience members to sleep, you can modify your message by shouting or speaking more softly, by turning to a different topic, or even by asking questions. Unfortunately, feedback that identifies noise in the mass communicative process comes seldom and then too late. For instance, if a reporter organizes a story badly, noise has entered the process. By the time the problems are called to the attention of the reporter, though, the story has been published or broadcast and the damage is done.

Worse, if newspaper readers telephone reporters to complain about the content of news stories, they are usually passed around, as one journalism critic put it, "like a sack of garbage" until they wind up with a news clerk who later complains to the editor that he has to handle all of the "nut" calls. For example, William A. Henry III, a Time associate editor who won a Pulitzer Prize in 1980 while at The Boston Globe, recalls wryly that complaint calls to the newspaper often used to be received by employees who—while transferring the call—would hold the telephone at arm's length and yell, "Nut on the line." To be sure, some newspapers have professional reader representatives who handle reader complaints effectively. In addition, a reader can always write a letter to the editor. But in general, news organizations seem to be universally inadequate at handling one-on-one consumer communication, the key way reporters learn about problems with their stories.

Television stations are seldom better than newspapers. One Midwest viewer, displeased at the way a weather forecaster for an ABC affiliate was pronouncing the capital of Iowa, called the newsroom to complain that the city was pronounced D-A' M-O-I-N rather than D-E-S' M-O-I-N-E-S. The reporter, trying a bluff, told the viewer, "I understand that there are two pronunciations." Actually, there is only one standard pronunciation, whether you're in New York City or Iowa City.

Communicative noise, then, whether it manifests itself as weak writing or inadequate delivery of the message (such as sloppy inking of a page or poor videotape editing), concerns reporters almost as much as lack of accuracy, objectivity, fairness and balance.

The amount of time the reader spends digesting the reporter's work also concerns print journalists. Studies show that the typical newspaper reader scans the paper in a scant 20 minutes, starting at the first page and working to the back. (Yes, some people do read their newspapers from back to front.) This minimal amount of time devoted to reading the newspaper creates a pattern of reading something like this: The reader reads most of the headlines on the front page, looks at the pictures, reads the cutlines under the pictures and even reads the first paragraphs of most of the front page stories. The reader with an interest in a particular story reads it to the "jump," or instruction to move to another page, and then mutters and gives up. Only the most serious readers make the "jump," studies show.

Then the reader works his or her way through the newspaper, looking at pictures, reading advertisements, headlines, first paragraphs and occasionally even reading entire stories. The reader who does tackle an entire story rarely reads beyond 25 column inches of copy, some studies show. (Four full lines of typed news copy more or less equal one column inch of typeset material.) Finally, the reader arrives at his or her favorite section, where the rest of his or her self-allotted 20 minutes is spent. That favorite section will vary, depending on the sex, geographic location, and interests of the reader. (For example, in cities with major league sports franchises or serious college athletics, the sports pages may be the final destination of many male readers.) Clearly, the reporter's masterpiece is read quickly if at all.

Broadcast reporters have similar concerns. Their distracted viewers and listeners are trying to digest often complex stories squeezed into 30- to 60-second time slots.

Furthermore, reporters have to try to communicate to a public which—according to the polls—is not enamored with the news media in general and newspapers in particular. The American Press Institute sponsored a seminar in 1984 for editors. In a report issued on the seminar findings, API noted: "A 1966 study by the Newspaper Advertising Bureau showed that 79 percent of adults in the U. S. read a daily newspaper. In 1984 that percentage had dropped to 66 percent. Meanwhile, the Harris Survey showed that confidence in the press (including newspapers) plunged from 29 percent in 1966 to 14 percent in 1982. Thus [said API's discussion leader], the decline in credibility in the press has paralleled the decline in newspaper readership."

The polls show the public prefers television as a news medium. To a large extent, experts suggest, consumers prefer television news because it is cheaper than a newspaper subscription. Television is also easier to use—viewing is passive and newspaper reading is active. And television is a more immediate news delivery system. If you felt an earthquake, for example, would you turn on the television or wait for your morning newspaper to be delivered?

The polls also suggest that the public finds television more believable than newspapers. The Roper Organization, in a 1984 survey comparing newspaper, television, radio and magazine credibility, asked this question: "If you got conflicting or different reports of the same news story from radio, television, the magazines and the newspapers, which of the four versions would you be most inclined to believe—the one on radio or television or magazines or newspapers?"

Fifty-three percent of those surveyed said they would believe the television broadcast. Twenty-four percent said they would believe newspapers, 8 percent said radio and 7 percent said magazines.

The low estimation of newspaper credibility may be linked to findings in a 1985 study by the American Society of Newspaper Editors, which ranked public attitudes of journalists' ethical standards. The findings placed newspaper reporters below clergy, doctors, police, television news anchors, teachers, television reporters and newspaper editors. Only advertising executives and used car salesmen ranked lower.

Many people—unaware of the remarkable capabilities of videotape editing—believe that the television camera does not lie. Television also promotes the trustworthiness of its news personalities with everything from on-set "happy talk" to shopping center promotions and all-night charity telethons. To put it another way, when was the last time you could place the face with the name of a newspaper reporter?

Finally, reporters know from the polls that the public is suspicious of them as a group. Reporters fear that the public sees them as rebellious political liberals who are out to find foxes in the hen house even when there's not a predator for miles around.

All of this suggests that reporters face many hurdles in presenting news to the public—and that there must be more prestigious, better paying, easier ways to make a living than being a newspaper or a broadcast reporter.

Complaints

The American Press Institute and the American Society of Newspaper Editors have been studying the problem of reader perceptions of newspapers and reader complaints about newspapers for many years. Hundreds of thousands of dollars have been spent surveying readers and non-readers, subscribers and former subscribers and almost everyone else who will offer an opinion. The result of all of this surveying and guessing is that editors suspect readers have four main problems with newspapers. The problems, sometimes called the "unholy four," are that readers think newspapers publish too much bad news, are guilty of sensationalism, invade the privacy of subjects and are biased. (Broadcasters have conducted many studies, too, and have found somewhat similar results.)

HOW TO IMPROVE THE CREDIBILITY OF AMERICA'S NEWSPAPERS

At a seminar sponsored by the American Press Institute aimed at improving the credibility of newspapers, participating editors offered numerous solutions to the growing problem of reader complaints.
Suggestions included the following:

1. improving reader access through the use of letters-to-the-editor, guest editorial-page columns, neighborhood meetings and reader representatives;
2. improving newsroom leadership and offering better community orientation programs for new reporters;
3. hiring more minority and female reporters;
4. strengthening coverage in under-covered parts of the community;
5. teaching reporters how to respond politely to reader complaints;
6. toning down smart-aleck writing;
7. monitoring the "bad news" stories on page one and section fronts, and if necessary, moving some "bad news" stories inside the newspaper;
8. improving the accuracy of headlines and reporting on mistakes made by the newspaper, through an "amplifications and clarifications" column.

The first complaint is the so-called bad-news syndrome, the notion that news organizations present little but gloom and doom. As we have seen, news is, to a large extent, a timely, local, unusual event of a controversial nature. Unfortunately, many consumers view any coverage of that kind of news event as inherently negative. Editors continually try to defend themselves against this charge, and in so doing, try to educate the public about the responsibilities of the media. Dave Ranney, formerly an editor of The Hillsboro Star-Journal in Kansas, and now a reporter for the Kansas-based Harris Newspaper Group, explained his newspaper's position on bad news in an editorial. Ranney said, in part, "Newspapers are not newsletters. A newspaper prints what it considers to be news, good and bad. A newsletter prints the good news in a format guaranteed to offend no one. Don't look for bad news in a newsletter or one-sided optimism in a newspaper."

In the API's examination of the problem, editors concluded that readers, in fact, enjoy reading bad news but that balance is important. Too much bad news on the front page and in front sections gives readers the perception of nothing but bad news.

Closely related to bad news is the charge that news organizations look for dust under the bed when the house is spotlessly clean. William Raspberry of The Washington Post, in a comment at a recent API seminar, explained the readers' complaint: "What I hear is criticism of negative reporting. We try to uncover scandal even when it is not there. We judge the worth of stories on this basis. [And] readers have been trying to tell us that our self-righteousness isn't justified." Ranney presented the editor's viewpoint in his Kansas newspaper: "An informed public is always more rational and more compassionate than one kept in the dark. Progress is based on information. Those who say, 'Oh, don't put that in the paper. Nobody needs to know, it'll only stir things up,' have missed the point. Controversies stem from secrecy, not disclosure."

The second criticism is sensationalism, typically defined as an overemphasis of some elements of a story at the expense of other, perhaps more important, elements. Critics also charge that news organizations sometimes cover stories *only* to boost readership or viewership. One ASNE study shows that the public believes that television news sensationalizes more than the print media. In fact, television reporters in some markets joke that "if it bleeds, it leads" the news program. Dan Rather put it another way in "The Camera Never Blinks." Rather noted that some television stations increase viewers by liberally covering "fuzz and was" stories. "Fuzz," of course, refers to police and crime; "was" refers to death.

Sensationalism is closely related to invasion of privacy, the third charge. Both are really questions of taste. Taste can only be defined locally. San Antonio, Texas, newspapers routinely carry more graphic stories and pictures than Wichita, Kan., newspapers, which are located only 600 miles away.

Will you offend your readers if you publish the name of a rape victim? The answer is yes in many American cities. In covering a drowning, can you show the uncovered body of the victim? In some cities readers will accept that picture; in others they will condemn you for using it. In writing about an automobile accident in which the victim is decapitated, do you mention the headless body? Do you publish a picture of it? Did the national television networks violate good taste in 1986 when they constantly replayed video tape of the grieving parents of astronaut Christa McAuliffe? Did the newspapers that printed a similar picture violate the parents' privacy?

Coverage of this kind often leads to charges of insensitivity toward the dead and injured, and of reporter discourtesy and arrogance. Are journalists ghouls? critics seem to be asking. Mike Moore, editor of The Quill, a magazine published by The Society of Professional Journalists, Sigma Delta Chi, says journalists are just doing their job, with the same kind of detached efficiency expected of a police officer:

"Something like a cat rolling in catnip, the press is occasionally pictured as reveling in human suffering. You've heard it all, I'm sure. The press loves a good murder, a sensational fire, a rampaging storm, even a plane crash.

"I'm always a little amazed when I hear such things. Though I've known many reporters and editors, I have never met one who derived pleasure from covering stories involving human suffering and grief."

Participants at the 1984 API seminar recommended toning down smart-aleck writing and treating reader complaints with courtesy, civility and sensitivity.

Ultimately, however, avoiding charges of sensationalism and invasion of privacy means staying in touch with the mood of the public. It's true, of course, that sometimes newspapers and television stations present pictures or stories that generate hundreds of critical telephone calls or letters, but that kind of public reaction is not common. If a journalist misjudges public taste, consumers may not indicate why they dislike or distrust the news organization. Rather, they will simply cease to purchase or watch the product.

Finally, we come to the fourth complaint, bias. That charge can be as simple as a conviction by readers that their hometown newspaper will not cover the activities of a particular civic club, or as complex as a belief that certain political candidates will always be denied reasonable coverage. Ranney, writing in his Kansas newspaper, articulates the editor's position well: "Deciding what is news is not easy. Something of interest to one group is usually meaningless to another. Striking a balance is almost sure to offend one or the other."

One study at the API seminar showed that 54 percent of readers thought news stories about political candidates were tilted to agree with the newspaper's editorial endorsement. At many newspapers, reporters do not even read the editorial page, let alone have the presence of mind to slant a story for or against a candidate. Editors are too busy correcting spelling, style and factual errors to worry about the fine points of whether or not the story is going to be read with displeasure by the editorial page writers or the publisher. (Many medium and small market broadcast stations avoid editorializing completely.)

Bias doesn't rear its head when journalists adhere to the traditional notions of accuracy, objectivity, completeness, fairness and balance. Though the public may perceive that bias exists, at most American news organizations it happens rarely and only when reporters or news executives have not been careful.

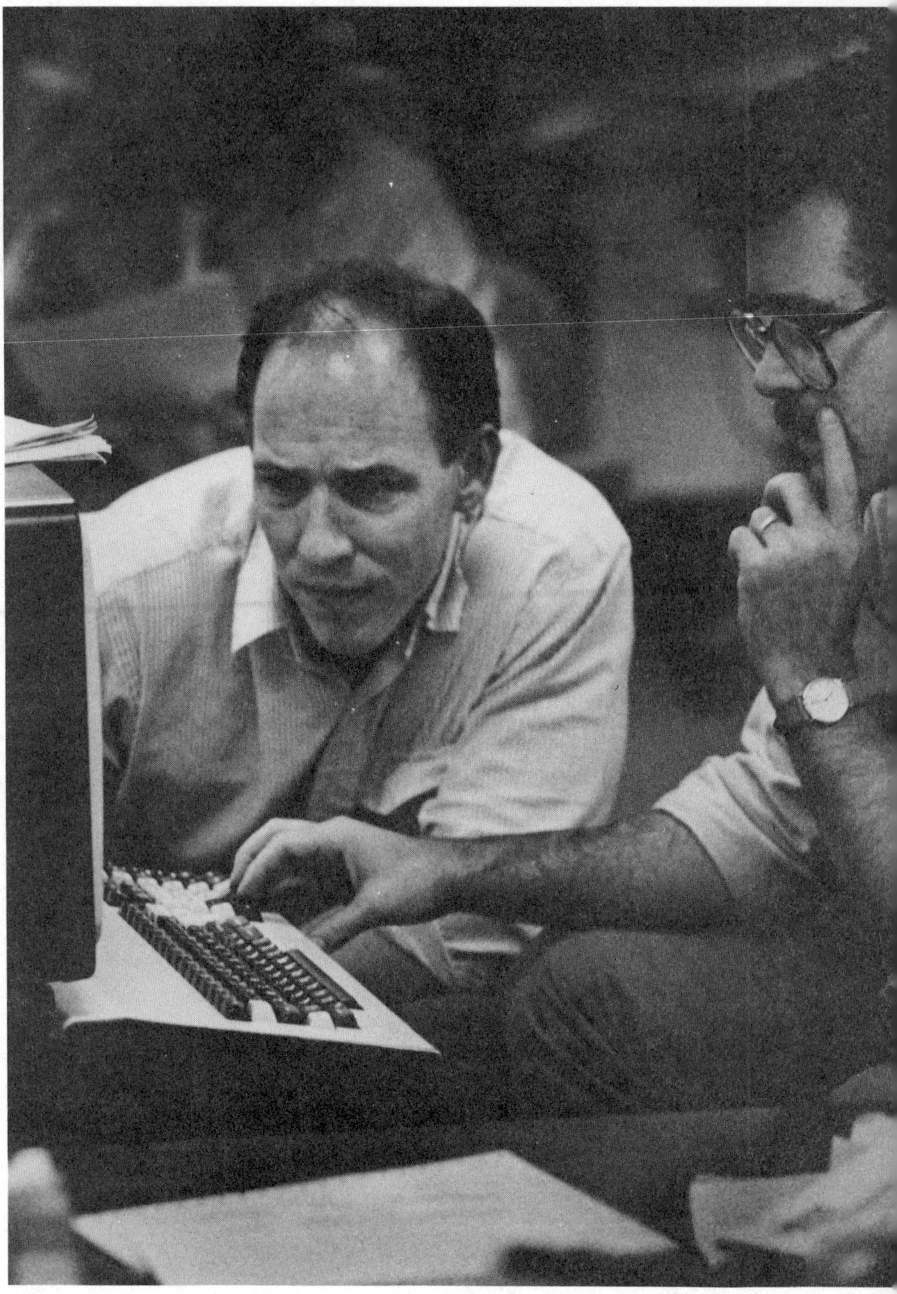

CHAPTER 2

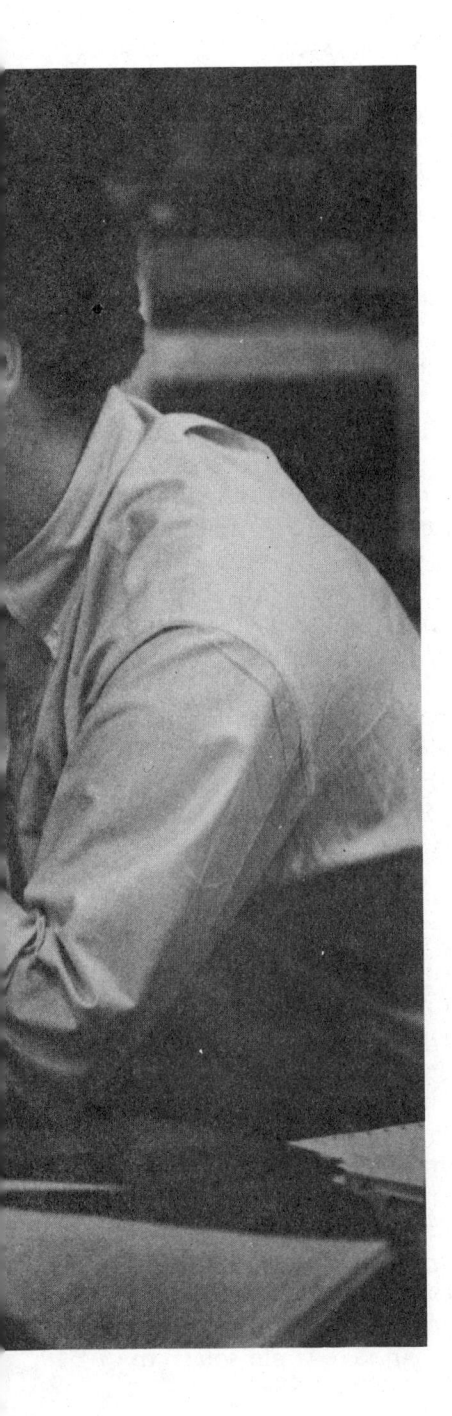

Newsroom Basics

The Reporter

Newsroom Organization and the Role of the Editor

More About the Copy Desk

How a Reporter Functions in an Electronic Newsroom

The Traditional Newsroom

Dealing With Deadlines

The Changing Newspaper

Broadcast News

The Reporter

If you're a typical American, you probably do not have a close friend who is a newspaper reporter. In fact, you have probably never even met a newspaper reporter. That's not because reporters eschew friends; it's because, statistically, there are not very many newspaper reporters around. Media experts, using Labor Department figures, estimate that there are about 75,000 full-time daily and weekly newspaper reporters in the United States. That's a small number if you compare it with the nation's more than 600,000 college and university teachers and the more than one million registered nurses. To put it another way, newspaper reporters are about as rare as geologists, the government says.

So, while journalists (and that includes radio and television reporters, magazine writers, editors and some public relations people) are relatively plentiful, newspaper reporters are, indeed, a little like the gray whale—a rare and perhaps endangered species.

Still, you probably have a clear image of a newspaper reporter: abrupt, aggressive, callous and possibly a little disheveled in appearance. Perhaps your "reporter" is actor Dustin Hoffman or Robert Redford playing Carl Bernstein and Bob Woodward in the movie, "All the President's Men," or Robert Walden or Linda Kelsey playing Joe Rossi and Billy Newman in television's "Lou Grant" series.

That's Hollywood, but what are newspaper reporters really like? A dozen studies completed in the last decade provide clues. Let's start with journalism students, who provide most of the raw material for the nation's newsrooms. In a study published in Journalism Quarterly, two Florida journalism professors found little difference between journalism students and those majoring in other fields. Compared with non-journalism students, the journalism students they surveyed spent about the same amount of time reading printed media, knew no more about current events, were no better typists, and were only slightly better spellers. The journalism students, however, were significantly better grammarians than other college students.

More than half of the 20,000 journalism students who graduated from U.S. colleges in 1985 found media-related work according to Dow Jones Newspaper Fund surveys. Twenty-two percent of the graduates went to work in public relations and advertising. Weekly and daily newspapers hired about 16 percent of the graduates. Wire services, magazines, and radio and television stations hired the rest of the graduates who found media jobs. One-third of the remaining journalism class of 1985 took non-media jobs or went to graduate school, and about 12 percent were unemployed or did not answer the survey.

The graduates hired by the daily newspapers accepted starting salaries of about $13,500 a year, while broadcasting, advertising and public relations graduates were offered about $11,000, $14,000 and $15,000 a year respectively, according to median national figures from the Newspaper Fund. Those eyeing newspaper careers can take some solace in

Chapter opening photo: Kansas City Times reporters Kevin Garrity and Mark Frazier confer about a story. (Staff photo by Gary Dunkin, Kansas City Times)

another 1985 survey—of 264 editors of dailies with a circulation of 25,000 or more—which showed that the typical starting salary of recent college graduates was a more encouraging $15,000 a year for reporters and about $16,000 a year for copy editors. Unfortunately, the best of those salaries is slightly below the median annual starting salary for the 1985 college graduate in humanities—and significantly below the average starting salary of the student who majored in business or engineering. The figures suggest that the graduate whose primary objective is making money ought to look for employment other than with a newspaper. The figures also suggest why the newspaper reporter may be an endangered species: Editors in some parts of the country say they have difficulty finding talented beginning reporters. In addition, those reporters they do find often leave the newspaper after a few years for a more lucrative field, such as public relations.

Surveys of practicing journalists indicate that the typical newspaper reporter is a married, college-educated Caucasian male (although this is rapidly changing, with journalism school enrollments currently about 60 percent female) who is a Protestant but rarely attends church. Most reporters surveyed say they are middle-of-the-road politically.

The studies imply that newspaper reporters are highly concerned with the quality of their work and with the overall quality of their news organization, but oddly, the reporters typically do not belong to a professional organization such as The Society of Professional Journalists, which is dedicated to improvement of that performance. And, the studies show that as a group, reporters feel that their work has allowed them to meet interesting people and perform a public service, but they are unhappy with the pay.

Newsroom Organization and the Role of the Editor

The nation's reporters work for one of nearly 1,700 daily or 7,700 nondaily U.S. newspapers. Each newspaper is typically divided into five departments—editorial, advertising, production, circulation and business—although the department lines are usually blurred at the nondailies. The editorial department, where the reporters, photographers and editors labor, is responsible for everything in the newspaper that is not advertising. The advertising department sells both classified and display (retail) advertising. The production department is responsible for typesetting and printing the newspaper. The circulation department distributes the paper. The business department, which may not even have a formal name, takes care of anything else that needs to be done at the newspaper, ranging from paying the electricity bills to keeping the floor clean. Each department is headed by a manager, who answers to the publisher (perhaps through a general manager).

The publisher may, but probably does not, own the publication, as America's daily newspapers are increasingly group owned. There were about 2,200 daily newspapers in 1910, but only a few were owned by groups. By 1974, groups held nearly 1,000 newspapers, or about 55 percent of the total number, and by 1984, groups owned 69 percent of America's dailies and controlled 79 percent of daily circulation. Studies have shown that groups will probably continue to grow and consolidate into more and more state, regional and even national groups. Group ownership is not intrinsically bad, but studies suggest that group-owned dailies tend to have fewer argumentative editorials on local controversial issues and somewhat similar major political endorsements.

Reporters typically work for the city editor, who answers to the managing editor. Many reporters begin their careers at small daily newspapers, often in the 10,000 to 25,000 circulation range. One recent study suggests that newspapers in that range usually have about 15 editorial employees. Typically, those 15 include the managing editor and city editor, as well as a news editor, a newswire or "telegraph" editor, a copy editor, seven reporters, two photographers and one librarian. A newspaper with a circulation of at least 500,000 usually has more than 250 editorial staffers, including 125 reporters.

Whereas reporters are typically male, young and moderate independents or Democrats, the typical publisher is male, middle-aged or older, conservative and Republican in his politics. So, what kind of person is the reporter's boss: the managing editor? That is an especially important question if news is exactly what the editor says it is, since the editor's views and attitudes may color his or her judgment, objectivity notwithstanding.

Are editors cut from the same cloth that reporters are? Surveys suggest they are. One survey of daily newspaper editors suggests that they

David Hacker, writing coach and staff writer for the Wichita, Kan., Eagle-Beacon, discusses a story with Clark Spencer, staff writer. (Photo by Mark Gale)

(like reporters) are typically married, college educated, Caucasian and male. In general, they're older than their reporters, as you might expect. A second survey, this one of 400 top editors from newspapers with a circulation of more than 50,000, shows that nearly three-quarters of the editors call themselves political independents, and decline either Democratic or Republican party identification.

Those are the key newsroom players. Now let's observe the entire team in action. That action, which is called the "copy flow," typically starts with an assignment from the city editor. The city editor is responsible for coverage of the newspaper's prime circulation area and is usually the reporter's immediate supervisor at all but the largest-circulation daily newspapers. Newspapers serving large geographic areas may also have metropolitan and state editors, who supervise reporters covering those territories. On large newspapers, the managing editor does not make assignments; he or she sets the tone for the newspaper, and does the hiring, firing and promoting. On smaller dailies, the managing editor does all of these things as well as shouldering some of the burden of the city editor.

The city editor then tells the reporter what and where the story is, and when it must be completed. The reporter writes the story based on information gathered either by telephone or in person, then turns the copy back to the city editor. The editor may approve the story as written, reject it, or more typically, ask for clarification and changes (less politely called a rewrite).

Then the story is sent to another editor (usually called a news editor, although this title varies a lot) who must make some basic decisions about the story. The news editor has already received a guide, or "layout," showing the available amount of space (the "news hole") from the advertising department. Is there enough space for this particular story? the news editor asks. Even if there is, should the story be condensed? Should a photograph be used with the story? On what page will the story appear? Where on the assigned page will the story be placed?

After the news editor makes these decisions, he or she forwards the story to the copy editor, who executes the news editor's instructions. The copy editor—or the copy editor's assistants, if necessary—reduces the story by removing paragraphs from the end of the article, writes a headline for the story and if a picture is to be used, may write instructions for the photograph size as well as explanatory information for the photo. Most importantly, the copy editor is the final quality control point for the story, checking and double-checking the story for accuracy, objectivity, completeness, fairness, balance, style, spelling, grammar and clarity. Then the story, in its new form, is sent out of the editorial department into the production department, where it is typeset.

It is obvious from the copy flow that the reporter does not participate in a number of critical decisions. For example, the reporter generally does not make assignments. The reporter does not determine deadlines or even the final appearance of the story. The reporter doesn't decide if the story is used in the newspaper or where the story is placed. Finally, the reporter does not write the headline or make any decisions regarding photo use or size. Reporting the news, clearly, is a group effort. This combined effort of the reporter and the editors is required if news is to be accurately gathered and written in the pressure cooker of publication deadlines.

More About the Copy Desk

If the managing editor sets the agenda for the kind of news a publication will cover, and the city editor administers that agenda, the copy editor and assistant copy editors make certain the coverage is accurate and readable.

The city editor will have already caught and corrected many imperfections in a news story, but the copy editor knows that if an error—anything from a spelling error to an ungrammatical sentence—is published, the copy desk workers will ultimately be blamed for missing the mistake. Without copy editors, however, many more errors would be printed, reporters and editors agree.

The copy editor reads a story like a turkey buzzard searching for carrion, and with good reason. News stories do frequently contain errors. For example, one national study showed that between 40 and 60 percent of news stories have errors, including spelling, grammar and typographical mistakes. In another study, editors estimated that 68 percent of news stories have at least one error. What kind of errors? A week-long study of one Florida newspaper showed that about half of the errors at that newspaper were mistakes in time, place, age, title or identity, with misspelling of names and disagreements between source and reporter accounting for a lesser number of mistakes.

The copy editing process depends on an experienced editor, who like the high school English teacher of your worst nightmare, scrutinizes every word in your story. You've written "Markham Street." Is Markham a street, an avenue, a road or a boulevard? the copy editor worries. You've written about a woman named Johnson. Is it Johnson or Johnston? Is it Miss, Mrs. or Ms. (assuming the newspaper is following Associated Press style)? The ultimate answers to these and other questions are the domain of the copy editor.

Reporters are still accountable for accuracy as well, although reporters are not usually fired for spelling, punctuation, grammar or similar mistakes, or even for factual errors, according to one national study. Only 30 percent of the editors surveyed said that they had fired anyone for a factual error, such as misspelling a name. A majority of those editors, however, said they have fired at least one employee for an interpretive mistake, such as misunderstanding a concept or failing to make it clear. The 100 or so editors surveyed said that during the course of their careers they have fired nearly 250 reporters, a sobering figure for a novice journalist. More importantly, reporters who make mistakes and manage to survive termination are reporters who do not know their craft, and who certainly will not excel in journalism until they learn their business.

One way to guarantee termination is to fabricate "facts" in a story, as did a young Washington Post reporter in 1980. The reporter wrote a story which unfortunately won the 1981 Pulitzer Prize for feature writing. The dramatic story, headlined "8-Year-Old Heroin Addict Lives for a Fix," did not use the real name of the young "addict" because the reporter told Post editors her life was in danger if real names were used. Without real names the copy editors could not double-check many of the facts. Later, after the Post won the Pulitzer Prize, the story was revealed as fiction and the Pulitzer committee withdrew the Prize. The reporter's career with the Post ended. We will return to the incident in Chapter 14. The point is that a dishonest or poorly trained reporter can sabotage a copy editor's best efforts.

How a Reporter Functions in an Electronic Newsroom

The techniques of reporting changed little from the 1600s, when the first newspapers appeared, until the early 1800s. After the introduction of the mass circulation "penny" press in the 1830s, however, numerous technological changes began to significantly affect the way reporters gathered, wrote and edited stories.

Not long after the invention of the telegraph in 1837, reporters discovered that the thin wires were a handy way to "file" stories from far away. By about 1900, typewriters, invented 30 years earlier, started appearing in newsrooms, and reporters soon found themselves abandoning their longhand in favor of hunting and pecking at keys. About the same time, reporters also began using the telephone to file stories to writers called "rewrite men" (at the time, most *were* men) who specialized in sculpting the raw clay of field reporting into the finished story. In addition, photojournalism, although technologically possible in the 1880s, found its way into the newsroom.

Later, radio and then television news began to change the way stories were written. Tape recorders—though even now not widely used by newspaper reporters—made reporting more accurate. During the 1950s and 1960s, a new faster, safer typesetting system called photocomposition helped push deadlines back so that reporters could have a little more time to write and edit their stories. All of these inventions changed the lives of reporters, but perhaps none changed reporters' techniques as quickly and as significantly as the introduction of the computer into the newsroom.

The computer appeared in newsrooms as an extension of photocomposition technology. Two hundred years ago, the reporter (who typically was also the printer and the publisher) wrote news articles by hand and then selected individual letters of wood or metal to create lines of type from which a page was printed. When Otto Mergenthaler invented the automatic typesetter or Linotype in 1885, the process became speedier but still required an operator to retype the reporter's story. The photocomposition typesetter, introduced years later, also required repeating the reporter's keystrokes. Before long, sophisticated photocomposition computers had marched out of the newspaper's production

Dennis Montgomery, Associated Press bureau chief in Richmond, Va., checks a reporter's copy. (Photo by Steve Helber, Richmond AP staff, courtesy of AP/Wide World)

department and had replaced the reporters' old worn-out typewriters. Today's reporters virtually typeset their own stories using a computerized process the industry calls "capturing keystokes."

Journalists soon found that capturing keystrokes has several advantages. They found they could write stories on video display terminals more easily than on typewriters, because errors made on the terminals could be easily corrected. In addition, the terminals' optional automatic spelling checker could alert them to possible errors. (Publishers found they could save money because fewer employees—particularly compositors—were needed. Thus, many compositors found that they were out of work, except where typesetting unions exacted re-training concessions from newspaper owners.)

Let's look at a typical newspaper terminal. It looks a lot like a personal computer, with a television screen and an attached keyboard. Typically, the reporter activates, or "logs onto," the terminal by typing the date and one or two special letters to let the machine know someone is using it. Then the reporter types his or her name and the story identification, or "slug," and begins the story in earnest. Periodically, the reporter usually sends the story electronically to the computer's master tape storage area, a process called "writing to memory." By writing the story to memory, the copy is usually preserved in the case of a power failure.

The reporter also may store notes on the terminal and may type notes directly onto the machine during a telephone interview. The notes can be printed on a newsroom printer before writing the story or can simply be used on the terminal screen as needed by alternating images of the story in progress with images of the notes.

In addition, portable terminals are available for the reporter who must file the story far from the newsroom. The reporter covers the story, types the copy into a battery-powered portable terminal, finds a telephone, clamps a cup-like device connected to the terminal onto the telephone mouthpiece, and sends the story electronically to the newspaper's main computer.

Once a story is written—whether in the field or in the office—it is electronically sent to the city editor, who can then send it back to the reporter for rewriting if necessary. After the city editor is satisfied, the story is electronically transmitted to the news editor, the copy editor and finally the production department, where it is assigned a type size and reproduced on special photographic paper. The photographic paper is then merged with all of the other stories for that particular newspaper page and eventually transformed into a printing plate.

The Traditional Newsroom

The electronic newsroom and electronic copy processing is now the rule at most of America's daily and non-daily newspapers. At a few newspapers, however, traditional copy processing is still the standard. All of the newsroom players are the same in a traditional newsroom, but their tools are different. Electric, and sometimes manual, typewriters stand in for computers, and pencils and rubber cement take the place of electronic manipulation of stories. The reporter writes the story on a typewriter, edits the copy with a pencil (using copy editing symbols) and if paragraphs must be rearranged, cuts the paper apart and glues new paragraphs into the existing story.

In addition, carbon copies are required at most newspapers using traditional copy processing. At some newspapers, this means using sandwiches of interleaved pieces of paper and carbon material called "books." Unfortunately, after the story has been typed, the reporter must then separate the multiple carbons for use by various editors. Reporters and editors have long complained that peeling and separating a "multi-book" story takes an excrutiating amount of time when deadlines are looming.

Some newspapers that have abandoned the glue-pot-and-pencil approach to copy editing but are not yet fully electronic have opted for using modified electric typewriters that can generate specially marked stories. This coded copy can be read by machines called optical character readers. The character readers transform the typewritten copy into electronic data that can be edited on video display terminals. Thus, the reporter's typewritten story is eventually turned into electronic information. Newspapers usually use this process in transition from traditional copy editing to the electronic newsroom.

Dealing With Deadlines

Three-quarters of America's daily newspapers are published in the afternoon. These afternoon, or PM, newspapers—many of which serve small communities—account for less than one-half of the nation's daily circulation, however. Many of the morning newspapers are large circulation metropolitan or national dailies, such as The Wall Street Journal (with a weekday circulation of two million), USA Today and the New York Daily News (with circulations of more than 1.2 million each), the Los Angeles Times (circulating about one million copies), The New York Times (with a circulation of more than 900,000), and The Washington Post (circulating more than 700,000 copies). Because jobs are significantly easier to obtain at smaller newspapers, it is likely that the reporter beginning a newspaper career is apt to find a job initially at a small PM publication.

PM papers call for reporters who are early risers. For the newspaper to be home delivered by late afternoon, noon deadlines are common. To meet a noon deadline, reporters must often come to work by 6:30 or 7 a.m. and produce the majority of their copy at a time when many people are still working on their second cup of coffee. Afternoons at PM newspapers are usually saved for feature stories and other copy that can be published the following day.

AM newspapers, on the other hand, must reach subscribers before dawn, which typically means midnight deadlines. AM reporters typically come to work in the midafternoon and labor until the copy deadline, a schedule that requires high energy when many people are wearing down. Of course, AM reporters who routinely cover offices with 9-to-5 schedules often work those hours themselves.

Even though PM newspapers still outnumber AM papers, there has been a long trend toward morning publication because of the difficulty of delivering afternoon newspapers in traffic-clogged urban areas, and the pervasive power of early evening television news programming.

Whether a reporter's deadlines are at noon or midnight, the pressure of coping with a daily inflexible completion time requires a little strategy and a lot of personal tranquility. Let's look at strategy first. Assume you're a reporter for a 25,000 circulation afternoon newspaper. You work from 7 a.m. to 4 p.m. You write under deadline until noon, after which you take a one-hour lunch break and then write stories for the following day's edition, or for the Sunday paper.

When you arrive for work on Tuesday, you find a stack of yet-to-be rewritten press releases left over from the previous afternoon. You rewrite four short releases, saving a fifth release that requires additional information for after 8 a.m. when you can telephone the public relations person who wrote the story. After that call, your city editor tells you to cover a press conference being held by the mayor at 8:45 a.m. The city editor tells you the conference is being held to announce receipt of federal funds to build an addition to the city's sewage treatment plant. You know little about that story, and spend 10 minutes in the newspaper library scanning the files for previous stories on the subject.

The newspaper library, also known as the morgue, is a required stop for most reporters on their way to writing a story. The library, often tucked away at the back of the newsroom, is the depository for scissored clips of all of the local stories the newspaper has ever published. Stories there are usually arranged alphabetically by topic ("sewer," for instance) or by the name of the individual involved in the story (the mayor, for example). The library may also be electronic, in that the reporter can call up the clips on the terminal, take notes from them, and then send them back to their electronic home. In addition, newspaper libraries have numerous reference books, ranging from encyclopedias and almanacs to sources such as the National Directory of Addresses and Telephone Numbers, which lists 150,000 names and addresses of U.S. businesses and government agencies.

After you find four relevant stories in the library and take notes on the issue, you drive over to city hall to cover the conference. You listen to the mayor's prepared statement, pick up the mayor's own press release, ask some questions and drive back to the office, arriving at 9:45 a.m., two hours and 15 minutes from deadline. As you walk in the office, the city editor gives you one more story to complete by noon: A trucking union that delivers new cars to dealers across the United States has just gone on strike, and the editor wants you to survey the city's dozen new-car dealers to see how long they can hold out without additional deliveries of new cars.

At 10 a.m., you analyze your problems. You have to write the press conference story, which requires integration of notes from the newspaper files, the mayor's conference and the mayor's own press release; you also have to call a dozen auto dealers and get responses from them on the national trucker's strike. If you write the sewer story first and then have to wait for dealers to return your calls, you may not be able to finish the strike story. On the other hand, if you place the strike story calls first, get a couple of quick answers but have to wait for others to call back, you can be working on the sewer story while you are waiting. That becomes your strategy for beating the noon deadline.

You begin the calls at 10:10 a.m. As you predicted, you get through to the sales managers of four dealerships, interview them, but find yourself awaiting return calls from the other sales managers. While you wait, you begin composing your sewer story on your video display terminal. Composing on a terminal or typewriter is one of the most basic secrets of surviving in the newspaper business; writing a story in longhand first and then transferring it to a terminal is a waste of precious time and a sure sign of an amateur.

As you write, the returned calls start coming in. The newsroom has three lines, but you anticipate that one will be busy most of the time, leaving you with the possibility of receiving no more than two calls at one time. You instruct the switchboard to put all calls through to you, even if you are already talking with one party when the next call comes. Juggling incoming calls is another deadline survival technique. If you're speaking on the telephone with one party when a second call comes, you put the first party on hold long enough to ask the second party to please wait, get back to the first party and quickly finish the interview, then return to the second party, and so on.

By 11 a.m., while juggling calls, you finish your sewer story and begin working on the dealership story. You have interviews with eight of the dealers, enough to get a consensus that the dealers have a sufficient quantity of new cars to serve customers for 60 days. With that information, you begin writing your story, knowing that you can incorporate additional information into the story as the remaining calls come in. Unfortunately, however, at 11:30 a.m.—30 minutes from deadline—the city's biggest dealer has not returned your call. You call the dealer's secretary again, and explain why you need to talk to the dealer and that you must have his comments within the next 15 minutes if he is to be included in the story. You do this because you know that many news sources are not aware of story deadline times and will make time for you if they know how much you need to talk to them. Your key dealer calls you back in 10 minutes, apologizing for the delay, answers your question and at 11:55 a.m. you complete your story.

The strategy for deadline survival has worked, and worked because of four techniques. First, you anticipated potential problems and organized yourself accordingly. Second, you composed your story at the terminal. Third, you accomplished two tasks nearly simultaneously—you wrote the sewer story while you interviewed auto dealers. Finally, you had the presence of mind to juggle telephone calls and were not afraid to be persistent with sources. Of course, there are numerous other techniques for conquering deadlines, many of which you'll discover only as you have to meet those deadlines.

The Changing Newspaper

Overall newspaper readership is still growing. Average daily newspaper circulation reached an all-time high of more than 63 million in the mid-1980s. On the other hand, studies suggest that readership is not growing with the population and that the American public may be slowly losing the newspaper reading habit. Studies indicate that in 1967, 73 percent of those surveyed said they read a newspaper every day; by 1987, that figure had dropped. Although television news is often cited as the cause, the reason for the slow decline is not absolutely clear.

However, here is a scenario of how television has gained its ground, as suggested by a number of mass communication researchers: Televi-

A printer examines a Tulsa World page. (Photo courtesy of the Tulsa World)

sion, which began operating experimentally in the 1920s, didn't begin to capture the nation's interest until the late 1940s. Because television

ANOTHER ANSWER: THE "TAILORED" NEWSPAPER

In 1983 the writing and editing committee of The Associated Press Managing Editors Association took a look at how editors were coping with the electronic age. As part of that study, Clark Hoyt, managing editor of The Wichita Eagle-Beacon of Kansas and Trueman Farris, managing editor of the Milwaukee Sentinel, researched customized or "tailored" newspapers, which may be technically possible by the mid-1990s.

"Thousands of words pour into newspaper offices every day that never see print," wrote Hoyt and Farris. "Many of the stories would have high appeal to a limited number of readers but are crowded out of the newspaper by stories of wider interest. Discarded stories are a waste. A needless waste?

"Every newspaper editor dreams of being able to get those stories of special interest in print and delivered to the readers who want them, who are willing to pay good money to get them.

"The 'tailored newspaper' may be an answer to editors' dreams in a few years. Some think that newspapers tailored for an individual reader or a specific group of readers may be the way to send newspaper circulation soaring to new highs.

"Listen to John Naisbitt, author of the best selling 'Megatrends.' In a recent edition of Editor and Publisher, he was quoted as telling a meeting of newspaper promoters that more dailies may be forced to concentrate on special editions targeted to specific audiences of readers. He based his prediction on the swing from a centralized to a decentralized society.

"Listen to Stanton Cook, publisher of the Chicago Tribune. At the same meeting he urged finding ways to use the 80 percent of information that newspapers receive but never publish. Cook said: 'Within the newspaper itself we must learn to speak more directly and authoritatively towards special segments of our readership and indeed, potential readership.'

"And listen to a message from the magazine world. In a story on the facelift of Rolling Stone magazine in Printing Impressions, it was claimed that new printing processes would permit Rolling Stone 'to meet advertisers' and even editors' increasing clamour for split demographic runs to cater to the needs and interests of specified reader and distribution groups.'

"As a managing editor, how would you like to produce pages or sections in your newspaper that vary from copy to copy? How about being able to give a reader who is a nut about automobiles a full section of auto news while his next door neighbor, who is a fishing fool, would get no auto news but a lot of fishing news in the same space? Can that be done? Maybe not that finely, but it can be done. Today."

Hoyt and Farris believe the keys to tailoring are techniques such as pagination, hard-copy photography, satellite hard-copy delivery, Standard Advertising Units and ink-jet printing.

Pagination is a computerized method of storing text and graphics for quick assembly in the form of a newspaper page. Hoyt and Farris cited one expert who believes pagination will be widely used by 1990.

Hard-copy photography refers to computerized non-film photographs made by newspaper photojournalists. The computerized photographs can be quickly transmitted by telephone and easily edited on editors' terminals.

Satellite hard-copy delivery will provide newspapers with the means for quick delivery of national advertising as well as special interest stories, such as stories for an auto news section. Standard Advertising Units, a uniform way of selling advertising space that is now in wide use, will allow pagination systems to work more efficiently, Hoyt and Farris said.

Finally, ink-jet presses will allow production personnel to stop printing one section of a newspaper almost instantly in order to print another. Now, such section changes are time-consuming and costly. Ink jet technology can also be used for marking subscribers' tailored newspapers.

Hoyt and Farris noted: "With computerized circulation lists, with pagination, with quick fix ink-jet presses, with sophisticated inserting machines, tailored newspapers might well become a fact before too many years. With one remaining problem; how to get the tailored newspaper delivered to the right customer?" Hoyt and Farris concluded that such circulation problems can eventually be solved, too.

was perceived as an entertainment medium, the first customers it took were radio listeners and movie patrons. Newspapers, in general, served an information function and were not initially affected. In 1959, for example, people in one national survey clearly indicated newspapers as their major source of news. By the 1960s, though, as network television newscasts expanded from 15 to 30 minutes and local newscasts also grew in length and frequency, viewers—and most of the nation watched television by that time—began to rely on television as their major source of news. Today, television is still the primary source, the surveys show.

These realities are causing changes in the ways newspapers look and are written. In fact, newspapers are changing in some of the same ways that radio and motion pictures changed when leaders of those industries saw audiences defecting to television. Radio, which once featured weekly dramatic and comedy programs, discovered music and the disc jockey. Hollywood developed color, wide-screen, stereophonic sound, three dimensional projection and even movies called "smellies," which emitted odors. Newspapers are fighting television and seeking to retain their audience through a similar variety of techniques, including color photography, improved design, shorter stories in some cases (such as USA Today's style of presentation) and longer, more thoughtful magazine-style stories in other cases. In addition, newspapers are switching to morning delivery in ever increasing numbers to avoid competition with television's afternoon news stronghold and the delivery problems found during rush-hour in metropolitan areas. Will these strategies work? Will newspapers as we know them today survive?

Broadcast News

The Reporter

Radio and television reporters do not differ markedly from their print brethren—with two significant exceptions.

First, minorities and women are more common in broadcast reporting.

Second, in small cities or markets, experienced television reporters seem to earn about the same salary as veteran newspaper reporters in comparable places. In large markets, however, television reporters earn a great deal more money than their newspaper counterparts, according to a 1985 study by Jean Gaddy Wilson at the University of Missouri School of Journalism. The study noted that television reporters in the nation's largest cities earned an average salary of about $45,000, compared with an average salary of $32,000 earned by newspaper reporters working for the country's biggest papers. That's especially interesting because the 1985 median entry level salary for radio

Television crews cover a California murder trial. (AP/Wide World Photos)

and television reporters—$11,000—was lower than that for newspaper reporters, according to Dow Jones Newspaper Fund figures.

Television news pays better than radio news, according to a 1985 survey from the Radio-Television News Directors Association. The survey, conducted by Vernon Stone of Southern Illinois University at Carbondale, noted that a typical reporter at a large market television station makes almost twice as much money as a radio counterpart. Although television and radio salaries vary by market size, television reporters in the nation's smallest markets still earn more than radio reporters in those markets, Stone reported.

Newsroom Organization and the Role of the Editor

The nation's broadcast reporters are employed by about 10,000 radio and television stations. Ninety percent of those broadcast outlets are radio stations, but many radio stations have very small news departments, often with only a part-time reporter or a full-time news director who also is the station's sole reporter. Radio newsrooms staffed and organized like newspaper newsrooms are usually found only in America's largest big-city stations.

Television stations, on the other hand—especially those in the nation's biggest 100 markets—often have newsrooms somewhat similar to those found at newspapers. For example, a large television station's news department is headed by a news director, who is roughly equivalent to a newspaper's managing editor. The news director reports to the station's general manager, who is similar to a publisher. The general manager also employs department heads to supervise advertising sales, engineering, production, programming and other smaller departments, much like a publisher employs department heads to oversee advertising, production, circulation and business operations. At a medium market television station—perhaps a network affiliate serving a city with a population of 200,000—the news director will supervise an executive producer who in turn supervises other producers. The producers coordinate the news programs, in conjunction with one or more assignment editors and numerous reporter-photographer teams.

While the news gathering process varies from station to station as well as by market size, it works something like this. Reporters are sent to cover stories by the assignment editor. When the photography is complete and the story is written and assembled on videotape, editorial control passes to the producer, who is responsible for the day-to-day content of a particular newscast. The producer can order changes—in writing, selection of videotape or length of story, for example—as can the executive producer and the news director.

In summary, television reporting, like newspaper reporting, is a collaborative effort often involving many editors: a news director who supervises the station's reporting, an assignment editor who decides what stories will be covered, numerous producers who help shape stories, and videotape editors who assemble the final product. Editorial collaboration is necessary because of the variety of skills required to get stories on the air quickly.

How a Reporter Functions in a Broadcast Newsroom

Reporters at medium market television stations often work more traditional hours than newspaper reporters. Typically, a television reporter comes to work about 9 a.m. and finishes the day at about 6 p.m. During that period, the reporter will often cover two or three stories, usually with a photographer. In some cases, the photographer shoots the story while the reporter gathers information by telephone. When the tape is returned to the station, the reporter watches it, and then writes a story to accompany the video.

To get a closer look at the process, let's suppose you are assigned to cover a speech. There are a number of ways to execute this kind of assignment, but here's a common approach. You and the photographer pack up the camera, recorder, batteries, lights and other necessary equipment, and take the gear to the place where the speech is occurring. When you arrive, you learn what the speech is about and decide how to cover the story. You choose to tape some of the main speaker's remarks and tell the photographer which segments of the speech you want to have taped. After the speech, you interview the speaker on-camera. Based on what you've seen and heard, you mentally write the story, including an introduction. Then you memorize that introduction, and the photographer videotapes your opening.

You return to the station, look at the videotape, select the portions you want to appear in the final "package" that will be aired and then write your story. You also write a set of instructions for the videotape editor, who assembles the tape. After the story, with its selections from the speech and the on-camera interview, is assembled, you record your narration where needed on the tape. Finally, you write a brief introduction to your story, which will be used—perhaps with revisions—by the person anchoring the newscast.

You may be asked to rewrite the story for use on a later newscast. News directors try to avoid identical stories on the early and late evening news programs.

If you work for a typical medium market station, you will repeat this process several more times during the day. The final story of the day—the story assigned at 3 p.m. for a 6 p.m. airing—is obviously produced under much more intense pressure than stories covered earlier in the day.

In addition to all of this, you may have noon or weekend anchor duties or may be required to go on the air "live" when a major news event occurs.

As you've undoubtedly noticed, broadcast reporters' tools are different than those used by newspaper reporters, but the principles of quality reporting and the importance of skilled editorial supervisors (whatever their titles) remain the same.

Now that you understand more about the basics of news and newsroom operation for both print and broadcast media, we will examine writing techniques, beginning in Chapter 3.

/p
BEIRUT, Lebanon (AP) _ An American who runs a private
kidnapped by four gunmen Tuesday on his way to play go
responsibility in the name of the Shiite Moslem group
The kidnapping was the first abduction of an American
months./p
The U.S. Embassy identified the victim as Frank Herbert
Mass., director of the Lebanese International School in
Islamic Jihad, which espouses the fundamentalist teach
Ruhollah Khomeini, has said it holds at least three oth
A spate of politically motivated kidnappings in west Be
most Americans and other Westerners to leave the city.
accused Reed of being a CIA spy./p
Police said the assailants, toting silencer-equipped p
dark blue Volvo, rammed Reed's chauffeur-driven car on
a.m. near the ruins of a supermarket in west Beirut's B
Reed was driving from his home in west Beirut's Manara
golf at the war-scarred course on the city's southern e
from the Volvo, forced Reed and his Lebanese driver at
kidnappers' car and sped off, police said./p
The driver was freed minutes later a few hundred yards
Syrian intelligence officers in charge of enforcing a s
law and order in west Beirut. Until Tuesday, no foreign
since Syrian troops moved into west Beirut on July 4./p

CHAPTER 3

Newswriting Basics

The Summary News Lead: Who, What, When, Where, Why and How

Varying the Lead

The Inverted Pyramid

Electronic and Traditional Copy Preparation

Writing Obituaries

An Overview of Wire Service Style

Rewriting the Press Release

Writing the Simple News Story

Attribution

Writing the Multiple Incident Story

Copy Editing for Clarity and Conciseness

Radio Newswriting

The Summary News Lead: Who, What, When, Where, Why and How

In the first two chapters, you were introduced to many complex and perhaps even disquieting aspects of news. You read about what makes news and how what is considered news varies from time to time and place to place. You learned that reporters and editors often decide not to use entire stories and that they almost always exclude some information from the stories they do cover—for which they are often harshly criticized. You learned that reporters must write accurately, objectively, completely, fairly and with balance. You also learned that readers often scan stories quickly and carelessly. And you learned that readers have a long shopping list of complaints against the news media but rarely communicate their anger to reporters.

Your job now is to take a deep breath, pump up your courage, sharpen your note-taking pencil and learn how to write and edit news stories in such a way that you convince readers that you and your news organization are reliable and worthy of their respect.

If every journey begins with a single step, the first step in writing a news story—after you organize your information—is composing the initial paragraph, or *lead*. (This is sometimes spelled *lede*.) The news story lead is typically one sentence containing fewer than 35 words. (Some editors insist that no lead exceed 25 words.) The task of the lead is to sum up the story by answering the six traditional questions of journalism: *who, what, when, where, why* and *how*. This kind of lead is called a *summary lead*. Reporters say the lead is usually the most difficult part of the story to write because the writer must have a clear understanding of every facet of the story in order to explain often complex information in one or two concise sentences.

Let's suppose you are assigned to write a story about a man in your city who has been injured in an automobile accident. Here is your lead, based on information you receive from the city police and the local hospital:

> Norman Whitehurst, 42, of 801 Vest Drive, was seriously injured Tuesday morning in a one-car accident near the intersection of U.S. 13 and Gay Street, according to Warrensburg police.

Let's test the lead to see if it does what it's supposed to do. Does it sum up the gist of the story in fewer than 35 words? It does, and it accomplishes the job with only 30 well-chosen words. Does it answer the question *who*? Yes; the *who* is Whitehurst, as well as his age and his address. The lead also answers the questions *what* (a one-car accident that seriously injured someone), *when* (Tuesday morning) and *where* (near the intersection of U.S. 13 and Gay Street in Warrensburg).

This lead fails to tell the reader *how* and *why* the accident occurred, however. Decades ago, a newspaper lead was unacceptable if it did not answer each of the six lead questions. Today, editors allow more flexi-

---

Chapter opening photo: The video display terminal is replacing the typewriter in most American newsrooms. (Staff photo by Gary Dunkin, Kansas City Times)

bility. Modern editors insist that the news lead summarize the story for the reader—usually by answering as many of the six questions as possible—but editors also realize that answering every question may result in an overly long, complicated sentence. Thus, the answers to one or two of the lead questions—frequently the *how* and the *why*—are now often saved for the second paragraph of news stories. Here is an example of such a second paragraph, complete with information about how and why the Whitehurst accident occurred:

> Police said the accident occurred when Whitehurst, who was driving north on U.S. 13, apparently fell asleep and lost control of his vehicle about 5:30 a.m. Whitehurst's car crossed the highway median and struck a telephone pole at the northeast corner of the intersection, police said.

Note that this second paragraph also gives the reader more detailed information about *when* and *where* the accident happened.

The lead should do more than merely answer the questions *who, what, when, where, why* and *how*. First, the lead should make complete sense to the casual reader who doesn't want to read in detail about Whitehurst's accident. In fact, newspapers serving large communities where many serious accidents occur would probably run *only* the lead of this story, if they use the story at all. In addition, the lead should provide the more serious reader with a loose table of contents of what can be expected in the rest of the story, peaking the person's interest to read further. Finally, the lead should suggest a good headline for the editor who may have time to read only the lead, before writing something such as: Local Man Hurt in Accident.

Varying the Lead

Not all leads, of course, must begin like the Whitehurst example, which is a *who* lead because it emphasizes the name of the person involved in the news event. A lead may also emphasize *what, when, where, why* or *how*. Let's take the Whitehurst example again and try variations of it. A *who* lead such as this is very common, which is one of the reasons it reads so well. Let's try a *what* lead:

> A one-car accident at the intersection of U.S. 13 and Gay Street Tuesday morning seriously injured Norman Whitehurst, 42, of 801 Vest Drive, according to Warrensburg police.

The *what* lead, which here emphasizes what happened to Whitehurst, also is common. Reporters find the *who* or the *what* lead is the best choice in most cases.

When leads are more unusual and so tend to read oddly. Here is a *when* lead:

> A Tuesday morning one-car accident at the intersection of U.S. 13 and Gay Street seriously injured Norman Whitehurst, 42, of 801 Vest Drive, according to Warrensburg police.

Reporters use *when* leads on those occasions when the time element is critical to the understanding of a story. For example, if an airplane crashed into a school an hour after all the children went home, a *when* lead might be the best choice.

Here is another variation:

> The intersection of U.S. 13 and Gay Street was the scene of a one-car accident Tuesday morning that seriously injured Norman Whitehurst, 42, of 801 Vest Drive, according to Warrensburg police.

Obviously this is a *where* lead, which is also a little unusual. A *where* lead is appropriate only when the location of the news event takes precedence over all other factors. In the Whitehurst story, this might be appropriate if that intersection was Warrensburg's most dangerous corner.

Next, let's look at a *how* lead:

> A one-car collision with a telephone pole at the intersection of U.S. 13 and Gay Street Tuesday morning seriously injured Norman Whitehurst, 42, of 801 Vest Drive, according to Warrensburg police.

This lead answers the question, How was Whitehurst injured?

Let's look at a final example, a *why* lead:

> Driver drowsiness was the cause of a one-car accident Tuesday morning at the intersection of U.S. 13 and Gay Street, Warrensburg police said. The accident seriously injured the vehicle's only occupant, Norman Whitehurst, 42, of 801 Vest Drive.

Notice that this *why* lead is two sentences and 39 words long and more than a little awkward. As a rule, if the lead is awkward and unusually difficult to write, it is because the writer is trying to force an unnatural sentence structure. Try writing *who* or *what* leads most of the time and combined *why* and *how* leads only when they are appropriate to the story and when their construction seems natural. By the same token, *when* and *where* leads will almost always seem unnatural and should be used with caution.

The Inverted Pyramid

Once the story is summarized in the lead, the typical news story presents the details in a declining order of importance. This structure is called the *inverted pyramid*. Many, though not all, news stories are written this way.

There are both historical and contemporary reasons for writing news stories in the inverted pyramid fashion. The form began during the American Civil War, between 1861 and 1865. Before then, the typical news story was often wordy and written chronologically. The inverted pyramid style of newswriting emerged as war correspondents filed stories over battlefield telegraph lines where wordiness meant extra expense and chronological order meant a story's critical ending was never received if the line was cut during transmission. These ingenious war reporters soon learned that the solution was to send a concise story with a summary lead and then other information more or less in the order of importance. When the war ended, stories continued to be sent by telegraph and later overseas cable. Gradually, the inverted pyramid style of newswriting gained widespread acceptance.

Today, stories are written in the inverted pyramid style for reasons that have nothing to do with telegraph lines or the Civil War. The inverted pyramid form makes sense today because it lends itself to newspaper readers who spend only 20 or perhaps 30 minutes with the day's printed news. These busy, fickle readers can scan headlines and, finding one with appeal, can then read the lead to see if the story does, indeed, contain information of interest. If the readers begin to dig into the story, they also can feel free to desert at any point, knowing that they have read the most important information.

A second reason for using the inverted pyramid today has to do with the hurried manner in which newspapers are assembled. The newspaper's advertising department has first crack at space in the newspaper; news goes in the left-over room, a space known as the *news hole*. The process is a little like having two trains on the same track; while ads are being sold, stories are being written, and eventually the two will collide. When that happens—when the news editor discovers that there are too many stories for too little space—something has to go. Advertisements are rarely removed, or *bumped*, so the news editor must either omit stories or shorten them. Some stories are sent to an electronic or real wastebasket, but many stories are just shortened to allow them to fit into the newspaper. Placing the least important information at the end of a news story greatly assists the harried editor charged with shortening the story. The editor can often remove a few final offending paragraphs of a long story without harming it much.

Like the lead, the inverted pyramid structure needs to be tested. Several questions should be asked of all stories written in the inverted pyramid form: Is everything promised in the lead actually delivered in the body of the story? Can the half-hearted reader stop at any point in the story without missing critical information? Are the paragraphs strung together with some kind of transitional unity, so that the story flows smoothly?

Let's look at the structure of the entire Whitehurst accident story:

Norman Whitehurst, 42, of 801 Vest Drive, was seriously injured Tuesday morning in a one-car accident near the intersection of U.S. 13 and Gay Street, according to Warrensburg police.

Police said the accident occurred when Whitehurst, who was driving north on U.S. 13, apparently fell asleep and lost control of his vehicle about 5:30 a.m. Whitehurst's car crossed the highway median and struck a telephone pole at the northeast corner of the intersection, police said.

Whitehurst is in serious condition at the Central Missouri Regional Medical Center, a hospital official said. Police said he was not wearing a seat belt.

Whitehurst's car was demolished, police said.

We've already examined the lead, so let's look at the second paragraph, which is designed to answer any questions the reader might have about *how* or *why* the accident happened. One-car accidents are often caused by weather conditions or by drunken drivers returning home in the early morning hours. This paragraph tells the reader the police believe neither was true in Whitehurst's case.

The third paragraph gives us information about the driver's medical condition and where he is being treated, and also suggests why he may have been injured. The fourth paragraph is barely necessary, although it does provide some information for curious readers.

Now for the test: Is everything promised in the lead actually delivered in the body of the story? Yes, and perhaps even a little more if you count the information about the degree of damage done to Whitehurst's vehicle. Can the half-hearted reader stop at any point in the story without missing critical information? Certainly, although the second, third and fourth paragraphs offer important information. Are the paragraphs strung together with some kind of transitional unity, so that the story flows smoothly? Yes, primarily because the paragraphs are linked with the recurring words *Whitehurst* and *police*.

The word *police* serves another function in this story; it attributes where the reporter got the information for the story. You'll read more about guidelines for attribution later in this chapter.

Electronic and Traditional Copy Preparation

Before you begin to write, you need to know something about the mechanics of writing a news story on a video display terminal or a typewriter.

The majority of American daily newspapers have replaced their aging manual and electric typewriters with video display terminals. To the untrained eye, the terminals look like personal computers. In reality, they are typically more akin to true word processors in that they have special conveniences for writers—such as a single key to insert or delete material—not available with all personal computers.

Here's how the terminals typically work. The reporter sits down at the machine, which appears to be little more than a keyboard and a blinking green or amber television screen, and types in his or her name, the date and some sort of story identification called a *slug*. The slug is a short word that allows the reporter or editor to retrieve the story later. Then the reporter begins the story.

As the reporter types, a blinking light called a "cursor" moves across the screen. At the end of each line, the computer automatically moves any word that extends beyond the right margin to the next line. This feature is called *word wrap*. If a word needs to be changed, the reporter simply puts the cursor on the first letter of the word and retypes a new word over it. If a word needs to be removed, the reporter can touch a special "delete" key, which, with the blink of an eye, whisks away the word—or sentences, paragraphs and entire pages if necessary, or if the reporter is clumsy. To insert a word, sentence, paragraph or page, the reporter taps an "insert" key at the chosen spot and a space opens up on the line. If paragraphs need to be transposed, the reporter usually marks the target paragraph with a special code, then marks the new destination of that paragraph, touches another key or two and the paragraph is transferred.

Other features are usually also available, such as "global search." With this feature, a reporter can tell the terminal to search throughout the text for an item such as a misspelled word. For example, if *embarrassment* is spelled *embarassment* in the story, the terminal will search for each misspelled word and ask the reporter if a change should be made as it finds them. In addition, some terminals have special keys that can be temporarily dedicated for special use. These keys, called *user defined keys*, can be trained to spit out stock phrases that are used again and again, such as "Soviet General Secretary Mikhail S. Gorbachev" or "Mayor Emmanuel E. Paraschos." Storing such stock phrases saves time.

After the story has been entered on the terminal, the reporter adds a special code to the end of the story to tell the computer the story is finished. Then the reporter electronically sends the article to the computer's master memory, where it is held in storage—a power failure notwithstanding—until an editor retrieves it for polishing. Later, the edited story is set into type.

Each newspaper computer system varies a little from this description, but in general, the procedure for using a terminal is similar to what has been described. Whatever the system, most reporters can master the equipment in a few days.

A few daily newspapers and some weeklies do not yet have terminals. At those papers, reporters write stories on typewriters and use special copy editing symbols to correct mistakes and make them understandable to editors. The reporter using this traditional system types his or her name, the date and the story slug (with single spacing) in the upper left hand corner of the piece of paper and begins the story (with double or triple spacing) about one-third of the way down the page. This space provides room for editorial instructions, such as headline and picture information, that will be added later. The reporter uses a 60-character line with a five-space indentation for paragraphs and does not hypenate words at the end of a line. If the story continues to a second page, the reporter makes certain that both the sentence and the paragraph conclude at the end of the page and types "MORE" at the bottom of the page. At the top of the second page, the reporter types his or her last name, followed on the next line by the slug and the words "1ST ADD," which means the first addition to the first page. At the end of the story, the reporter types "— 30 —," a traditional symbol that dates back to at least the 1870s and means the story is complete. Finally, the reporter circles all editorial information, such as the names and slugs. (See figure 3–1)

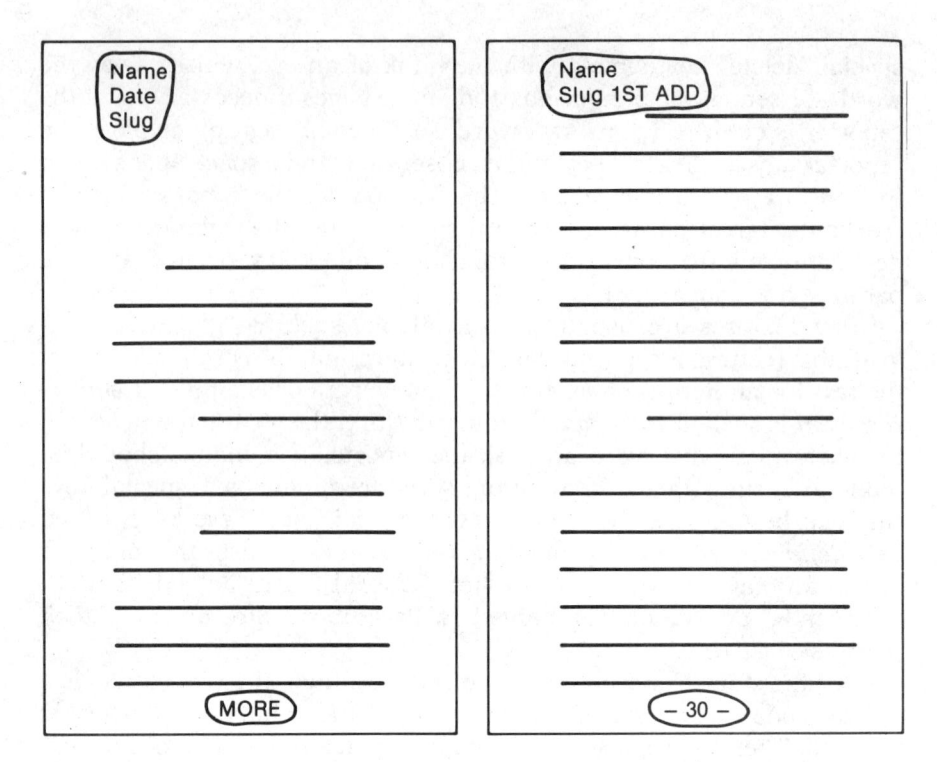

Figure 3-1: *This figure shows the way typewriter-produced copy should look.*

After typing the story, the reporter uses a pencil to edit it with copy editing symbols. These symbols are used to correct typing, spelling and newspaper style errors, as well as to improve the clarity of the story. A pen is not recommended for copy editing, because good stories aren't written—they're re-written. Editing and re-editing in ink will make the copy look like a chicken stepped in an ink bottle and walked across the story. Many of the copy editing symbols and the way they are used in the reporter's story are shown in the following table.

Meaning	Use
New Paragraph	police said. Whitehurst is
Remove Material	Warrensburg city police
Remove Inside Letter	Gay Streeet
Remove Letter At Word End	Warrensburge police
Insert Word	of 801 Drive
Insert Letter	Norman Whithurst
Insert Punctuation	Norman Whitehurst, 42,
	Whitehurst's car
	I'm not hurt, he said.
	one car accident

Close up space	Nor man Whitehurst
Create space	Norman‎Whitehurst
Change to capital letter	Norman whitehurst
Change to lower case letter	Warrensburg Police
Transpose words	Whitehurst in is serious
Transpose letters	Whitehrust is in serious
Abbreviate	(United States) 13
Spell out	U.S. 13 and Gay (St.)
Use numerals	U.S. (Thirteen)
Use letters	(1)-car accident
Remove and condense	spokesman said. ~~He was not thrown from the car.~~ Police said he
Remove paragraph	~~Police said he wasn't hurt.~~

Writing Obituaries

Beginning reporters usually have to prove themselves capable of handling small assignments before more significant stories are sent their way. Often, the new reporter will spend weeks and perhaps even months writing obituaries, rewriting press releases and handling simple stories before the editor nods approval. That's because the editor knows that writing these kinds of stories is an excellent way for the reporter to learn the newspaper's terminals and procedures. The "junk desk"—there's actually a somewhat less polite word usually used in place of "junk"—also is an excellent place for the editor to learn if the reporter is accurate.

An obituary is a news story about a person's death. A death notice is usually written and paid for by relatives, while the obituary is staff-written and usually free.

As a reporter, you typically write about most people only three times: when they are born, when they get married and when they die. Birth notices usually only occupy a line or two. Engagement announcements and wedding stories usually are also very short and are often written according to a fill-in-the-blank formula. The obituary, however, is often a much deeper story, providing readers with a profile of the deceased, and while it may have a fill-in-the-blank quality about it, it also offers you the opportunity to give readers a lot of interesting information. Most importantly, you learn accuracy, because the obituary is the last time most people are mentioned in the newspaper and getting the information right is critical. If you misspell a deceased's name, you—and the newspaper—will never be forgiven by relatives.

While the obituary structure varies some from newspaper to newspaper, it has a fairly consistent organization used across the country. That structure—a *modified inverted pyramid*—starts with a summary lead that tells the reader who died, and when, where and perhaps why the death occurred. The second paragraph is biographical and may be organized either in chronological order or in order of importance. The next paragraph usually lists the survivors, often in this somewhat sexist order: husband or wife; sons and daughters; parents; brothers and sisters; and grandchildren. The fourth paragraph gives the reader at least two pieces of information: when and where the funeral will be and where the burial will take place. This structure is a modified inverted pyramid, because unlike the true inverted pyramid, the obituary really cannot be trimmed from the bottom without losing important information. On the other hand, the obituary does have a summary news lead like the inverted pyramid.

Obituaries are based on information supplied by the family. You may receive that information on a special obituary form that the newspaper gives to funeral homes, or the funeral home may call you. Whatever the delivery system, as a reporter, you should be ready to ask questions rather than merely accept the family's prepared information. Unfortunately, asking questions frequently means you must contact family members while they are grieving. That can be unpleasant, but accepting information without asking these questions is like telling a news source, "Tell me what you think I need to know." You might get all the information you need for a story, but chances are you will only get a portion of the story.

Let's take a look at an obituary and dissect it.

Otto Arthur, 70, of 1412 Marcum Terrace, died Thursday at University Medical Center.

Arthur was born in the Bronx, a borough of New York City, and graduated from the U.S. Merchant Marine Academy. He was an officer on merchant ships until 1942, when he joined the Army as a warrant officer. After the war, he was an officer on oil tankers sailing from East Coast to Gulf Coast ports. He retired in 1972 and moved to Huntington. He was a member of the American Legion.

He is survived by his wife, Marguerite, of Huntington; a son, Jay Arthur of Little Rock, Ark.; and two brothers, Edward Arthur of Troy, N.Y., and Sidney Arthur of New York City.

Funeral will be at 2 p.m. Thursday at Willis and Sons Funeral Home in Huntington. Burial will be at Roselawn Memorial Park.

First, let's look at the lead. The obituary uses a traditional summary lead that answers the questions *who* (Otto Arthur, 70, of 1412 Marcum Terrace), *what* (he died), *when* (Thursday) and *where* (at University Medical Center). If the circulation area of the newspaper you are writing for is large enough, you may have to clarify in which city the home address and medical center are located. Note, too, that the cause of death is not given. That's because the information is usually not available. However, the cause of death is news; it is *not* in poor taste. In fact, many newspaper readers say they look for hints of the cause of death, such as places to which memorial donations may be sent, in stories without that information. In short, if you obtain the cause of death, use it unless your newspaper has a policy against its publication.

The second paragraph provides biographical information. Here is where you need to dig for information. The biographical portion of an obituary is the meatiest part, and yet, it is the place where information from the funeral home may be the scantiest. For example, what would you, a thorough reporter, do if the funeral director had telephoned the obituary information and had said Arthur was born "in the New York City area"? New York City is a big place. Where was Arthur born, specifically? you would ask. If the funeral director had said Arthur didn't have any training after high school but was a ship's officer, you would call Arthur's family to ask for clarification. If the funeral director had said Arthur didn't belong to any organizations, you would again make a note to call the family for clarification. An absolute statement like that is rarely true—it should not be accepted at face value.

The third and fourth paragraphs of the obituary almost write themselves. They follow some strict rules of style. First, note in the third paragraph that relatives are set off in groups by semicolons. Next, note that some cities have state abbreviations and some do not. The story follows wire service style, which you will read about shortly. Third, note that the words *funeral* and *burial* are not preceded by the word *the*. That's because news writing is concise, and unnecessary words such as *that* and *the* can be omitted under certain circumstances. Finally, note that the basic facts about the funeral service are given in order of the time of day followed by the day of the week followed by the place. That order is used in almost all news stories.

An Overview of Wire Service Style

You may have noticed that the Arthur obituary follows specific rules for abbreviation, capitalization and use of titles. Most newspapers have a *style manual* that reporters are required to learn. The style manual answers questions such as what states to abbreviate and how to abbreviate them, whether to use numerals for the age of Arthur in his obituary, and whether the country in southeast Asia is Viet Nam or Vietnam.

The goal of following a consistent style is to save time, space and money, as well as to create a more professional-looking publication. Reporters work faster because they know exactly how to solve style problems, and editors save time because less editing is necessary. In addition, expensive space is saved because most style rules—such as using *Dr.* instead of *Doctor*—favor brevity. All of that adds up to a

58 Newswriting Basics

Jon Hall, an investigative reporter at the New Haven, Conn., Register, edits a story. (Peter R. Hivzdak/Jackson Newspapers, New Haven)

more economically efficient newspaper. Finally, a uniform appearance throughout the newspaper created by a consistent style suggests professionalism, a commodity newspapers seek to nurture in readers' minds.

At one time, reporters who moved from newspaper to newspaper were confronted with learning new style manuals the size of telephone books at each place of employment. In 1960, The Associated Press and United Press International wire services compiled a slim common stylebook, which many newspapers also adopted. In 1977, the common stylebook was expanded and has been regularly revised since then. While the two wire service style manuals have different appearances and features,—for instance, the AP manual has a 20-page entry on libel and invasion of privacy—the rules are almost the same. For example, at last count, there were fewer than a dozen significant variances between the AP and UPI books. How does this affect a reporter who does not work for a wire service? Simple. Most daily newspapers today use the joint wire service style, with minor local variations. Thus, the reporter who moves from one newspaper to another typically must master only a few special, local style rules.

An excerpt of the joint wire service style manual appears in Appendix A.

Rewriting the Press Release

After mastering the use of the terminal and the obituary, with its reporting and style problems, often the next reportorial hurdle is rewriting the press release. Press, or news, releases arrive at the typical newsroom by the hundreds each day. The releases are usually written by public information, public affairs and public relations specialists working for businesses, institutions, governmental bodies and civic organizations. Sometimes writers at expensive public relations and advertising firms write releases; sometimes poorly trained but well meaning civic volunteers do. Whatever their source, most releases wind up in newsroom trash cans, either because they are not newsworthy at all or because they are newsworthy somewhere but not where they have been sent.

The releases that survive the gauntlet of editors' eyes are usually rewritten. They are rewritten because they are too long, are not sufficiently local, have the lead buried somewhere deep in the story, lack necessary information or do not follow newspaper style. They may also mention the sponsor's name too frequently. Release writers are trained to mention the sponsoring organization's name once in every paragraph or so, and reporters are trained to remove those names wherever possible. It's a guerrilla war of words, and reporters try to win.

The technique for rewriting a press release—or most types of news stories for that matter—is simple. First, separate fact from opinion. Opinion has little place in a news story; if it is used, it requires attribution to a source. Some reporters merely cross the opinion out, and they are left with the body of the story. Next, figure out what the story is about, and write the lead. Finally, search the release for unanswered questions. If you find any, call the release writer for more information. Here's an example of a release sent to a daily newspaper in a state capital:

Roberta Burford, 31, has been named special counsel to Attorney General John Stevens, it was announced Tuesday.

Miss Burford, who previously held the title of chief of staff for Attorney General Stevens, will assume her duties next Monday.

Prior to joining Attorney General Stevens' office, she was an intern for the antitrust division of the attorney general's office and before that was an administrative assistant for the Legislative Joint Performance Review Board.

What is wrong with the release? On the positive side, it's in English. On the negative side, there are numerous unanswered questions that a thorough reporter should ask: Is it necessary to mention Stevens three times? What will Burford do as special counsel and what did she do as chief of staff? Is the job change a promotion or just a reshuffling of personnel? What is the Legislative Joint Performance Review Board, other than five long words? Where did Burford graduate from law school—and undergraduate school for that matter? What is her address, in case the editor wants that in the story? All of these questions should be answered—and perhaps included in the rewrite of the release.

Writing the Simple News Story

Graduation day. No more obituaries; no more press releases. On to meatier news stories, though short ones, to be sure. Actually, you've already read a short news story—the article about the Whitehurst accident. Other types of short news stories include advance stories about meetings, speeches and civic events, as well as stories about accidents, crimes, fires and weather damage. Of course, any story can be short. It is conceivable that a reporter could cover a three-hour council meeting and be told to write a three-paragraph story about the event. Some stories, though, simply deserve to be brief, such as the Whitehurst accident. Let's look at how you gathered the information and wrote the article.

Most large daily newspapers routinely assign experienced reporters to make daily visits to area police and fire stations to cover this kind of story, among others. Smaller newspapers also cover police and fire agencies, but on a more random basis and often with less experienced reporters. Size notwithstanding, virtually all daily newspapers have an available reporter—usually a beginning reporter—make routine telephone calls to public safety agencies just before deadline. That's how this story came to be. The procedure in making these newsgathering telephone calls to police is usually to call the radio dispatcher and ask that officer or the ranking officer on duty—often called a watch commander—if anything newsworthy has happened in the last few hours.

In this case, the watch commander tells you, the reporter, that a personal injury accident has occurred within the past hour. You ask for more information, and the watch commander supplies it from the accident report written by the investigating officer. As the officer reads portions of the report, you ask for clarifications. How is Whitehurst's name spelled? At what speed was Whitehurst driving? Was anyone else in the vehicle? Did Whitehurst tell the investigating officer why he drove into the telephone pole? Where was Whitehurst taken for treatment? After talking with the watch commander, you call the hospital where Whitehurst is being treated. Whitehurst's admission and condition must be confirmed before you can write the story.

These questions are absolutely necessary; without them, the story would be incomplete or possibly inaccurate. The ability to gather complete information—whether the information is for an accident story, an obituary or the rewrite of press release—is a critical component of excellent newswriting. The thorough reporter must look for gaps in every story, because without understanding every facet of what happened, it is impossible to write an article accurately and clearly.

Writing the Whitehurst story is not particularly difficult. The only significant writing decision you must make is whether to use the traditional news lead, which is also called a *summary news lead*, or a variation called a *general lead*. The general lead answers the traditional *who, what, when, where, why* and *how* questions, but answers them in a nonspecific or general way. The general lead must be followed by another paragraph—in reality, a summary lead—that explains the events in detail. Here is an example of the Whitehurst story, written with the general lead and the second or sublead.

A Warrensburg man was seriously injured Tuesday in an auto accident downtown, Warrensburg police said.

Norman Whitehurst, 42, of 801 Vest Drive, was injured at 5:30 a.m. in a one-car accident near the intersection of U.S. 13 and Gay Street, police said.

As you can see, using the general lead takes about twice as much space as using a summary lead. Even so, reporters frequently use the general lead in two situations. The first occurs when a story is extraordinarily complex and cannot be adequately explained by a short summary lead. Consider this situation: One committee of the state Legislature, the Legislative Joint Performance Review Board, a watchdog group, recommends the abolition of another state committee, the state Board of Embalmers, which licenses funeral home workers, because the work of that group is duplicated by a third board, the state Board of Funeral Directors. Using a summary lead for this alphabet soup mixture of boards would probably confuse the average reader. A general lead such as this might help solve the problem:

> A state watchdog board recommended Tuesday that the state committee licensing funeral embalmers be disbanded because those workers are already licensed by a third state group.

The other occasion for using a general lead is when the *who, what, when, where, why* or *how* of a summary lead would have little meaning to the average reader because of the size of the community. Many wire service stories are written with general leads because the "community" is often the entire country. Even locally, the community may be so large that an individual in a story is virtually anonymous. That situation dictated the following general lead in a Denver newspaper:

> A driver for the Capitol Cab Company was beaten to death early Sunday outside a Brighton bar. Police have arrested four men for investigation of homicide.

The Whitehurst story, however, deserves a summary lead, because it is not complex and the town Whitehurst lives in is small enough for some readers to recognize his name or at least the location of the accident. Once you have decided on the lead, the structure of the Whitehurst story is simple: you give an explanation of *how* and *why* the accident occurred, followed by slightly less important information about Whitehurst's injuries, and finally, even less important information about the damage to his car.

All simple stories follow this procedure. As a reporter, you carefully and quickly gather information. You identify and often eliminate opinion; if you leave it in the story, you attribute it. You check and re-check your information for gaps. If you don't understand part of a story, you gather more information. When you are satisfied you completely understand the story, you write either a summary or general lead, followed by the rest of the story in an order of declining importance.

Attribution

Attribution is identification of the source of information. Readers—and editors—require it so that they can determine that a source said something rather than a reporter. The favored word for attribution in news stories is *said*, because it is absolutely neutral. Other nearly neutral possibilities include *added, asked, inquired, noted, pointed out* and *responded*. Other attributive words, such as *alleged, charged, claimed, divulged, hinted, proclaimed* and *stated*, are significantly less neutral and should not be used unless they are appropriate.

The rules of attribution are simple: All information that is not universally known should be attributed. Reporters probably do not need to attribute the fact that the Earth is round; that is universally understood and will not change. On the other hand, if a police officer says that an accident victim, Whitehurst for example, is in serious condition at a local hospital, the source should be attributed, for Whitehurst's condition may change. Attribution is even more important when writing about events that may be subject to various interpretations, such as Whitehurst falling asleep while driving.

All quotations should be attributed as well. Reporters use three kinds of quotation: *direct, indirect and partial quotations*. The following paragraph contains all three:

> "I won't be a candidate for county commissioner," McCuen said, adding that he wouldn't consider "any office" in the next two years. McCuen said the party should consider him unavailable until 1990.

"I won't be a candidate for county commissioner" is a direct quotation. Direct quotations require attribution in every paragraph or so for the sake of clarity. (In single source stories with two or more successive paragraphs of direct quotation, one attribution every other paragraph may suffice.) The phrase *"any office"* is an example of a partial quotation, and *the party should consider him unavailable until 1990* is an example of an indirect quotation. For clarity, partial and indirect quotations require attribution every time they appear.

Writing the Multiple Incident Story

At 9:05 p.m., a black funnel cloud drops from the sky and a tornado sweeps through the oldest residential area of your town. After splintering a few dozen homes, the storm passes over downtown and makes its way to a water pumping station, where it swallows part of the city's water treatment facility. As it moves out of town, the storm destroys two high tension towers, which carry power into the city. The town is left with three fatalities, hundreds injured and homeless, and no electricity or water. The quiet of the night returns. The tornado has finished its work, but as a reporter, your work is just beginning. You face a special kind of story—a *multiple incident story.*

The multiple incident story presents itself when two or more events of equal weight occur within a short period and each event rightfully belongs in the lead of the story. Examples include natural disasters that result in human injury and property destruction, complicated city council meetings, and dramatic situations such as fires with fatalities, bank robberies with captures, and suicides linked to homicides or accidental deaths.

When a multifaceted story breaks, you are faced with a complex writing task. There are two approaches to writing the multiple incident story, and both assume the use of a general lead because of the complexity of the story.

One option is to tell the multiple stories in alternating paragraphs. First, you use general lead to sum up *all* of the elements of the story, including as many of the *who, what, when, where, why* and *how* answers as possible. A sublead for the first event and then a sublead for the second event (assuming there are only two key events) fill out the details of each event. Then, and this is the hard part, you must alternate between events in an order of declining importance until you have told the story. The following story about the deaths of a husband and wife is an example of the atternating paragraph approach:

A Boulder couple died in their home Friday—the husband from a self-inflicted gunshot wound and the wife from injuries received in an accidental fall.

Police identified the dead man as William T. Smith, 44, of 5959 Marshall Road. Smith, apparently grief-stricken over the accidental death of his wife earlier in the morning, shot himself at 12:34 p.m., police said.

His wife, Ellen Smith, 43, of the same address, apparently fell down the basement stairs of their home after tripping over a loose board, according to W. T. Malek, Boulder County coroner. Malek said Mrs. Smith died of a broken neck sometime between 8 a.m. and noon. He ruled the death accidental.

After discovering his wife's body, Smith called police, authorities said. While Malek and Boulder police officer William Comstock were investigating Mrs. Smith's death, Smith left the basement, then returned shortly with a handgun. Before Comstock or Malek could speak with him, Smith shot himself in the head, police said.

Comstock said Smith reported the death of his wife at approximately noon. When Comstock and Malek arrived at the home, Smith told them he had returned home, searched for his wife and found her at the bottom of the basement stairs. He called an ambulance and police, he said.

The couple moved to Boulder four years ago when Smith became an assistant professor of botany at the University of Colorado, police said. They had no children.

Funeral arrangements are pending.

Let's look at this story in detail. The first paragraph is a general lead, which answers the questions *who, what, when, where, why* and *how* for both deaths in general terms. The second paragraph—a sublead for Smith, who is the story's first element—provides the reader with more details about *who, what, when, where, why* and *how*. The third paragraph, another sublead, is devoted to Mrs. Smith and answers the same questions about her. The fourth and fifth paragraphs provide more details about Smith's activities, because little is left to be said about Mrs. Smith. The sixth and seventh paragraphs provide details about both of them.

The advantages of the alternating paragraph approach are that the casual reader can easily abandon the story and the editor can edit it just as easily. The disadvantage is the resulting organizational complexity.

There are variations of the alternating paragraph method. For example, reporters can alternate facts in multiparagraph chunks after providing the lead and subleads. Or, after introducing the story through the lead and subleads, reporters can even tell about *everything* that happened in one event before proceeding to another event.

The second approach to writing multiple incident stories is the chronological method. As with the alternating paragraph method, you begin with the general lead and two (or more) subleads. After the subleads, a transition paragraph tells the reader the story is about to become chronological. After the transition, you write the story chronologically. Here is an example of a transition to a chronological story:

> Police said the events that led to the death and suicide began shortly after Smith went to work at about 8 a.m.

The advantage of this approach is that it is logical and, consequently, easy to read. The obvious disadvantage is that, because this is a highly modified inverted pyramid style, the reader must finish the story in order to understand it. In addition, the editor cannot trim the story by killing the final paragraphs, because they are significant.

There is certainly not one way—or even a best way—to write the multiple incident story. With the exception of the necessity of a summary or general lead, your creativity is your only restraint.

Copy Editing for Clarity and Conciseness

Copy editors often improve stories, as you read in Chapter 2. Reporters shouldn't rely on copy editors to clean up journalistic messes, however. The reporter's copy should be as good as possible before it is given to the copy editor.

"Good" means newsworthy, accurate, objective, complete, fair and balanced. A story should also have clarity. Clarity means a story should be understandable and precise. To see the importance of clarity, look at the second paragraph of the following story:

> A 16-year-old Central High School sophomore is in satisfactory condition at University Hospital after being treated for smoke inhalation Tuesday.
>
> Douglas Masters, son of Robert and Mary Masters, of 19 Foxcroft Lane, was overcome by acrid smoke in the family garage after pouring solvent in his car, according to police.
>
> He was discovered by his sister, Dana, 19, who called a city ambulance after finding Masters unconscious on the garage floor at 9:30 p.m.

If clarity means understandability as well as precision, the second paragraph of the story is a journalistic disaster because readers will be confused. First, the paragraph assumes too much about the readers' knowledge of cars. Auto mechanics would understand that solvent is often poured into a running motor's carburetor intake to clean the device and that the process usually produces tremendous smoke, which is dangerous in a closed garage. But you can't assume that readers are mechanics. Furthermore, this paragraph merely suggests that Masters poured solvent *somewhere* in his car. Where did he pour it? The paragraph also uses a word—acrid—that many readers may not understand. In addition, acrid is not the right word for this circumstance. Acrid means harsh to the taste or smell. The exhaust fumes may or may not have been harsh. Mark Twain might have had a word like *acrid* in mind when he said: "The difference between the right word and the almost right word is the difference between lightning and the lightning bug." The paragraph (and the story) also fails to mention that the garage was closed, a situation that contributed to the accident.

A corrected second paragraph might look something like this:

> Douglas Masters, son of Robert and Mary Masters, of 19 Foxcroft Lane, was overcome by automobile exhaust fumes in his family garage, according to police. Masters, working in a closed garage, had attempted to clean the car's carburetor with a solvent which produced dense fumes, police said.

Conciseness also improves a story. Be alert for unnecessary words. In the sentence *Whitehurst's car was totally demolished, police said*, the word *totally* is redundant. Redundancy is boring and a waste of precious space.

Radio Newswriting

Whether the reporter writes for print or broadcast the fundamentals of reporting remain the same. Broadcast newswriting does present other challenges and constraints, though. Television newswriting, because of its visual dimension and more complex technological hardware, needs to be studied separately. We will focus here on radio newswriting.

Radio differs from print in several ways. First, time is king in radio. While a newspaper story might be acceptable at 10, 20 or even 30 paragraphs, radio reporters think in terms of 10, 20 or perhaps 30 seconds. About 16 typewritten lines of copy—about 150 words—use up a minute of valuable air time. That means that the average 30-second story needs to be written in about eight lines, or 75 words. When you recall that the average newspaper lead is perhaps 30 words, you can begin to see the difficulty radio reporters have when they must squeeze complex stories into bite-size chunks that listeners can digest.

Print reporters are surprised to discover that radio stories are not structured in inverted pyramid style. Instead, radio reporters use a general lead to tell listeners *who, what, when* and *where* something happened, and then, if story length allows, they explain *why* and *how* the event happened in subsequent sentences. In essence, the radio story is a general lead followed by a sublead. Often, paragraphs aren't even marked, because the stories are usually too short to warrant them.

Radio Newswriting Style

Radio writing follows a conversational style, using contractions and colloquialisms in most parts of the country. The stories are usually written in the present tense whenever possible, because radio's forte is immediacy and the present tense gives the illusion of on-going events. Detail such as ages, initials, street addresses and exact numbers are often dropped. Titles usually precede names, as opposed to the opposite practice often used by newspapers. These conventions are necessary, radio reporters say, because the typical radio listener is often distracted and listens only half-heartedly. "Just assume you're writing for a half-deaf child," suggests one radio news director. "You need to write like you talk, but also simplify, repeat and write in short sentences of about 20 words."

Radio reporters should write in the active voice, as should newspaper reporters. In the active voice, the subject of the sentence acts on the verb; in the passive voice, the subject is acted upon by the verb. For example, here is a sentence in the passive voice, followed by one in the active voice:

> PASSIVE: The food was eaten by the cat.
>
> ACTIVE: The cat ate the food.

The second sentence is shorter and has more energy. Both broadcast and print reporters are occasionally forced to use the passive voice—or use it because they're not paying attention—but the active voice is still a worthy goal.

Copy is usually capitalized and is rarely abbreviated. Exceptions are well-known designations such as U-S. Numbers below 10 are spelled out. Numbers from 10 through 999 use numerals. Above 1,000, the form is 2-thousand or 3-million. Difficult words are explained phonetically, such as this: CAIRO (KAY-ROH), ILLINOIS. Similarly, words requiring special emphasis are underlined or set off by commas.

Like newspaper reporters, radio reporters identify each story with their name, the date and a slug in the upper left corner of the terminal screen or paper. They also write their stories on a terminal or typewriter with margins set for a 60- or 65-space line. They need to pay special attention to the way sentences are completed. For example, compare these two sentences:

FARGO RESIDENTS CAN EXPECT RAIN AND WINDY
WEATHER FOR MOST OF APRIL.

FARGO RESIDENTS CAN EXPECT RAIN AND WINDY WEATHER
FOR MOST OF APRIL.

The second sentence is better because it is easier for an announcer to read. The radio reporter must write for the ear.

Unlike stories for newspaper use, only minimal copy editing is acceptable for radio news. This is necessary because much radio news is read without rehearsal, and the copy must not confuse the announcer. It is acceptable to remove one or two words from the copy and perhaps to insert one or two words. Other than that, mistakes call for retyping the copy.

Types of Radio Stories

Radio stories come in at least two forms. The most common type is the *reader story*, which is simply a short version of a newspaper story. The second type is variously called an *audio story*, a *wrap*, a *package* or a *doughnut*.

This kind of story has additional audio—usually a second voice—recorded on a tape cartridge, or cart. Most often the cart sound is a short quotation from someone mentioned in the story and is designed to be played in the middle of the story. The audio story opens with a description of what happened and to whom, then features the cart-based quotation—which is called a *sound bite*—and closes with more information from the reporter or announcer. Quotations gathered by the reporter and featured in the story but not recorded on tape must be clearly identified or the listener (who can't see the quotation marks on the reporter's copy) will think the reporter or announcer is editorializing.

Let's look at a 20-second radio reader story. Here's the Whitehurst story again, written for newspaper, followed by the radio version:

Norman Whitehurst, 42, of 801 Vest Drive, was seriously injured Tuesday morning in a one-car accident near the intersection of U.S. 13 and Gay Street, according to Warrensburg police.

Police said the accident occurred when Whitehurst, who was driving north on U.S. 13, apparently fell asleep and lost control of his vehicle about 5:30 a.m. Whitehurst's car crossed the highway median and struck a telephone pole at the northeast corner of the intersection, police said.

Whitehurst is in serious condition at the Central Missouri Regional Medical Center, a hospital official said. Police said he was not wearing a selt belt.

Whitehurst's car was demolished, police said.

Now let's compare it with the radio version, a 20-second radio reader story.

WARRENSBURG POLICE SAY A LOCAL RESIDENT IS IN SERIOUS CONDITION THIS MORNING AFTER AN AUTO ACCIDENT DOWNTOWN. THEY IDENTIFY THE MAN AS NORMAN WHITEHURST. POLICE SAY HE WAS DRIVING NORTH ON U-S 13 WHEN HE APPARENTLY FELL ASLEEP AND LOST CONTROL OF HIS CAR AT THE GAY STREET INTERSECTION. WHITEHURST'S CAR HIT A TELEPHONE POLE, POLICE SAY. HE'S IN CENTRAL MISSOURI REGIONAL MEDICAL CENTER.

Note the changes. The radio version is not paragraphed, and it is shorter than the print version. It is conversational. Present tense and active voice have been used as much as possible. Details such as age and address have been omitted. The story is written in all capital letters. In addition, there are style changes, such as the change from *U.S.* to *U-S*.

Aside from those cosmetic changes, reporting, after all, is reporting. The primary differences are not between print and radio reporting, but rather between mediocre and excellent reporting.

PART 2
Reporting News

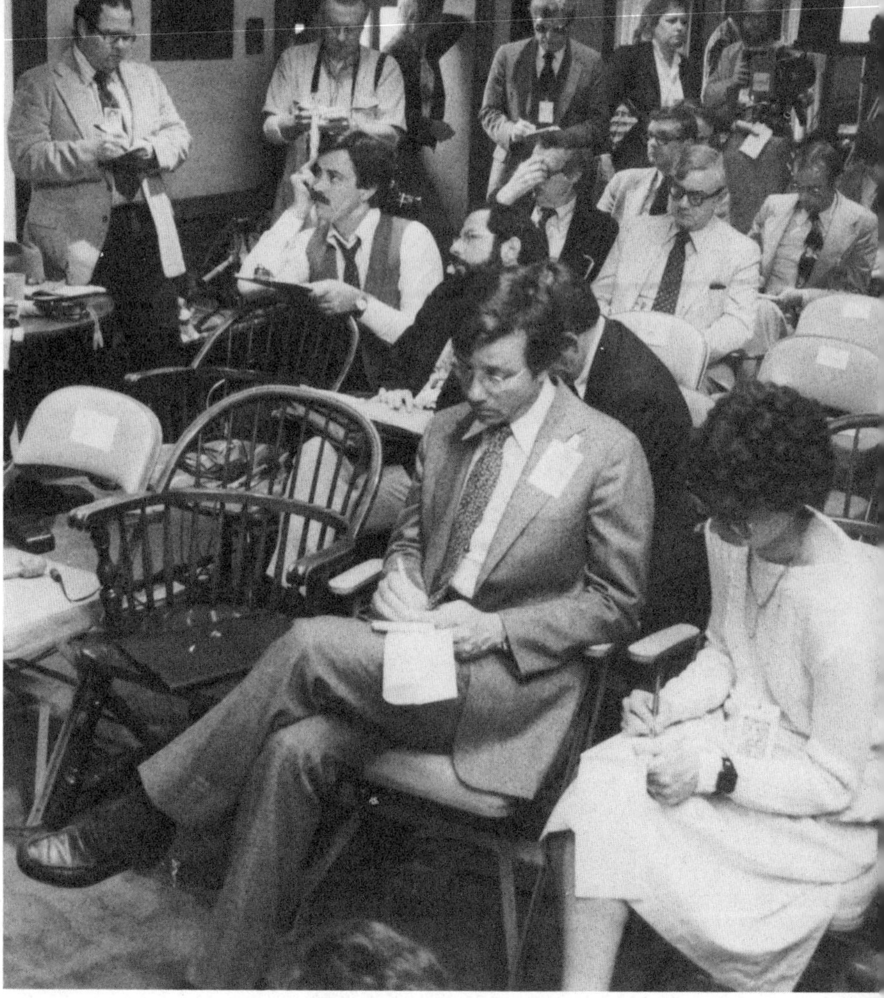

CHAPTER 4

General Assignment Reporting

The General Assignment
The Advance Speech Story
Covering the Speech
The Advance Meeting Story
Covering the Meeting
Covering the Press Conference
Writing Under Deadline
Winning a Pulitzer Prize Under Deadline

The General Assignment

Karen is a general assignment reporter at the Times, a morning 100,000 circulation newspaper published in the state capital. Her "office" is a desk in the Times newsroom, a large carpeted area furnished in chrome and plastic and dotted with the glowing green squares of video display terminals.

Karen, who graduated from journalism school only a month ago, is a little intimidated by her surroundings because she knows the Times has a first-rate reputation in the state and demands excellence from its reporters. Thus far, like most other beginning reporters, Karen has been trusted only with writing obituaries and rewriting press releases, in order to learn the Times' departures from wire service style, as well as the techniques of writing stories on the Times' terminals.

But today is different. Karen gets her first significant assignment.

"I want you to cover a speech at the state Volunteer Firefighters Association," the city editor tells her.

"As you know, the Leeton volunteer fire department refused to fight a fire last week and let a man's new house burn down," the editor explains. "The man hadn't paid his fire association dues for that year, and the firefighters say they won't fight fires at the homes of people who don't pay dues. So the fire department just went out there and watched. Well, the attorney general is going to be speaking this afternoon at a meeting of all the state's volunteer firefighters, and he might say something newsworthy. So cover it."

Karen, a little nervous, barely remembers how to write a speech story. Walking to her desk, she strains to recall the speech stories she wrote in college.

The technique, she recalls, is to use a summary or general lead that uses a direct, indirect or partial quotation to sum up the essence of the speech and answers the basic questions of *who* said *what* to *whom*, as well as *when, where, why* and *how*. And she has to do all of that in the usual single paragraph containing fewer than 35 words. After that, Karen recalls, she must cover the event accurately, objectively, completely and fairly so that the reader who perhaps had wanted to attend the event but could not will understand the gist of the speech.

Karen did not do well on speech stories in college. She remembers that on numerous occasions her toughest journalism professor gave the class a little background information, played a long video tape recording of a complex, boring speech, and then ordered the students to write the story in 30 minutes. She also remembers having had difficulty taking notes fast enough to get accurate, memorable quotations. Nonetheless, she remembers surviving the college exercises and even writing a few good speech stories.

The main problem with writing a speech story, Karen knows, is that you are often covering someone you don't know, haven't even heard of, at a place you've never been to, with a group you don't know anything

---

Chapter opening photo: White House reporters wait for a presidential conference to begin. (AP/Wide World Photos)

about. That dilemma, however, is what general assignment reporting is really all about. You are always covering topics you know little about. Today, you might cover the attorney general talking about state law and how it affects firefighters; tomorrow you might be interviewing a world famous biochemist. As a general assignment reporter, you have to be all things to all people; you have to be a renaissance person. Thus, when Karen was studying journalism, the university required her to take many liberal arts, fine arts and science courses in addition to her journalism courses. This was necessary, her journalism advisors warned, because even if she mastered the techniques of journalism, she might fail miserably as a reporter unless she knew a lot about her world—including a melange of subjects such as the biological and physical sciences, history, political science, philosophy, psychology, sociology, government, business, mathematics, literature and the fine arts.

As Karen thinks about the impending VFA assignment, she hopes writing this story will be like riding a bicycle after years of little practice; she hopes her speech story writing skills will return to her quickly.

The Advance Speech Story

Karen's first stop on her way to covering the speech story is the newspaper library, or the morgue, as some of the older Times reporters call it. There she finds reference books of all kinds, ranging from an encyclopedia set and scores of state telephone directories to biographical references such as Who's Who in America and city directories with cross-listings of names, occupations, addresses and telephone numbers. Most important, she finds a clipping file of previous Times stories written about virtually every local subject—from aardvarks on the loose to zebras at the zoo—all alphabetically arranged. Karen pulls out envelopes containing information on the attorney general and on the Volunteer Firefighters Association.

The Volunteer Firefighters Association, she notes from the file, was incorporated three years ago and is a lobbying group for about 300 of the state's 350 volunteer firefighting associations. Karen learns that not all fire departments are members of the VFA, but that the organization does include a majority of them. More interesting, she notes, the VFA has gone on record supporting the actions of the Leeton volunteer fire department, which refused to fight the house fire that precipitated the upcoming speech from the attorney general.

The file of the attorney general, John Stevens, is about a foot thick, consisting of literally hundreds of short stories crammed into an accordian folder. Karen notes that the attorney general has made no previous comments about the Leeton fire. That is good news for Karen; it means the speech might be particularly newsworthy if Stevens takes a position on the legal obligations of volunteer firefighters. The most helpful item in the attorney general's file, however, is an advance speech story written by another Times reporter.

The advance speech story is just what it sounds like it should be: a short article alerting readers to an upcoming speech. The story should have a summary or general lead. (Often, *how* and *why* in a news story are answered in the second paragraph, you recall.) The rest of the material in the story is usually background information on the speaker, the topic, the group the speaker is addressing and why the speech is occurring.

Here is the advance speech story Karen finds in the file:

State Attorney General John Stevens will speak to the Volunteer Firefighters Association at 3 p.m. Tuesday in Room 222 of the Tower Building at Capitol and Harbor streets.

The speech, which is open to the public, will occur on the second day of a three-day annual meeting of the VFA. The association represents 300 of the state's 350 volunteer firefighting departments, according to Ralph Watson, VFA president.

Most of the state's communities with populations of fewer than 1,000 have volunteer fire departments, Watson said.

Stevens has not yet selected a topic, Watson said.

Karen scans the rest of the file, takes some notes, locates the Tower Building on a city street map and then hurries out the door to cover her first significant news story.

Covering the Speech

Karen arrives at Room 222 of the Tower Building 15 minutes before the speech is to begin. She counts about 250 people in attendance and then begins asking for Watson, the VFA president. Karen knows that she needs to talk to both Watson and Stevens, but she suspects that the attorney general will arrive just before the speech, leaving no time for

---

SPEECH COVERAGE TIPS

- Don't be late.
- Introduce yourself to the speaker and ask for an interview after the speech.
- If you don't have a reporter's notebook, fold a dozen sheets of 8-by-11-inch paper into a 4-by-11-inch size to take advantage of the narrower width.
- If you are a poor note-taker and a transcript is not available, use a tape recorder and take notes simultaneously.

- If you don't understand what the speaker said during the talk, obtain a clarification after the speech.
- Find out where you can reach the speaker after the talk, in case you or your editor have questions.
- When you write your story, remember that you are writing it for the person who wanted to hear the talk but wasn't invited or didn't have time to come. Be inclusive but don't bore the reader.

an interview. Because she is writing for a 6 p.m. deadline, Karen knows she should interview Watson *immediately*, Stevens *after* the speech, and then, if necessary, Watson *again* for a reaction.

Helpful VFA members find Watson for Karen, and Karen asks him if he has changed his mind about volunteer fire departments fighting fires only on the property of members. She also asks Watson if he has talked to the attorney general about the issue. As Watson is answering the second question at 2:55 p.m., Stevens enters the room.

Stevens delivers his remarks in an almost classic speech-making pattern, Karen notes. The typical speech begins with an attention-getting device, such as a joke, an anecdote, or a challenge to the listeners (such as "I'm going to tell you something you don't want to hear, but I know that you will listen to what I have to say"). That opening device is usually followed by background information or more anecdotes to orient the listeners to the subject. From there, the speaker makes a transition into the body of the speech, with a major point followed by subpoints and comments to support the subpoints. If there are subsequent major points, the speaker uses additional transitions with additional subpoints and comments. Finally, the speaker brings the audience to the conclusion, which often includes some easily remembered device, such as a joke or anecdote or phrase.

Karen takes a seat toward the front of the room, so that she can hear clearly. Then she takes notes on Stevens' speech and jots down two or three questions to ask him after the presentation. His main point is that firefighters have to fight all fires because that action is required by state law. At 3:20 p.m. Stevens finishes. Stevens receives sparse applause that is at best polite, Karen notes. Afterward, Karen and four broadcast reporters corner Stevens and bombard him with questions. Then Karen finds Watson again and asks him for a reaction statement.

Karen returns to the Times by 4 p.m. with 15 pages of interview notes in her reporter's notebook. By 5:30, the story of the attorney general's speech and the firefighters' reaction is written. It will appear the next morning on page two of the newspaper's first section. With that, Karen has successfully passed one more test of her first job in journalism.

Note-Taking Techniques

How Karen covered and wrote that story is a story in itself. First of all, Karen had to have excellent notes to write her story. Unfortunately, the act of taking notes is more an inexact art than a logical science.

To get good notes, the reporter typically depends on self-taught note-taking techniques, a swift pen and a good memory to capture a speaker's language accurately.

Let's look at self-taught note-taking techniques first. Most British and European reporters know some version of shorthand, but most American reporters do not. In the absence of shorthand, a tape recorder might seem to make good sense. However, most national surveys show that the majority of American newspaper reporters do not routinely use tape recorders for deadline news stories. Experienced reporters say that using a recorder seems to increase the amount of time needed to write a story because of the extra minutes spent searching for key taped quotations. They add that recorders seem to have an uncanny tendency to malfunction after reporters start depending on them too much.

Attitudes, however, are changing, and eventually tape recorders may become as indispensable as video display terminals. If you do use a tape recorder, take accurate notes at the same time. Your notes are the best insurance policy against machine failure. For more tips on recorder use, see the next chapter.

Transcripts are usually not available for local speeches. John Stevens, the state attorney general, probably made his speech from little more than a few notecards. Worse, a news-wise source such as the attorney general might have secretly taped his own speech with a pocket recorder and is probably prepared to send the tape to your editor if you misquote him. (Some speakers, the president of the United States, for example, often follow a prepared text, which is available to reporters in advance. Even then, you should follow along and look for variations.)

So, if you are a typical reporter, you have no shorthand skills, no tape recorder and no transcript. To get your notes, you should use the procedures followed by America's most experienced reporters.

First, experienced reporters try to get to the speech site a little early. There, they often listen to the language of the speaker for a few minutes before the speech begins, so they will be able to capture phrasing accurately. If a speaker routinely uses contractions, for example, the quotations should reflect that usage.

Reporters also try to take notes on something resembling a reporter's notebook, which is a pad of paper bound by a spiral at the top and commonly only four inches wide by eight inches long. The narrow margins allow for faster note-taking, the journalists say.

Reporters typically try to capture the speaker's main points with a personal shorthand for individual words as well as an overall telegraphic style for complete sentences. For example, a reporter might scribble, "Hr 2 tell u 2day u must obey law," for "I am here to tell you today that you must obey the law." Another approach is to leave out all vowels. Thus, "I am here to tell you today that you must obey the law" becomes "m hr t tll u tdy tht u mst by th lw." The skilled reporter takes complete notes for all numbers.

After the speech, the reporter tries to interview the speaker to get clarifications of main points and additional and perhaps more accurate quotations. The post-speech interview also allows the reporter to check spellings of names mentioned in the speech and obtain additional background information on the speaker.

Finally, the reporter needs to get to a video display terminal or typewriter quickly, because reading one's own notes and reconstructing quotations becomes increasingly difficult with the passage of time.

It is important to quote accurately. "When in doubt, check it out," experienced reporters say. Checking it out may mean calling your source to get a clarification of a clarification, using an indirect quotation if you are sure of what your source said but not exactly how he or she said it, or leaving the quotation out of the story entirely if you are unsure of the language and unable to double check it.

Writing the Story

A skilled reporter will probably have the lead of the speech story in mind by the time he or she gets back to the office. In this case, Karen knows that Stevens has stunned the firefighters by telling them that they must fight every fire in their district, whether the fire occurs on the property of a member or not. Karen has confirmed that Watson, the VFA president, expected Stevens to support the association and has also confirmed that Watson was shocked by Stevens' speech. Finally, she has asked Stevens if he really meant what he seemed to say, and the attorney general has reiterated his remarks in an interview.

With these corroborating facts, Karen's lead is clear-cut:

> Attorney General John Stevens Tuesday surprised several hundred volunteer firefighters assembled here for an annual meeting when he told them they were legally required to fight all fires in their district.

Karen has selected a *who* emphasis lead because she thinks the source of the comment is slightly more important than the comment. However, a case could also be made for a *what* emphasis lead. The lead would look like this:

> Volunteer firefighters are legally required to fight all fires in their district, Attorney General John Stevens said Tuesday to several hundred volunteer firefighters assembled here for an annual meeting.

In this version, the *what* (the legal requirement facing the firefighters) is paramount. The *who* (Stevens) is still in the lead, of course, as are the *when* (Tuesday), the *how* and the *why* (at an annual meeting of the firefighters), and the *where* (here).

After the lead, the speech story typically features a paragraph answering or amplifying any of the questions not addressed in the lead, then another paragraph—if necessary—providing background information about the speaker, the group the speaker is speaking to or the issue being spoken about. From there, the reporter uses alternating direct, indirect and partial quotations (for the purpose of variety) to amplify the lead.

If the speaker talked about two matters, a transition to the second major concept is required. The transition is usually simple. Two possibilities in the Stevens story are *"Stevens also said"* or *"Stevens, addressing concerns that firefighters might go bankrupt, said."*

Karen is also concerned with working Watson into the story for balance. After all, Watson has another view, even though the VFA president has admitted he is not a legal expert. Moreover, that balance needs to come fairly soon in the story to be fair to the reader who may not finish reading the story.

Here is Karen's complete story:

Attorney General John Stevens Tuesday surprised several hundred volunteer firefighters assembled here for an annual meeting when he told them they were legally required to fight all fires in their district.

Stevens made the remarks on the second day of a three-day convention of the state Volunteer Firefighters Association at the Tower Building. About 300 of the state's 350 volunteer departments are VFA members. The VFA previously told its members they did not have to fight fires on non-members' property, according to VFA President Ralph Watson.

Stevens also told VFA members that Leeton firefighters were legally liable in refusing to fight a house fire there last week that resulted in a non-member's $75,000 home burning to the ground.

"The state law is very clear on this matter," Stevens told the firefighters. "If you operate a fire department and are called to a fire, you must try to put it out. I realize that putting out fires of non-members may discourage membership, but the law is the law."

Watson said after the speech that he was "stunned." He also said he thought Stevens was wrong.

"We have our own lawyer, and he came up with a different conclusion. We may have to test this one in court," Watson said.

"If Stevens is right, I think this development will lead to the destruction of hundreds of small volunteer departments," Watson added.

Stevens also said volunteer departments could charge non-members for the costs of putting the fires out, "no matter how big the bill is."

"As a matter of fact, the attorney general's office will even help you collect those bills," he said.

"I feel sorry for them," Stevens said in an interview after his speech, "but I have to enforce the law."

Let's look at the story paragraph by paragraph. In the second paragraph, Karen includes more background about the *why* and *how* of Stevens' remarks. Why were the firefighters meeting? How many state firefighters are members of the association? Why were firefighters surprised by Stevens' remarks? In addition, Karen needs to establish Watson as a source for the story early, and this is a good place for that initial attribution.

Having finished with what is essentially lead material, Karen moves into the primary theme of the speech, the liability of the firefighters, in the third and fourth paragraphs. The third paragraph sets up the primary theme. Karen's research in the newspaper library comes into play with figures for the burned house in Leeton. Karen places information about the destruction of the home in this paragraph rather than the first, because that story was covered extensively a week ago. News is timely. The house fire is no longer timely. What is news is the requirement that firefighters fight all fires, as Karen wrote in her lead.

The direct quotation in the fourth paragraph supports the indirect one of the previous paragraph. Karen chose to use the direct quotation in the fourth paragraph because it is a complete and accurate recitation of what Stevens said: *"The state law is very clear on this matter,"* Stevens said. Use this form when the quotation is both concise and forceful.

(The indirect quotation is a paraphrase of what the subject said, and is often used to shorten a long quotation or to hedge when the reporter knows what was meant but is not certain of the exact language. For example: *The state law is clear*, Stevens said. The partial quotation is a combination of the direct and indirect quotation. Here, quotation marks are used around the exact language and the rest of the language is accurate but may not use the exact words of the speaker. For example: The state law is *"very clear,"* Stevens said.)

Direct quotations require attribution, such as *Stevens said*, at least once every paragraph or so for clarity's sake. However, as a general rule, attribution can be more sparse in a single source story with direct quotation than in a multiple source story with direct quotation. On the other hand, indirect and partial quotations require attribution after *every* use. And *said* is the best choice for all attribution. Karen used *said* in six of 11 instances in her story, for example. (She also used *told*, *according to*, and *added* for variety. Note that she did not used *stated* because it has a different feeling and a different meaning. Most ordinary people *say* things; pompous people *state* things.) Look at Karen's story for examples of attribution.

Let's return to the VFA story.

Karen introduces Watson's view in the fifth, sixth and seventh paragraphs to balance the story. The attorney general, Watson told Karen, is entitled to his opinion like any other lawyer. And an opinion, Watson said, is just that and does not carry the force of law. Thus, Karen feels she must include Watson's remarks.

In the last three paragraphs, Karen introduces the second major theme of the speech, the idea that Stevens will help firefighters collect money owed them by people who are not members but who have fires on their property. The word *also* is a transition to the second theme of the speech. The remaining two paragraphs can easily be cut without any damage to the story. As a matter of fact, this story could be edited at any point after the second paragraph and it would still make sense to the casual reader.

The Advance Meeting Story

Writing the advance meeting story is essentially the same as writing the advance speech story. Both stories require a general or summary lead that answers the traditional questions of *who, what, when, where, why,* and *how*. Both stories require some background information. In a speech story, the reporter typically explains who is making the speech and the topic of the speech. In a meeting story, the reporter gives the reason for the meeting or the issue to be discussed.

If you are assigned to write a story about an organization seeking coverage, you may have a press release to use as a starting point. The press release should raise some questions that you can answer by calling the contact listed on the release.

For example, suppose that you receive this release and must write an advance story:

For Immediate Release

Educators To Meet
In City

Contact:

Robin Harrell
569-3250

The State Education Association will hold its annual meeting all day October 10 and 11 at Johnson Convention Center in the city.

Special invited guests will be United States Representative Mark Hoddes, Washington University education professor Robert Burford and University of Delaware law professor Eric Arnold.

Teachers from all over the state are expected to attend.

— 30 —

The release has more holes in it—unanswered questions—than a doughnut factory. What are the invited guests going to talk about? When? Where? What are the issues facing State Education Association members? Will the issues be discussed at this convention? Who is the president of the group, for purposes of attribution?

You need answers to all of these questions before you can write your advance story, and Robin Harrell, who wrote the release, is your immediate source. You call Harrell, who answers your questions and also gives you the name of the association president, Elmer Duncan. You find out from Duncan that more than 3,000 teachers are expected to attend the event, which will focus on censorship in school libraries. You check the newspaper library and discover that many stories have been written about attempts at censorship in rural school libraries in your state.

With all of this information in hand, you write the advance meeting story. Here it is:

Censorship of school libraries and newspapers is the theme of the annual convention of the State Education Association, to be held Oct. 10–11 at the Johnson Convention Center.

"There have been a number of incidents involving censorship in this state during the last year," according to Elmer Duncan, SEA president. "This convention hopefully will give teachers a perspective on the problem."

Speakers will include U.S. Rep. Mark Hoddes, Robert Burford, a professor of education at Washington University in St. Louis, and Eric Arnold, a law professor at the University of Delaware.

Burford, whose topic is "Censorship in the School Library," will speak at 7:30 p.m. Oct. 10 in Room 119 of the Convention Center. Arnold, speaking on "Censorship and School Newspapers," will address the group at 11 a.m. Oct. 11 in Room 220 of the center.

Hoddes will deliver the convention's keynote address, "The Supreme Court and Censorship," at 7:30 p.m. Oct. 11 in the center's Great Hall.

Other discussions dealing with censorship of school libraries and newspapers will be held in various center meeting rooms, according to Duncan.

More than 3,000 teachers from throughout the state are expected to attend, Duncan said.

The lead is a straight *what* emphasis summary lead that answers the questions *what* (the meeting on censorship), *who* (the SEA), *when* (October 10–11), and *where* (at the Convention Center). The *why* (incidents of censorship) is answered in the next paragraph, and the *how* (the speakers) is answered a bit too late—in the third paragraph.

The fourth and fifth paragraphs of the story are a laundry list, but are still fairly important. They could be cut from the story if necessary. The last two paragraphs of the story are less important and could easily be cut without damaging the story.

The other common kind of advance meeting story involves coverage of an organization that does *not* provide you with a press release. A city council meeting is one example. In covering organizations such as a city council, you usually have only a notice of the meeting, a notice that may have been grudgingly sent to your newspaper because the state open meetings and records law—commonly called a freedom of information law—requires advance notice.

In that kind of situation, your first task is to learn what will be discussed at the meeting. You learn that information by calling the city clerk and asking for an agenda, a list of items to be discussed. You may also want to ask for the minutes of the previous meeting. (You also have the option of having the clerk read you the information, if deadlines demand that procedure and if the clerk's temperament allows it.) With the agenda, the previous minutes and clippings from the newspaper's library about the last meeting, you can usually write an advance story in much the same way as the SEA advance story was written.

Covering the Meeting

Covering a meeting can be somewhat more difficult than covering a speech, especially if the meeting is long and deals with a variety of complicated issues. In addition, events generally happen more slowly at a meeting—which is good for the reporter—but there also are more participants, which makes identification more of a task.

Let's imagine that you are assigned to cover the main business meeting at the convention of the State Education Association. What do you do first? You call a source at the SEA—probably someone in the organization's public information office—to get background on what is likely

---

MEETING COVERAGE TIPS

- Once again, don't be late.
- Arrive with an agenda and an understanding of some of the matters to be discussed and the players who will be discussing them.
- Make a friend at the meeting who can identify people and explain issues.
- If you're covering a city council meeting, it may be taped by the city clerk. If so, use the tape to make certain your quotations are exact.
- Have the telephone numbers of key participants in case you need to call them later for additional information.
- Know the state freedom of information law, if it applies to the meeting you are covering. Carry a copy of it with you. Protest when public groups try to break the law.

to be discussed at the business meeting, who the principal players will be and when and where the meeting will be held. Then you check your newspaper's library for clippings with background on the issues that will be discussed and for examples of how previous SEA business meetings were covered.

At the appointed time, you go to the SEA business meeting. You're in a huge auditorium, with perhaps 2,500 people. The SEA public information person, who can spot a reporter like a dog can find a bone, locates you. The public information representative hands you an agenda. You quickly see that you are primarily interested in two issues: how SEA votes on a resolution to condemn attempts at censoring high school newspapers and school libraries and who is elected SEA president and vice president for the coming school year.

The SEA vote occurs first. That's easy. Two names are put into nomination for the position of president and vice president. You write down the names and make a note to check the spellings and school affiliations later. Then, a paper ballot vote is taken, and the audience is told that the election results will be announced at the conclusion of the business meeting.

Meanwhile, a jumble of old and new business is discussed, little of it of interest to your readers. Finally, the key resolution is brought up, at just about the exact time your SEA source told you it would be presented. People come forward to a microphone to speak for or against the resolution. You have difficulty catching names, but you can understand school names. You make a note to locate someone from each school after the session and obtain accurate identification of the speakers. You get some good quotations, representing both sides of the issue. The actual vote is taken, and the resolution is passed by a wide margin.

A few minutes later, the outgoing SEA president announces the results of the election. You now have everything you need except for identification of some of the speakers. As the meeting is adjourning, you get that information by interviewing a number of participants. Then, you're off to your video display terminal.

Actually, covering the SEA business session is easy compared with covering a multifaceted, fast-paced board meeting where virtually every action is newsworthy. Suppose, for example, that you are assigned to cover a board meeting at the local zoo.

Your job begins with identifying zoo board members so that you will know who is speaking for or against each agenda item. Ask someone, such as the board secretary, to help you. Then you must listen carefully as each issue is presented and as various oral votes are taken. You should mark quotations in your notebook with a personal code to identify who said what to whom. After the meeting, you must locate someone who can explain the issues to you in detail so that you can explain them to your readers. If you don't understand the issues, you can be certain that you can't explain them to your readers. Your problems—if you have them—will be caused by numbers, by a large number of players and a larger number of issues. This kind of cast-of-thousands story can even confuse experienced reporters.

Worse yet, at some meetings, many equally significant events occur, all of which must somehow be squeezed into the lead. For example, suppose that at one session the zoo board votes to fire the zoo director, increase the zoo admission fee by 25 percent and sell the snakes because they're no longer popular.

What is the solution for this story, which, like all other stories, requires a simple lead? Experienced reporters know that they must usually write a general lead to explain meetings such as this one, where everything happens except for the parting of the Red Sea.

Here is an example of a possible general lead:

> In a flurry of activity, the Lakeland Zoo board voted Tuesday night to fire the zoo director, increase admission fees to $1 and sell the zoo's 139 snakes.

The *what* emphasis lead spells out in general terms the major board activity, as well as telling the reader about *where* (Lakeland), *who* (the zoo board) and *when* (Tuesday). The *why* and *how* will be saved for the subsequent sublead.

The second paragraph will be a sublead detailing the specifics of *what, where, who,* and *when,* as well as the *why* and *how,* if there is room. If not, *why* and *how* are covered in the third paragraph. Then each of the main issues will receive one or more paragraphs.

Reporters sometimes write separate, or *sidebar,* stories for especially complicated speech or meeting stories. For example, if the firing of the zoo director is too complicated to be adequately explained in the main story, a separate story should be written. That story can be a news story or a feature account, depending on circumstances. (you will read more about feature stories in Chapter 7.)

Covering the Press Conference

The press, or news, conference is a little like the old joke that begins, "There is good news and there is bad news." The good news about the press conference is that the news is conveniently packaged for the

---

PRESS CONFERENCE TIPS

- Get to the press conference early so you can request an exclusive interview after the session.
- Pick up any available press releases or press kits.
- Listen to questions asked by broadcast reporters, but do not spoil their audio quotations (sound bites) by interrupting answers.
- Be persistent. If the interviewee does not answer your question the first time, politely rephrase the question and ask it again.
- If you have an exclusive interview after the press conference, save your best questions for then.
- If possible, listen to your competition's exclusive interview, but don't let your competition listen to your exclusive interview, even if it means buying your subject a soft drink somewhere else.
- If you think that there may be an information gap in your story, request a telephone number from the interviewee so that you can contact him or her later for additional information.

media; the bad news is that the news is also grossly managed in favor of the news source, and worse, the competition gets the news at the same time.

From the source's viewpoint, the press conference is an efficient and fair way to spread the word. The press conference is efficient, because it allows the person staging the event to gather reporters from all of the community's news organizations in one room at one time. The press conference is fair, because every news organization in the market is invited, although some may choose not to attend.

The press conference varies from situation to situation, but there are some constants. The ritual begins with the delivery of a press release to the news organization some days before the event. Often, a representative of the group holding the press conference calls the city editor on the day of the event and asks whether a reporter will be sent to the meeting.

At the press conference—often held in the office of the individual or organization sponsoring the event—the reporter is given additional copies of any press releases and fact sheets pertaining to the issue at hand. The sponsoring group may even hand out a press kit, which is an elaborate folder containing a number of releases, brochures and perhaps even photographs.

Light refreshments such as coffee or soft drinks or even sandwiches may be provided, although the code of ethics of The Society of Professional Journalists and the ethical code of conduct of many news organizations discourage accepting anything (including a free lunch) that might influence coverage.

The person who calls the press conference usually opens the event with a short statement, then takes questions from reporters. Unfortunately, press conference questioning is usually neither easy nor logical. In an interview, a reporter typically asks a specific question, then follows with several even more narrowly defined questions. At a press conference, however, a reporter is competing for attention with other reporters who also have questions they must ask. The typical result is often irritating to both the reporter, who is trying to get a complete answer to a question, and the questioner, who is trying to give one. The good reporter solves this problem not by monopolizing the questioning, but by remembering the partially unanswered question and returning to it as many times as necessary.

Another persistent problem with the press conference format is competition from other reporters. Obviously, if a reporter from one newspaper asks a question with other reporters present, the response may show up in everyone's story. Reporters sometimes try to combat this by saving their best question for an interview after the press conference. Television reporters are particularly apt to corner a subject after the conference because they want an exclusive videotape interview. This tactic only works if the reporter is positive the subject will, indeed, be available after the conference for questions. Thus, experienced reporters make prior arrangements with subjects for such exclusive interviews.

So much for press conference strategy. How is a press conference story written? Because the press conference is really a short speech with an interview afterward, the speech story structure seems to work best. The speech story, you will recall, features a summary or general lead that answers most of the six questions and includes a direct, indirect or partial quotation that sums up the essence of the conference.

Let's suppose your city editor has told you to cover a press conference today at City University. The person who has called the conference is Larry Newth, who is scheduled to lecture about unidentified flying objects the following day at the university. The editor gives you a news release from Newth with little helpful information other than the time and place of the press conference.

Newth, you learn, believes the government has acquired disabled UFOs and the corpses of some of the occupants. Because Newth is a paid lecturer, he is probably from out of state, you guess. You do a quick check of the newspaper files both for Newth and for UFO sightings in the state. You find nothing. Then you call the university public information office, which refers you to the university lecture-booking office where biographical information is available on Newth. A secretary reads the information to you over the telephone.

Newth, you discover, is 29 years old, a graduate of Michigan State University with a degree in business and a "self-employed UFO researcher," whatever that means. You also learn that he charges a flat $500 in expenses and no fee for his lecture. That is unusual, you are told, because typical university lecture fees range from a low of $1,000 to a high of $10,000, plus expenses.

The press conference is being held in a room at the Student Union. There, you see reporters and photographers from each of the city's two television stations. You also see a wire service reporter and a reporter from a weekly newspaper. Finally, you spy the photographer from your own newspaper. You also see Newth, who is well-dressed and poised. You introduce yourself to him and ask him for a 10-minute private interview after the press conference. He agrees to your request.

Newth begins the conference promptly at 2 p.m. with a five-minute prepared statement. After the statement, he is peppered with questions about his statement, his background and why he is making charges of governmental obfuscation. After the group questioning, he gives private interviews for both television stations. Then it's your turn. You have saved what you think is the best question for last: Has he ever seen a UFO himself?

As you go back to the office, you ponder possible story approaches. You know that Newth's story would make a good feature, but the city editor told you he wanted a traditional news story. The traditional news story format demands that you summarize Newth's position, which is that the government of the United States is lying to its citizens about the presence of UFOs. You also decide that you must include the information about the lecture fee in the story because it adds some credibility to an otherwise incredible charge. Finally, you know you must include the specifics of Newth's upcoming lecture because you are also writing an advance speech story. You confer with your editor to explain your decisions and write the story. Here is the finished story of the UFO press conference:

Unidentified flying objects have crashed in the United States and bodies of aliens have been recovered, but the American government won't admit their existence, Lawrence Newth, a UFO researcher, charged at a press conference at City University Tuesday.

Newth, who will lecture about UFOs at 7 p.m. Wednesday in Rogers Hall, said government security agencies such as the National Security Agency and the Central Intelligence Agency have recovered "both UFOs and bodies of non-human beings" who were found inside the vehicles.

"The bodies found were of non-human creatures about two feet tall," Newth said. The creatures were recovered from a UFO that crashed in New Mexico during the early 1960s, he said.

Newth said he learned about the crashes from information obtained under the federal Freedom of Information Act from agencies such as the NSA, the CIA and the Federal Bureau of Investigation.

Newth read from what appeared to be a censored May 15, 1985, memorandum from an unidentified FBI field agent to FBI headquarters that said: "Three so-called flying saucers have been recovered in New Mexico." He refused to release a copy of the memo.

The memo also said that "three creatures of human shape but only about two feet tall" were recovered from the crash site, according to Newth.

Newth refused to speculate on what happened to the alien bodies but said he presumed they were being held "by a government agency somewhere."

"This is absolute proof that UFOs do exist and that aliens from another world have visited the planet Earth," Newth said.

Newth, who is on a lecture tour of college campuses, said he accepts only $500 in expenses for his appearances because telling the world about UFOs is his "passion."

"I have never seen a UFO myself," he said, "but I have seen the evidence, and the evidence has convinced me that this is a topic that needs to be talked about.

"This effort may lead to world peace if we come to realize there are other forces more powerful than our own in the universe," he said.

Let's look at the story paragraph by paragraph to see why material is placed where it is. The first paragraph is a *what* emphasis summary lead, using an indirect quotation and answering the questions *what* (the presence of the UFOs, the presence of the bodies and the government denial), *who* (Newth), *where* (City University), *when* (Tuesday) and *how* (the press conference). The word *charged* is used rather than *said*, because Newth made a strong accusation.

There are two other acceptable ways to write this lead. Some reporters would either omit the reference to the press conference or save it for the second paragraph. That would shorten the lead from 38 words to a more palatable 34 words. Other reporters would use a general lead because Newth's name would have little meaning to readers. That approach would shorten the lead even more but lengthen the overall story.

The second paragraph answers the question *why*: Why is Newth in the city and at the university making the charges? The sentence also provides readers with the equivalent of an advance speech story. The quotations in the second and third paragraphs fill out the charge Newth made in the lead. Because this story is written in a modified inverted pyramid style, the reader could stop at this point and still make sense of the article.

The fourth and fifth paragraphs give more information about where Newth got his information. He showed reporters a copy of what, indeed, did look like a government memo but would not make any copies available for the reporters. The reporter's goal is to indicate that Newth had something that looked like proof, but that it may not have been authentic.

The partial quotation in the sixth paragraph about some government agency is in response to a question asked by another reporter at the press conference. The direct quotation that follows it amplifies that Newth was not dismayed by his inability to locate the bodies of the aliens.

The eighth paragraph is necessary to explain what all of the readers must now be asking themselves: Is this man doing this for the money, or does he really believe what he is saying? The last two paragraphs of direct quotations are in response to questions you asked in the exclusive interview. But Newth's answers, while interesting, did not warrant more prominent coverage, you decided.

In short, you have written a story about an ordinary looking fellow with some extraordinary opinions. You also have tried to communicate to the reader that Newth is making his collegiate tour not for the money he earns but because he believes in what he is doing.

You have covered a press conference—a short speech followed by an interview—and written it much as you would a speech story. In the process, however, you have learned that the press conference story is often easier to write than the speech story because you have the opportunity to ask questions until you thoroughly understand the answers.

Writing Under Deadline

People face deadlines everyday. If you have an appointment with a friend at 9 a.m., you are expected to be at the appointed place at the appointed time. If you're a few minutes late, your friend may call the tardiness to your attention but the friendship will probably continue.

In the news business, however, reporters must take deadlines seriously. News is a perishable commodity. Hundreds of men and women—editors, press operators, delivery van drivers, carriers—are poised to produce and transport a newspaper. Timing is critical if the paper is to be delivered when the reader wants it.

If a reporter works for an afternoon newspaper and the final copy deadline is noon, the news story that is finished at 12:45 p.m. is of little value. (The editor may soon decide the reporter is of little value, too.) The tardy story could perhaps be used the following day, but unless it is an exclusive, it will already have been told by competing media. Thus, it will probably not be used, ever.

So, next to accuracy, meeting deadlines is the reporter's greatest challenge. The process is almost like weighing something on an old-fashioned scale. The great weight of a deadline is placed on one pan of the scale. The weight of accuracy is placed on the other pan. The job of the reporter is to balance the scale while telling the story.

Balancing the scale takes practice. As you have read, a majority of America's newspapers are published in the afternoon. That means the typical newspaper reporter arrives at work before dawn and writes perhaps five stories before the typical noon deadline. Reporters for morning newspapers have the same problem, though they tend to come to work at 2 or 3 p.m. and face a first edition deadline of 7 or 8 p.m. In either case, the reporter has perhaps five hours in which to develop a number of major stories, five hours before facing a deadline beyond which there is no reprieve.

Reporters have different techniques for dealing with deadlines. However, America's best reporters cope by simply organizing themselves and by not procrastinating. If you are a morning newspaper reporter facing an evening deadline, that means starting work on your toughest story as soon as you get to work. Plan to cover your story by telephone if at all possible. Place your calls early and leave messages with those people you are unable to reach that you are "on deadline" and need to have calls returned by a specific time. Tell your newspaper telephone operator or city desk clerk that you are willing to accept two calls at one time, and be prepared to put one party on hold while you are interviewing another source.

You may find yourself juggling two or three stories at the same time and two or three sources for each story, also at the same time. This kind of circus act is facilitated by video display terminals, which can store one story in memory while you are working on another story. In fact, you can store your notes for your first story on one memory, the story itself on another memory, and your second story and second story notes on additional memories. Some terminals will even allow "split-screens," where notes and stories can be seen side-by-side. The reporter assembles the story by simply drawing from alternate screens.

Frankly, all of this takes some degree of personal tranquility. If you are the kind of person who foams at the mouth when you have to wait in line for five minutes at the grocery store, you will probably have difficulty coping with the nail-biting deadlines that are endemic to the news business.

Winning a Pulitzer Prize Under Deadline

The story of excellence in modern American newspaper reporting is, to some extent, also the story of the Pulitzer Prizes. Joseph Pulitzer, a Hungarian immigrant who pushed the St. Louis Post-Dispatch and later the New York World to national prominence, drafted an agreement in

1903 with New York City's Columbia University for the creation of a journalism school and for "annual prizes to particular journalists for various accomplishments, achievements and forms of excellence." (There are also prizes in letters and music.) Pulitzer died in 1911. The first of his prestigious prizes were awarded in 1917 to Herbert Bayard Swope of the New York World for a then-timely series of articles, "Inside the German Empire," and to the New York Tribune for an editorial on the first anniversary of the sinking of the ocean liner Lusitania. More than 500 Pulitzer Prizes for journalism have been awarded since then.

Today, Pulitzer journalism juries typically make two to four nominations in numerous categories for work done during the previous calendar year. The nominations go to the Pulitzer Prize board, which makes the final decision in each category.

Journalism prizes in recent years have been awarded in the following categories: public service, general news reporting, investigative reporting, explanatory journalism, specialized reporting, national reporting, international reporting, feature writing, commentary, criticism, editorial writing, editorial cartooning, spot news photography and feature photography. Most of the prizes carry a $1,000 award. Sometimes the Pulitzer Prizes go to individuals; sometimes news organizations receive the award. A prize is not awarded in every category every year.

Mt. St. Helens' erupts in 1980. Coverage of the eruption brought a Pulitzer Prize to The Daily News in Longview, Wash. (AP/Wide World Photos)

Reporting, of course, is the basis for all newspaper work. Pulitzer Prizes for reporting have been awarded since 1917, but a separate category for reporting under deadline was created in 1953. (Deadline reporting now is included in the general news reporting category.) Even though previous prizes for deadline reporting had been awarded, the first official deadline reporting prize went to the editorial staff of the Providence, R.I., Journal and Evening Bulletin for coverage of a bank robbery and the subsequent police chase and capture of the bandit.

A more recent and more spectacular example of that same kind of reporting occurred in 1981, when the news staff of The Daily News in Longview, Wash., was awarded a Pulitzer Prize for their round-the-clock coverage of the eruption of nearby Mount St. Helens. The 1980 volcanic eruption, which was 500 times more powerful than the first atomic bomb dropped during World War II, left about five dozen area residents dead or missing and disrupted life in the Pacific Northwest for months.

The Daily News editorial staffers rushed to work on a Sunday morning as soon as they heard about the eruption, editor Ted Natt recalls. The 25 staffers worked virtually around the clock for 10 days, Natt says. Staffers worked wherever they were needed. For example, a computer technician took photographs and news clerks conducted interviews. Between May 18, when the 9,677-foot mountain exploded, and the end of the year, more than 1,000 stories about the eruption were written and published, and more than 500 photographs were taken, according to Natt.

On the day following the devastating explosion of Mount St. Helens, Daily News staffers Linda Wilson and Tom Paulu described rescue efforts. Here is their Pulitzer Prize-winning story:

Toutle School Turns Rescue Site

By **Linda Wilson**
and **Tom Paulu**
The Daily News

PULITZER PRIZE WINNER

A Toutle Lake School playground resembled a war rescue effort Sunday.

Throbbing Huey helicopters dropped in and out with precision.

Emergency personnel stood ready with first aid equipment. Anxious families leaned over the wire fence waiting for relatives and friends trapped by the raging Toutle River to be airlifted out.

The first news from Mount St. Helens was not good.

Ten-year-old Sherry Vining burst into tears and hugged her mother when she realized her missing grandmother wasn't on the first few flights.

"We're real worried about them," Goldie Vining said as she comforted her daughter. "There is a bunch of people standing in a field up there, and no one can find them."

The Vining family waited a long time for their grandmother to step off the helicopter. But her arrival was not completely joyous, because two persons from her group still had not been found.

Helicopter pilots who had flown around the area told stories of acres of obliterated trees, dead wildlife and inhabited cars with no sign of life.

"The heat and the wind was so powerful it looked like the area had been clear cut," one pilot reported.

"It looks like an atomic bomb—it wiped out cars, bridges—it's just outrageous," another said.

The noise from the copters was pounding. Two or three would arrive at a time, sending blasts of dust through the air.

Waiting parents shielded their babies' eyes and children hung onto fences. Finally the first load of evacuees landed.

Survivors poured out of the cavernous helicopters in a crouched run with bags of clothes and valuables. Many looked like ghosts. Their clothes, hair and shoes were coated with a fine gray ash.

The Withers family of South Toutle Road was among the first to be airlifted out.

Marvin Withers said his family tried to drive out but the roads were blocked by mud. So they stuffed a few clothes in plastic bags and waited for the copters.

Like the Withers, most evacuees left in a hurry with only the items they could grab in the last minutes.

Many had no idea where they were going or where they would stay.

Kevin Page said he hadn't planned to leave his Kid Valley home until he saw trees, two cars and a log truck trailer bobbing down the Toutle River.

Patrick Kilgore, who lives near Camp Baker, stepped off a copter with a six-pack of Pepsi and his South American boa constrictor, named Josephine. Known as "Snake-Pit-Pat," he said the only reason he came out was because of rumors of poisonous gases.

"We were safe, I know we were safe," he said with the snake cradled under one arm.

The pilots kept going back to the stricken area for more.

They were hampered by confusing reports about missing persons and ash and gas in the air.

Those waiting at the playground could only hope and watch. They milled around, watched the choppers and traded stories.

The pulsating helicopters continued to deliver their cargo with regularity.

One older evacuee, Don Hammond, was given oxygen immediately after getting off a helicopter and then carried to another to be flown to a Longview hospital.

A Seattle couple who had just been out for a Sunday drive arrived on the copter with "Snake-Pit-Pat."

"We were up there having a beer with him and then we heard the CB and it was coming right down on top of us," Terry Clayton, a Seattle teacher said.

"Breathing it hurt your lungs, and we were really sweating. We were trying to drive across a bridge and there was mud splashing on the windshields."

He and his companion, Pam Siddens, finally gave up and left their car behind.

The rescue effort went on all afternoon. Dozens of people were flown out of the area above Toutle and taken by bus to Castle Rock and Kelso.

Wilson and Paulu's story is exceptional reporting in many ways. First, it utilizes reportorial detail from interviews and observation to create a mood. Here are two examples:

INTERVIEW:

Helicopter pilots who had flown around the area told stories of acres of obliterated trees, dead wildlife and inhabited cars with no sign of life.

OBSERVATION:

Survivors poured out of the cavernous helicopters in a crouched run with bags of clothes and valuables. Many looked like ghosts. Their clothes, hair and shoes were coated with a fine gray ash.

Second, it features a series of strong, carefully selected quotations to tell the story of the explosion and the resulting flood in the words of those affected better than it could be told in the third person. Here are two examples:

> "The heat and the wind was so powerful it looked like the area had been clear cut," one pilot reported.

> "It looks like an atom bomb—it wiped out cars, bridges—it's just outrageous," another said.

Third, it is packed with hard-hitting words that paint portraits for the reader, such as the following sentence:

> Throbbing Huey helicopters dropped in and out with precision.

Although the explosion of Mount St. Helens is unusual, the experience of the reporters for The Daily News is not at all unusual. Reporters—whether they are experienced or fresh from college—are expected to be able to cover virtually any kind of news story during their first months on the job, particularly at a small or medium circulation daily

---

SOME CHARACTERISTICS OF EXCELLENCE

Teresa Carpenter, who won the 1981 Pulitzer Prize for feature writing, is herself a study in excellence. After earning a bachelor's degree in English from Graceland College in Lamoni, Iowa, and a master's degree in journalism from the University of Missouri at Columbia, she became a Hawaii-based reporter for a Japanese business publication. Then, after more than two years in Hawaii, she returned to the mainland for a three-year stint as a writer for a New Jersey monthly. By 1979—when she was in her early 30s—Carpenter found herself free-lancing articles for the New York City-based Village Voice, which circulates about 160,000 copies weekly all over the country.

Carpenter's first significant assignment for the Voice was a lengthy news feature about a Long Island housewife who was murdered by her husband. She soon followed that with a story about the murder of prominent New York state political figure. Six months later Carpenter's third murder story was published: an article about the killing of Playboy "Playmate of the Year" and aspiring actress Dorothy Stratten. The Stratten story, titled "Death Of A Playmate," was the basis for the 1983 movie, "Star-80." The three stories together earned Carpenter the coveted Pulitzer Prize.

Even though Carpenter won her prize for feature writing, the three murder stories are fascinating case studies in thorough reporting. As a reporter, Carpenter has strong views about what characteristics be-ginning reporters should have. For example, she says journalism students should have strong language skills. "Why [would] someone without a basic command of English go into journalism?" she asks.

Students should also enjoy and appreciate reading, she says. "There are people who are brought up in households where reading is the rule and have been read to as children and [who] read for pleasure. Obviously, the language skills of someone like that are going to be superior to someone who has never cracked a book," she explains.

But if reading is important, curiosity is critical, Carpenter says. "It's important to hire people who have curiosity. You can't learn curiosity. Reporters have got to be driven by a really sincere desire to find out what happened in any given instance. I think a young person going into the business should ask himself: 'Am I curious and do I really want to know what happened?' [Curiosity] solves a lot of problems [such as] going into an interview [and worrying], 'Will I be thought dumb? Will I be rejected?'

"Someone said this to me when I was a very young reporter and I was nervous going into an interview: 'It really doesn't matter. The important thing is that you know the information you want to get and get it.' And it's true. It's nice to be thought smart, but it's better to get your story."

newspaper (such as The Daily News, which has a circulation of only about 25,000).

Yes, it is true that a few newspaper editors eschew journalism school graduates in favor of liberal arts graduates and say that they are prepared to "train" these new reporters. But in reality, virtually all newspaper reporters are expected to hit the ground running, to be able to produce acceptable copy from the outset. Thus, newly hired and liberal arts graduates untrained in journalism may find themselves in the unemployment line if the editor's promised training is absent or inadequate.

The Pulitzer Prize work of The Daily News staff is, on the one hand, exceptional. It is a glistening journalistic ideal produced under the most difficult circumstances. On the other hand, that work is the meat and potatoes of general assignment reporting—that is, ordinary reporting under extraordinary conditions. The Daily News reporting sets a tone of excellence to which every reporter should aspire.

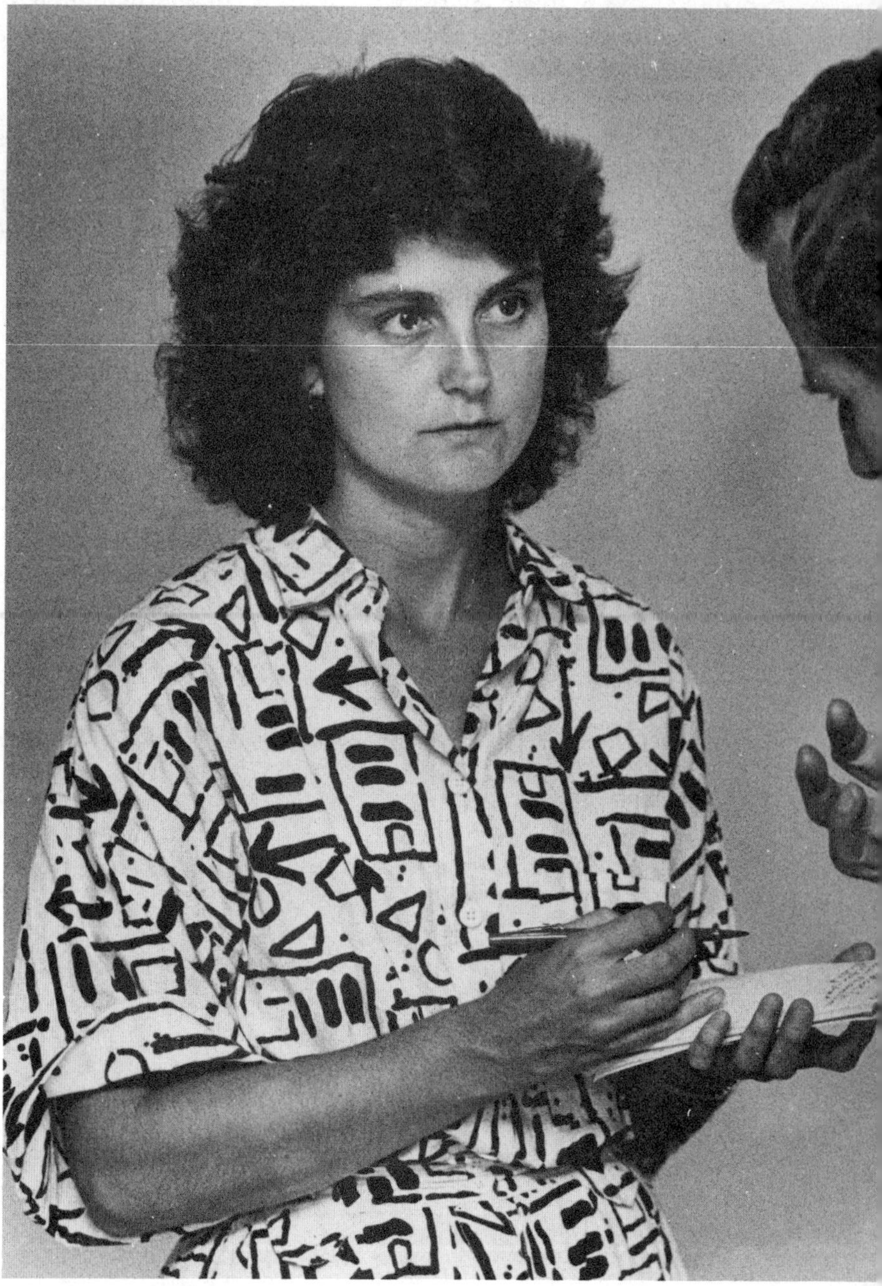

CHAPTER 5

Interviewing

A Documented Conversation
Preparing for the Interview
The Effective Interview
Further Attribution Guidelines
Using Recording Devices
Advice from Pulitzer Prize-Winning Reporters
Putting It All Together
Keeping an Open Mind

A Documented Conversation

With the origin of human beings came an insatiable urge to share information and knowledge: in short, to communicate. The crude cave drawings that were the earliest means of written communication have now been replaced by the modern marvels of video display terminals that flash endless data streams from one point to another in a matter of seconds. The technology of communication has changed over the centuries, but the basic techniques for extracting information from human beings have not.

This chapter discusses the journalistic methods for achieving the goal of communication. A reporter's interview, in the broadest sense, is nothing more than a documented conversation, blended with an ability to accurately and skillfully relate that information to an audience, whether they live in San Diego, Austin or New York City.

The interview is the backbone of most news and feature stories. In fact, the interview process is so crucial that if you do not like talking to people, you should forget about becoming a successful journalist. As a journalistic interviewer, you need three other crucial characteristics as well:

- A resolve to listen and, most of all, to *hear* what is said—and sometimes what is *not* said.
- The ability to understand the interviewee and his or her perspective.
- An absolute unwillingness to settle for anything less than a complete and thorough interview, even to the point of repeating questions or critical points as necessary.

Preparing for the Interview

There are three common kinds of interviews. The *face-to-face interview* is the most desirable. This allows the reporter to establish rapport with the subject and witness reactions to questions. The disadvantage of a face-to-face interview is that it takes longer to conduct than the telephone interview. The *telephone interview* is quick, but many people are reluctant to talk at length over the telephone with a stranger. A *group interview*—interviewing a husband and wife together, for example—offers the accord of a face-to-face session, but it can also be difficult to manage. If a reporter has sufficient time, the single subject face-to-face session is best.

Once you have decided on the type of interview, the next task is deciding whom to interview. Let's suppose there has been a minor earthquake in a remote part of your state. Your editor orders you to

Chapter Opening Photo: Kansas City Times education reporter Lynn Byczynski interviews a subject. (Staff photo by Gary Dunkin, Kansas City Times)

write a story about the effects. Whom do you interview? The mayor of the affected town? The city police chief? The county sheriff? A source at the state office for disaster planning? Victims? Witnesses? Ideally, you should interview all of these people, but you probably lack the time and resources to accomplish that. You must make a selection.

In many cases, editors make the decision for the reporter. Consider a recent journalism graduate named Marsha and her first assignment at the Times. Like most of her counterparts, she is bright, energetic and filled with enthusiasm about her first reporting job. The city editor has assigned Marsha to write a supplementary, or *sidebar*, story to accompany a main news article about Tom Flake, the chairman of a giant retail corporation, who is scheduled to address the local Rotary Club.

The interview with Flake is less than two hours away. The editor has told Marsha to concentrate on Flake's innovative plan to sell only American-made merchandise in his 700 discount stores. Marsha has never heard of Flake, much less prepared herself with intelligent and pertinent questions about his plan or his life. An understandable anxiety sweeps over her. She wants to make a good impression on the editor, but she doesn't know where to turn.

Perhaps the most common mistake made by fledgling reporters like Marsha, when they embark on an interview, is the lack of preparation. Unfortunately, and all too often, such reporters believe it is enough simply to show up on time and think of questions as the interview progresses. While more interviews than not are conducted in that fashion, the final product generally reflects the lack of preparation in lackluster stories, which with just a little groundwork might have been molded into exemplary pieces.

If you were Marsha, what would you do? Here are some time-tested methods for preparing for an interview under such a deadline. First, check the latest edition of Who's Who in America in the newspaper library. Flake is certain to be listed there, along with a summary of his career achievements. This will give an indication of his interests, when he began his career, any professional recognition and perhaps even a brief statement about his business philosophy.

Check the newspaper library's clipping file for any previous stories about Flake. You'll be surprised how many times someone's name turns up here. The stories can provide valuable background and quotations that will help form the basis for pertinent questions. If you have time, trade journals from Flake's profession can help provide a wealth of information about him.

Next, make a quick call to Flake's hometown newspaper and see what reporters there can tell you about him. Reporters are generally eager to help each other.

If these checks fail to turn up any background on Flake, you could place a call directly to his office and ask a secretary to provide facts from his resume, which is likely on file in the office. By doing this as a last resort, you save yourself from going into the interview cold. In addition, you might also pull some interesting personal observations about Flake from his secretary.

During the interview, you must remember you are a reporter, not a stenographer or press agent. Although it is perfectly acceptable to let Flake drone on about his achievements during the interview, you must be prepared to do more than merely record his words and repeat them for your readers.

As a journalist, you have a responsibility to place the interview in perspective, to blend the facts that shape the story into more than rehashed notes. You must also be prepared to lead Flake with relevant questions that probe into specific areas. As a reporter writing a sidebar story, your main concern is not the news account of Flake's visit. Another reporter will write that story. Your primary job is to provide—through the interview—an understanding of the thinking behind his plan to sell only American-made merchandise in his stores. To be first-rate, your interview and story must delve beneath the surface facts to reveal what motivations have propelled Flake to his decisions: Patriotism? A dislike for foreign merchandise? A business gimmick?

The message is simple. Preparation is worth the effort. By preparing, you probably will discover many interesting and provocative facts about your subject and therefore be able to formulate intelligent and revealing questions.

The Effective Interview

The career journalist will conduct thousands of interviews with a wide range of people: from convicted murderers on death row, to politicians, to bag ladies who wander the streets in search of their next meal. Consequently, the mastering of interview skills and techniques are a necessity for any journalist. Here are guidelines for making your interview and the resulting product the very best it can be:

- Allow 30 minutes longer than you expect for any interview.
- Never keep a subject waiting. Always be on time for an interview.
- Have at least a hastily written script in your notebook of crucial questions that you gleaned during preparation. Make certain that these questions have been answered before ending the interview.
- Attempt to position yourself so there is no large object, such as a desk, between you and your subject. Information flows more freely and comfortably when people are neither intimidated nor subconsciously hiding behind such an obstruction. In that same respect, it is advisable to interview an executive or official outside of his or her office, away from the distractions of daily work life.
- Always have two pens and an adequate notebook. Borrowing these items reflects a lack of preparation and professionalism.
- Put the date, time and place of your interview on your notes. Note any other people present and their telephone numbers.
- Begin your interview with conversational remarks without your notebook in hand or a recorder running. Put your subject fully at

A Tulsa World reporter interviews a news source. (Photo courtesy of the Tulsa World)

ease. Smile. It tends to set a far more relaxing mood than a frown. Of course, your demeanor should always be determined by the type of interview.
- Begin the real interview with a simple, yet probing question. For example, you might ask: "Mr. Flake, you are listed as one of the 10 highest paid corporate executives in the nation, yet I couldn't help but notice you're driving a 1973 Volkswagen. Why is that?"

Since interviewing simply means asking questions, it is important to understand the basic categories of questions. Reporters routinely use seven kinds of questions.

1. *The Open-ended Question.* This is generally asked in order to break the ice in an interview and is not intended to probe for relevant information. "What's been happening in your life lately?" is an open-ended question that gets the interviewee talking.
2. *The Direct Question.* As the interview progresses, your questions become more specific. A direct question seeks to discover the nature or condition of a topic. If you ask the mayor, "How is the budget progressing?" you have asked a direct question.
3. *The Closed Question.* Direct questions often precede closed questions, which carry interrogation one step further. Here's a closed question for the mayor: "How much has been budgeted for travel next year?"

4. *The Probe Question.* This query frequently follows direct and closed questions and is even more specific. Again, using the budget example, here's a probe question: "Why have you budgeted 20 percent more for travel this year?"

5. *The Bi-polar Question.* This is asked to get a yes or no answer without additional comments. "Will the budget be released to the media by 9 a.m. tomorrow?" is an example.

6. *The Mirror Question.* As reporters gain experience, they learn to carve out time in the flow of an interview to catch up on comments and points they have mentally noted but not yet recorded. To do this, they restate earlier questions and permit the subject to briefly review. The answers usually add to a reporter's understanding of a given point. "So what you're saying, mayor, is that there is a need for officials to travel more in the coming year?" is an example of a mirror question.

7. *The Hypothetical or Suggestion Question.* Toward the end of an interview, reporters frequently ask subjects to speculate on a topic or issue of interest. If you ask the mayor to speculate on what he or she believes would happen if the travel budget were eliminated from city government, you've asked a hypothetical question. If you phrase the same question, "Have you ever considered eliminating the travel budget in order to save revenue?" you have asked a hypothetical question in the form of a suggestion.

- Don't attempt to transcribe every word the subject utters. Paraphrase those things you find interesting and directly quote the points that seem vitally significant. Ask the subject to repeat answers, if necessary.
- After asking a question, keep quiet and listen. Let your subject answer fully before continuing with the interview. Often the best statements given by your subject will come at the end of a particular point just made. Resist the temptation to step on the answer in an attempt to impress the subject with your knowledge of an issue.
- If your subject touches on an area of particular interest and then moves on, make a note to return to that topic. All too often, valuable points are irretrievably lost in the give-and-take of the interview exchange, because the reporter fails to note them for a calculated return.
- If the subject is reluctant to answer a particular question, move on to another area and return to the touchy subject later, possibly by using more carefully constructed questions.
- Note all contradictions during the interview. Ask the subject to explain such discrepancies to your satisfaction.
- Place identifying marks in your notes by interesting or significant comments the subject made. This makes it much easier to locate pertinent material later. Keep in mind that your editor may want to pull a particular quotation out for use with a photograph or to break up the story visually.
- Number questions in advance in the margin of your notebook. As the subject addresses those questions, number the responses in your notes to match the number of the question. If the subject

returns to an earlier question late in the interview, it will be easy to note that fact.
- At the conclusion of the interview, it is wise to ask the subject if there is anything else he or she wishes to add or discuss. This can occasionally turn up even the lead for your story. It also closes the door for any possible criticism later that the subject wasn't given an opportunity to explain a point. When you feel the interview is over, take five more minutes to ask at least two additional questions. The answers to these final questions often wind up in your lead paragraph.
- Above all, as in all newspaper writing, where time often is an enemy of complete accuracy, never be reluctant to call your subject back to check facts before publication. This only reflects your concern for accuracy and thoroughness. As mentioned earlier, to save time, always note the subject's phone number at the beginning of your notes.

If you're writing a feature story, here are a few additional interviewing tips:
- Make notes on your subject's appearance and distinctive personality traits or mannerisms that obviously or subtly set him or her apart from others. Be observant.
- Ask for the names and whereabouts of several of the subject's closest friends and perhaps an enemy as well. Quick telephone interviews with these people can provide valuable depth and perspective.
- Ask the subject to share some personal thoughts about himself or herself—perhaps a habit or custom—that few people know. These can provide additional insight into his or her personality and behavior.
- Inquire as deeply as possible into the subject's family life. Sometimes it is advisable, when possible, to conduct at least a telephone interview with the spouse as well for added depth.

Further Attribution Guidelines

Frequently, a subject will want to provide a reporter with secret information that may help the reporter better understand the subject's position. The reporter can use these "revelations" by following time-honored guidelines recognized by The Associated Press Managing Editors Association and other press organizations. In addition, some newspapers have specific attribution policies.

The highest level of attribution is *direct quotation*. Direct quotation means exactly what it says. The words in the quotation are the interviewee's words. When the subject speaks on-the-record, you may use direct quotation without restriction.

The next two rungs down the ladder are *not-for-direct-quotation* and *not-for-attribution*. The first refers to an agreement to identify the source but to quote that source only indirectly. This technique allows the source to later say he or she was misquoted, if an embarrassing situation develops. Not-for-attibution means the subject can be quoted but not specifically identified. For example: *A White House official said* the President will fly to Moscow within the next two weeks.

Lower still is *background*. Generally, background means the reporter can use the material but cannot link it in any way to the original source. Thus, using background material requires a confirming source.

Finally, at the bottom of the ladder is *off-the-record* attribution. This one is easy to understand. If a reporter accepts off-the-record material, it's secret. Period.

This hierarchy of attribution should guide you in handling special information. Let's look at how to use the guidelines in a few situations. First, if someone asks you to go off-the-record in advance of giving you quotations or background information and you agree to that stipulation, you must honor that restriction.

PROTECTING YOUR SOURCES

Police officers value reliable sources like gold. So do journalists. Because good sources are crucial, journalists must be willing to sacrifice their freedom and face a jail cell to protect sources when it becomes necessary.

In the course of gathering facts, you will often encounter people willing to help you only if you guarantee their anonymity. These people generally have a lot at stake, including their reputations, their jobs or maybe even their lives. Consequently, once you have given your word not to identify them, you must keep that promise at all costs. To violate your word virtually assures you that you will not get others to provide confidential information in the future.

Many states have realized the need for reporters to protect sources and have enacted so-called shield laws. These laws basically say the reporter does not have to reveal sources of information to state courts or grand juries under most circumstances. However, these laws do not always apply.

In 1984, editorial writer Richard Graves of the St. Louis Globe-Democrat spent three days in jail in Belleville, Ill., for refusing to disclose the names of confidential sources who provided information for a 1980 editorial he wrote while employed at The Belleville News-Democrat. Graves had been named in a libel suit against the Belleville newspaper that was spawned by his controversial editorial. He was the first U.S. newsperson since 1958 jailed for contempt in a civil libel case. His two sources eventually came forward voluntarily.

Afterwards, Graves warned that journalists should never believe that the jailhouse door couldn't close on them. "No one except a newsman can understand another newsman's sense of ethics," Graves told The Society of Professional Journalists, Sigma Delta Chi, in 1985. "But all the newsmen you know and trust will either be involved in the case, covering it and therefore unable to get involved, allowing their own confidential sources to cut you up in print, or afraid to offer meaningful advice because they know, as you do, what you must do and the price you might pay for doing it. So my advice for anyone considering getting into journalism is to decide now if you can pay that price. Once it happens to you, it's too late to back out."

In an effort to fight back, increasing numbers of journalists are making up-front arangements with their sources to guarantee protection unless the story results in a trial, at which time the source would be willing to come forth voluntarily. The best tactic, though, is to avoid using unnamed sources unless it is absolutely necessary, to convince your sources to go public with their information and be named in the story.

However, instead of readily agreeing to such an off-the-record promise in advance, experienced reporters often try to move the subject up the ladder to at least a not-for-attribution level. As you recall, this means the information provided by your subject can be used if attributed to a "source," or some other vague reference that would not disclose your subject. Some reporters use this form by simply saying "it was learned."

Problems sometimes develop when a subject freely gives the reporter direct quotation information then later says the statement is supposed to be off-the-record. Unfortunately, there are no established guidelines to follow when this occurs. If the reporter is far enough into the interview to have already obtained relevant information from the person being interviewed, he or she may decide the disputed quotation is just too significant to overlook. The reporter then must inform the subject that no agreement for confidentiality had been made beforehand and the quotations and information are fair game. However, if the interview is still in the early stages and the reporter needs the subject's full cooperation, it is probably wisest to consent, with the understanding that any further comments offered without advance off-the-record agreement will be considered fair game.

The universal code among journalists is that off-the-record agreements made in advance of the statements are the only ethically binding agreements. Yet, it is the reporter's responsibility to make the subject clearly aware of that fact before the interview begins.

Using Recording Devices

In this age of increasing litigation, reporters who once relied entirely on their notes for accuracy are slowly turning to recordings to support their stories. While recording devices can sometimes inhibit the subject of an interview from fully opening up to the reporter, many of America's best reporters say tape recorders generally appear no less threatening than a notebook and a pen when they explain that the recorder is necessary to preserve the integrity of the interview.

Subjects who open up to reporters in interviews are sometimes surprised to see the way their words sound in the context of the overall story. It is not unusual for them to claim that they were misquoted. A tape recorder not only insures and substantiates the accuracy of the quotation, but also discourages false claims against the reporter's credibility.

When you use a recorder for interviews, it is wise to supplement the tape with notes. That protects you in the event of a malfunction and pinpoints specific quotations for easy reference. Try to get a recorder with a built-in microphone, a footage counter and an audible "forward cue" function. The built-in mike helps ease the intimidation factor, and

> **SECRET TAPING OF TELEPHONE INTERVIEWS**
>
> Do you in fact violate the law when you audiotape a telephone interview without advising the subject that the call is being taped? The answer isn't clear.
>
> On the one hand, the 1968 Omnibus Crime Control and Safe Streets Act says a telephone conversation may be tape recorded as long as one party—the reporter, for example—is aware of the taping. On the other hand, at least 11 states restrict such one-party recordings of telephone conversations, according to The Reporter's Committee for Freedom of the Press. Those states are California, Florida, Georgia, Illinois, Maryland, Massachusetts, Montana, New Hampshire, Oregon, Pennsylvania and Washington. In addition, the Federal Communications Commission and local telephone company operating rules usually forbid one-party or secret taping. However, some communication lawyers have argued that the 1968 federal law overrides state law and that FCC regulations and local rules are also legally unenforceable because they conflict with the 1968 act.
>
> In practice, most daily and many non-daily newspapers have written or unwritten guidelines regarding reporters secretly taping telephone conversations. A recent survey of editors of 150 daily newspapers suggests that most believe that secret recording is unethical. The best advice is not to do it unless you are certain of state laws, or both sides have agreed to the recording.

the footage counter and the cue will assist you in quickly finding quotations on the tape.

In some states it is legal for one party to record another's voice over the telephone without the second party's knowledge. Other states require that both parties be aware that the conversation is being recorded.

While you may wish to record important face-to-face, telephone and group interviews in the event a quotation is later challenged by the subject, you should never violate the law or the newspaper's policy in this regard.

Advice From Pulitzer Prize-Winning Reporters

Some of the best interviewers in journalism, those who have earned the Pulitzer Prize, share certain traits that enable them to reach deeply into their subjects' experiences and extract those things that will most interest readers.

The Baltimore Sun's Jon Franklin, who won his first Pulitzer Prize for feature writing in 1979 and a second for explanatory journalism in 1985, prefers, whenever possible, to witness and document the fine, textural details of an event firsthand, and then buttress his stories with solid interviews.

That's exactly what he did in his story that won the 1979 Pulitzer Prize. In that article, he wrote about a woman undergoing brain surgery for a tumorous mass she called "the monster." Franklin not only witnessed much of the surgery itself, but also observed how the surgeon began that fateful day and the patient's fears before surgery. He brought their lives together in the operating room and built suspense to the point where the doctor, with the brain exposed, realized his patient's condition was inoperable. She later died.

In his 1985 Pulitzer Prize-winning series entitled "The Mind Fixers," Franklin gives us an example of how to consolidate pertinent information from several interviews. Here is an excerpt from the first story of that series. Note how he asks questions and sets up his interview quotations with marks, or *bullets*. These are both effective techniques.

**Chemical Workings of the Brain
Herald Psychiatry's New Frontier**

By **Jon Franklin**
The Baltimore Evening Sun

PULITZER PRIZE WINNER

Since the days of Sigmund Freud the practice of psychiatry has been more art than science. Surrounded by an aura of witchcraft, proceeding on impression and hunch, often ineffective, it was the bumbling and sometimes humorous stepchild of modern science.

But for a decade and more, research psychiatrists have been working quietly in laboratories, dissecting the brains of mice and men and teasing out the chemical formulas that unlock the secrets of the mind.

Now, in the 1980s, their work is paying off.

They are rapidly identifying the interlocking molecules that produce human thought and emotion. They have devised new scanners that trace the flickering web of personality as it dances through the brain. Armed with those scanners, they are mapping out the terrain of the human psyche.

As a result, psychiatry today stands on the threshold of becoming an exact science, as precise and quantifiable as molecular genetics. Ahead lies an era of psychic engineering, and the development of specialized drugs and therapies to heal sick minds.

But that's only the beginning: The potential of brain chemistry extends far beyond the confines of classic psychiatry.

Many molecular psychiatrists, for instance, believe they may soon have the ability to untangle the ancient enigma of violence and criminality.

Further, there is the promise that the current technology will lead to the development of drugs capable of expanding the workings of the normal mind—enhancing memory, heightening creativity and perhaps, one day, even increasing intelligence.

Ultimately, interviews with more than 50 scientists indicate, the revolution may offer us the most important gift of all: a dramatically improved understanding of who we are, why we are that way, and what it means to be human....

What is this new science? What are its principles? From what promises flow its optimism and appeal?

The flavor is conveyed most dramatically in the words of the scientists themselves as they strive to convey their view of the brain and their hopes for the future:

- Dr. Michael Kuhar, a brain chemist at the John Hopkins Medical School: "The working unit of the brain is the [receptor]. You can think of the receptor as a button. Chemicals come and push that button and make things happen.

"The brain is this complex array of buttons. You give certain drugs which hit certain receptors and certain things happen in the body. It might be an emotional experience, a thought experience—it might be a constriction of blood vessels, or a release of gastric acid. You know, stuff like that."

- Dr. Marcus Raichle, neurologist and radiologist at Washington University in St. Louis: "This is very seductive stuff ... for the first time we have the prospect of looking [inside the brains of] living patients with emotional disease, and looking at specific regional changes in their brains.

"I think we are going to find that there is a biological basis for many behavioral disorders."

- Dr. Paul Mandel, at the Center for Neurochemistry in Strasbourg, France: "People don't realize that psychology is a result of chemical behavior. That's why alcohol changes behavior ... it acts on the other molecules. A lot of behavior has relatively simple physical causes...."

- Dr. A. John Rush, a brain scanner expert at the University of Texas Health Science Center in Dallas: "I would think that within 10 years we'll have at least one or two biotechnologies that will tell us a great deal about the probabilities that someone will in fact develop a [psychiatric] illness. I think we're going to be able to identify people with a reasonable degree of reliability ... say 70 percent."

As you can see, using several hundred words pulled from detailed, far-ranging interviews in three states and France, Franklin neatly condenses and surveys the concept of molecular psychiatry. This should serve as one example of how reporters can use large amounts of information in a compact format.

Says Franklin of his work: "My best advice in interviewing is to take good, accurate notes, then pick and choose your best quotes carefully when it comes to writing the story. The best story, whether news or feature, is one that is neither overloaded with too many quotations nor too much narration.

"It flows in a balance. Above all, you cannot be reluctant to ask tough questions, the questions you're afraid might hurt a subject's feelings or offend them. But you should always, of course, ask those questions with tact."

Nan Robertson, a 1983 Pulitzer Prize-winning reporter for The New York Times, has discovered over the years that her best technique for

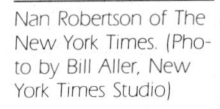

Nan Robertson of The New York Times. (Photo by Bill Aller, New York Times Studio)

obtaining information for her stories lies in putting her subjects at ease early in the interview process.

"I talk with them and let them know it's OK to open up, to tell me their true feelings," she says. "Pretty soon, most of them begin revealing all sorts of things about themselves. It is these details that give life and flair to your writing, that sets it apart from the mundane and makes your reader want to continue reading past the first five or six paragraphs."

The art of effective interviewing boils down to efficiently gathering information from person or persons and presenting your findings in the most interesting and informative manner. Although Franklin and Robertson are primarily feature writers, a news reporter has much to learn from them. For interviewing purposes, the only difference between the feature story and the news story reported under deadline pressure is the type of information the reporter is seeking and the questions the reporter must ask to obtain it.

For example, when Marsha was sent to interview Tom Flake, she was primarily seeking information about his new business scheme. If she had wanted to turn the sidebar story into a feature—to make Flake more human to the reader and paint a word portrait of him—her approach would have been similar, but her questions different. She would have noticed, for example, whether Flake wore penny loafers or wing tips. Was he clad in a traditional, conservative three-piece suit or a flashy sport coat with a pastel shirt and gold chains dangling from a well-tanned neck?

Pulitzer winners Loretta Tofani and William K. Marimow are reporters who usually write about breaking news under extremely tight deadlines. But like their feature counterparts, they are also masters at getting often reluctant subjects to talk about delicate matters. Often they save the potentially alienating questions until after they have obtained the basic facts to lay the story's foundation. A subject who becomes immediately alienated and defensive by a reporter's tough, adversarial questions is not likely to open up during the remainder of an interview.

Tofani, a Washington Post reporter, demonstrated an exemplary ability to convince reluctant subjects to talk when she interviewed both the victims and perpetrators of 24 jail rapes that occurred in 1982 in Prince George's County Jail. For her tenacity in interviewing, she received the 1983 Pulitzer Prize for investigative reporting.

In that series, Tofani obtained the victims' names from sources in the jail, and the rapists were identified by their victims. She then persisted until she had convinced sources on both sides to speak on-the-record—to let her use their names in describing the crimes. She interviewed most of the rapists in prison; some talked in their homes after being released. She also conducted in-depth interviews with law enforcement officers and judges. As a result of the admissions contained in Tofani's stories, some men were later prosecuted and convicted for those rapes.

Marimow, of The Philadelphia Inquirer, won a Pulitzer Prize in 1985 for investigative reporting about police brutality in Philadelphia. Here is Marimow's advice on interviewing:

"Explain exactly why you're calling and why you think the interview is important," he says.

"Prepare carefully for your interview by reading all available clippings, bringing with you public records which will support some or all of your questions. Make a list of each question you want to ask and don't be afraid to refer to the list before stating that you've completed the interview.

"Make every effort possible to conduct the interview in person. It gives the interviewer a better chance to establish personal rapport and, thereby, obtain more detailed information. More importantly, it helps the interviewer gauge the credibility of the interviewee," Marimow explains.

"In one-on-one interviews, I think the reporter should seriously consider *not* taping the interview unless the subject of the interview is taping the session. I believe that the presence of a tape recorder sets up an additional inhibition to good communication. Instead, review with the subject of the interview the most critical answers and check back again before publication.

"It's always helpful to begin an interview with a question about procedures—whether it involves *how* municipal bond issues are sold, *how* service connected disability pensions are granted or *how* a candidate can be recalled from office. This puts the interviewee in the position of being the expert and allows him to discuss a neutral subject.

"Telegraph most of your moves. For instance, if you're going to ask some innocuous, seemingly irrelevant biographical question, explain why you feel this is necessary before you begin the question.

"If you haven't obtained the information previously, make sure that you do get biographical data—such as birth dates, schools attended, parents' names and occupations—from all interviews. One can never tell when such information will be useful later," he says.

He adds: "If you believe the important question has been evaded, ask the question again by stating that you want to be 100 percent certain that you understand the answer. Or, ask the question in a way in which you suggest, but do not state explicitly, that the answer was dishonest. For example, I interviewed a real estate investor who owned a particular property. I was given what I considered to be a dishonest answer. After the question was answered, I said, 'Are you telling me that no one else, not anyone, has any ownership interest, however slight, in the property?' This time, the subject of the interview changed his answer."

THE ART OF INTERVIEWING

Although interviewing techniques are often a blend of logic, personality, sensitivity, empathy and timing, Pulitzer Prize winner James Polk of NBC News, David Hayes of the Kansas City Times and Steve Weinberg of the Investigative Reporters and Editors group believe there are definite guidelines to "the art of getting people to tell you the truth."

In their pamphlet entitled Sourcery, they offer this practical advice about interviews and fact gathering:

- Ask for help. If you ask people to tell you everything they know, that is a precious possession not readily surrendered. But people like to be asked for their help. Ask them to help you understand what is happening. That is what you want, isn't it? You're a little confused and lost, and you need help in figuring things out. In helping you, people just may tell you what they know.

- Be prepared. Know what you're talking about. Know what they're talking about. Study the subject—and the terminology of the topic. Know what your questions are. Know what the answers could be. Don't parade your knowledge. But use it to prompt discussion—and replies.

- Listen. Shut up and listen. A good reporter is a good listener. You shouldn't be trying to tell people everything you know. You want to get what they know. Sometimes the best questions are "Uh-huh," "Why?" "How?" "What do you mean?" and "I don't understand," the short questions which keep people talking, while you keep listening.

- Be honest. You want your sources to be honest with you, don't you? Be honest with them, if you want to build mutual trust. That doesn't mean putting everything out on a platter before the first question. But do try to be candid, rather than coy. If you're working on a story, say so. Take people part of the way into your confidence. Maybe they will do the same for you.

- Talk to everyone. There is no magic formula for finding sources. Figure out everyone who might know something about what you're looking for. Talk to them all. Keep asking. Go back and forth. You may find a piece here, a piece there. Getting stories is akin to assembling puzzles—without knowing how many pieces there are or what the final picture may look like.

- See people face-to-face. You can't look a telephone in the eye. And if you're in someone's office or living room, they can't hang up or put you on hold or ask you to call back another time—when they won't be in. In fact, few people know how to throw you out gracefully. So stay, and try to keep asking questions. Walk into an office two minutes after quitting time, when the secretary has gone but the boss with all the work to do is still there—and has no more appointments or ringing phones to interrupt him or her at that hour. Knock on doors at home at night and on weekends. Show up unexpectedly. Often people will see you to find out what you want.

- Go back. Go back again and again. Keep knocking on doors. You may feel foolish, but be polite and persist. Keep asking for help. It may seem hard to ask questions when you may feel foolish, but remember one rule: the only way you're certain of never getting the answer is to be too embarrassed to ask the question. One reporter's axiom: "There aren't any embarrassing questions—just embarrassing answers."

- Be pleasant. Make small talk. Be humble. After all, you don't know everything, you need help, or you wouldn't be there. And you should try to be sympathetic, when it's merited. Try to be a friend—but always remember you are a reporter.

- Remember the obvious question. That's not as easy as it sounds. You can get caught up in the small talk, the story-telling, the new angles, the listening, the good humor and charm of a source. But remember what you came for. Identify the question before you go in, and keep working on it, keep asking. If people ignore or evade your key questions, or lead you down another trail, you have to come back. Reword your question, rephrase it, ask it in different ways, as many times as you must until you do have an answer that's understandable and believable.

- Challenge your sources. Contradict them a little. Don't accept the easy explanation. Say you don't understand, say it doesn't make sense from what you know from other people. Ask them, "How can you be certain?" Let them prove it to you—with more details, other names, any documents.

- Never trust your source, at least not completely. Double-check. Look not only for corroboration, but also for contradictions, for evidence to the contrary. Not even your best source has a perfect memory.

- Don't socialize with reporters all the time. Socialize with people whose stories have not already been in print. Remember all the friends you ever met. Sometimes the person you once dated in college will grow up to be a top official of the Justice Department. Never underestimate anyone as a potential source.

- If you want to protect your sources, don't tell anyone, particularly your fellow reporters who are (with the exception of you, of course) the worst blabbermouths in the world. If you want a sensitive source to talk with you, he or she has to decide whether to trust you. And your word must be golden. A bad reputation will quickly ruin even the best reporter.

- You set the rules, and you clarify the terms on which you're talking. If this is background, or not-for-attribution, make certain you and the sources have the same definition of that, and recognize that the information will be used. It's up to you to avoid any misunderstanding. Spell out the terms, if necessary, at the outset so you both understand them. Don't take off-the-record information—that's unusable in any form, and let your sources know that. Most of them want to tell you something anyway, and will do so, at the least, on a background basis that allows you to pursue confirmation elsewhere. Don't let the source change the rules at the end of the evening. Your job is to tell stories to the public, not to your grandchildren someday.
- Give your worst enemy a fair shake. Always give someone his or her best defense in the printed story. Even if you don't believe it, let the readers have a chance to judge for themselves. You may earn that person's respect. He or she may even tell you the full story later on.
- Be cruel. This is the unwritten rule. When all is done—but not yet said—let the facts fall where they may. You have no friends now. You are a reporter—tell the truth. But don't pass judgment on people unnecessarily. You're a reporter, not God. Let people's deeds speak for themselves.
- Always say thank you. Say thank you at the end of the day. Go back when the story is over and say thank you again. Say thank you to sources even when nothing is happening. An honest thank you is as rare and as encouraging as a good listener.
- Keep trying. Keep working. It is the drudgery of making sure of details that uncovers the unexpected. A sage of this profession has said, "I've met a lot of lucky reporters. I've never known a single lazy lucky reporter."

Putting It All Together

Organizing the Interview Story

It's noon. Paul, a Times reporter, has returned from a two-hour interview with a convicted murderer who is sentenced to die in the state's gas chamber next week. His reporter's notebook is filled with exciting quotations and interesting facts. The story is due in four hours, and Paul is worried that he's about to botch the best potential story of his young career because he doesn't know how to fit the pieces together neatly.

Paul sits at his terminal staring at the pages of notes. On the back flap, he has scribbled the name and telephone number of the doomed man's wife and young son. There is also the name and number of the prisoner's mother and brother. Planning ahead, Paul has already obtained the phone number of the wife of the man murdered by the inmate.

"My gosh," Paul thinks. "They're only going to allow me 40 inches to tell the story in tomorrow's paper. I've got plenty of notes to do that already. Do I really need to call the others and collect even more notes?"

In all likelihood, the answer is an emphatic yes. The objective of quality reporting is depth, detail and rhythmic flow. One-dimensional interview stories generally fall far short of that standard.

Considering Paul's four-hour time restriction, here's what he should do to prepare the kind of story he will be proud to see his name on the next morning. In his first hour, he should interview as many of the other sources as he can, soliciting their responses to the impending execution and any other insights about the doomed man.

Next, Paul should take 30 minutes to relax and clear his mind of all else, allowing the information he has gathered to synthesize and organize itself, a practice that seems to become more commonplace as reporters gain experience.

With two and one-half hours remaining, Paul should make a rough outline of how his story can flow best from beginning to end. He can scribble this on a notepad or anywhere, just so the thoughts become roughly organized into some framework.

Should he begin with the convict's boyhood and work steadily toward his demise in linear fashion? Would it be more effective to begin with the inmate's thoughts of impending death, then flash back to his boyhood? Where can he best incorporate the thoughts of others? What are the very best quotations he collected during the interview? Paul should also ask himself, "Why am I writing this story?" and "What are the most significant things I learned today?" Most importantly, he should ask, "How can I make the readers feel what my subject is feeling?"

Writing the Story

With two hours left, Paul should begin writing his story. By budgeting 90 minutes to write, he allows himself just over two minutes for each column inch of the story. By following his rough outline, he makes sure he stays on track and keeps the story flowing, using transitional paragraphs when necessary.

At the end of 90 minutes, with a half-hour left before deadline, Paul still has ample time to carefully rework any rough spots in the story before submitting it to the editors.

This situation is not unique. Deciphering interviews within tight deadlines is standard fare. Unfortunately, younger reporters are inclined to want to skip the period of reflection in the aforementioned process, fearing the limited time will catch them several paragraphs short. But reflection and the perspective it brings is crucial for a full understanding and professional presentation of such stories. It frequently separates an ordinary story from the award winner.

With an interview story, the reporter has many decisions to make about the quotations he or she has gathered: How many should be used? Which ones should not be used? How can they best be incorporated into the story?

Consider this excerpt from Marimow's 1984 series on the police misuse of K–9 dogs in Philadelphia. This series won the 1985 Pulitzer Prize for investigative reporting. Examine how Marimow incorporates his interview quotations into the early part of the story. Would you have done it differently?

The K-9 Cases

By **William K. Marimow**
The Philadelphia Inquirer

PULITZER PRIZE WINNER

Even today, 2½ years later, Ronald Whitt says he can understand why a Philadelphia police officer stopped to question him one night in Center City as he and a friend were examining the dents in Whitt's 1978 Camaro.

What Whitt cannot understand—and what he still describes as the "worst thing that ever happened to me in my life"—is what happened after a second policeman, officer Stephen Gubicza, and his K–9 dog Stormy arrived on the scene at 12th and Appletree streets.

"I saw the dog running from the jeep toward me," said Whitt, now 23, who was standing spread-eagled and defenseless against the front of a police car. "I tried to jump on top of the car because I've been a paper boy, and I've been bit before."

But Stormy was too quick. In an instant, the K–9 dog sank his teeth deep into Whitt's left calf and kept biting. "I screamed at the top of my lungs, 'Get this dog off of me!'" recalled Whitt.

After about 30 seconds, Whitt said, Gubicza fought the dog off his body. "He actually pulled that dog's teeth out of my leg," Whitt said.

Then, as Whitt, bleeding and in pain, backed timidly away from dog and handler, Stormy broke away from Gubicza and again bit the helpless Whitt, this time in the right thigh. After another struggle between handler and K–9 partner, Whitt was extricated from Stormy's jaws. Whitt was then driven by a police officer other than Gubicza to Hahnemann University Hospital, where he was treated for about six hours for multiple puncture wounds of the left calf and right thigh.

Not only does Marimow artfully blend his interview information from Whitt into the second paragraph, but he also uses the third paragraph quotations and Whitt's words to build suspense and set up the actual dog bite.

Marimow saved a powerful quotation for the fourth paragraph immediately after Whitt had been bitten. He could have used the quotation earlier, but it is most appropriate as used because it adds impact to the description of the attack.

Some newspapers seem to almost follow a formula for introducing quotations into stories. For example, there are newspapers that refuse to use a quotation from an interview in the lead paragraph, regardless of how strong or relevant that quotation might be. The quotation invariably appears in the story's third or fourth paragraph. This is because some editors and reporters believe the third or fourth paragraph quotation lends a vital personalization early in the story, while also permitting a more traditional, information-laden lead paragraph.

Here's another example of that approach. This excerpt is from the first installment of Peter Rinearson's Pulitzer Prize-winning "Making It Fly" series in The Seattle Times. As you recall from Chapter 1, the series chronicles the building of the Boeing 757 jetliner. Note the effective use of a partial quotation in the third paragraph.

Boeing loses millions of dollars on every new 757 it sells.

But someday—if fate cooperates, if the wager pays off, if enough of the twin-engined jetliners are sold—the 757 will become hugely profitable.

Or at least that's Boeing's hope.

It's all part of what Sanford McDonnell, chairman of McDonnell Douglas, has called a "sporting business that rivals Las Vegas."

Sometimes minimal use of quotations is the most effective technique. For example, take this portion of a 1983 interview with Palestine Liberation Organization leader Yasir Arafat, which was written by David Zucchino of The Philadelphia Inquirer. This story was one of several that won the American Society of Newspaper Editors 1984 award for best newspaper writing on deadline. Note how Zucchino masterfully interweaves interview material with description to form a vision in the readers' minds and does so with only three direct and two partial quotations.

Yasir Arafat Tries to Dodge the Bullet

by **David Zucchino**
The Philadelphia Inquirer

TRIPOLI, Lebanon—The shells were falling closer by the time the man called Abu Ammar finally appeared, poking his bearded face from the side window of a dirty blue Chevrolet.

Yasir Arafat, *nom de guerre* Abu Ammar, had been chased in by the shells. He and his bodyguards ducked inside a converted school building on a shabby side street yesterday, trailed by a mob of photographers who had waited all day to document what appeared to be another step in the demise of the world's most famous guerrilla leader.

There was not much Arafat could say. He was boxed in. Only about 60 Palestinian Liberation Organization fighters loyal to him still clung to the southwest corner of the Beddawi refugee camp above this grimy city. The crunch of PLO rebel artillery drowned out Arafat as he spoke.

He tried to smile, but it was a gray and hollow effort. He had just spent the first full day without control of a single Palestinian refugee camp since he assumed leadership of the PLO in 1969.

He smiled again and described, as he always does, his will to fight. But the fact that he had sought refuge in Tripoli itself was mute evidence that his military leadership of the Palestinian cause had all but evaporated.

Someone asked if all of Beddawi had fallen yet. Arafat brightened. "As you can hear, there is still fighting," he said, and he playfully rubbed a reporter's head as he would a child's.

Although he could not acknowledge it in words, it was clear that he knew Beddawi was finished for him. He is now bottled up in Tripoli, where the few thousand men still under his command have prepared new redoubts inside buildings like the converted school.

His heavy guns have been pushed back to the very shore of the Mediterranean, and he is reduced now to ranting against the Syrians, who arm and direct his former troops. The Syrians, he said, have given "a signal that they intend to invade the city," moving a new brigade into Lebanon.

Although some rebel leaders yesterday repeated assurances that they would not harm Tripoli, other mutineers threatened to bomb Arafat's hideouts "down to the earth" if he did not abandon the city.

Arafat himself said again that he would leave only when asked by Tripoli's officials, although he has said it before and has ignored their subsequent pleas to do just that. In any event, by yesterday most city officials had fled.

As he spoke, Arafat raised his right hand, and everyone noticed that it was bandaged. "This?" he said. "Don't worry. It is still working, you can be sure." Someone asked if he had been wounded. He smiled and wiggled his fingers. There was no sign of blood or bruises—and, anyway, it was a small bandage.

He was turning to leave when he was asked if Tripoli was his last stand. "How can you ask me this when there are five million Palestinians in the world? . . . The PLO is the sole representative of five million Palestinians. No one can liquidate the PLO."

His security men shouldered him to the Chevrolet. He slipped inside, hopped right out to kiss the cheeks of two Palestinian girls and two fighters, then dropped back into his seat, to be driven to yet another very temporary hideout.

He flashed a V sign and was gone, followed down the street by the thud of shelling in the lost camp of Beddawi in the smoky hills above.

To put it another way, reporters should realize they are not obligated to relay every fact and quotation they acquire from a person during an interview. In fact, the wise reporter might even save the overflow quotations for his or her "future file" in the likely event the subject's name turns up again.

For example, let's say you have just completed a long, fruitful interview with a state senator. The story is due tomorrow and you have far more information than you actually need for the piece, particularly after you make the additional contacts to flesh out the article.

Why not select the very best quotations for your upcoming Sunday story and hold back a few for a fascinating year-end feature article about old-timers in the state Senate? You will save valuable time on the latter story and find it much easier with such a head start. It pays to think ahead and creatively on the stories that can be considered timeless. In the same vein, perhaps the senator told you in the interview of a hobby he enjoys or an antique shop his wife owns. You might also file that portion of the interview away and make a note to dig it out for a lighter feature story someday on the state's antique stores or perhaps the hobbies of famous people in the state.

The key words for successful interviewing skills and techniques are preparation, consideration and organization. When you prepare properly, consider your approach, and organize your material, success is bound to follow.

Keeping an Open Mind

If asking the right questions in the right way of the right people is critical to the success of the journalistic interview, there's at least one stumbling block that can guarantee an interview's failure—a closed mind.

For example, a young reporter once interviewed an old man from a small, poor southern town, not expecting to find much quotable from anyone in the area. The elderly man in question was the mayor of the hamlet. The reporter found him seated on some farm machinery near the little post office in town. When the man began to speak, a fountain of knowledge spewed forth from his weatherbeaten lips. His unguarded words flowed freely and fit neatly together, like those of a poet, although he had little formal education. The power of his sheer common sense was astounding and his self-taught vocabulary enormous. The old man's words eventually became a powerful interview in a well read newspaper story.

The nation's best reporters agree that the most effective and significant stories they produce are born in open, receptive minds free from the clutter of preconceptions and rumors. They go into a story well prepared yet objectively allowing the story to unfold before them. It is only in this way that the newspaper reporter can effectively mirror human life through effective interviewing techniques.

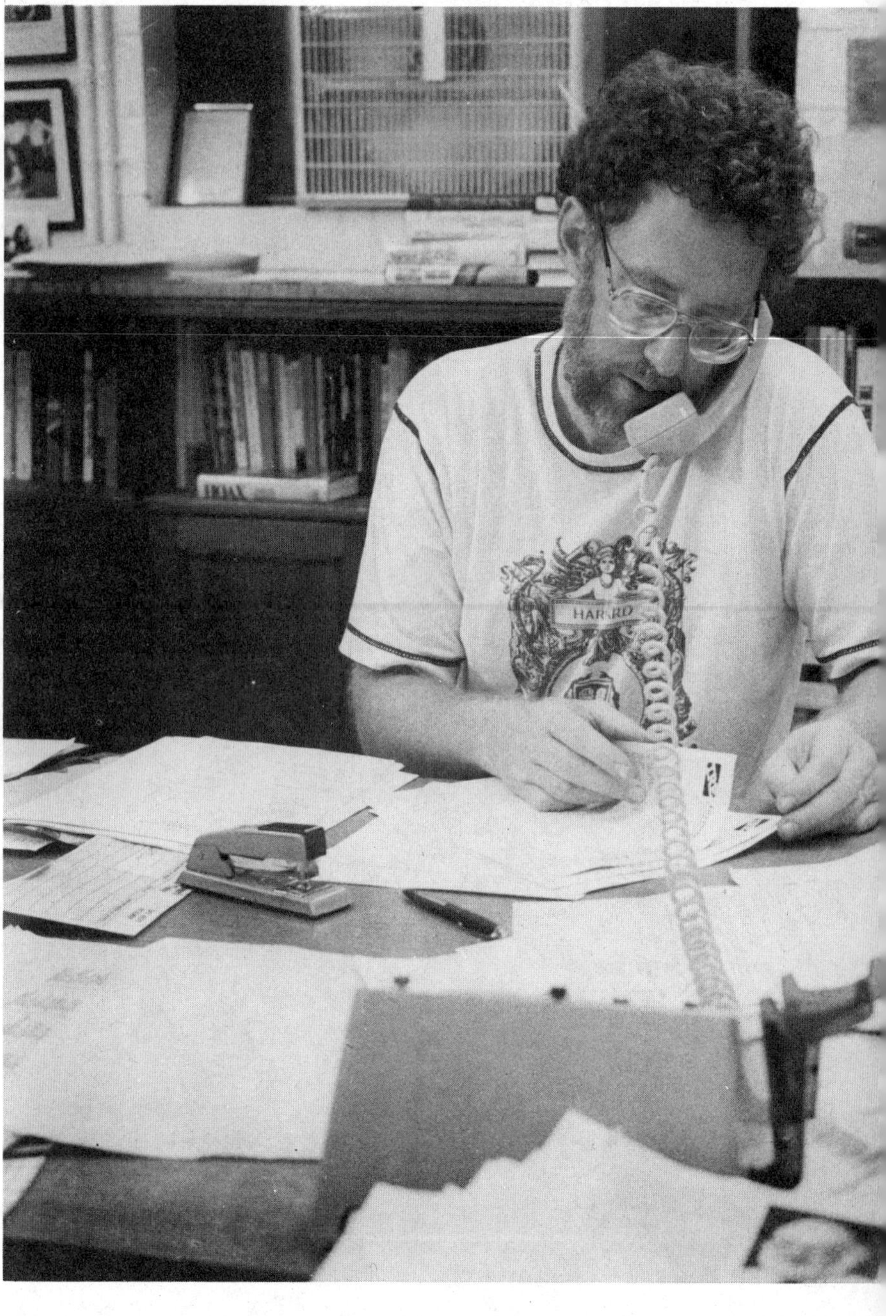

CHAPTER 6

Using Documents Effectively

The Paper Trail
Practice Makes Perfect
Sources for Documents
Using Data Bases and Libraries
Keeping an Eye on Public Officials
Pursuits of the Paper Trail
Using Freedom of Information Acts

The Paper Trail

Interviews collect vital oral data, yet written records are often even more valuable because they offer tangible evidence for the points in your story. Public records are essential for documenting the truth of a story. Local, state and federal bureaucracies generate mounds of paperwork about even the most trivial matters. Journalists have come to call these recorded tracks the paper trail.

From the time of our birth, records that document our lives are kept on file. Doctors keep our inoculation records as we grow. Public schools routinely verify our progress through report cards and yearbooks. As adults, written accountings of our annual earnings are required by state and federal governments. We write checks for things we purchase, and we regularly disclose information about ourselves in credit card applications. When we buy property, the purchase is recorded in the tax assessor's and collector's offices. Our marriages are permanently recorded in certificate form. A run-in with the law generates paperwork in police departments, and driving a vehicle on public thoroughfares necessitates a state driver's license. If we're hospitalized, records are kept. If our house burns, there are detailed records on file with the local fire department. Divorces often initiate a flurry of court records that might contain income tax information, depositions, property lists and much more. When we die, the paper trail lives on. A death certificate and perhaps an autopsy or coroner's report—is filed. The funeral home keeps records. Probate court records may contain information we held secret during our lifetime.

Think about the sizeable paper trail you have already left behind: school registrations, your previous performance in schools, forms you've completed for scholarship applications or perhaps a work history with the campus placement office if you applied for a part-time job.

Steve Weinberg, executive director of the Investigative Reporters and Editors organization based at the University of Missouri School of Journalism, is one accomplished journalist who places great stock in these trails of paper. "It's a catchy phrase that many journalists do not even know," wrote Weinberg in the Washington Journalism Review. "[But] many of those who know it and preach it rarely practice it. Only a small number of journalists are accomplished users of documents. And that's a pity."

In a study of capital correspondents titled "The Washington Reporters," Steven Hess of the Brookings Institution found the journalists he interviewed used no documents in about three-fourths of all stories, Weinberg noted. As partial evidence, Hess quoted a Washington bureau chief who said his experience showed not many reporters excel at documents research: "They think they are [excelling], but they're not.

Chapter opening photo: Steve Weinberg, director of the Investigative Reporters and Editors group at the University of Missouri, answers a reporter's question about locating documents essential to a story. (Photo by Duane Dailey)

Most reporters don't know how to compile a financial record on an individual because they've never been taught." Even the renowned Watergate exposé, which among other feats traced and exposed the laundering of presidential campaign money, did not originate from original research by the press but rather from the FBI leaking the information, Weinberg quoted Hess as saying.

Unfortunately, when newspaper and television reporters are given more time, they simply do more interviews, Hess said. John Ullmann, an editor at the Minneapolis Star and Tribune, echoed this and noted that the average insurance investigator knows more about digging into documents than most journalists, Weinberg wrote.

Weinberg also noted in the WJR article, that some reporters who do use documents skillfully have risen to the pinnacle of the profession. Pulitzer winners Donald Barlett and James Steele of The Philadelphia Inquirer, Rich Robertson of The Arizona Republic, Mary Hargrove of The Tulsa Tribune, and Chuck Cook of the Los Angeles Herald Examiner are a few. Each of these reporters is disciplined enough to spend long hours pouring through mounds of files and papers to document their stories. You will read more about them a little later.

Practice Makes Perfect

The paper trail often vanishes over the horizon, but experience generally tells you when you have sufficient documentation to substantiate your story. If you have done your homework before you interview your subject, you will likely be better informed than he or she is when it comes to discussing specifics. This preparation gives you not only added perspective, but also the ability to catch inconsistencies and discrepancies during the interview.

Weinberg of the IRE organization believes the best way to become adept at following a paper trail is to practice on someone you know. He suggests collecting as much paper as possible in a week on a particular person.

For example, let's suppose your subject is a teacher at a state university. Start with the college catalog to find out the rank of the professor. The catalog also tells you about her academic degrees. Next, check the university budget to find out how much money she makes. Then ask the university public relations office for a copy of those parts of the professor's résumé that are public. Check the city directory to find out the professor's telephone number and address and the occupation of her spouse. Next, survey the clipping files of your newspaper to see what has been written about the professor and also check the department of motor vehicles to see what kind of car she drives and whether her driver's license shows suspensions or revocations. Call the tax collector to see if she is delinquent. Check with the secretary of state to see if she has made political contributions for the last election. Run her name through the civil, criminal and bankruptcy courts. As you can see, the list of possibilities is nearly endless.

As with anything else worthwhile, hard work is required. Getting your hands dirty in the documents themselves is critical to success. Document searches will often prove futile in one area but rewarding in another. Beginning reporters learn the box canyons of the search process by doing their own digging. Eventually, the astute reporter creates shortcuts to long hours of paper searches by establishing professional relationships with public employees who can find what is needed in a matter of minutes.

Sources for Documents

The purpose of this chapter is not to provide an endless list of checkpoints along the paper trail. Rather, it is to prompt you, as an aspiring reporter, to begin recognizing every potential avenue of information in your quest to be the best journalist possible. Researching documents holds little glamour and can prove tedious. Yet you needn't don the hat of a certified public accountant when you research documents. The task primarily requires sheer tenacity and the creativity to discover and mine the wealth of documented facts that probably exist for any subject you want to examine. A good reporter can conceive of any number of places where various records about a story subject might be found. Leave no stone unturned.

Granted, not all documents are considered public information. Income tax information is not publicly available; neither are adoption records or hospital files in most states. The records of a private business do not fall under the purview of free information in our society either. But the persistent reporter generally finds a way to legitimately obtain the information he or she is seeking if the record exists.

For example, tax returns and credit card purchases sometimes surface in the records of bankruptcy court, U.S. Tax Court or even a civil suit. These court records *are* public documents. To find who is suing whom, check plaintiff and defendant indexes in municipal, county, state and federal court. There are also computerized data bases, such as Lexis and Westlaw, that list most lawsuits of significance filed in the United States for the past several years. These data bases are explained later in the chapter.

"Empire," a book by Donald Barlett and James Steele of The Philadelphia Inquirer, about Howard Hughes, the late reclusive multi-millionaire, is an example of how records can be used effectively to examine a person. Hughes certainly was a difficult subject to investigate. No one saw him or spoke with him for decades. What kind of paper trail could such a fanatical phantom leave? As it turned out, the trail of records was both wide and long. The two reporters examined 250,000 pages of documents, may of them public records. Here is what they said about public records in their book:

> The great majority of records and documents ... were drawn from three general areas—the courts, government agencies and private sources. Scores of criminal and civil legal actions involving Hughes, his companies, past and present Hughes executives and others connected with the Hughes' empire were examined in two dozen state and federal jurisdictions from New York to Los Angeles.

Any journalist embarking on a paper trail of an individual or institution needs to know what categories of documents exist. Take some time to analyze where you are going and what documents are likely to exist in the courts and public agencies. For example, if you're looking at a nursing home, you should know to check for local and federal inspection records as well as deficiency or complaint reports.

Usually, it is best to begin your records search with secondary sources such as clippings in your newspaper's library or the nearest public library. You can also scan magazines. Newspaper and magazine articles are generally more accessible today than in past years because of computerized data base searching. University libraries usually have trained data base researchers.

If the person you are researching has achieved status in society, chances are that he or she is listed in the annual Who's Who in America. The entry gives specific information about schools attended, degrees received and other interests and accomplishments. It can also offer valuable clues about the person. The information is usually provided by the subject of the entry and says something about what the person thought was important to offer publicly.

From there, you can move to community resource documents. These might include church bulletins, family genealogies and newsletters of fraternal groups or offices.

Documents of education are another critical resource to investigate carefully when following the paper trail. Don't overlook the student newspapers and annuals from the time your subject began school until graduation. Check alumni association records and any information available through the registrar's office.

Next, look in the county courthouse for real estate documents. They will include home purchases and sales, mortgages, tax assessments, landlord-tenant disputes, zoning variances and more. Such records are nearly always considered public. Public documents also exist for certain personal property, such as cars, planes, boats, horses and even guns.

Travel always spawns paper. Hotel registrations, airline and ship manifests, passport and visa applications, car rentals, travel advances and reimbursements are all recorded somewhere, although most are not likely to be filed as public records. At this point, having good sources can be extremely valuable.

Reporters often overlook campaign contribution lists, which are also matters of public record and are of particular interest when examining politically sensitive stories or issues of political influence.

Let's examine a specific example. It's another hectic day at the Times. The editor has just assigned you to find out all you can about Max Parker, a local attorney who has just announced his candidacy for state attorney general. After checking the newspaper's library, where should you look? Here are some suggestions, in addition to the ones you've already read about:

- Check the records in probate court, chancery court, bankruptcy court, circuit court, traffic court and even federal court to see if Parker's name appears as either a plaintiff or defendant. If so ask the court clerk for the transcript of that proceeding and analyze the facts contained therein. In today's litigious society, it is not unusual for a person to have been swept up into the current of lawsuits.
- Visit the tax assessor and the tax collector to gather records on what Parker has claimed as his material possessions and property.
- Check with the secretary of state or corresponding agency in your state to learn if Parker's name shows up as a partner in any non-profit corporations. If so, what are the stated purposes of that corporation? Is Parker's wife's name on any partnerships? What about other relatives?
- Since Parker is a lawyer, stop by the state Supreme Court building and the area bar association to see if his name shows up on any lists of commendations or complaints. If there a record indicating that Parker was ever censured by either group?

YOUR COMMUNITY'S VITAL STATISTICS

For stories that reflect the economic and social complexity of a community there is perhaps no better source than the U.S. Bureau of the Census. You can obtain facts and statistics from the bureau that can help buttress interviews and firmly establish the point of your article. An especially helpful census document is the widely available Statistical Abstract of the United States, published yearly. The 1,000-plus-page book provides detailed data relevant to virtually every sphere of human endeavor including population, housing, health, education, employment, income, business, science and government finance, often on a state-by-state basis. This book, and much of the other detailed census information—such as the Census of Housing, the Census of Population and the Census of Economics—is usually found at several locations in each state, including state employment offices, colleges and major libraries.

If you work in a community with a university near by, contact the school's research and extension service, which can often provide a wealth of social and economic information about the state and region.

Vital statistics such as birth certificates, marriage licenses and death certificates are generally filed either with your local health department or at area courthouses. Many state health departments publish a booklet that deals solely with vital statistics, listing deaths by cause, death rates, birth rates and other detailed social information about your state and individual counties.

- Check with the state health department or other appropriate agency to obtain Parker's birth certificate. This will give you his exact age, parents' names and place of birth.
- Learn which state agency maintains marriage licenses. If Parker is married, obtain a copy of that document. It should list his wife's maiden name.
- If Parker drives a car, he is bound to have a driver's license. A check with your state licensing department will reveal further information from that document. In addition, your department of motor vehicles should list the description of vehicles owned by the candidate. In some states, driving records are public documents.
- Don't overlook the obvious. A call to Parker's office can produce a résumé that will list his career history and professed accomplishments in one fell swoop. Take time to write or call the educational and professional listings for verification. Such background checks on individuals have often produced stories about false or misleading statements made by people in positions of public trust.

For example, an Arkansas candidate for state representative once handed a reporter his campaign card, which listed his alleged accomplishments on the back. One of those was a cum laude degree from the college he attended 13 years earlier. The reporter wound up with a front page story three days later after researching the candidate's claims and discovering he had barely maintained a "C" average through college. The candidate claimed a "printing error"; he also lost the election.

Reporters Rich Robertson and Jerry Seper used hundreds of public documents to expose corruption in diploma mills for the investigatively-oriented Arizona Republic in Phoenix. The investigation revealed details about 11 phoney "universities" in Arizona. The series led to indictments and changes in Arizona laws regarding such schools.

Using Data Bases and Libraries

America's best reporters recognize that virtually every story has a information pothole that needs to be filled in. No small or medium circulation newspaper library will have all of the required repair materials—the reference books and periodicals.

Reporters have many library resources available to them besides the newspaper library. One of the most important but least commonly used resources is the computer-accessed electronic data base. Data bases provide reporters with instant access to what has already been written about specific subjects in the nation's largest periodicals and most specialized journals. Using a data base is a lot like having the world's best encyclopedia—which is constantly updated—at your fingertips.

The data base is a fairly recent addition to the journalistic arsenal. As a matter of fact, most weekly newspapers do not yet have access to data bases. The reason, of course, is money: Access to data bases can cost from a few dollars to several hundred dollars per hour, depending on the time of day the data is accessed and other factors.

However, most daily newspapers subscribe to a wire service such as The Associated Press. The AP library in New York City will conduct a search for wire service stories on a given topic at the request of member organizations. AP can search its files for wire stories dating back to the late 1970s and, using a second data base, can also search for stories in various periodicals. For example, for a 1985 series on dangerous cast-off school buses, the AP service provided two Arkansas Democrat reporters with vital information about the crashes of these buses in the United States and foreign countries during the previous decade.

In addition, members of the IRE organization can have data base searches made on virtually any subject worldwide for a reasonable charge.

Data bases electronically tap into wire service files, newspapers, magazines, trade newsletters, congressional hearings, government documents, legal decisions, scholarly papers, bibliographical material, scientific information, press releases and much more.

Three general kinds of data bases are appropriate for reporting purposes: complete text, statistical and bibliographical data bases. These data bases have exotic names like CompuServe, The Source, Nexis, Lexis and Westlaw. The complete text data bases provide full texts of speeches, legal decisions, wire service and news stories, and magazine articles. The statistical data bases provide numerical facts and information. The bibliographic data bases lead reporters to other sources where full text information about people, places and things may be found.

Here's how some data bases work. Let's assume that you are writing a story about unidentified flying objects. You want to scan the wire services, major national newspapers and magazines for the latest UFO sighting in the United States. Your video display terminal, or perhaps a special dedicated computer, is connected by a telephone line and a device called a *modem* (for modulator/demodulator) to a central data base in another city. You instruct the terminal to dial the data base and a *menu*, or list of potential items to be ordered, appears on the terminal screen. You ask the menu for full text of major periodicals, then type in "UFO." The computer automatically searches the data base for all recent stories regarding UFOs. When it finds a story about the latest sighting, it notifies you. Then you have the option of putting the information into the memory on your terminal, having it automatically typed out on an office printer or taking notes from what you read on the screen. The process is fast, but the dollar clock is ticking while you and the computer search through the data base.

The technology of data bases is advancing more rapidly than books can be published. Consequently, by the time you read this, many additional breakthroughs in this field will have been made. Check with your editor to see what computerized data is available to you.

A slower but cheaper alternative to electronic data base searches is a trip to the local library. Your life will be easier if you get to know the reference librarian at the best public or university library in your city. The good public or university library has a wealth of non-electronic data bases that more or less duplicate the electronic ones in every way but speed and timeliness. For example, if you were doing the story about UFOs and wanted to know about recent sightings in the United States, you could check the The New York Times Index or the Official Washington Post Index. Both indexes would give you references to stories in the respective papers, which would allow you to find the microfilm on which the stories were located. You could then either take notes from the microfilm or make a copy. While you were there, you could also check the Reader's Guide to Periodical Literature, which catalogs numerous popular magazines. However, because magazines often have a lead time of many months, the newspaper indexes would probably be more helpful.

In addition, the public or university library may have many reference books not held in the newspaper library. For example, if you need to know the name of actor Edward G. Robinson's last movie, call your local reference librarian. The librarian will probably check a book such as the Dictionary of American Biography and tell you that the film was "Soylent Green," a science fiction movie about dead people who were made into little green food pellets. If you want to know when "Soylent Green" was made, call the librarian again, who will no doubt check Leonard Maltin's TV Movies. (The 100-minute-long movie, directed by Richard Fleischer and starring Charlton Heston and Robinson, was made in 1973, the librarian will tell you.)

Remember, however, that the reference librarian is not your slave. Your hysterical telephone requests may be justified when you have an impossible deadline. At other times, you should do your own research in the library's reference department.

A few reference works you will find at many large public and university libraries are listed here. The books can prove useful in quickly providing background information about an unfamiliar subject.

<u>Biographical References</u>
Biography Index (for sources of biographical information)
Current Biography Yearbook and Current Biography (for biographies of individuals in the news)
Dictionary of American Biography (for biographies of dead Americans)
Dictionary of National Biography (for biographies of dead British and international figures)
Directory of American Scholars (for biographies of some American college and university scholars)
International Who's Who (for biographies of international figures)

Webster's Biographical Dictionary (for short biographies of living and dead individuals)
Who's Who (for biographies of living British and international figures)
Who's Who in America (for biographies of living Americans)
Who's Who in American Politics
Who's Who in the East
Who's Who in the Midwest
Who's Who in the South and Southwest
Who's Who in the West
Who's Who of American Women

Business References
Million Dollar Directory (for information about small, medium and large companies)
Moody's manuals (for condensations of annual report information)
Standard & Poor's Register (for information about major corporations)
Standard & Poor's Corporation Records (for more detailed information about major corporations)
Thomas' Register of Manufacturers (for information about major manufacturers and their products)
Wall Street Journal Index

Other References
Almanacs and encyclopedias from various publishers
The Book of American Rankings
The Book of World Rankings
Facts on File (for a weekly news digest of many metropolitan daily newspapers)
Names and Numbers (for a listing of hard-to-find telephone numbers)
National Directory of Addresses and Telephone Numbers
Reader's Guide to Periodical Literature (for a listing of articles by subject from nearly 200 major periodicals)

Keeping an Eye on Public Officials

The First Amendment to the U.S. Constitution intended that the people remain free to question the machinery of politics and government. Without such questioning, any government is free to sink to its lowest level of performance and perhaps become thoroughly corrupt. A major part of this vital questioning depends on reporters understanding and using public records effectively.

When examining any public official, the first step should be to obtain a copy of the relevant codes, regulations, ordinances, and laws that pertain to the performance of that official. What is the official supposed to be doing to earn his or her salary? This provides you with both perspective and a firm foundation upon which to stack the volumes of information you will invariably obtain.

When you are looking at the performance of a public official, there are many records to examine. For example, there are campaign contribution reports. Politicians in most states are required to list those who made significant contributions to their campaign. A quick call to your state election commission or to the secretary of state's office can tell you exactly where to find these reports in your state. Federal candidates must file similar reports with the Federal Election Commission in Washington, D.C. Has your official been involved with any legislation or regulations that benefited such a contributor?

In addition, some states also require their elected officials to list their economic interests, which show their ownership of property and origins of income. Again, check with your local election commission for these files.

Don't overlook court records. Municipal, probate, chancery, bankruptcy and federal court records should be listed with the clerks of each court. Has your official been involved in a lawsuit that may affect his or her public performance?

There are also financial disclosure records, usually kept by county clerks, which provide detailed financial information on all mortgages filed within a county within the past few years.

Business applications and licenses can also prove invaluable in tracking an official if the individual is involved in a business or profession that requires licensing. Does the information gleaned from these records corroborate other facts you have gathered or lead you elsewhere along the paper trail?

Corporation records—for both for-profit and non-profit corporations—should be on file at your secretary of state's office. They may yield the names of partners in business with a public official. If you find the names of such partners, check to see if they have contracts with any state or local governments or if their corporation receives public funds of any kind. This could represent a serious conflict of interest. Remember that the name of the "Acme Corporation" means little. It's the *who* behind Acme that matters.

Looking at zoning and planning records sometimes pays dividends. Check zoning change requests made by corporations to discover the true players behind such requests and perhaps the motives. These files are usually located in your city or county planning and zoning commission offices. Is your official putting pressure on zoning boards to help financial contributors or a business in which he or she owns a part interest?

Finally, there are governmental inspection reports. If you find that your public official owns all or part of a facility subject to inspection, valuable information can be collected from files at local, county and state inspection departments. For example, in a Tulsa Tribune investigation, reporters discovered one Oklahoma nursing home owner who was claiming a new Corvette each year on the public cost reports as a legitimate operating expense. Cost reports are routinely filed with state health agencies.

Corresponding records for some businesses, such as nursing homes receiving Medicaid, also exist at the federal level at your nearest regional U.S. Department of Health and Human Services agency. HHS conducts its own follow-up inspections that are matters of public record and may vary greatly with your state inspection records in what they reveal. Look for contradictions between those reports to find significant stories.

Pursuits of the Paper Trail

Once a reporter has learned where and how to look and has cultivated sources, little information is beyond reach. For example, when Oklahoma's Penn Square Bank failed earlier this decade, thousands of depositors and financial institutions were injured. Mary Hargrove, the award-winning special projects editor of The Tulsa Tribune, covered the story better than anyone in the country because of her knowledge of records. Hargrove, whose grasp of document usage is among the best in the nation, is a prime example of how effective use of the paper trail is not limited to only those who work in the biggest newspaper and television markets.

Hargrove has many suggestions for where we might look for business records on a corporation: "Let's call it the the Crosstown Towing Company," she says. "The secretary of state, located in the state capital, will have articles of incorporation. These are the papers creating the company and will provide the date of incorporation. Ask for the [office] service agent, who is often an attorney, and double-check for any amendments, such as mergers with other companies. The articles will list the price per share of stock and several pages of standard jargon about the purposes the company is created for.

"A franchise tax record is kept with the state tax commission.... It's the best source for getting to the real owners. The folks who pay the bills and their addresses will appear on the back of the tax form. Go back several years and see if those names change in case you can get a lead on former employees," Hargrove explains.

"Both the state and federal courthouse may have dozens of areas to check. Look for lawsuits under 'Crosstown Towing', and all of its executives. Check for material liens in the state courthouse in case the individuals haven't been paying their bills. The company may surface in Small Claims Court; a list of unhappy clients could be very useful."

Hargrove adds: "Regulators at all levels could hold reams of documents. For example, Crosstown Towing in Oklahoma must be licensed by the city and the state corporation commission. The state Department of Public Safety also has some jurisdiction over towing companies. Look for applications for licenses which often include financial data on the companies and backgrounds on the executives. Complaint files may be kept separately, so ask specifically for them. Names of customers or former employees could be tucked away in the file drawers of any of these regulators. Also, any actions by the government against the company could be included in depositions or other exhibits.

"Annual reports may be kept in the business section of the local library or a nearby university library. Don't dismiss these glossy yearly statements. They list officers and often have pictures of people who don't want to pose for you. The towing company's financial picture will be laid out, although it may not be very thorough. Go back several years

RESEARCHING GAIL SMITH

Hargrove knows how to search for information about people as well as businesses. Here are her tips on backgrounding a subject named Gail Smith:

- Check newspaper clips in all cities in which Gail Smith has lived or worked. Don't dismiss the social section. It is often the best source of news. In wedding announcements, for example, it will list long-term friends in the wedding party who can describe Smith's family and personality. It will probably include education and employment at that period in her life. Be careful to check the facts yourself, especially when the clips come from another city and you don't know the reporter who covered that story.

- A city directory probably can be found in your newsroom library or the city library. The directory will list job, address and possibly family. If Smith is not a wealthy or prominent person and has no clips in your news library but has lived in town, go back at least 10 years in the city directory and come forward. As you see her move, you can tell by the area of town that she is making more money. This will help you track her jobs and you can go back to the companies and ask about her habits and work performance. Also, if her husband disappears from the listing, check the courthouse for the probate or divorce files.

- Divorce records found at the county courthouse yield tons of information. The divorce record looks like a lawsuit and will list spouse, date of marriage, any children and their ages and perhaps even who gets what property. This could include real estate, boats, cars and other items which can give a glimpse into Smith's financial condition. Some states permit this information to be sealed, but it's worth asking about.

- Civil suits and depositions filed at the county or federal courthouse with those suits can be crucial if Gail Smith refuses to talk to you. Find out who is suing her and get to that person and his attorney. They may have papers of Smith's or know others who dealt with her. Depositions may not be in the file so be sure to ask the attorney if they have been put somewhere else. These are sworn statements and often begin with biographical data. It would be hard for Smith to allege statements you use from a deposition are wrong.

- Professional associations usually in the state capital offer another source of good background. Organizations for nursing home owners and operators, beauticians, funeral home directors, bail bondsmen, attorneys and doctors require members to fill out applications which include date of birth, education, any lawsuits or convictions and often a picture. Many times, Smith may put down references, so there are additional sources to call.

- Death certificates are found at the state health department and offer a wide range of tips including birthdate, place of birth, cause of death, next of kin, doctor and funeral home. The funeral home might tell you that Gail Smith's expenses were paid by a life insurance policy listing a nurse at the nursing home as a beneficiary.

to see which officers in the towing company don't reappear. Chances are, they'll be willing to talk to you if they're ex-employees. Sometimes, these reports brag about their clients and give a handy checklist of those people or firms the company does business with—more sources to run down," Hargrove says.

Hargrove also notes that "competitors are the cream of all sources. They know which clients have been snatched away, which shortcuts the towing company is using and can point out how the industry is supposed to work. You can't spot what's strange if you don't know what the norm is. They probably belong to the same professional organizations so they can tip you off to other disgruntled competitors or customers. Also, if regulators are asking questions, the competitors will be able to tip you off," she adds.

When The Tulsa Tribune investigated the empire of evangelist Oral Roberts and his City of Faith hospital in 1986, reporters made good use of three crucial public forms: Articles of Incorporation and IRS forms 1023 and 990. Samples of the forms are reproduced as figures 6.1 through 6.4. The series revealed how financially strapped the Oral Roberts organization had become despite Roberts' vast personal holdings.

Chuck Cook of the Los Angeles Herald Examiner, who has twice received the IRE's national award for the best investigative reporting in America, is also an expert at using public documents to build his stories. As a reporter for The Register in Southern California's Orange County, Cook teamed up with another reporter on an award-winning effort to expose questionable deaths in the county jail. Here is how Cook explains the importance of records both to that series and to a more recent exposé of questionable recruiting practices at Memphis State University.

"In Orange County, California, we used hundreds of records to detail suspicious circumstances surrounding the deaths of more than 20 inmates at the county jail," Cook says.

"Law suits against the county provided a list of survivors of dead inmates and their complaints against the county. Additionally, claims were filed with the county Office of Risk Management. These provided valuable information about cases that were settled before they reached court.

"In Orange County and many California counties, the sheriff is also the coroner. We became suspicious of this natural conflict in jail deaths, and obtained autopsies and coroner's investigative reports.

"We had our own medical expert review the autopsy reports. He found many of the reports were self-serving and the pathologist and coroner reached implausible conclusions," Cook says.

"[However] the coroner's investigative reports proved valuable in detailing the circumstances that led to the deaths. We also found errors in these reports. For example, the sheriff-coroner ruled that one prisoner died after going into a stupor from drinking too much alcohol. But his investigators noted in their reports that the prisoner walked from one cell block to another while supposedly passed out. In this particular

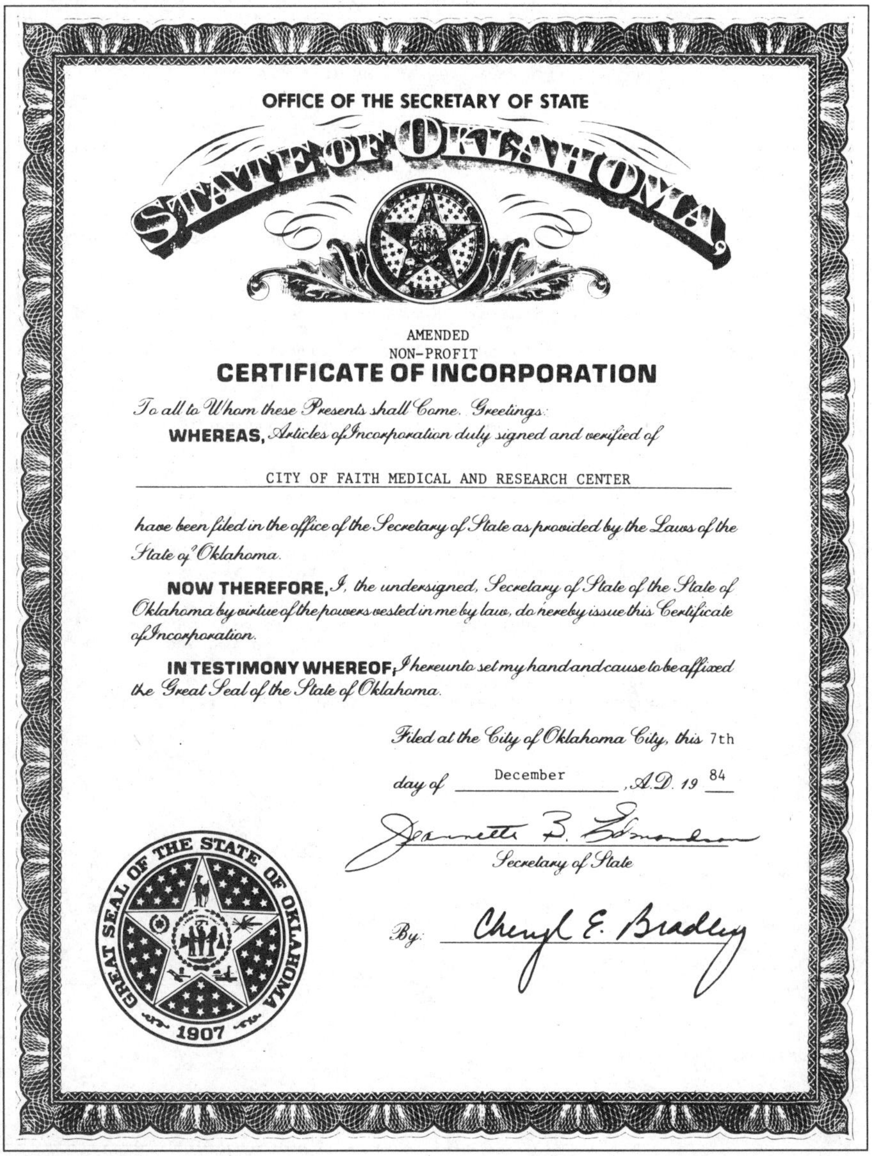

OFFICE OF THE SECRETARY OF STATE

STATE OF OKLAHOMA

AMENDED
NON-PROFIT
CERTIFICATE OF INCORPORATION

To all to Whom these Presents shall Come, Greetings:

WHEREAS, *Articles of Incorporation duly signed and verified of*

CITY OF FAITH MEDICAL AND RESEARCH CENTER

have been filed in the office of the Secretary of State as provided by the Laws of the State of Oklahoma.

NOW THEREFORE, *I, the undersigned, Secretary of State of the State of Oklahoma by virtue of the powers vested in me by law, do hereby issue this Certificate of Incorporation.*

IN TESTIMONY WHEREOF, *I hereunto set my hand and cause to be affixed the Great Seal of the State of Oklahoma.*

Filed at the City of Oklahoma City, this 7th

day of December *, A.D. 19* 84

Secretary of State

By:

GREAT SEAL OF THE STATE OF OKLAHOMA 1907

Figure 6-1 Certificate of Incorporation

case, the autopsy also provided clues that the sheriff-coroner's death ruling was wrong. The sheriff-coroner's autopsy showed a .19 blood alcohol content, legally drunk but less than many people arrested for drunken driving. Our experts said that was less than half the alcohol content normally associated with alcohol death. The pathologist apparently ignored signs of bruises on each side of the neck, a ruptured windpipe and a frothy blood clot blocking the trachea. Our medical experts said those were indications the prisoner died from a chokehold.

Figure 6-2 Articles of Incorporation
Articles of Incorporation, found in the secretary of state's office, usually include the date the company was formed, its stated purpose, directors and other information. This example is one of eight pages in the Articles of Incorporation for the City of Faith Medical and Research Center.

"Records from the state Department of Corrections and budget requests from the sheriff to the county board of supervisors helped document overcrowding that led to three [additional] deaths.

"Public records can be valuable in most stories, and their value and importance is not limited to just crime and death stories," Cook adds.

"For example, public records were important in exposing recruiting violations and other irregularities involving the Memphis State Univer-

Form **1023** (Rev. April 1984)

Department of the Treasury Internal Revenue Service

Application for Recognition of Exemption

Under Section 501(c)(3) of the Internal Revenue Code

For Paperwork Reduction Act Notice, see page 1 of the instructions.

OMB No. 1545-0056

To be filed in the key district for the area in which the organization has its principal office or place of business.

This application, when properly completed, constitutes the notice required under section 508(a) of the Internal Revenue Code so that an applicant may be treated as described in section 501(c)(3) of the Code, and the notice required under section 508(b) for an organization claiming not to be a private foundation within the meaning of section 509(a). **(Read the instructions for each part carefully before making any entries.)** If required information, a conformed copy of the organizing and operational documents, or financial data are not furnished, the application will not be considered on its merits and the organization will be notified accordingly. Do not file this application if the applicant has no organizing instrument (see Part II).

Part I.—Identification

1 Full name of organization

2 Employer identification number **(If none, see instructions)**

3(a) Address (number and street)

Check here if applying under section: ☐ 501(e) ☐ 501(f)

3(b) City or town, State, and Zip code

4 Name and phone number of person to be contacted ( )

5 Month the annual accounting period ends

6 Date incorporated or formed

7 Activity codes

8 Has the organization filed Federal income tax returns or exempt organization information returns? . . . . ☐ Yes ☐ No

If "Yes," state the form number(s), years filed, and Internal Revenue office where filed. ....

Part II.—Type of Entity and Organizational Document (see instructions)

Check the applicable entity box below and attach a **conformed** copy of the organization's organizing document and bylaws as indicated for each entity.

☐ Corporation—Articles of incorporation and bylaws. ☐ Trust—Trust indenture. ☐ Other—Constitution or articles of association and bylaws.

Part III.—Activities and Operational Information

1 What are or will be the organization's sources of financial support? List in order of size.

2 Describe the organization's fund-raising program, both actual and planned, and explain to what extent it has been put into effect. (Include details of fund-raising activities such as selective mailings, formation of fund-raising committees, use of professional fund raisers, etc.) Attach representative copies of solicitations for financial support.

I declare under the penalties of perjury that I am authorized to sign this application on behalf of the above organization and I have examined this application, including the accompanying statements, and to the best of my knowledge it is true, correct, and complete.

(Signature) (Title or authority of signer) (Date)

Figure 6-3 Internal Revenue Service 1023 Form

The 1023 Form, an Internal Revenue Service public record, is an application for tax exempt status. It may include the articles of incorporation, an expansion on the list of directors, purpose of the organization, funding sources and anticipated revenues.

sity athletic department, when I was a reporter at the Memphis Commercial Appeal. A routine driver's license check revealed several traffic tickets issued to athletes. By checking those, we found the star 7-foot

Form **990** Department of the Treasury Internal Revenue Service

Return of Organization Exempt from Income Tax
Under section 501(c) (except black lung benefit trust or private foundation) of the Internal Revenue Code or section 4947(a)(1) trust
Note: You may be required to use a copy of this return to satisfy State reporting requirements. See instruction D.

OMB No. 1545-0047 **1985**

For the calendar year 1985, or fiscal year beginning , 1985, and ending , 19

Use IRS label. Otherwise, please print or type.		
	Name of organization	**A Employer identification number** (see instruction L)
	Address (number and street)	**B State registration number** (see instruction D)
	City or town, state, and ZIP code	C If address changed, check here . . . . ▶ ☐

D Check type of organization—Exempt under section ▶ ☐ 501(c) ( ) (insert number), OR ▶ ☐ section 4947(a)(1) trust
E Accounting method: ☐ Cash ☐ Accrual ☐ Other (specify) ▶
Check here if application for exemption is pending . . ▶ ☐
F Section 4947(a)(1) trusts filing this form in lieu of Form 1041, check here ▶ ☐ (see instruction C10).
G Is this a group return (see instruction J) filed for affiliates? . . . . ☐ Yes ☐ No
Is this a separate return filed by a group affiliate? . . . . ☐ Yes ☐ No
If "Yes" to either, give four-digit group exemption number (GEN) ▶

☐ Check here if your gross receipts are normally not more than $25,000 (see instruction B11). You do not have to file a completed return with IRS but should file a return without financial data if you were mailed a Form 990 Package (see instruction A). Some States may require a completed return.
☐ Check here if gross receipts are normally more than $25,000 and line 12 is $25,000 or less. Complete Parts I (except lines 13-15), III, IV, VI, and VII and only the indicated items in Parts II and V (see instruction I). If line 12 is more than $25,000, complete the entire return.

501(c)(3) organizations and 4947(a)(1) trusts must also complete and attach Schedule A (Form 990). (See instructions.)

Part I Statement of Support, Revenue, and Expenses and Changes in Fund Balances		(A) Total	(B) Unrestricted/ Expendable	(C) Restricted/ Nonexpendable
			These columns are optional—see instructions	
Support and Revenue	1 Contributions, gifts, grants, and similar amounts received:			
	a Direct public support			
	b Indirect public support			
	c Government grants			
	d Total (add lines 1a through 1c) (attach schedule—see instructions)			
	2 Program service revenue (from Part IV, line f)			
	3 Membership dues and assessments			
	4 Interest on savings and temporary cash investments			
	5 Dividends and interest from securities			
	6a Gross rents			
	b Minus: rental expenses			
	c Net rental income (loss)			
	7 Other investment income (Describe ▶)			
	8a Gross amount from sale of assets other than inventory (Securities / Other)			
	b Minus: cost or other basis and sales expenses			
	c Gain (loss) (attach schedule)			
	9 Special fundraising events and activities (**attach schedule**—see instructions):			
	a Gross revenue (not including $ of contributions reported on line 1a)			
	b Minus: direct expenses			
	c Net income (line 9a minus line 9b)			
	10a Gross sales minus returns and allowances			
	b Minus: cost of goods sold (attach schedule)			
	c Gross profit (loss)			
	11 Other revenue (from Part IV, line g)			
	12 Total revenue (add lines 1d, 2, 3, 4, 5, 6c, 7, 8c, 9c, 10c, and 11)			
Expenses	13 Program services (from line 44, column (B)) (see instructions)			
	14 Management and general (from line 44, column (C)) (see instructions)			
	15 Fundraising (from line 44, column (D)) (see instructions)			
	16 Payments to affiliates (attach schedule—see instructions)			
	17 Total expenses (add lines 16 and 44, column (A))			
Fund Balances	18 Excess (deficit) for the year (subtract line 17 from line 12)			
	19 Fund balances or net worth at beginning of year (from line 74, column (A))			
	20 Other changes in fund balances or net worth (attach explanation)			
	21 Fund balances or net worth at end of year (add lines 18, 19, and 20)			

For Paperwork Reduction Act Notice, see page 1 of the instructions. Form **990** (1985)

Figure 6-4 Internal Revenue Service 990 Form
This is the first page of a 990 Form, a four-page document the IRS requires all non-profit organizations to file annually at IRS regional offices. It includes all direct public contributions, the five highest paid employees, a general balance sheet and sometimes a list of the directors.

center on the basketball team had three traffic violations in separate cars—a Jaguar, a Continental and a Corvette. We ran the license numbers from those cars, which revealed they were owned by prominent MSU athletic boosters, an NCAA violation.

"In most states," Cook says, "records of state universities and colleges are open the same as any other state agency. I have found that many universities are never asked to provide these records to the public. That was true at Memphis State where the newspaper had to file a lawsuit against university officials to get them to comply with the state open records act.

"But the results were worth the effort. Documents we obtained as a result of the lawsuit showed sloppy business practices, over-awards of more than $60,000 in federal grant funds to athletes, credit card abuses and an attempt by unversity officials to cover up those problems. Letters and memos obtained from the athletic department showed university officials were aware of a secret slush fund used by boosters to funnel money to athletes. Those documents showed university officials failed to report the illegal fund to the NCAA.

"Other documents revealed allegations from another university that Memphis State officials had illegally recruited a star lineman from their team. The records showed the lineman had enrolled at Memphis State without paying tuition and when the NCAA began to investigate the transfer, the athlete paid $2,100 in tuition fees with money allegedly hidden in a shoe in his closet," Cook says.

Cook and Hargrove—while among those who continually achieve high standards of excellence in their reporting—are certainly not alone when it comes to using paper trails in journalism effectively. Consider these other achievements stemming primarily from a thorough use of records:

- Clark Hallas and Robert B. Lowe teamed up to write a 1981 Pulitzer Prize-winning story at The Arizona Daily Star when they found

---

USING POLICE RECORDS

Access to various records in a police department or sheriff's office varies from city to city and county to county. Much depends on the specifics of each state's freedom of information law. Access also depends on the reliable sources a reporter can cultivate within a police department.

Law enforcement agencies typically generate the following documents in the aftermath of a typical arrest:

- The original complaint or call for assistance, whether it is a crime or a car accident.
- The incident report filed by the investigating officer, describing the details of the situation at the scene. (For an accident, this is often called the Uniform Accident Report.)
- The arrest and disposition report, completed for anyone charged in a crime or an accident. The arrest report provides information on the actual charge, the name of the arresting officer and the date of the incident. The report frequently documents the number of court appearances and continuances if they are granted.
- The jail log, which lists the name of any person confined there and the date of confinement. Bail bond information is also recorded on this log.
- Any court records maintained by police about their cases.

In addition, law enforcement agencies create dozens of other records worth checking, such as regular income reports, which detail monies they collect from fines and other sources. Annual budgets provide detailed views of salaries and capital expenditures in a police or sheriff's department. Documents are also on file that describe the number of complaints and arrests reported in a given period.

documents that exposed corruption in the athletic department at the University of Arizona.
- In 1982, Paul Henderson of The Seattle Times received the Pulitzer Prize for a story that combined revelations from crucial documents and records with compelling interviews to prove the innocence of a man charged with rape.
- In 1985, Lucy Morgan and Jack Reed of the St. Petersburg Times earned a Pulitzer Prize for their exposé of corruption in the county sheriff's department, which led to indictment of the sheriff. Their stories were based to a large degree on incriminating documents and records obtained during their examination of the sheriff.

Writing in the Washington Journalism Review, Weinberg says that in his position as executive director of IRE, he regularly reviews reporters' in-depth stories from both the United States and Canada. He said he is continually amazed at how some reporters are using documents in new ways to get better stories. "But I am also depressed at the thousands of questions I get each year from other journalists who have no idea how to learn who owns a piece of property or who sits on a local business's board of directors."

Using Freedom of Information Acts

A good portion of the paper trail can be unearthed using your sources and your creativity. However, sometimes you must literally pry the information from city, county, state and federal agencies. Freedom of information, or "sunshine," laws make that possible. Such laws refer to the right of citizens—and reporters—to see public records and (with open meetings laws) attend public meetings. Both state and federal versions of these laws exist.

Just a few years ago, the majority of states did not have statutes that guaranteed citizens access to public records and meetings. At the 1956 national convention of The Society of Professional Journalists, Sigma Delta Chi, one report said this about the situation: "In 26 states, it is possible for the politician, at his will, to close the records of the citizens' government at any time, and in 38 states it is possible for him, at his will, to conduct the business of the people in secret sessions behind closed doors."

Today, virtually every state has approved laws to ensure both open records and meetings, as has the U.S. government. That has not stopped many elected and appointed officials at every level of government from acting to circumvent or even violate those laws, however. A survey of newspaper accounts from around the nation reveals a steady stream of suits filed by media against officials accused of violating their states' open records and meetings laws. The media most frequently sues police departments, school boards and local city and county boards and commissions for access.

The specific laws governing the nature of access to public information vary widely across the country, which complicates the issue. For instance, in Alaska, the personnel records of public employees are off-limits, while in other states some public personnel records are open. The enforcement penalties for violating the statutes range from virtually no criminal penalties in New Mexico and Indiana to the possibility of removal from office, a maximum of three months in jail and a $500 fine in Nebraska. In Texas, violators can get up to six months in jail with a fine.

During the summers of 1983 and 1984, Society of Professional Journalists interns Rick Dent and Barney Kilgore compiled the specifics of each state's freedom of information laws. Their study provided, for the first time, a comparative overview of each state's commitment to open records and meetings. A condensed version of their findings is included in Appendix B.

Sometimes it is necessary to submit a special request to get the information you need. The steps for making a freedom of information request, whether to a local or state agency or to the federal government, are basically the same. First, address your request to the agency's FOI officer and identify the statute number under which you are making the request. Then thoughtfully and accurately identify exactly what information you need. A vaguely worded FOI request simply opens the door for a denial or brush off.

By the same token, make your request sufficiently broad to encompass any related material, because much more information may exist on the subject than you imagine. For example, if you ask the U.S. Justice Department for specific reports on a particular crime that occurred five years ago, also include a related request for any further documents on the individual in question or any additional pertinent reports they may have filed with other law enforcement agencies.

Close the request either by agreeing to pay for the search and copying costs or by requesting a waiver of the fees on the basis that you are seeking the information as a reporter in the public interest. Finally, tell the recipient how soon you need the information. The response time will vary from state to state and agency to agency.

Tonda Rush, the former director of the FOI Service Center in Washington, D.C., and now a lawyer with the American Newspaper Publishers Association, notes that you have the option of appealing if your request is denied or if no response is forthcoming. The final option is a lawsuit to obtain the information. Increasingly, media organizations have had to resort to such lawsuits to overcome continual delays or stonewalling for some public records. If a suit is successful, courts usually force the government to pay court costs and lawyers fees.

There are exemptions to all FOI laws. At the federal level, for example, there are nine traditional reasons the government may use for refusing to disclose records. Information may be kept secret because release would violate national security, or because the material is specifically exempted by law, or because it is an internal agency personnel rule, a trade secret or an internal agency report or proposal. An agency also may withhold FOI-requested information because release would violate personal privacy, because the information is part of a current or pending law enforcement investigation, or because it deals with federally regulated banks or with oil and gas wells.

Be aware, though, that federal agencies customarily believe their exemption status is far broader than you will believe it to be. Consequently, it pays to be persistent and innovative when filing FOI requests. If you are denied by a federal agency, you can appeal the denial to a higher authority within that agency. Your appeal should consist of another letter clearly stating why you believe you are entitled to the information in the public interest. The agency official then has 20 days to respond to the appeal. If the request is again denied, your only alternative is a lawsuit.

Sample FOI Request Letter

The letter in Figure 6-5 is appropriate for a federal FOI request. It is prepared by the FOI Service Center. See Appendix B for details on open records in various states.

```
                                            Your address
                                            Day time phone number
                                            Date

    Freedom of Information Office
    Agency
    Address

        FOIA Request

    Dear FOI Officer:

        Pursuant to the federal Freedom of Information Act, 5 U.S.C.
    § 552, I request access to and copies of (Here, clearly describe
    what you want.  Include identifying material, such as names,
    places, and the period of time about which you are inquiring.
    If you think they will help to explain what you are looking for,
    attach news clips, reports, and other documents describing the
    subject of your research.)
        I agree to pay reasonable search and duplication fees for
    the processing of this request in an amount not to exceed  $___.
    However, please notify me prior to your incurring any expenses
    in excess of that amount.¹
        (Optional Fee Waiver request) The FOI Act provides for a
    waiver or reduction of fees if disclosure could be considered as
    "primarily benefiting the general public."  I am a journalist
    (researcher, or scholar) employed by (name of news organization,
    or under contract with ____ publisher, etc.), and intend to use
    the requested information as the basis for an article
    (broadcast, or book).  (Here you will want to add detailed
    information about the public's interest in the information you
    are requesting and your expertise in the subject area as well as
    your qualifications to disseminate the information broadly to
    the public.  See p. 6 for list of topics which must be covered
    here.)  Therefore, I ask that you waive all search and
    duplication fees.  If you deny this request, however, I am
    prepared to pay reasonable fees up to $___, but please notify me
    of the estimated charges before you begin to process my
    request.²
        If my request is denied in whole or part, I ask that you
    justify all deletions by reference to specific exemptions of the
    Act.  I will also expect you to release all reasonably
    segregable portions of otherwise exempt material.  I, of course,
    reserve the right to appeal your decision to withhold any
    information.
        As I am making this request as a journalist (author, or
    scholar) and this information is of timely value, I would
    appreciate your communicating with me by telephone, rather than
    by mail, if you have questions regarding this request.³  I look
    forward to your reply within 10 business days, as the statute
    requires.
        Thank you for your assistance.

                                            Very truly yours,

                                            Your signature
```

```
                              Footnotes

    1 Most agencies will not consider your request properly filed unless you state something about
    the fees -- either your willingness to pay or your request for a fee waiver.  By setting an amount
    up front, the agency will begin to process your request, and you can retain some control over the
    ultimate amount you will have to pay.
    2 By stating this in the alternative, the agency must begin to process your request in order to
    give you an estimate of the fees.  If they deny your fee waiver, you then must choose either to
    appeal that denial or agree to pay the fees.
    3 It is always a good idea to call the agency's FOI office several days after your request is
    mailed, to be sure of its arrival and to talk directly with the officer processing your request.
    Quite often you can resolve any minor problems concerning your request at that time and avoid delays.
```

Figure 6-5 A Sample FOI Act Request Letter

PART 3
Beat and Specialized Reporting

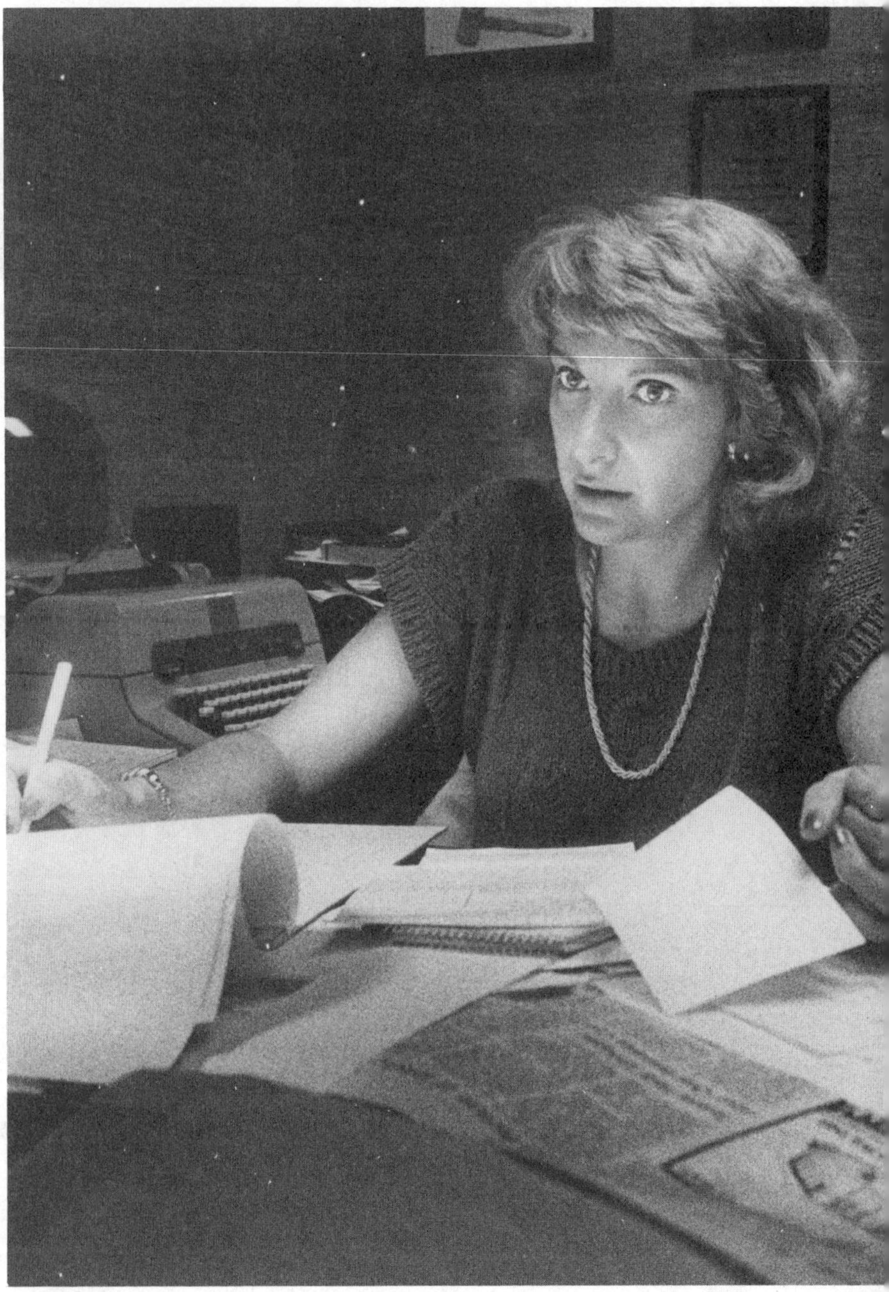

CHAPTER **7**

Beat Reporting Techniques

The Beat
Making Friends and Influencing People
Transforming the Press Release
Mastering Five Tricks of the Trade
Covering Southern Illinois
A Pulitzer Prize-Winning Beat Series

The Beat

Police officers once patrolled communities by walking the streets. These strolls were called *beats*. On his beat, the officer would admonish or congratulate citizens of the community (depending on the activities of those citizens during the preceding 24 hours) and rattle doors and windows of businesses at night to make certain that all was well. The arrival of the patrol car saw the demise of the foot beat in many American cities, though in a few places the beat never disappeared and in others it disappeared and has now returned.

Newspaper reporters, unlike police officers, have never discarded the beat as an effective way to keep an eye on community events.

Traditionally, the reporter's beat has been arranged by either geography or subject area. For example, in a geographic arrangement, the beat reporter might cover all of the offices within a specific building, such as a federal building. There, the reporter typically might find offices of the state's U.S. senators and representatives, as well as the offices of the Internal Revenue Service, the Federal Bureau of Investigation, the Department of Commerce, the Veterans Administration and other agencies. From this list, you can see that a federal building beat can be a mixture of often incongruous elements. For example, in one day, the beat reporter might cover a press conference given by a senator, a tax change story and a story about an FBI bust involving money laundering.

The Arizona Republic's political beat reporter Keven Willey prepares a story on deadline as a university journalism student looks on. (Photo by Earl McCartney, The Arizona Republic)

Chapter opening photo: Mary Hargrove of The Tulsa Tribune ponders a problem in a story. (Photo by Sherry Brown, The Tulsa Tribune staff)

Beats are more commonly arranged by subject matter. Examples include the police, fire, court, city hall and education beats. A reporter covering the police and fire beat might have to cover both city and county police, as well as numerous fire districts within the city and county. Since the city and county police departments are rarely located within the same building, different faces and procedures have to be mastered for each police agency. The court beat reporter might have to cover the municipal courts in one location, the state courts in another location and the federal courts in a third location. In a small community, the city hall reporter might be lucky enough to find all municipal offices within one building. Larger cities usually have many satellite municipal offices, all of which must be covered. Education beats are usually far-flung. Most cities have several school districts, each with their own superintendent and board. The education beat reporter might even have responsibility for covering community colleges and universities within the circulation area.

The structure of the beat system depends on the reporter, the editor and how the areas can be most effectively covered. Newspaper editors usually organize beats along practical lines. One reporter might cover the local university, a geographic beat, while another reporter covers city, county and state police, a subject area beat. Still another reporter might cover most federal agencies except the federal courts, which are covered by the same person who covers the municipal courts.

However the beats are organized, the newspaper reporter's goal is virtually the same as that of the policeman on the beat—to keep an eye on things, and take action when necessary. The police officer's action often is making an arrest; the reporter's action is writing a story.

Making Friends and Influencing People

Let's assume that Karen, the reporter introduced in Chapter 4, has been at the Times for two years now, first handling general assignment work and then some relief police beat reporting with aplomb. Her minor in college was political science and she likes covering politics, so Karen is pleased when she is asked to join the four-person capitol bureau. The new job means a promotion, increased pay, and more predictable working hours. Karen has been working afternoons and evenings; because the offices in the capitol complex are open from 9 a.m. until 5 p.m., she will now typically work from about 10 a.m. until 7 p.m., which is the early deadline for the Times.

On her first day on the new job—a Monday—Karen finds herself at the state capitol, about two miles from the main newspaper office. The newspaper's capitol bureau is on the first floor of the capitol building, near the entrance to the impressive, domed building. In the small room are about a dozen desks, four of which belong to the Times. The other desks are used by capitol correspondents from The Associated Press,

United Press International, an out-of-state newspaper that covers state politics occasionally, and five radio and television stations.

Helen Burford, the Times' bureau chief, gives Karen a tour of the capitol building, pointing out where various state offices are located. Helen, who has been a reporter for the Times on every beat from the police station to the courthouse, tells Karen she will be responsible for covering the offices of the state treasurer, the secretary of state, the attorney general and the lieutenant governor. Other reporters cover other nearby state offices; Helen covers the governor's office. Of course, Helen adds, everyone splits up the work during elections and in emergencies.

"Let me spell it out for you," she says. "In the treasurer's office, you'll pick up some occasional stories about strange expenditures, things people are trying to get the state to pay for that are out of line. Often this information will be leaked to you by sources who do not want to be interviewed.

"The secretary of state maintains the building. Cleans the floors, that kind of thing. But he also keeps election records, so the main news out of his office is around election time. Candidates have to file their expense forms with him. He also validates petitions and referendums that may wind up on the ballot.

"The real, everyday action is all going to be in the attorney general's office. The attorney general is quietly running for governor. You'll see consumer fraud complaints, death penalty litigation. Big cases. If the cases make it to court, our courthouse reporter will cover them. But while they're pending trial, you cover them."

"What about the lieutenant governor's office?" Karen asks.

Helen smiles. "It's a part-time job. He doesn't have very much to do, except during the legislative session. Other than that, he'll call an occasional press conference to lament the problem of drunken driving, or excessive spending, or whatever."

Helen then takes Karen around to meet key people on her beat. Karen meets the lieutenant governor's secretary, and Helen reminds her privately that the secretary is often the key to covering any office. She meets the secretary of state and his chief aide. She meets the state treasurer and the chief of staff for that office. Finally, Karen is taken to the biggest and most important office on her beat, the attorney general's office. There she meets important secretaries in each division of the office, as well as a few attorneys who head various divisions.

Karen spends the rest of the day in the bureau memorizing names and placing those names with faces. She pours over organizational charts of each office and checks the file of stories left by her predecessor, who has been promoted to assistant city editor. She also reads a long memorandum on the beat that her predecessor left. The confidential memo includes notes on peculiarities of the beat—most importantly, instructions regarding whom to see for what information and how to deal with them. She pays special attention to a portion on the attorney general's office, specifically a note about the office's second ranking lawyer, a man named Joe King. "King," the memo says, "has been at the attorney general's office for the past 15 years. He is brutally frank, accessible, irascible, but will tell you anything you want to know about anything, including any case in progress, if you ask him nicely. Asking him nicely means treating him as the dean of lawyers in the office, which frankly he is."

Karen also looks at clips of stories written about pending issues in each office, issues Karen will have to follow up. Finally, she tests the video display terminal link to the Times office. She will use the terminal each day to mail her stories electronically to the Times before deadline. But now it's 7 o'clock and time to go home.

Tuesday morning. Karen is ready to go to work, win friends and influence people. Karen, who has been thinking about what she can do to establish herself as a good reporter in the minds of her sources, realizes she will ultimately prove herself by her stories. She also understands that her skill in human relations will determine her initial success on the beat.

Karen had read Dale Carnegie's book, "How to Win Friends and Influence People," and over the weekend, she tried to recall his principles for getting people to like you, as they might apply to a beat reporter. Karen recalled that there are only six basic concepts and that they are deceivingly simple.

First, Carnegie said, people who deal with the public should be genuinely interested in others. If you're not interested in people, you're in the wrong business, Carnegie warned. You should learn people's likes and dislikes, their interests and their passions, Carnegie said.

Rule Two was even easier, Karen remembered. Smile when you are talking to people.

Rule Three? Learn and use the names of your sources. The sweetest sound in the language is your own name, Carnegie said.

Rule Four was custom made for the reporter: "Be a good listener. Encourage others to talk about themselves," Carnegie wrote.

Rule Five suggested that Karen should talk about what the other person—the source—wants to talk about. That's a good idea, but Karen also reminded herself that she shouldn't let her news sources steer her off the track. Carnegie's fifth rule needs to be tempered with moderation.

Rule Six: If the source is important to you, tell the source how much you value his or her help. Appreciate the person, and don't hide your feelings.

These six rules are simple suggestions, Karen thinks, yet valuable.

Karen's first stop on Tuesday is the attorney general's office. She knows the attorney general is planning a press conference for 2 p.m. to discuss his latest election plans, and Karen wants some background before the meeting. Karen walks into the main office and sees Joe King talking with the receptionist. King should know what's going on, Karen says to herself.

"Mr. King," Karen says, introducing herself, "I'm the new Times reporter covering your office." Karen makes sure she is smiling. "I hear you just got back from a vacation in Colorado. How was it?"

"Do you know anything about Colorado, young lady?" King asks.

"Yes, I grew up in Dillon, a little town just over the Divide from Denver."

"Yes, I know Dillon well. I was just there as a matter of fact," King says. "I love it out there."

"Do you ski or hike?" Karen asks.

"Some. But mainly I just like to walk, enjoy the scenery, watch the trees turn at this time of the year. It happens so fast at that altitude, you know. And the aspen trees—they seem to quake with the slightest breeze."

"I know," Karen admits. "You make me miss it, just talking about it."

"Well, what can I do for you?" King asks.

"I need a little background on this press conference the attorney general is going to be having this afternoon," Karen says. "Can you help me?"

"Sure," says King. "Come into my office. We'll talk about it."

Twenty minutes later, Karen emerges with enough background to ask three or four intelligent questions at the press conference. She has also developed a source in the attorney general's office, not because she has been devious, but because she has simply followed some basic rules about dealing with people, rules she will need to refine during the coming months and years.

Transforming the Press Release

Many beat stories come from old-fashioned digging and unsolicited tips. Press releases, however, provide reporters with many of those tips. As a matter of fact, some editors estimate that as much as half of the local news in a newspaper originates directly or indirectly from releases, which are short unsolicited "news" stories that offer information from businesses, governmental agencies, schools, clubs, organizations and individuals. These releases arrive daily from both local and national organizations by the hundreds in every newsroom in America.

Most of the releases are thrown away because they do not have significant news value. The releases that are used are news sources but often unreliable ones, because the releases are little more than *plugs*, or free advertising, disguised as news stories. Because they are plugs, the releases that do have news value usually have to be rewritten.

Karen, like most reporters, receives dozens of press releases every day by mail and hand delivery. On Tuesday, she gets one from the lieutenant governor's office that solemnly announces the formation of a task force against drunk driving. That might be worth a two-paragraph story, Karen thinks.

There are five releases from the attorney general's office, including one warning Karen of the upcoming press conference on the attorney general's political ambitions, which King has already briefed her about.

The other releases deal mainly with consumer protection—one is filled with dire warnings from the attorney general about purchasing land from mail order developers. Each release requires some coverage. Karen will merely rewrite some releases, filling in unanswered questions by telephoning sources and interviewing them. One release, however, suggests a long news story to Karen, and she makes a note to set up interviews with various staff members and assistant attorneys general. This is the release that intrigues Karen:

For Immediate Release   For Information Please Contact

Attorney General   Ron Lee
To Create Task Force
For Missing Children   371-2007

 Attorney General John Stevens Tuesday announced the formation of a special six-person task force to recommend ways the state can assist parents with missing children.
 Currently, the state has no service agency to assist parents with missing children, Stevens said.
 "If a child disappears, all the parents can do is report the disappearance to their local law enforcement agencies," Stevens said.
 "We think that the state should be more involved in the case, that parents should be able to deal with someone who can assist them in entering their child's name on the state computer, making sure that it stays there, tracking the case, putting the parents in contact with national child-find organizations, and generally helping," he said.
 Stevens added that his office would arrange for voluntary fingerprinting of children throughout the state. The fingerprinting would be done by an attorney general's office staff member, who would travel around the state.
 "The fingerprinting will help parents with positive identification of their children," Stevens said.
 Stevens said he has named two businessmen, three state legislators and one other person to the task force. The force will meet monthly for the next year. Those who have agreed to service on the task force are Don Horace and Ralph Watterson, local businessmen; Harry Roberts, Gordon Kumpe and William Hopkins, state legislators; and Virginia Merrill, a consumer representative from Mountain City.

— 30 —

The press release raises some questions, Karen decides. Why has the attorney general suddenly become so interested in missing children? Karen wonders. And what are the benefits of fingerprinting toddlers? she asks herself.

She calls her new source, Joe King, who tells her that the attorney general started the task force because of the problems of Virginia Merrill, the woman from Mountain City named to the group. Karen calls several more sources in the attorney general's office, who tell her that Merrill's daughter ran away from home about a year ago and that Merrill became frustrated with state agencies while searching for her. Karen also learns that after the daughter voluntarily returned home, Merrill met with the attorney general to convince him that the state needs to help parents with missing children.

With that information, Karen knows that she has stumbled onto a major Sunday feature story that she can develop from interviews with the attorney general and with Merrill. A feature is generally a descriptive, quotation-filled story that humanizes the news. Although beat reporters usually concentrate on news stories, they must also be alert to feature possibilities. For the time being, however, Karen must write her news story for Wednesday's newspaper.

The next day, her story—derived from the original press release and a telephone interview with the attorney general—is published. Here it is:

Parents with missing children currently get no help from the state, Attorney General John Stevens said Tuesday in announcing the formation of a special six-person missing-children task force.

The lack of state resources in helping parents with missing children is approaching a critical stage, Stevens said, because the number of missing children in the state is doubling each year.

Stevens said 25 children were reported missing by their parents last year. This year's total is 49, with "even more" expected before the end of the year, Stevens said.

Some of the missing children are runaways, Stevens said, while others are abducted by parents and strangers.

"If a child disappears, all the parents can do is report the disappearance to their local law enforcement agencies," Stevens said.

"We think that the state should be more involved in the case, that parents should be able to deal with someone who can assist them in entering their child's name on the state computer, making sure that it stays there, tracking the case, putting the parents in contact with national child-find organizations, and generally helping," he said.

Stevens said he is assigning a member of his staff to travel throughout the state to provide free fingerprinting of children.

Stevens said he has named two businessmen, three state legislators and one other person to the task force. The force will meet monthly for the next year.

Stevens said he hoped the task force would survey other states with more sophisticated missing-children programs and recommend "innovative ways to help parents."

Those who have agreed to serve on the task force are Don Horace and Ralph Watterson, local businessmen; Harry Roberts, Gordon Kumpe and William Hopkins, state senators; and Virginia Merrill, a consumer representative from Mountain City.

Let's compare Karen's lead with the lead from the press release. Here is Karen's lead:

> Parents with missing children currently get no help from the state, Attorney General John Stevens said Tuesday in announcing the formation of a special six-person missing-children task force.

Karen uses an indirect quotation lead because her editor has cautioned her against a direct quotation lead. Direct quotation leads are not improper, but they tend to make the overall lead too long. Karen's lead emphasizes parents with missing children and still answers the other questions required of the summary lead. In addition, Stevens' name provides an attribution for the lead.

Here is the press release lead:

> Attorney General John Stevens Tuesday announced the formation of a special six-person task force to recommend ways the state can assist parents with missing children.

This lead, though not wrong, is less desirable because it emphasizes Stevens, which is the emphasis you would expect from a writer on the attorney general's staff. Karen's lead has more impact and provides more information.

Karen is generally happy with her initial story, but the fingerprinting portion of Stevens' program still disturbs her. Would child-care physicians approve of this? Karen wonders. Karen notes that the state's leading pediatrician will speak the next day at University Hospital and makes arrangements to interview the doctor after his speech.

On Thursday, the doctor tells Karen he has grave reservations about two aspects of Stevens' program. Karen then interviews Stevens and writes a Friday follow-up story to her first story. Here is the second story:

Although missing-children programs are usually established with good intentions, they probably scare and scar children, Dr. Allen Lane, pediatrician and author of seven child-care books, said here Thursday.

Attorney General John Stevens, who recently created a task force to help parents with missing children, is encouraging parents to fingerprint their children and teach them to avoid strangers.

Lane, interviewed following an address to the State Pediatric Association at University Hospital, said he was "particularly concerned about the value of fingerprinting, because it's not going to keep children from being abducted or molested."

"The only real value of fingerprinting is for identifying dead children," Lane said. "Having somebody from the attorney general's office fingerprint them scares them for no good reason."

Stevens said he disagreed with Lane. "All we're trying to do is help parents accumulate identifying materials, such as fingerprints, recent photographs and perhaps even videotapes of their children. All of this material, taken as a package, will help law enforcement agencies should the child disappear," Stevens said.

Lane also criticized school programs featuring lectures on molestation and abduction.

"There are two problems there," Lane said. "First, parents should be the ones to talk to their children about those kinds of matters, because they understand their child's fears. They will be careful not to overdo it.

"The other problem is that in telling children to avoid everyone they don't know, you're telling them every stranger is a potential criminal—that everyone who says 'hello' is a fiend. A child who grows up thinking everyone he doesn't know is an enemy is a child who will be scarred for life," Lane said.

Stevens said Lane apparently "misunderstood the thrust of the state missing-child program."

"The program is positive. We are not doing what he thinks we are doing. We are only telling children that they can make a choice about speaking to a stranger, and that they don't have to take a ride with a stranger just because he is an adult," Stevens said.

Stevens' plan includes a six-person task force to survey other state missing-children programs and then make recommendations about how state government can assist parents with abducted children.

In addition, a member of Stevens' staff will provide free fingerprinting for parents who request the service.

This story begins with a summary news lead that emphasizes *what*. The next paragraph gives background to the story. Subsequent paragraphs give Lane a chance to speak his piece and allow Stevens a rebuttal. Finally the story includes some background paragraphs on the attorney general's overall program. The last two paragraphs are "throwaways" in that they can be removed from the story without damage, should it run too long. In fact, the story could readily be edited to about half of its original length and still make sense and have balance.

Enough about Karen. Let's integrate what she's learned with some advice from experienced beat reporters.

Mastering Five Tricks of the Trade

Aside from practicing good human relations and digging for stories, there are other tricks of the beat reporting trade you'll need to know about.

Peter Rinearson, a Pulitzer Prize-winning beat reporter for The Seattle Times, offers the first tip. "Learn the language of the speciality" you're covering, he says. "There are several reasons why that's helpful. One is that it will make your communication with people a lot more efficient. You'll know what they're talking about; they'll know what you're talking about. Another thing is that it sort of makes you part of their community, part of their profession. The trick is that in the writing stage, you can't use the [beat] jargon."

Next, learn how the organization you are covering functions, who reports to whom and why. The easiest way to get that information is from an official organizational chart, kept by almost all bureaucracies. If you're covering a city, county or state agency, ask the chief of staff or personnel officer for the chart. Since beats often involve covering public or quasi-public groups whose staffing is a matter of public record, this shouldn't be difficult. When you get the chart, memorize names and job titles.

Third, make rounds on a daily basis in the same way a physician makes rounds at a hospital. You should visit your beat sources at approximately the same time every day, renew acquaintances, and gather information. Use your human relations skills to make friends. Remember to befriend secretaries, who often know more about the organization and upcoming events than the boss. Secretaries will sometimes divulge, or *leak*, information to you because they like you and want to help you. On the other hand, your sources may also include unhappy employees who are willing to leak only information that might prove damaging to real or imagined enemies. Within any large bureaucratic structure, you will find people who have been passed over for promotion or are jealous of co-workers and bear a grudge. Your beat sources may even include people who leak information simply because they cannot keep a secret. Whatever the reason for the source helping you, experienced reporters caution, be prepared to hear a great deal of gossip—some of it valuable, but most of it useless.

In the process, do not expect the secretaries (or other sources) to put their jobs on the line to help you, but if you can gain their confidence and, if necessary, guarantee them anonymity, you will probably get help when you need it.

SEEKING THE TRUTH

Pulitzer winner James Polk of NBC News, David Hayes of the Kansas City Times and Steve Weinberg, director of the Investigative Reporters and Editors organization at the University of Missouri, offer these tips from an IRE pamphlet to beat reporters on sorting out what is the truth:

Never assume. Check everything. Most journalism mistakes are simple mistakes, not complicated errors but careless oversights. Double-check. Always doubt. A Chicago adage: "You say your mother loves you? Check it out."

People will tell you what they only think they know. Few people distinguish between what they actually know and what they only assume. Sources may tell you what they suspect, think, speculate, or have heard from others, without really knowing. It's up to you to recognize the difference and go find the facts. A handy test to use: ask the source—and yourself—"How do you know that?"

Use your common sense. There are times you may have to make judgment calls about where the truth falls. People may, with honest intent, tell different versions of the same event. Look for what makes good, simple common sense. Develop a logical mind. Try to look at things as they are—not as you hope them to be. One warning: A story that sounds too good to be true often is just that—not true.

People rarely tell 100 percent lies. Usually there is a kernel of truth in every tale. Most people are not capable of fabricating total falsehood. They may change, color, exaggerate, omit, selectively use, misstate or misunderstand certain facts. As a rule, people will tell the version which best serves their position. But the tale will be woven around some pieces of truth. A simple "no" may be a complete lie; a longer sentence usually contains some fact. It is the reporter's job painstakingly to strip away the layers to find what is true.

Look for what is missing. At any stage of a story, it may be helpful to draw up a checklist of what you do not know. Avoid being so proud of what you have found that you aren't alert to what isn't there. Develop a sense for what doesn't add up—and always look for the holes.

Don't rush the truth. Yes, you must meet deadlines. But a deadline is never an excuse for writing what you don't know. Manage your time. Have the patience to pursue the facts. If you must write, and don't know all the answers, tell your readers so. Success does come with being both first and right. But it's still better to be second than wrong.

Run scared. Worry about what you may not know, what you may have missed. If you are a reporter who is worried about being wrong, you have a much better chance of getting the story right.

In most instances, after you have consistently made rounds on your beat for awhile, you can begin to collect more and more information by telephone. This saves time, but it also allows sources to avoid you. One way of handling this is to be frank with your sources: Tell them when you are working against a deadline and by what time you must have information. Remember, though, that you are not the only one who is busy; your sources may have twice as much to do as you have.

Fourth, do not get too close to your sources. When you're a good friend of a news-making source, you may get to the point where you can no longer report objectively. It is easy for that source to ask you to kill or slant a story and very hard for you to refuse. Imagine that you're a police reporter. You have done your job well and the police officers trust you. Unfortunately, they trust you so much that they beat up a suspect in front of you, and then expect you not to report the incident. That's one example of getting too close to a source. Some news organizations prevent such situations from happening by transferring beat reporters at regular intervals.

Rinearson warns: "Never fall into the trap where you're a pal with anyone" on the beat. "You never want to worry about what they think of you. I do not want to create the kinds of relationships with my sources that I'm worrying very much about.... It's got to be an accurate portrayal and a fair portrayal," but beyond that Rinearson says he lets the reporting chips fall where they may.

Finally, ask plenty of questions. "It's always better to look dumb to your sources than to your readers," says Rinearson.

Covering Southern Illinois

Like Rinearson, Dennis Montgomery has pounded beats for years and has mastered the intricacies of beat reporting. Montgomery is now the chief of bureau for The Associated Press in Richmond, Va. During his 15 years with the newsgathering cooperative, he's been a reporter, a correspondent and a news editor as well as an administrator. Here Montgomery talks about the techniques he used to cover one of his beats—the southern third of the state of Illinois:

"To cover a beat you have to be on it. That sounds obvious. But, the point is lost on some reporters.

"You can't telephone the prison spokesman, tell him to call you if something breaks and call that covering your beat. Sure, you want to get on his call list for press releases and the like. But taking press releases and passing them off as stories isn't covering a beat.

"In Southern Illinois there are three prisons to cover: the state prison at Menard, the federal prison at Marion and the minimum security prison the state runs at Vienna. Marion was built to replace Alcatraz and it has about 300 stories in it waiting to be written. So, how do you get them?

"Well, you don't rely on the prison spokesman, or 'flack.' You make contact with the inmates. You write letters to them. You give them your telephone number and tell them to call you collect. You listen and write and talk to their wives and sweethearts. You go to their Thanksgiving dinners, the prison Jaycee Christmas programs and you attend the federal court trials for the folks who are accused of trying to escape, or of smuggling in drugs, or whatever.

"And you do it long enough, with persistence and it pays off. Prisoners don't have a lot to do. They love to get letters and they love to write letters.

"It doesn't take long for your name to make the rounds. And pretty soon you're hearing all sorts of interesting things. Some of them are even true.

"One of my 'pen pals' showed me that information on the atomic bomb is so easily accessible that he could get to it even inside the nation's most secure prison. It took a year, but he sent me a working set of drawings for a nuclear bomb you could build in your basement. Government agencies sent him the information. Boom.

"Another guy was a Puerto Rican nationalist who attacked the House of Representatives back in the 40s. He'd been refusing pardons for 10 years because they wanted him to admit he was wrong. Heck of a story. He was prepared to sit in prison for the rest of his life rather than turn his back on his principles.

"And, when I changed states a few years later, I was able to use those Marion names and connections to land the first not-for-pay interview granted a print journalist by James Earl Ray. He hadn't spoken to anyone but Mike Wallace and a Playboy writer with a checkbook in the decade that had passed since Dr. Martin Luther King was killed. Nice anniversary exclusive.

"Keeping up those contacts pays off. Ray still writes once in awhile. His wife called last year about something.

"But, you know what? Three times in four years in Southern Illinois the prisoners at Menard rioted and I never got one of the stories. I was on vacation every time. I think they waited for me to get in my car to give the signal. It was uncanny. But, see, I didn't get the story because I wasn't there. That's the point. Simple. Drove me nuts.

"No, I'm not saying you can't take vacations if you are a beat reporter. I'm saying you've got to be on the scene, at the gates, that you have to have access, to produce copy.

"And the only way to get that access is to go pull on the door handles, literally as well as figuratively.

"Let's say the courthouse is your beat. You can't do much of a job covering it if all you are doing is dropping by to read the opinions in the afternoon. Some reporters will say, 'Sure, you've got to do things such as learn the names of the secretaries.' Well, that's true, as far as it goes. The better reporter sees that he not only knows their names but their birthdays and the names of their kids and how to get a thank-you bouquet to them quickly. An account with a good florist, one who delivers a couple of times a day, can be a real asset.

"That's a trick. There are lots of them. Everybody makes up their own as they go along. But there is something you can't ever lose sight of and no pocketful of tricks and no amount of clever toil can supply the place of. You want to go by and see the secretaries every day. You want to stop by and mention to the judge that since you've been reading his opinions you've developed a new interest in jurisprudence. You want to teach yourself to read documents upside down. You want to know where the trashcan next to the copying machine gets emptied. And you want to be sure to take your lunches in the cafeteria with the rest of the courthouse crowd. But there is nothing you can do that's more important than this:

"Never forget that you are there to observe, that there are at least two sides to everything, that you don't have a story unless you have them both, and the second you become a player, the moment you take one side or another, you've destroyed your ability to report on that beat. Whatever it is.

"If the prison flack opens his newspaper in the morning to learn for the first time that the prisoners say his penitentiary is a hotbed of drug dealing, you've probably lost him as a way to get access to the administration. You've blindsided him, embarrassed him in front of the warden. His defense, when the warden calls him in to explain the bad press, is going to be to attack you, and probably your newspaper. The next time you call to set up an interview with an inmate, you're going to be surprised how hard the arrangements are to make. And you're going to learn about the next escape from the radio.

"What's worse is that the flack has an honest gripe. Fairness requires you to go see him and ask him whether his prison is a hotbed of drug dealing. If he denies it, you've got his comment for the story. And if his comment is wrong, you may have a second story—one about the adequacy of the monitoring of the prison's contraband interception. Of course, he may surprise you and say, 'Lord, yes. There's nothing you can't buy inside these walls. The legislature won't give us the money we need to guard this place like it should be.'

"You get the idea. Whatever he says makes the story better. You've done yourself a favor—a dividend—for being fair, for getting the other side, for not forsaking the role of a reporter for one of an advocate. The flack has to think of you as just as much his friend as do the inmates and the guards and the prisoners' wives and all of those other people. They've got to know that they can trust you to be fair, that you just aren't going to print whatever they happen to tell you, that you are going to check it out and get the story straight.

"Remember that you are going back to that beat tomorrow for another story. If you think readership credibility is a general problem in the news industry, think how much of a problem it is going to be for you personally and professionally when you get back to the courthouse and

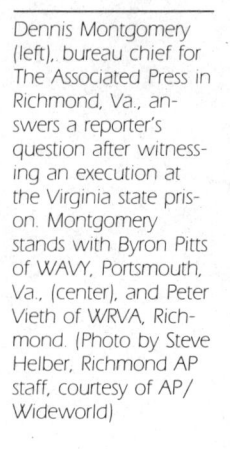

Dennis Montgomery (left), bureau chief for The Associated Press in Richmond, Va., answers a reporter's question after witnessing an execution at the Virginia state prison. Montgomery stands with Byron Pitts of WAVY, Portsmouth, Va., (center), and Peter Vieth of WRVA, Richmond. (Photo by Steve Helber, Richmond AP staff, courtesy of AP/Wideworld)

find out that a half-dozen of your most interested readers are so mad they won't speak to you anymore because you've published something that isn't fair. You're the victim of a self-inflicted wound.

"So there are things to think about. Elementary stuff, really. It's the elementary stuff that pays off. Watergate was broken by two guys who started knocking on doors—just like they teach you in journalism school. A story isn't a story, no matter what the subject, unless it says who, what, where, when, why and how. Just like they teach you in j-school. And covering a beat is just the same. Just like they teach you in j-school. Be there, plow the ground, use your wits, get in straight and write it right."

A Pulitzer Prize-Winning Beat Series

Some beat reporters believe they are earning their keep and serving the public if they simply keep up with the major events occurring on their turf. America's best beat reporters, however see their job as more than just providing daily coverage of breaking news. They go beyond the minimum necessary because they believe *extra* effort is required to effectively explain often complex issues involving their beats.

Peter Rinearson's beat is aerospace, an industry that is extremely important in the Seattle area, thanks to the Boeing aircraft company. Rinearson—who began his association with the Seattle Times as a University of Washington journalism intern in 1976 and was hired as a full-time reporter in 1978—spent seven months cataloging the victories and defeats of the Boeing 757 jetliner. When the 757 finally flew, the Seattle Times printed a 12-article, seven-part series called "Making It Fly." Rinearson describes the series as "the story of 30,000 people making 130,000 pounds of high technology fly. It is also a tale of world political and financial forces, risk, painstaking compromises, and the complexities and subtleties of the industrial process." Rinearson won a Pulitzer for the series in 1984. He was 28 years old when he wrote the series, and 29 when he won print journalism's most coveted award.

Though much of Rinearson's work is written in traditional news style, "Making It Fly" is a feature, encompassing description and quotation. Still, the articles are, in essence, just good beat reporting. Here is the prologue:

Making It Fly

By **Peter Rinearson**
The Seattle Times

PULITZER PRIZE WINNER

During a 2½-mile drive skirting the edge of Miami's international airport, Frank Borman and Tex Boullioun agreed to an enormous gamble.

Borman, president of Eastern Airlines, and Boullioun, then president of Boeing's commercial airplane division, knew the gravity of the decision they were making. But it wasn't apparent from their casual, confident manner during the four-minute automobile ride on a sun-drenched August day in 1978.

Boeing and Eastern had talked for much of 1977 and 1978 about a new airplane, one on which both Borman and Boullioun would risk the futures of their companies.

They had some ideas. The airplane would be a much-updated derivative of the popular single-aisle Boeing 727, with two engines instead of three. It would have about 160 seats. Eastern and British Airways together would launch the airplane, giving Boeing the sales orders and cash to begin production.

Then, on that August morning in Miami, Borman surprised Boullioun and other Boeing executives who had gathered at Eastern's headquarters at the edge of the airport. Borman asked to see data on a hypothetical plane about 15 seats bigger than they'd talked about earlier.

Boeing officials, though not eager to increase the size of the plane, obliged and laid out the material for Borman, who was noncommittal. Boullioun had to leave early, and Borman said he'd see him to the airport terminal.

Once together in the back seat of the car, Borman told Boullioun he liked the bigger airplane design and was willing to gamble on it.

"All at once Borman had a flash that a 175-passenger airplane was what Eastern wanted," Boullioun recalled. "He said, 'If you'll build that, we'll go.'"

Boullioun replied: "You've got it."

And so, with a handshake—just as the car jiggled over some railroad tracks—the Boeing 757 was born.

"It was a recognition of months and months of negotiation," Borman recalled recently. "Finally we had an accommodation. We knew we were going to be able to do it. They laid out just the airplane we wanted."

Launching a commercial airplane project sobers an airline because it must hazard millions of dollars on a plane that won't fly for years.

But an airline's risks pale next to those of an airplane manufacturer, which may spend $1.5 billion or more on a new design. Not many new aircraft are launched, because a sales flop literally can drive a manufacturer out of the commercial airplane business, as Lockheed proved with its L–1011 jetliner.

"It's the world's biggest poker game. The risks are fantastic," said Ken Holtby, a top Boeing vice president. "We bet the company over and over again in terms of our net worth."

Today the 757 is in service with both Eastern Airlines and British Airways and is proving claims that it would be the world's most fuel-efficient airplane.

But bringing together the elements to make a new idea fly is an immensely detailed process. In the case of the 757, it began well before Borman and Boullioun shook hands, and still isn't finished.

"Sometimes I sit back in amazement and look up at an airplane flying overhead," said Malcolm Stamper, president of the parent Boeing Co. "It's flying people at these tremendous speeds over long distances. And, you think, it was just a bunch of parts, pieces of paper on the ground.

"I think when you build an airplane for the first time it's an excitement, because it didn't exist. Take the 757. Somebody said, 'We'll cut out this piece of sheet metal and we'll bend it this way. And we'll go get this wire and we'll string it this way. And this pipe and bend it.'

"And they put all these things together and they're inanimate. Nothing's moving. Then they fill it up with fuel, light it up, and it takes off and flies! It becomes alive all of a sudden."

The prologue, which prepared the reader for the expanse and tone of the story, was published in tandem with the series' first installment, called "The Big Gamble," which explained that Boeing was prepared to lose millions building the 757 in return for a payoff later. Subsequent installments detailed how Boeing made the decision to build the plane, how the company designed the aircraft, how Boeing assembled workers and materials, how the company tested the plane, and how Boeing sold the plane. Finally, the first 757 was ready for delivery to Eastern Airlines. The last installment, "The Delivery," masterfully mixed detail and color with solid reporting to describe that delivery. Here is Rinearson's feature. Study it, and see how it differs from a news story.

The Delivery
It Was Two Weeks Late and Eastern Was Impatient

By **Peter Rinearson**
The Seattle Times

PULITZER PRIZE WINNER

It hardly looked like an airplane about to enter commercial service.

Some passenger seats were missing. A rack jammed with electronic equipment was strapped to the floor in the first-class section. Technicians and engineers swarmed over the airplane, inside and out.

Seats were pushed forward on their tracks, with carpets rolled back and mechanics climbing in and out of floor recesses. Six technicians were crammed into a cockpit meant for two pilots.

A team of mechanics worked on a recurring problem with the right-wing forward flaps. A heavy-set man looked up at the tail, eyeing the airplane's rudder alignment. A pair of workers used an array of photo-electric cells to aim the airplane's landing lights.

It was Friday, Dec. 17, 1982, and Boeing was late delivering its first 757 to Eastern Airlines. Not contractually late, because the manufacturer had given itself a cushion of extra time. Such buffers, both in projected dates of completion and projected airplane performance, let Boeing almost always point to "better than anticipated" results.

Nevertheless, it already was two weeks past the date Eastern had been told it would receive the first of its silver-and-blue 757 twinjets.

The airline, which had launched the 757 project, was getting impatient. It had announced plans to begin 757 service Jan. 1 and had purchased television advertising to herald the new jetliner during the Rose Bowl and other New Year's Day football games. Even more important, millions of dollars in safe-harbor-leasing tax benefits to Eastern were riding on getting delivery before the end of 1982.

On that overcast day a week before Christmas, while technicians scurried and chiefs paced impatiently, Boeing had yet even to acquire Federal Aviation Administration certification which would allow the 757 to be operated commercially.

An engine-icing problem on a test flight a month earlier had sidetracked certification. The engine had been modified, but was yet to be proved in icing conditions.

Deadlines and timetables were being revised continuously. The target had been certification by Nov. 23, but the days and numbers kept changing. Hundreds of Boeing employees were destined to keep working on the program during the traditional long Boeing holiday recess. There was even talk of working Christmas Day.

Things were, in short, a mess.

"Every time you set a number, it slips. I don't even want to set another one," lamented Bill Robison, director of manufacturing on the 757 project.

Robison was standing with Paul Johnstone, then senior vice president of operations for Eastern, since retired. Johnstone is an amiable man, but he was growing perturbed by the delays in delivery of the jetliner.

Johnstone was head of a delegation that had come to Seattle from Eastern's Miami headquarters to look over the new Boeing jet before accepting it. Every Boeing airplane is subjected to such inspections when it is delivered to an airline. Just as a careful car buyer scrutinizes a new automobile carefully before driving it off the lot, an airline examines a $30 million airplane before flying it home.

Eastern's inspection of the 757 program really had begun in 1979, when the airline sent an ex-Boeing engineer, Ben Gay, back to Seattle to be Eastern's on-site representative. Gay had an impossible job, keeping track of an enormous program, but he was assisted by Boeing employees whose sole job is to help represent the interests of airlines.

Gay's mission was to make sure the airplane would meet Eastern's needs—that every light bulb could be replaced easily, that the cockpit would please Eastern's pilots, that the carpets were the right colors.

"You can't see it all," Gay said. "I can go out quite a bit, but I can't cover all of it. Too much for one man."

But one man is enough when Boeing's high level of quality control is considered, Gay said. "If we had doubts about Boeing's ability to build a decent airplane, not only design-wise but quality and workmanship-wise, we'd have people up here. But they've proven to us in the past that they can build a good airplane with good workmanship, and if it isn't right they fix it."

Gay's activities were reaching a high pitch in the closing days of December as the first 757s were being readied.

The particular airplane under inspection on Dec. 17 was No. NA007, the newest of the new 757s. It had flown for the first time only two days earlier.

On that shakedown flight, 39 problems had been detected—not big problems, but typical little first-flight problems: an annoying sound of hissing air around a seat in row 20, an electrical-access panel that fell off the first time the airplane ever landed.

Now Johnstone, Gay and other Eastern personnel waited for a planned 1 p.m. demonstration flight of the airplane which, in just two weeks, was supposed to carry the first paying Eastern Airlines 757 customers.

Hours ticked by. Mid-day came and went and still the airplane sat outside Plant 2 at Boeing Field. Technical problems kept cropping up. Even the modest 1 p.m. timetable could not be met.

Johnstone recognized the possibility Eastern might not get its first two 757s certified and in service by the end of the month. Every minute seemed precious. "We're down to moving hours out of the schedule, not days or weeks," he said.

Many of Johnstone's thoughts that Friday afternoon were 900 miles south at Edwards Air Force Base near Los Angeles, where another 757 was facing obstacles of a more substantial nature.

It was Boeing 757 No. 3, a flight-test airplane flown by pilot Kenny Higgins. The pilot and his crew were almost desperately trying to build up ice on the airplane's engines to prove that the icing problem had been remedied.

On a routine flight test Nov. 16, both Rolls Royce engines on 757 No. 3 had been damaged when ice built up on their spinner cones, hubs for the forward set of fan blades. The ice had broken off in chunks large enough to bend blades and cause dangerous engine vibration.

After a sometimes-heated debate with Boeing over the cause of the problem, Rolls responded by installing heated spinner cones to prevent ice build-up, and it was presumed the problem was solved. But presumption alone would not win an FAA airworthiness certificate. The "fix" had to be proven.

Boeing and Rolls worked out a strategy in which they would take FAA personnel on a flight through the same sort of supercooled weather conditions that caused the engine damage on Nov. 16. The jetliner would use one engine with a heated spinner and one without—as a control—for the test. The idea was to damage the unmodified engine as before, while demonstrating the safety of the engine with the heated spinner.

But proof was elusive. Day after day, 757 No. 3 flew across the western United States seeking appropriate weather conditions, and day after day it had no luck.

"We had a week of totally dry weather in this half of the whole United States," said John Hodson, a Rolls Royce vice president.

Finally, Boeing asked the Air Force to help it make ice. At Edwards, a KC–135 tanker was loaded with water. The tanker, a derivative of the Boeing 707, normally is used to refuel another airplane in flight with an arm-like boom. This time, however, the tanker dispensed water into the freezing air.

The 757 flew about 70 feet behind and the water had turned to ice by the time it hit the airplane and its engines. It was a last-ditch attempt to create icing conditions, prove the engine modification, win certification and get the first two airplanes to Eastern by the end of the year.

Johnstone knew the test was under way as he paced around the 757 on Boeing Field, but he didn't know how it was going to turn out.

He would have been relieved to know that, in fact, over the next few days the test would succeed, certification would be granted, and Eastern would receive its first two 757s before the end of the year.

December's ill winds weren't the first turbulence the 757 program weathered during its five-year flight.

By 1981 the health of the airline industry was fading, and Boeing faced the prospect of canceled orders for the new airliner. Some airlines, such as American, eventually withdrew plans to buy the new and expensive 757. They couldn't afford it.

Eastern President Frank Borman went before Congress in 1981 and 1982 to plead for tax breaks so that his company's "launch" order for the 757 could proceed.

"The performance of the (airline) industry in 1980 and 1981 jeopardized not only Eastern's participation in that (757) program, but the entire Boeing program," Borman told Senate Finance Committee on March 18, 1982.

Borman told the senators he had been in Seattle in July 1981 attempting to cancel or delay a third of Eastern's order for 757s. Then Congress passed safe-harbor leasing, which improved the situation.

"We went back and did our numbers and found that with the provisions of safe-harbor leasing we could indeed continue the $909 million capital (757) order," Borman testified. "And we went to Boeing and said, 'With the new tax law, it's go,' and Boeing is in fact producing our airplanes. And they are coming down the assembly line, ready or not."

Safe-harbor leasing was an ingenious, controversial mechanism which allowed unprofitable companies to sell unusable tax breaks to profitable companies. Fortune magazine called it "an obscure form of tax-avoidance boogie-woogie." Here's how it worked:

With or without safe-harbor leasing, a company acquiring capital assets (in this case, airplanes) is entitled to tax breaks such as depreciation. But tax breaks are little good to an unprofitable company which pays no tax anyway. In fact, they can even hurt a money-losing airline.

That's because a profitable airline might get a $10 million tax break on a $30 million Boeing jetliner, making its true cost only $20 million, while an unprofitable airline would have to pay the full $30 million for the same airplane.

Under safe-harbor leasing, an unprofitable company could sell its tax breaks to a profitable company for cash. In the hypothetical case of the $30 million jetliner, ABC Airline could sell its $10 million tax break to XYZ Oil Co. for, say, $8 million.

The $8 million in cash for ABC Airline would reduce the true out-of-pocket expense for a $30 million jetliner to $22 million. XYZ Oil, meanwhile, would get a $10 million tax reduction for the $8 million it paid—a quick $2 million profit.

Technically, ABC would temporarily sell the jetliner to XYZ, then lease it back. It is a complicated shuffle of paperwork in which nothing really is exchanged except tax breaks and cash. Both the profitable and unprofitable company are sheltered from taxes in a "safe harbor."

No one loses—except the federal treasury, which, in this hypothetical example, would be out the $8 million.

Safe-harbor leasing was pushed through Congress in 1981 by Borman and others, who argued that unprofitable companies like Eastern were suffering and could not afford to buy needed equipment, such as Boeing 757s.

By early 1982, however, it was clear that Uncle Sam was being taken to the cleaners.

Alan Greenspan, a conservative economist, labeled safe-harbor leasing "food stamps for American business." Profitable companies were gobbling up available tax credits from unprofitable companies, and some big profitable companies—including General Electric—used the loophole to pay no taxes at all for 1981.

In February 1982 the mood in Congress was turning against safe-harbor leasing. Senate Finance Committee Chairman Robert Dole called for repeal of the tax loophole.

Borman and leaders of other unprofitable companies returned to Congress. Borman's argument was compelling: Eastern had proceeded with the 757 order only on the promise of safe-harbor leasing, and revoking that promise would be unjust and disastrous.

Congress chose a middle course, eliminating much of safe-harbor leasing but allowing a timed phase-out for several key and depressed industries, including airlines.

The 757 seemed safe again, although as Eastern's financial picture continued to deteriorate there were other doubts whether it would be able to complete the purchase of 757s.

By Dec. 17, when Johnstone was examining the first of the new jetliners, financial packages involving safe-harbor leasing had been assembled. Once the jetliner was ready, Eastern would have money available for transfer to Boeing, Johnstone said.

The actual purchase of a completed Boeing jetliner is conducted in a variety of ways.

Typically about a third of the price has been prepaid to Boeing during the course of manufacture. But increasingly, as airlines have fallen on hard times (or developed shrewdness in such dealings), Boeing itself has provided financing for part of the purchase price and the whole deal has grown more complicated.

In the case of the sale to Eastern, final funds were to be transferred by wire, with telephone conference calls between several cities confirming the movement of funds from one New York bank account to another. The moment the money changed accounts, the airplane changed hands.

For competitive reasons, Boeing and the airlines tend to obscure the details of such financial transactions. But Eastern's 1982 annual report provides some details.

For instance, the report reveals that the British government provided roughly $10 million financing per 757 "at an attractive interest rate" because of the purchase by the airline of Rolls Royce engines. More to the point, the report said Eastern made $12.8 million on the sale of the tax benefits associated with the first two 757s.

The report says Eastern will raise another estimated $130 million through the sale of the tax benefits associated with 13 additional 757s and four Airbus A-300s due for delivery this year.

"We would have had to cancel the (757) program had we not had safe-harbor leasing," Borman said in an interview last month. "There's no question. It's fact."

Eastern Airlines is looking to the 757 as part of the solution to its financial woes. The 757 is the world's most efficient jetliner, on a per-seat basis, and the airline hopes that its position as the only U.S. operator of the airplane for two years will give it some competitive advantage on costs.

"Frank Borman sees it as a vehicle to thwack his competition with," said Alan Smith, a Rolls Royce official.

Boeing has faced lean years recently, too, and also is looking to the 757 to help restore the strong profitability of the past. Announced total orders for the 757 actually have fallen rather than risen during the past two years, but Boeing claims the airplane eventually will be the world's all-time best-seller.

This is a point of speculation and dispute. While Boeing contends the 757 is about the right size to capture a large share of future sales, other aviation-industry forces—notably Europe's Airbus Industrie—believe the still-to-be-built 150-seat airplane will be far more attractive than the 185-seat 757.

The Airbus view, shared by many others, is that the 757 is a technological success but is likely to be a financial failure—the same bittersweet combination that characterizes the European Concorde SST.

"The 757 would sell beautifully if it had 150 seats," said Reinhardt Abraham, chief technical executive of Lufthansa German Airlines. "My personal opinion always was that the 757 was too close to the 767 and A-310, and it is meeting its own (Boeing) competition. Only huge airlines will be able to fly both the 757 and 767."

But M. J. Lapensky, president of Northwest Airlines, offered a sharply contrasting view. "I don't know what's magic about 150 seats," he said, adding that the 757 is sized perfectly at 185 seats to fill the gap in capacity between the 140-seat 727s and 290-seat DC-10s.

However, Lapensky added that Northwest won't order any 757s until it becomes apparent which of three available engines (two made by Rolls Royce, one by Pratt & Whitney) offers the best economy.

Wolfgang Demisch, an aerospace analyst for the Wall Street firm of First Boston, takes a middle view.

Demisch suggests that the 757 will be a money-losing burden for Boeing in the short run because the company will sell relatively few in each of the first few years of production.

But he believes that the long run will show Boeing has sized the airplane correctly—that the 185-seat airplane will prove more valuable than the 150-seat airplane, because the shortage of air-traffic controllers and growing congestion in air space will force airlines to fly fewer flights with larger-capacity airplanes.

And although it is costing Boeing a bundle to build an airplane which isn't yet selling well, it could have cost Boeing much more not to build the 757, Demisch contends.

Airbus elected to build its second jetliner, the A–310, at the same 210-passenger size as the 767—a size where there is a known strong market and where appropriate new-technology engines already were under development.

In Demisch's view, Airbus probably would have sized its airplane smaller, at about 160 seats, if the 757 hadn't already been under development to fill that need.

"I think in essence that the 757 has ... rattled Airbus sufficiently by its presence that they didn't launch a competitive entry," Demisch said.

"There was a time when Airbus was feeling pretty buoyant a couple of years back, and if there hadn't been a 757 at that point there would have been a large, gaping hole between 140 seats for the 727 and 210 seats for the 767," he said. The temptation to build an airplane in the middle "would, I think, have been irresistible."

"As it is, that opportunity was preempted, and as it stands now I think Airbus is probably regretting that they didn't go ahead and do it anyhow," Demisch said. "Basically, I think it means Boeing is going to be gaining market share, courtesy of the 757, which protected them at the short-to-medium-haul length."

Successful jetliner models seem to stay in production about 20 years. When a jetliner is retired it generally is because its technology is outmoded, not because it is physically worn out.

By incorporating state-of-the-art technology in the 757, Boeing attempted to create an airplane that would be flying well into next century. In fact, the 757 and 767 share a cockpit design which Boeing calls, ambitiously, the "Century 21 flight deck."

The cockpit can be updated readily by replacing computer software (programs), eliminating the need for challenging or impossible hardware changes. This simplicity and flexibility should add to the longevity of the 757.

But a Boeing airplane design is not static. As long as the 757 is in production it likely will be refined. Derivative versions of the airplane are under study, so one day soon men and women may be creating 757 freighters, or stretched or shortened passenger models.

In Renton and around the world, people continue laboring to make the 757—and make it a success.

The range of human endeavor on any given day is impressive.

On Wednesday, April 20, 1983, a day picked at random, Barry Buckworth was running a 90-foot-long milling machine at the Hawker de Havilland plant in Bankstown, Australia.

The machine, first of its kind in Australia, was automatically shaping three 757 wing-shear ribs simultaneously. The ribs were destined for the 40th Boeing 757, and Buckworth's job was to monitor a video screen and blow away metal shavings with an air hose.

That same day, in Burbank, Calif., Ken Tuttle was running a similar milling machine, although he was sweeping away the metal shavings rather than blowing them off. Tuttle is an employee at Menasco, another Boeing subcontractor, and his milling machine was simultaneously shaping the outer housings of the left-hand main landing gears of six 757s.

In Derby, England, 20-year-old Martin Spooner squirted lubricating oil onto carbon-hardened steel he was milling for Rolls Royce. Working in oil-laden air, Spooner was creating tooling for the manufacturer of the 757 engines.

In Minneapolis, Richard Butler, a group leader at a Honeywell factory, was looking after a high-technology machine which used ultrasound energy to drill and mill dense glass. The glass would become the heart of a laser-gyro inertial navigation system used on the 757.

At the Boeing plant in Wichita, Kan., Sharon Baily drilled holes and mounted parts of ribs in the nose section of 757 No. 33, while Jessie Bishop Jr. cut out wheel-well door panels of graphite, using a concentrated spray of water at 50,000 pounds of cutting pressure per square inch.

At Boeing's Vertol Division in Philadelphia, which mostly makes helicopters, Larry Troutman supervised assembly of the fixed leading-edge structure of the right wing for 757 No. 37. The structure is a 2,100-pound device, 64 feet long and containing 700 parts.

On that day, Art Flock of Delta Airlines was in Everett pondering how his airline wanted its 60 757s painted. And near Boeing Field in Seattle, Rob Wood, chief pilot of Britain's Monarch Airlines, was giving a test to two of his pilots in a 757 full-flight simulator.

At Renton Municipal Airport, Eastern's Ben Gay told Boeing to send 757 No. 6, destined for his airline, back into the paint hangar for more polishing.

"My main effort since those early deliveries has been to look for early in-service problems," Gay said. "There's a lot of little things. But overall, you'd give the airplane an excellent grade."

Nearby, top officials of Rolls Royce and Pratt and Whitney laid out for Boeing executives the first glimpse of the "I-2500," a collaborative engine proposed to power a 150-seat airplane Boeing and other manufacturers are considering building.

And on that day, April 20, Tom White finished two sketches of a proposed control box that airline personnel could use to load the 757's cargo hold automatically. Late in the day, he and his coworkers began a new project, a theoretical redesign of airplane passenger cabins in which convention is tossed aside and new ideas are given free reign.

In the Renton plant, Ken Baesler climbed from the inside of a 757 wing which he had been checking for leaks with a mixture of pressurized air and ammonia. In another building, Paul Duxbury was helping assemble the wings, driving titanium fasteners with a rivet gun.

In the final-assembly hangar at Renton, Bill English installed a wing part, tightening a ¾-inch nut to 100 foot-pounds of pressure. A Boeing inspector, J. J. Johnson, witnessed the operation and then stamped a seal on the nut to signal his approval. The pressure on the nut cannot be altered without breaking his personalized seal.

On the underside of the same 757, Dennis Kitchen spent an hour installing a nose landing gear, pushing the 3,000-pound installation dolly away like Superman when he was finished (the dolly was riding on a cushion of air).

And inside yet another 757 that day, Tanjer Gillard filled a Dixie cup with shiny white acrylic enamel and began to paint the heads of screws in a doorjamb. A finishing touch.

All these men and women, and thousands more, were contributing to the 757 program, an industrial venture of massive proportions—whether measured by the yardstick of economics, technology, politics, utility, or even romance.

All these men and women, and tens of thousands more, were helping to make it fly.

Features come in two broad categories—timeless and news features. Timeless features typically are human interest stories which may be published weeks or months after they have been written. News features, on the other hand, are tied, or "pegged," to specific news developments. "Making It Fly" falls somewhere in between the timeless and news categories, because while it has a timeless quality, the story was published soon after the December, 1982, delivery of the first 757.

Note that this feature story does not use a summary or general lead. Most features use specialized leads, ranging from descriptive ones, such as the lead of "The Delivery," to a lead using a direct quotation. The purpose of the feature lead is not to summarize; instead it should draw the reader into the story and set a tone for the story. The feature lead may extend for several paragraphs before the body of the story begins.

The feature story is not written in an inverted pyramid style. Instead, it has a distinct beginning, middle and end. Editing for length must be done carefully.

Finally, features liberally use quotations, description and creative structuring such as surprise endings.

Rinearson had only worked on the aerospace beat for a few months before he began his Pulitzer Prize-winning series. In a sense, "Making It Fly" was a way for him to get to know his beat better, he explains.

Rinearson, who had covered the legislature and city hall for The Seattle Times, says he was in the market for a significant beat by the summer of 1982. "I was interested in broad issues," he says. "If you want to cover national politics, you really need to be in D.C. What can you do of a broad nature in Seattle? Aerospace was the obvious beat."

Rinearson got what he wanted: He was offered the aerospace beat in July, 1982, but he didn't get an introduction to his sources because his predecessor had retired.

"So I am sorting of sitting there saying 'How do I do this?'" Rinearson explains. "Boeing is not a terribly open company. They're not terribly closed [either]. I had this new beat and I didn't know how to go about it. It's a pretty closed society. Very difficult to get an overview, even within the company. People tended to [specialize, and] very few people seemed to have a broad sense of what the company did. They understood their areas.

"And so I was groping around for some way to acquaint myself with the company. And I have lived [in Seattle] my whole life. I've been around Boeing, but you sort of take it for granted in Seattle. But I didn't really understand what it was they did in a real sense, and I knew my readers didn't understand. And so, I was here one day standing talking to another [reporter] and I was saying 'I don't know how to get into this thing,' into the beat. I was having some success. I was getting stories into the paper every couple of days, but I didn't really feel like I had gotten a hold of it in a broad sense. He and I had both read "Soul of a New Machine" by Tracy Kidder and he said, 'Maybe you ought to do a

Pulitzer Prize-Winner Peter Rinearson of The Seattle Times writes a story using a portable video display terminal. (Photo by Craig Fugii of The Seattle Times)

"Soul of a New Machine" on a jetliner.' No sooner had he said it than [I thought] 'That's it.'"

Rinearson's breakthrough probably came while he was attending the Farnborough Air Show in England, he says. "Suddenly I was in the midst of 50 of the company's top people. A lot of people were there and they were away from Seattle and accessible." Rinearson says that he asked a lot of questions there, and showed an honest interest in what Boeing officials were saying. Perhaps as a result of his articles on the air show, some people may have said, "Maybe this guy's okay," Rinearson speculates.

Rinearson envisioned "Making It Fly" as a six-week project, with three weeks for reporting and three weeks for writing, which would fit into 100 inches of newspaper space, perhaps in the Sunday magazine.

"After I got into it, I realized that what it took to build a jetliner far exceeded three weeks, six weeks or 100 inches." The project, which Rinearson sandwiched in between his regular beat reporting responsibilities, took seven months of up to 18-hour long days.

You're probably wondering how Rinearson accomplished his April 20 around-the-world trip described at the end of the article. Did he travel from Renton, Wash., to Bankstown, Australia, to Burbank, Calif., to Derby, England, to Minneapolis, Minn., to Wichita, Kan., to Philadelphia, Pa., and back to Everett, Wash.?

Rinearson explains his laborious technique: "It was difficult because obviously I couldn't be all of those places at once. So I did the very best I could. For the Seattle area, I went down for part of that day and personally watched people painting screws, the door and other things that didn't make it into [the story]. I also got on the telephone that day and called a number of people at Boeing, [and] basically spent the whole day on the phone. Some of them I had warned and others I just called and said, 'Hey, I'm curious in what you're doing right now.' And I picked some of the more interesting ones.

"As far as the out-of-town ones go, I had picked that date long in advance. The people around the country—Wichita and so on—I got on the phone and arranged it initially with the [Boeing public relations] office. I would have to let them select someone for me. I suppose there is some potential for manipulation, except that it's only two or three sentences. Not a lot of damage could be done."

Rinearson also asked the Rolls Royce public relations representative in England for help. "I let a PR person be my eyes and ears there and that didn't worry me too much because I knew that all I would be using would be two or three sentences. [Then] prior to using the material, I went to [Derby] England and went to the factory and talked to the person whose name I had used. So I wasn't able to be there on April 20 ... but I had it wired in advance so that I had someone there who was watching. Very little of that actually made it into the series."

And what about Australia? "I didn't go to Australia at all," Rinearson explains. "You see, Australia has a time zone advantage. It was April 19 in Seattle, but it was April 20 in Australia. In that case, I was able to get on the phone [and talk to] people. Once again, I think it wound up being a sentence in the series, but I did a fair amount of reporting for it. I also had them send me a packet of material which shows photos of the plant."

Rinearson ultimately wound up with so much detail that he turned "Making It Fly" into a book of the same title.

Reporters like Rinearson will tell you that beat reporting is a lot like majoring in criminal justice in college without ever bothering to become a police officer. You learn what police work is like, why some criminals commit crimes, how the courts function and about the theory of punishment. But you're never really a policeman; you're always the inquiring student. You come as close to being the subject of your reporting as you can without crossing over. As a reporter, you have another job—to explain.

Now that we have looked at general techniques of beat reporting, let's look at the specific demands of various beats.

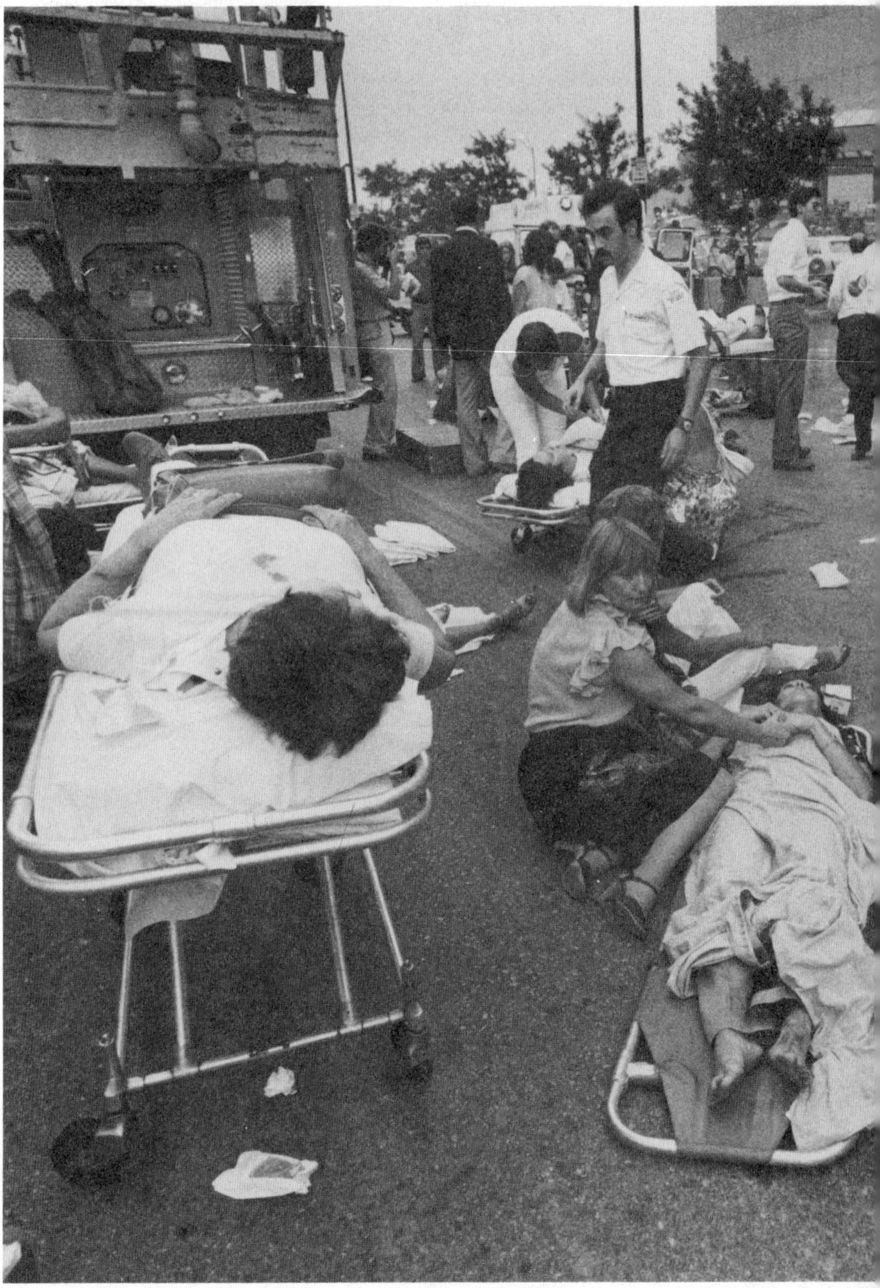

CHAPTER **8**

The Basics: Fire, Police and Court Reporting

Covering Fires
Covering the Police Beat
Covering the Courts

By now you realize that reporting requires many skills—language skills, interpersonal communication skills and skills in determining what is worth reporting. Developing the skills is a lot of work; so is doing the reporting.

Maintaining the correct attitude also is a part of all reporting. Diet experts tell us that "You are what you eat." It's more philosophically correct to say, "You are what you think." A reporter is a person who *thinks* reporting. A reporter thinks letting the public know what is going on is far better than keeping the public in the dark. A reporter thinks about almost every experience that comes along in relation to its news value.

After covering general assignment stories for awhile, reporters often get their next important reporting experience in covering the staples of news: fires, police and courts. By developing expertise in these basic areas, reporters become even more valuable members of their news organization.

Covering Fires

Covering fires and the fire department is rarely a beat by itself. For example, the police reporter may regularly check the fire department for routine stories on its operation and scan and cover the reports on minor fires. On major fires, however, an ad hoc group of general assignment reporters and photographers usually covers the story. Covering a fire is often the first taste a reporter gets of disaster coverage, for almost every uncontrolled fire is a disaster to those who are injured or suffer property damage.

An uncontrolled fire automatically has human interest and drama. Will it rage on? Was anyone killed or hurt? Has something irreplaceable been destroyed? How can it be put out? A big fire is a spectacle, hurling a column of smoke into the sky and spewing flames, out of doors and windows. It may be accompanied by reverberating explosions and crashing walls and roof timbers. Fires attract interest.

Learning to cover a fire teaches a reporter how to operate under stress—the reporter's own stress and the stress the sources are experiencing as they fight the blaze or watch their homes, businesses and possessions go up in smoke. The reporter needs a combination of patience and a sense of urgency accompanied by a single-minded concentration on getting the story without becoming a spectator or participant in the event.

Fire departments have two functions: responding quickly and adequately to fire emergencies, and preventing fires. While the educational

Chapter opening photo: Firefighters and police officers aid victims of the 1981 Hyatt Regency Hotel disaster in Kansas City, Mo. Coverage of the disaster won a Pulitzer Prize for the Kansas City Star Company. (Photo by Greg Smith/Kansas City Times)

and inspection aspects of preventing fires are appropriate subjects for news stories, the interest here is in covering fires.

First you must learn how the fire department works. Companies, one or more to a firehouse, are spaced out over a city. Each is headed by a captain who reports to a battalion chief who reports to the fire chief who heads the department. For routine matters the person designated by the chief for public relations activities is the person to start with. For major matters, the chief is the prime spokesman. At the scene of a fire, the company chief, battalion chief or department chief runs a command post where information known about the fire is available. This individual usually is the kind of calm and cool person who can find time to tell you what you need to know.

At the dispatcher's office a log is kept of fires reported and of the department's response. The number of companies dispatched, for example, will give you an idea of the size of the fire. An example of a story developed from a dispatcher's log is part of this chapter. The department keeps other records which provide information for stories: number and location of fire safety violations, cumulative totals on number of fires, property damage, death and injuries, geographical location of fires, and incidence of arson.

Also keep in mind that the fire department has an interest in and a legal responsibility for learning the answers to many of the questions reporters have about fires. This is true of most stories involving government agencies.

Several basic categories of questions are pertinent to any fire story:

- *Time factor.* When did the fire start? If someone can answer that question specifically, that person probably also knows how it started; often an approximation is the best anyone can give. When was the fire reported and by whom? When did firefighters reach the scene? When was additional help (if any) sought and when did it appear? When was the fire brought under control and when was it extinguished? The answers to these questions will provide the framework of most fire stories.
- *Deaths or injuries.* Everyone has burned a finger at some time or another and can empathize with a fire victim. Reporting on why or how someone got caught in a fire makes the magnitude of the event real.

Accurate identification of each victim is important for two reasons. It pinpoints the tragedy to those actually affected and reduces rumor and the fear of not knowing if a loved one was hurt or killed. Second, knowing names eliminates duplication in compiling the totals of those killed or injured in the fire. Most news media prefer to delay reporting the names of those killed or injured until a relative has been notified in person.

If there are serious injuries, when did the injured get off the critical list? When were they released from medical care? Knowing about fatalities or injuries determines the importance of the story and what will be in the lead.

- *Harm to property.* What was destroyed? What was damaged? What was the dollar value? The owners and occupants best know the answers to these questions, but fire and insurance officials may be the first to be able to give you a firm and reasonably accurate figure. Harm to property goes beyond the dollar value: What business will no longer have a place to operate? Who is left homeless? What landmark or historic site is gone? What artist lost all the paintings for his or her next show? What child lost the teddy bear that he or she can't go to sleep without? These kinds of things have intangible but real human value. More than the dollar figure, these facts make the fire real to your audience. The occupants can tell you these things, if you have the tact and compassion to ask in the right way.
- *Cause.* Why was there a fire? The causes can range from a bolt of lightning to arson. Arson—the intentional burning of property and endangering of life by fire—is a crime. The question automatically comes to the mind of every reader, as well as to the victims of the fire, the fire department and the state fire marshal's office (in the case of a major or suspicious fire). The fire department and the state fire marshal are usually the best sources though quoting an eyewitness might be even better.
- *Discovery.* Who spotted the fire and what did he or she do? Heroism may be involved. This person may be your best eyewitness, the one who first saw the blaze and perhaps the one who prevented many from being injured or killed.
- *Extinguishing the fire.* How was the fire put out? Did the neighbors form a bucket brigade? Did the fire department use an exotic chemical or a unique tactic? Was additional help summoned? How much did it cost to put out the fire? Were firefighters hampered by freezing temperatures, chemical fumes or lack of water?

An alert reporter will follow up on a fire. Did that business get rebuilt? How many teddy bears did friends of that little girl give her to make up for the one that was lost? Have the homeless found decent dwellings? What has been done to prevent a recurrence of this kind of fire?

Using Fire Department Records

The importance of the records a public agency keeps is illustrated by the following example. The Kansas City Star and Times discovered the value of the dispatcher's log, a record which rarely makes the news. In covering a major apartment fire in the early 1980s, reporters found that the dispatcher's log indicated when fire trucks and other emergency vehicles responded to an alarm and ensuing emergencies. This knowledge benefited the Star and Times when a far larger emergency occurred in the summer of 1981. The fire dispatcher's log provided the chronology of how the community responded to a tragedy that killed more than 100 local citizens.

At 7:05 p.m., Friday, July 17, 1981, two walkways spanning the lobby of the new Hyatt Regency Hotel in Kansas City at the second- and fourth-floor levels collapsed onto hundreds of people at a tea dance in the lobby. By the time the last of the concrete rubble was cleared away on Sunday, the death toll was 113 and 188 were injured.

The Star and Times received the Pulitzer Prize for their comprehensive coverage of the tragedy. Part of the coverage focused on the city's response during the first hour after the debacle. To write the story, reporters listened to the tape recordings at the police and fire department dispatchers' desks and interviewed the dispatchers.

Read this story to learn four things: how a reporter can turn a matter-of-fact official document into an interesting story, the way fire dispatchers work with the public and the media in an emergency, the value of knowing what records are available and how a fire story can capture the full attention of a reader.

Here is Robert Trussell's story, from the fire department as it appeared on page 2 of the Sunday, July 19, Star.

By the Minute, Dispatchers Hear Tragedy Unfold

By **Robert C. Trussell**
© 1981 The Kansas City Star Company

PULITZER PRIZE WINNER

Dispatchers at the Kansas City Fire Department alarm office, located almost within throwing distance of the Hyatt Regency, were jerked from relative quiet to frenzy at 7:08 p.m.—about three minutes after the collapse of two walkways in the lobby.

"We can be sitting around not lifting a pencil one minute and the next minute all hell can break loose," said Phillip Wall, a dispatcher who worked the Friday night shift along with Dean Gurney, supervisor, and Larry Gonnello.

"And that's what happened."

Wall answered the first call from a woman he believes was a hotel employee.

Wall: "Fire Department."

Woman (distraught): "Yes, please come to the Hyatt Regency. Have you been called yet?"

Wall: "No. What's the problem?"

Woman: "OK, three of our sky bridges have fallen."

Dispatcher: "Three what?"

Woman: "... yes, and hurt people. Could you come right away ...?"

Wall: "Are you talking about the elevators?"

Woman: "No. The three sky bridges ..."

Wall: "All right. We'll be right there."

Immediately after the woman's call, the police and an ambulance dispatcher called to alert the Fire Department. A battalion chief, three pumper trucks and a ladder truck were dispatched. At 7:12 p.m. a firefighter on Pumper No. 8 reported: "We have people trapped ... we need heavy equipment to move it, and we need ambulances."

Wall: "How much heavy equipment, what kind and how many ambulances?"

Firefighter: "... people in the lobby, the main lobby."

At 7:15 p.m. a second alarm was sounded. A second battalion chief, three more pumpers and two more ladder trucks were sent.

By 7:19 p.m. firefighters at the scene were calling for cutting tools to pry rubble away to free victims.

"We're gonna need all the (cutting) tools down here we can get," a firefighter called from the scene.

By 7:21 p.m. firefighters were also calling for more heavy equipment—cherry pickers. Two minutes later a fireman requested a forklift.

Soon after the firefighting crews were dispatched, Wall said, the alarm office alerted the

St. Joseph Life Flight helicopter and alerted area hospitals to prepare their trauma units.

"You develop a sixth sense for emergencies," Wall said. "We knew we had a big fish by the hook."

By 7:23 p.m. firefighters estimated there were 50 injured persons in the lobby, an estimate that would soon rise with no apparent end.

At 7:26 p.m. a Life Flight dispatcher called to ask about landing space for the helicopter.

At 7:32 p.m. residents began calling with questions about the catastrophe. The dispatchers could offer only a rough sketch of the calamity.

Firefighters reported at 7:33 p.m. that some of those trapped could not be reached by the cutting tools. Only heavy lifting equipment would do the job.

The Kansas City, Kansas, Fire Department contacted the alarm office at 7:34 p.m. to tell dispatchers its firefighters were bringing two more cutting tools. Four minutes later the dispatchers learned a rescue unit was on the way from Lee's Summit.

A man who did not identify himself called and offered the use of two helicopters. He was turned down for the moment.

"I don't think it would do us any good, Larry," a battalion chief told his colleague, Gonnello. "We can't gain access to the roof here, we're going to have to go in through the front windows."

"We do appreciate your offer," Gonnello told the man.

Within the next six minutes, the Belton and Lee's Summit fire departments called with offers of assistance, offers which were accepted.

During the first hour of the accident, residents and private companies called offering heavy equipment. Some were given police escorts to the scene. Offers also came from fire departments in Raytown, North Kansas City, Independence and Johnson County. Other assistance came from fire departments in Liberty, Mission, Johnson County, Shawnee, Merriam, Leawood and Central Jackson County.

Gonnello informed firefighters at the scene at 8:01 p.m. that the "helicopter man" was back on the line, offering the use of a chopper that could haul 40 victims at a time. This time the offer was accepted. The "helicopter man" turned out to be Robert Mullin, emergency preparedness director for Lenexa, who arranged for the use of two Army Reserve helicopters. Only one was used, the other was considered too large to maneuver in midtown Kansas City.

Wall said the horror began to sink in.

"It was something else," he said. "It wasn't too long ago the MGM Hotel fire (in Las Vegas) broke out. We were amazed by something that wasn't even in our city. Who knew a few months later we'd have a similar situation here?"

Wall walked to the hotel when his shift ended at 11 p.m. He extricated victims from the rubble and stacked lumber under the fallen walkways. He worked at the scene until 5 a.m.

"I couldn't believe the amount of blood everywhere," he said. "There were pools of blood down on the hotel floor. You could smell it—a real stagnant kind of pungent smell, just hanging in the air."

Here is the recipe for the previous story: Take the entire dispatcher's log for the crucial hour. Eliminate the incomprehensible and absolutely unimportant parts. Mix in the dispatchers' comments obtained at a later interview. (Obtain the comments by asking such questions as: "When did you first realize ...?," "What did you think was ...?" and "What did you do then?" and let the firefighter talk.) Write a lead that sets the scene. Write an ending that sums up the dispatcher's reaction to the tragedy. And sprinkle in words that tell how the people talking to the dispatcher sounded.

Knowing how to cover a fire prepares you for a story you may later be thrust into—such as a tornado, an earthquake, a hurricane, a volcanic eruption or an aerial bombing attack. The magnitude is vastly greater, but the questions remain the same—questions about the time factor, the persons involved, the destruction in both monetary and human terms, and the causes and effects.

Covering the Police Beat

Covering law enforcement—the police beat—is one of the universal specialties in the mass media. There are good reasons why.

Police officers investigate accidents, acts of violence and disturbances. They keep streets, buildings and lands under surveillance. They control crowds and traffic. They carry out the orders of the courts. They operate 24 hours a day. They know what is going on in public and they are obligated to share their extensive records with the public.

Reporting on police activities signaled the beginning of universal journalism. What the police and the courts do is of interest to everyone. When Benjamin Day began publishing the New York Sun in the 1830s, people who had never before read newspapers began to do so. "The Sun shines for all" was the paper's motto. People read the Sun because it cost only a penny an issue and because it published news about ordinary folks who had ordinary problems with the police and the courts.

Reading the police news during the 19th century and the first half of the 20th century was equivalent to watching soap operas today. The minor foibles of humanity that appear in police records today are no longer considered important enough to be covered by most of the media, but major crimes, accidents, public disturbances and happenings that require police assistance are interesting to everyone and often are big news.

Many new reporters have had little contact with the police. They have grown up in middle-class neighborhoods, gone to school and found a job. The police beat is often their introduction to a broader world: the world of people who have not adjusted to society, who have had misfortune or who have in other ways run afoul of the law. Much of what the police reporter sees is sad. Almost all of it is vitally important to the people involved. A great deal of it is interesting to the public, and some of it is very important.

Police Department Organization

The first thing a reporter new to police coverage needs to learn is how the law enforcement agency or agencies to be covered are organized. The municipal police department is the most common law enforcement agency. It consists of an appointed chief or commissioner and of patrol and investigative branches. The police department is organized along military lines, with a clear chain of command. Major cities are divided into police precincts, each with its own uniformed patrol officers and plainclothes detectives. In addition, special units—vice, homicide, narcotics, for example—operate citywide.

Every police department has at least one person who is assigned the public relations function and serves as the official spokesperson. In a small town this person is usually the chief. Big city departments have sophisticated public relations departments that deal with the media and with community groups and individuals. The official spokesperson is a good source, but not the only one the reporter depends on. Many police records are open to the public. The reporter monitors them daily—and then talks to the police officers who have first hand knowledge of a crime or accident. They have more information than the official spokesperson does.

In addition to municipal police departments, almost every political subdivision may have a law enforcement officer. Constables may serve the justice of the peace or municipal courts in small jurisdictions. In rural areas, the county sheriff and deputies may be the most important law enforcement agency. (The sheriff is an elected official who appoints deputies.) On the state level, the highway patrol or state police may have law enforcement responsibilities beyond enforcing the traffic laws. On a national level, U.S. marshals, the Federal Bureau of Investigation and the Secret Service enforce federal laws. The marshals basically are officers of the U.S. District Courts. The FBI investigates possible violations of federal law. The Secret Service protects the president and other officials and investigates the counterfeiting of money.

Specialized police ride the subways and some airliners, enforce the game and fish laws, look for moonshiners and bootleggers, enforce the laws in national parks and carry out a variety of other responsibilities. They may be county, state or federal officers. The armed forces have police who enforce the Uniform Code of Military Justice, a separate set of laws for the military.

The police in their relations with reporters are similar to other organizations in routine matters: how they will control crowds at the big game, who has been promoted, what data have they on crimes or accidents from the past year. However, in the case of possible crimes, laws come into the picture. Some restrict the amount of information available to the public and others assure that the public can find out what's going on.

The police record provides an authoritative report that informs the public and allays false rumors. Crime statistics can indicate changes in the nature of neighborhoods or in the behavior of certain segments of society. Traffic accident statistics sometimes indicate inadequate streets or signals. You can use the police record as a weather vane to find out what is happening and as a base of information on which to build stories.

Each police officer submits a report on every incident investigated. This report is almost always available to the public. It records the time and place of the incident, who was investigated and briefly tells what happened. It is the starting point for many stories.

You need to be careful in using names or otherwise identifying persons mentioned in any police report. A report of trouble with the police means a person's reputation or ability to make a living may be impaired. This is called libel, one of the limitations on the First Amendment. You or the company you work for can be sued for damages in a libel case. On the other hand, if the account is accurate and if the alleged offense results in charges being filed, the accusation becomes a public record. Reporting the contents of a public record is usually protected from successful libel actions by the defense of privilege.

In a news story about a crime, be careful to separate the charge from the description of the crime. Witnesses and the victim may be quoted at length about what happened but be wary of quoting them about who did it. In a separate paragraph it is safe to say who was officially charged with breaking a specific law. A person who is accused of a crime is likely to file suit unless a formal charge has been filed against him or her.

Police officers and other officials are forbidden to reveal the contents of some files they keep, and a reporter can be found in contempt of court for getting information from such records. Be particularly careful about records dealing with children and teenagers and with evidence that the police present to a grand jury. Laws specifying which records are restricted vary from state to state. Learn what your state's laws are about sensitive records.

Steve Yozwiak is the day police beat reporter in Phoenix for The Arizona Republic, the state's largest newspaper with a daily circulation of more than 300,000 papers. Yozwiak is a 1977 graduate of the University of Arizona in Tucson. He worked for the Daily Republic in Fairfield, Calif., for two years covering police, courts and city hall. He returned to his hometown of Phoenix in 1980, where he covered retirement communities, transportation, city planning, and both day and night police beats for over three years. Here he describes his daily schedule.

A DAY IN A POLICE BEAT REPORTER'S LIFE

I dress to the sound of a police radio scanner. I'm already late no matter what time it is. The cop beat never stops. Who knows what happened last night? In a metropolitan area like Phoenix with nearly two million people, something crazy happens every single day.

Besides the scanner, I arm myself with a two-way radio to stay in touch with the photographers and a portable telephone to stay in touch with editors, sources and everyone else.

Once in the office, I check the wire services. Then I make my rounds. I check jail booking slips and talk with local and state police, sheriffs and fire officials. Every agency has a designated spokesperson. They are often helpful, but they never know the whole story.

If possible, I talk to street cops, detectives, fire paramedics and witnesses.

In almost any event, there is a victim and family, friends or employers of the victim to track down. They have part of the story, too. They come in two types: ones who talk, and ones who won't. I can be as nice as you want, but some people are just hostile. And some people just need to get some things off their chest.

Cops are like that, too. Some love me. Some seem to hate me. All of them are suspicious.

If someone is arrested, there is a chance for a jailhouse interview. I never know what they're going to say. Sometimes they confess. Often they say they were framed. Most of the time they refuse to talk.

From homicides to teddy bears, the story ideas are endless. They come from sources, anonymous phone calls, letters and court records. Rarely do they come from my editors.

There are issues to cover, too. Crime statistics, police discipline, new types of weapons. I try not to forget that those issues revolve around people, and I look for examples.

I write on deadline almost every day. I remember when I was a sophomore in college. It seemed a chore to write one story a week. Now, I routinely do three or four stories each day. Even after deadline, there's always one more fact to check, one more phone call to make or one more source to call back.

I go home bushed, but my stories get good play.

Steve Yozwiak
The Arizona Republic

Interviewing Witnesses and Victims

Witnesses and victims present the police reporter with special concerns.

Do not hesitate to try to interview persons who witnessed accidents, crimes or tragedies. Identify yourself and be polite. Understand that they have witnessed something traumatic—they may be excited or even belligerent. Be sensitive and patient and willing to back off if the interview is unproductive. Try to lead each witness chronologically through the incident. Write down each witness's name and address—and phone number if possible. Keep your notes on each witness separate from the others. Particularly at the scene, keep notes sparse, then flesh them out immediately after your interviews. Try to interview witnesses as soon as possible after the event.

Interviewing victims and their close relatives requires even greater sensitivity. Publicity has the potential of causing further harm to the victim. For example, victims of rape and other sexual crimes may be spurned by members of the community if they are identified. Some state laws prohibit the publication of a rape victim's name. Know the law and the policy of your news organization toward making the names of rape victims public. Let the victim know what the policy is and be willing to decide in your own mind the best compromise between informing the public and protecting the innocent. When there is great public interest in a crime, straightforward reporting is the best way to allay rumors and, in the long run, to end public ridicule of the victims. Get to know what the people in your town will accept as legitimate reporting. If your words repel them, they won't get your message.

There are times when victims—like witnesses—simply cannot talk coherently about major traumatic events. They do not want to think about such events, much less talk about them. But there also are times when they need to talk. Your understanding of human behavior in such stressful situations will enhance your abilities as a reporter. (Some psychology courses may help you. Experience will help, too.) Many a good story has resulted from a sensitive reporter's patience, and many a distraught person has benefited from being able to tell a story he or she thought the public should hear.

The example that follows is not directly connected with a police investigation, but it is exactly the type of situation police reporters face daily in getting the facts about accidents and crimes from those who have experienced them.

David Hacker, a reporter for the Kansas City Times, talked to four widows on the Wednesday after their husbands were killed in the Friday evening hotel tragedy mentioned earlier. His story, "The Day the Music Stopped," was part of the Pulitzer Prize-winning coverage of the sky walk collapse. The story is important because the editors of the Star and Times recognized that the Hyatt Regency tragedy differed from other catastrophes. The 113 people who died when walkways crashed down on them in the hotel lobby were not a random group of hotel guests. Almost all of them were hometown people. Groups of friends had come to enjoy the music and drinks at the tea dance.

In Hacker's opinion, if he had tried to talk to the four widows a day earlier or a day later, he would not have gotten the story. By talking to them when he did, he got the interviews and made some friends. In describing the routine activities of the last day in four long, happy marriages, he was able to show the impact of sudden death on individual lives.

As you read the story—a news feature—try to reconstruct the questions David Hacker asked. Think about how you could ask them sympathetically and at the same time encourage your source to speak freely. This is the key to successful interviewing in stressful situations.

The Day the Music Stopped
By **David Hacker**
© 1981 The Kansas City Star Company

PULITZER PRIZE WINNER

When Nancy Jonas poked her husband, Bob, in the back to wake him up the morning of Friday, July 17, her elbow touched skin. It was hot, and Bob was wearing as little as possible, which was next to nothing. In fact, the only thing he had on was his beard, under which was tucked a double chin.

"I encouraged him to grow it," Nancy said. "He had this double chin, and the beard covered it up. Besides, I'm turned on by beards. After he grew it, he said to me, 'Do you like it?' He always trimmed it shorter than I liked. But if it was long and bushy, he didn't feel it fit his image."

Bob got up and went into the bathroom, where he had his first cigarette of the day, one of only 10 a day he was down to. He was on the Dr. Marshall Saper quit-smoking diet, where you cut in half each day the number of cigarettes you consume. Nancy dozed while Bob showered. Their children, Laura, 20, and David, 17, were asleep in their bedrooms. At 7 a.m., the temperature already was a sticky 79, promising another 90s day. The ranch house at 9619 Lamar, in Overland Park, was astir, but not by much. Lightning, the 9-week-old, coal black cat, hadn't appeared. He slept on the rug, next to the patio door in the dining room....

Eight o'clock. The temperature was still 79 degrees. Eleven hours left.

Because Bob was out of sight but not out of sound, Nancy Jonas lay in bed, her back to the middle, as so many married couples do when the years walk so quietly by and the thrill of touching during the night isn't so thrilling anymore.

"Oh, we'd wake up sometimes in the night and touch, but usually we slept back to back. He snored like no one." Later she would say, "I wish he'd been there to snore these last three nights."

In the kitchen was waiting morning coffee. It was Brim, fixed the night before. "God forbid that he should make the coffee himself," Nancy said with a laugh as she reflected on this last day of their life together. When he had finished his Kent King cigarette in the bathroom, he came back into the bedroom, got dressed, leaned over the bed and gave Nancy a kiss. "He could hardly make it without that first cigarette in the morning," she said. "He'd been smoking, I guess, 44 years."

When she got up and put on her green terry cloth robe, cut short with short sleeves, Bob already had gone out to the driveway and gotten the morning newspaper. He was sitting in his usual green chair at the kitchen table, reading. His favorite comic was Guindon. Nancy fixed him a piece of Russian rye toast, a small glass of orange juice and a glass of milk. Bob was on a diet.

That night they had plans to go to the tea dance at the Hyatt Regency, an evening out that they began talking about in April. They wanted to dance and then go to the Peppercorn Duck Club for dinner. "I was treasurer of our bowling league," Nancy said, "and I got $40. We were going to use that to help pay for the evening. But he got so busy, and there were a lot of crises, and we kept putting it off. Last Friday, he said, 'If we don't go, we'll never make it.' He was a big fan of the 1940s music. He said, 'As long as we're going down there, let's do it early.'"

After that breakfast, neither Nancy nor Bob had a bite to eat all day. "In fact, I didn't eat all week," Nancy said. "I was going to pig out that night. I have a weight problem. Life is so unfair."

Bob got up from the table, leaned down and gave Nancy another kiss, and they told each other to have a good day.

"He was a person who liked to be different," Nancy said. "He was really a religious person. The beard was kind of symbolic with his studies of Judaism. He started it after he had minor surgery."

Bob left the quiet house shortly after 8:30, and it took him 10 or 15 minutes to drive to his office at 2210 W. 75th St. He drove off in his 1981 blue AMC Concord. A few minutes before 9, Nancy, dressed in a yellow seersucker pantsuit, said a silent goodbye to the still-sleeping Laura and David, got into her 1980 white Chevy Citation and drove to her secretarial job at 87th and Switzer....

And then it was noon. The temperature was ... 88. Seven hours left.

When it was all over, Nancy Jonas, her soul wrapped in a chamois-cloth memory of her husband, said as she reflected on his effort, after 44 years, to give up smoking, "Why is it that the things you worry about never happen?"

He didn't die of lung cancer. He died of something that couldn't happen.

His work with children, the eighth-graders at their temple, B'nai Jehudah, brought him as much satisfaction as did teasing Nancy and telling friends bawdy jokes.

These were on Nancy's mind later.

Midmorning, Friday, July 17, she humdrummed her way through her secretarial work, typing, filing, answering the phone and figuring out what she'd do at lunch. She didn't want to eat; that was for the Peppercorn Duck that night and, oh how she'd let loose. At noon, she left her office and drove to Oak Park Mall five minutes away where, at J. C. Penney, she bought four sheets and two pillow cases for Laura, who was entering Kansas State University in the fall. She paid $2.99 each for the sheets, and the pillow cases were $1 more each. "I thought it was the best bargain." She charged it. "I don't pay cash for nothing," she said. "My husband worked on commission, and you never knew how much cash you'd have. I got the sheets for Laura because she'd been to the dorm and came back and said how yucky the sheets there were."

Nancy took a Coke back to the office with her. That was her lunch. She didn't want to spoil the Peppercorn Duck dinner after the tea that evening....

Three o'clock. The temperature had crept up another degree to 89. Four hours left.

About 3:30, back at her office, Nancy got a call from Bob. "He pretended I was a customer. He said, 'Mrs. Jonas, would you please type the document you have in your purse?'"

It was a paper she had been carrying for several weeks and just had not gotten around to typing. She promised to do it on the weekend.

"I love you," he said before ending the conversation.

It was a common greeting, a common message he gave her.

"All of us were aware of the family, and we always went to the extra effort to say things like this. We kissed a lot and said things like that. Bob's biggest concern was keeping the children happy. Our son, David, was grounded a few weeks ago when he was late coming home. Bob said, 'There's nothing a 17-year-old can do at 4:15 in the morning without getting into trouble.' He was being very good."

Bob's last words to Nancy on the phone, after he said he loved her, were, "I'll see you at home."...

When Nancy got home from work a few minutes after 5, she found Bob lying on the couch reading the newspaper. "Have you had your shower yet?" she asked. He nodded yes. David already was at work at the Red Lobster Restaurant, 9475 Metcalf. Laura was home. Nancy went into the bedroom and undressed and then went into the bathroom and filled the tub. "I don't like showers," she said. She used Dial soap. "I put on my favorite dress. It was a navy-and-white sun dress, with stripes and pink flowers and a white linen jacket." Her shoes were white sandals with high heels. Bob had gotten dressed. He wore a navy-blue blazer with gold buttons, tan slacks, a white shirt and black loafers. "He looked so gorgeous. So gorgeous." Their reservations at the Peppercorn Duck were for 8....

Six o'clock. One hour left. The temperature reached 90, the hottest hour of the day. Clouds had drifted in and out of the sky all day, sometimes hanging low, sometimes flying high. But they provided no shade. It still was muggy, uncomfortable, but it was time to leave for the tea dance, which had been going on since 4:30. . . .

It was hot when they walked into the Hyatt through the small, south entrance, Nancy Jonas said. "He walked faster than me. There were 4 million people, it seemed like. A record was playing. The band was not on the bandstand. Bob went to the restroom. He left me standing there, right under the walkway. I knew that if I moved, he'd lose me. We stood there for a few minutes, listening and watching. There were an awful lot of people. They all were smiling. I think as soon as we arrive, the band's on a break. That seems to be our kind of luck. I also noted that some people had badges that said, 'I'm a regular Hyatt Regency tea dancer.' He had a Scotch. I had a bourbon and 7-Up. He had to buy tickets from a girl at a card table. Then he went to the bar and gave the guy the tickets. Bob said, 'Let's go back in the corner.' He liked to watch the musicians because he once was one."

Indeed, Bob Jonas was a band drummer in World War II. "He raised a lot of hell when he was young," Nancy said later. "I think he was busted four times in the Army."

Bob sat on the arm of a lobby chair, where Nancy was sitting. The band had just started "Satin Doll." "My foot was doing the same thing his was, tapping. He finished his drink. He turned to me and asked whether I wanted another one. I'm a slow drinker and said no. He said he was going to go and get another drink. He got up and went over to the bar. People were all jammed together. I didn't watch him leave."

In less than an hour, they'd be sitting down at the Peppercorn Duck for the long-awaited elegant dinner. Nancy had given Bob the $40 from her bowling league chores. He had a few extra dollars too. Nancy didn't tell him, but she had stuck a $20 bill in her purse before they left the house. "When we parked the car, Bob said to me, 'Why don't you leave your purse here?' "

She said no, she'd take it with her. That $20 bought her a taxi ride home early the next morning.

"I didn't know that would be the last time I'd see him," she said. "The next thing I heard was this man saying in a normal voice, 'Get back, get back.' I was sitting about 10 feet away, and I stood up. I really didn't hear a thing. All of a sudden there was all this trash and people under the trash. I had the presence of mind to reach over and grab my purse. I noticed it was really weird. It was so quiet. It seemed like a long time. Here I stood like a dummy with a drink in my hand. I saw one little girl. I offered her my drink. She refused. I looked at myself, and there didn't seem to be anything wrong with me. It smelled like chemicals. It hurt your lungs. I just kept looking over at the bar, to see if I could see my husband. A young man smashed the window, and I saw the bartender climb out. But I didn't see Bob."

In a story like this, there is no epilogue. The story goes on and on and on.

When David Jonas heard that his father was missing, he elected to stay on at his job at the Red Lobster. "I heard about it," he said, adding that he thought, "If I stay here I'll be better off." Nancy Jonas made it through the night, aided by Marilynne and Sherwin Rosenthal and Alice and Tom Lewinsohn. When David got home at 1:30 a.m., he went straight to his room. He said, "When I wake up, Daddy will be here."

About 9 the next morning, Lewinsohn went to the morgue at Truman Medical Center and identified his friend Bob Jonas.

A few days later, when Nancy Jonas opened her torn self to share the moments of that awful Friday, she ended two hours of conversation with, "This is one tough lady."

She looked out the window, out to the patio. Lightning, the coal-black kitten, was exhausted and sleeping off three days of being petted too much by the children of the grieving. It was raining.

"Why is it raining?" Nancy said. "It never rains in Kansas in July."

Although the word "police" does not appear in "The Day the Music Stopped," the story has *everything* to do with police reporting. The police must take violence, tragedy and other forms of travail and reduce it to reports and forms that can be processed by the courts. The reporter operating out of police headquarters knows that behind every report may be a Nancy Jonas who hurts and whose life has taken an awkward turn. A police story expressed in human terms is always more interesting than a bare statistical report. More importantly, accidents, crimes and natural disasters understood in human terms are more likely to lead to a more careful, more law-abiding, more compassionate society.

When David Hacker talks about writing "The Day the Music Stopped," he emphasizes how the widows took the time and spent the emotional energy to tell him their stories. But the reporter's eye for detail and the writer's ability to weave a story are there. He didn't have to ask Nancy Jonas how hot it was at each hour of the day; he checked the weather reports. He took the trouble to inquire about Lightning the kitten, and to introduce the pet into the story early. He asked about the details of the daily family routine and of the special errands and chores that were done in preparation for the special evening. The brand of cigarettes, the breakfast menu, the make and model of the cars all went into his notebook. But, he emphasizes, letting the subjects tell their stories in their own words was the key to his successful interviews.

As a new reporter on the police beat you have three responsibilities:

- To learn the organization, records, personnel and policies of the law enforcement agencies you are covering.
- To establish yourself in the minds of news sources in these agencies as a diligent, fair-minded reporter committed to accuracy and completeness in every story.
- To establish yourself as an independent professional, willing to weigh all the pros and cons of what information should go in your stories, and also willing to stand up for what you think the public should get.

Spending time at the station houses, getting news and feature stories, and talking to the chief, lieutenants, patrol officers and clerical people will help establish you. Frank explanations of why material was published that was critical of police activities will pay off as time goes by.

As you become experienced on the police beat, you have a responsibility to remain sensitive to the trauma of routine accidents and crimes—sensitive in the way that Hacker was in interviewing and writing about Nancy Jonas. Most importantly you must remain a reporter, a representative of the public, and not a quasi-police officer caught up in the law enforcement profession.

Covering the Courts

If police news stories were the soap operas of the 19th and early 20th centuries, the courtroom was the stage where daily dramas of domestic, neighborhood and commercial conflict were made public, argued and resolved. It still is. Where else do people air their disagreements before

Reporters write stories in the Westchester County, N.Y., courthouse press room during the trial of Jean Harris. (AP/Wide World Photos)

the public, with most of what is done and said immediately available to the media? The courts remain a fertile setting for interesting and important news.

If you have never attended a trial, try to do so. You will see a judge keep lawyers for two opposing sides in line. You will see evidence presented and hear testimony as to guilt and innocence, fault and damage with years of people's lives or thousands of dollars hanging on the decision of a jury or the judge. Real money. Real years. Real people.

For the moments of high drama, there are days and weeks of waiting. The good reporter on this beat keeps scrutinizing the records of all the different courts. On a given day, a reporter may see a suit filed that may delay construction of a new shopping mall, a criminal case with high interest postponed for a month because the defense attorney's wife is ill, and a prominent citizen pleading guilty to a reduced charge just before the end of the day, hoping all the reporters have gone home early. But nothing gets past our good reporter because he or she knows how the courts operate, talks regularly with judges, lawyers, bailiffs and clerks, and has a workable knowledge of criminal and civil law.

Types of Court Systems

Note those two words: criminal and civil. Where two individuals or organizations are in disagreement, a civil suit may result, particularly if one or both can show some financial damage. If a law may have been broken, a criminal proceeding often begins, with the state or federal government charging a person, persons or organization with the violation. The court is there to make sure both parties are dealt with according to the law and impartially.

Two court systems exist in the United States: state courts and federal courts. In general, federal courts try those accused of violating federal laws. They also try civil cases in some circumstances. State courts (including municipal and county courts) handle everything else.

Federal judges are appointed by the president of the United States and hold office for life. The method of selecting state court judges varies. In some states judges are elected and in others they are appointed. In some states the voters determine whether appointed judges are retained. Usually, judges are appointed from a list prepared by members of the bar. Judges want to maintain good relations with their colleagues in the legal profession and behave in the patterns learned in law school and private practice. An elected judge is likely to maintain a popular image with the voters and often has a less disciplined courtroom than an appointed judge. All these considerations affect how reporters and photographers are allowed to cover court cases. In general, federal courts have more rigid rules of conduct than state courts.

HINTS FROM A VETERAN COURT REPORTER

The day begins at 8 a.m. in a breakfast restaurant shop near the Metro Justice Building in Miami. Judges, lawyers, and court personnel are talking shop and providing tips about what's likely to happen in court.

The day may end near midnight if a jury, deliberating behind closed doors, returns a late-night verdict that will be front-page news in the next day's paper.

The pace in Miami's criminal courts is frantic, frustrating, and filled with excitement. In a 12-month period, 20 Circuit Court judges review more than 35,000 felony cases involving crimes that range from car theft to murder. Other judges are assigned to nearly 500,000 traffic court and misdemeanor cases.

Here are a few suggestions for breaking into the courthouse beat:

1) Learn the in's and out's of the court clerk's office, which is where court documents are filed. Many court offices now have computers to keep track of cases. Court files are generally open for public inspection. The files often contain background information about criminal defendants, witness lists, and pre-trial motions.

2) Study the court system by tracking several cases during the pre-trial process. Many cases never go to trial but end with plea bargains to reduced charges during pre-trial hearings.

3) Keep a calendar. Note the dates when important cases are scheduled for hearings and trials, the names of attorneys in the cases, and the assigned judge. If possible, review the court file a day before hearings are scheduled. The file may provide information for an advance story.

4) Arrive early for hearings and trials. Lawyers, and even witnesses, may have time before court begins to discuss what's about to happen.

5) Identify the "movers and shakers" in the local court system. The presence of a prominent attorney or a chief prosecutor in court, or in a meeting with a judge, often signals that something newsworthy is happening.

6) Ask questions. Listen to the answers. Remember that there are two sides in most court cases. A reputation for fairness, by presenting both sides, and accuracy open doors.

7) Watch for trend and even statistics-type stories. What's the average fine a speeder pays? Are some judges dismissing more cases than others? The courthouse computer often can provide the answers.

8) Set up a filing system. Notes or documents from one hearing may be important for a follow-up story months later.

Al Messerschmidt,
The Miami Herald

In each of the court systems, there are levels of courts. Less serious crimes or *misdemeanors*—such as traffic violations, drunkenness, petty theft and disturbing the peace—and small claims civil suits may be tried before a magistrate (who does not have to be a lawyer) without a jury. These courts may be named "magistrates" courts or "justice of the peace" courts. Often the defendant will not have a lawyer. No one keeps a transcript of the testimony, and the magistrate determines guilt or innocence. In some jurisdictions, on the other hand, even the most minor case is tried before a judge in a courtroom and a transcript is kept. In either case, decisions may be appealed to the next court level, the court of record.

The court of record has different names in different states: district court, circuit court, even supreme court. Whatever its name, it is a court where evidence is presented, testimony is heard and the law is explained. A stenographer, called a court reporter, records the proceedings. That's why it is called the court of record. Often a jury—most often 12 persons selected from the citizenry of the judicial district in which the case is heard—decides which side wins the case. Juries may also determine the sentence or damages in a case, though in some states the judge makes those decisions. Serious criminal charges, *felonies*, are tried at the court of record level. In the federal system, the court of record is the U.S. District Court.

If a defendant in a criminal trial or either party in a civil suit believes the law has been misinterpreted, the verdict in the case can be appealed. The federal system and most states have two levels of courts to handle appeals. In many states, the first level is called the court of appeal, and the second level is the supreme court. In the federal system, the first level is the U.S. Court of Appeal, which is divided into 11 circuit courts; the U.S. Supreme Court is the highest court of appeal. In both the state and federal courts, the appeals courts do not rehear testimony. The judges or justices examine the record, study briefs and hear oral arguments by the attorneys for the parties. The appeals court may decline to hear the case, send it back for a new trial, overturn the lower court decision or uphold the decision.

When an interpretation of the Constitution of the United States is involved, appeals from federal or state courts may go all the way to the U.S. Supreme Court. Its nine justices are appointed for life. The supreme courts of the states, as well as the U.S. Supreme Court, have administrative responsibilities for the court systems in their jurisdictions, that is, they set policies for how the courts will operate.

As is the case with law enforcement agencies, a variety of specialized courts, or quasi-courts, exist. Courts-martial, made up of military officers, determine guilt or innocence under the Uniform Code of Military Justice. Tax courts handle cases involving the Internal Revenue Service. There are others. In addition, in high-population jurisdictions, the courts of record may have specialized responsibilities. Some judges may hear only criminal cases, others only juvenile cases, and so on.

Courts are involved with the lives of people and the conduct of business in many ways. The cases they hear may involve divorce and domestic relations, damage suits, probate and administration of estates, guardianships, conservatorships, care of the mentally ill, juvenile matters and all kinds of criminal actions from murder to violation of the antitrust laws. Records of domestic relations cases, particularly where children or juveniles are concerned, are often unavailable to the public. Almost all other records are open to the public—and available to reporters.

The rationale for open courts is embedded in the foundations of democracy. Impartiality and justice are protected when the officers of the court, the witnesses and others must carry out their responsibilities under public scrutiny. The concepts of habeas corpus (where the state must "produce the body" of the accused and tell him or her what the accusation is), of the accused being allowed to confront his or her accusers, of a fair and speedy trial, and of a jury of one's peers are all safeguards to the justice system. The alternative is the "Star Chamber" (named after a secret court in Britain with the same title), where accusation, trial and verdict are carried out in secret. Good coverage of the courts results in a better informed public and a fairer court system. As the representatives of the public, reporters sometimes become participants in court cases when attorneys try to close proceedings to the public. The Associated Press Stylebook includes a motion that reporters are able to bring to the attention of the court to prevent or delay court hearings behind closed doors.

A Criminal Case Step by Step

A reporter just beginning to cover the courts needs to know what happens step-by-step when a person is accused of a crime. Let's use a hypothetical case to explain how you might follow this process as a reporter. Remember as you read the example, though, that state court procedures vary some by jurisdiction.

Professor Jones, who is on sabbatical while writing a textbook, is discovered in the apartment of his graduate teaching assistant, Mary Smith, by Smith and her boyfriend, Tom Brown. The door has been broken open, Jones is taking money from a desk drawer and Smith's stereo components have been put in a box and placed outside the door. Brown tries to keep Jones from leaving the apartment, but Jones hits him, breaking his jaw, and runs away. Smith calls the police, who go to Jones' home and take him into custody.

Your examination of the police records shows that Jones has been charged with breaking and entering, grand theft, and assault and battery. You write a story for the college newspaper describing what happened at the apartment without naming Jones and then stating that Jones faces the charges in connection with the incident. You have been able to talk to the two students, but not to the professor, who has an attorney and will not talk to reporters.

A preliminary hearing and arraignment bring Jones before a magistrate to hear the charges (sometimes only one proceeding is used). The magistrate questions police, witnesses and a lawyer from the county attorney's office to see if enough evidence exists to "bind the prisoner" over to the grand jury. Remember that no record of the testimony is taken during an arraignment, so be sure to take careful notes if you are going to report what was said. The magistrate decides there is adequate evidence and sets bond so that Jones can get out of jail. If you think it is newsworthy, you report the amount of bond and other information from the hearing. In this case, the bond is pretty high because the charges now include attempted murder—Brown suffered a skull fracture and is still hospitalized.

Jones' case then appears before the grand jury. A grand jury is composed of citizens of the judicial district and is convened in each district on a regular schedule to consider felonies. It meets in secret to protect the accused. (In some states, Jones' case might be sent to another court with jurisdiction over felonies.) As the state's prosecutor, the county attorney presents the evidence. The accused and his or her attorney are not present nor is a judge. At the end of its considerations, the grand jury presents to the presiding judge a report which lists cases that have been *no-billed*, that is, the charges have been dropped, and those for which a bill of indictment has been issued. Jones is indicted.

He is arraigned again and a new bond and a trial date are set. The trial date can be delayed on motion of the prosecutor or Jones' attorney for good cause. Jones could plead guilty at this time and at other times during the case if he chose and, after a hearing, receive a sentence. He chooses not to.

On the day the trial begins, a panel of prospective jurors is assembled in court. Jones, his attorney, the prosecutor, the court reporter, news

A man charged with murder stands before a Florida judge during a pre-trial hearing in West Palm Beach. (AP/Wide World Photos)

reporters and members of the public are also present. As the judge enters, the bailiff—an officer who sees that things are done in good order and swears in witnesses—asks everyone to rise. After all are seated, the charges are read and the defendant pleads not guilty, prosecuting and defense attorneys ask prospective jurors questions that are intended to assure that they are impartial and capable of interpreting the law. Both sides may ask that prospects be rejected for cause. In addition, each is allowed some peremptory challenges, whereby they may reject a certain number of prospects without giving a reason. Eventually 12 jurors are seated.

The prosecuting attorney and Jones' defense attorney make opening statements in which they tell the jury what they expect to prove. The prosecution says it will show that Jones deliberately committed the alleged crimes and should be convicted. The defense says it will show that Jones was the victim of a mental breakdown, that he was incompetent at the time the crime occurred and that he should not be convicted.

The prosecution then presents its case. Evidence includes items taken from the apartment and found on Jones' person when he was arrested. Testimony includes the statements of Smith, Brown and the police. Jones' attorney cross-examines them and questions them closely about Jones' behavior. Smith says Jones was erratic. At times he was very affectionate toward her; at other times he was belligerent, but never abusive. At the end of the day the prosecution rests its case. The jury is sent home for the night and forbidden to discuss the case or read, watch or listen to news stories about it.

In that day's story, you indicate what the lawyers said they intended to prove, describe the items placed in evidence and quote the testimony. You also describe Jones' behavior as he sat beside his lawyer—morose and almost as if he were not listening.

The next day, the defense brings a psychiatrist, colleagues and Jones' wife to the stand. The psychiatrist says Jones is showing schizophrenic tendencies, Mrs. Jones says her husband has been despondent about his progress on his book. His colleagues say he has been behaving oddly. On cross-examination, none of the witnesses go so far as to say Jones is insane or that he does not know the difference between right and wrong.

Early in the afternoon the defense rests. Prosecution and defense make closing statements in which they say they have proved their points and ask for a jury verdict in their favor. The judge now instructs jurors as to the law in the case. They are sent into a jury room to deliberate guilt or lack of it. In a room near the courtroom, you write your account of the day in court and, using your portable terminal, transmit it by telephone to your newspaper. Early in the evening, the defense attorney asks the judge to bring the jury back in because he has new evidence. The judge calls him to the bench; they discuss the matter so no one can hear and the judge rejects the motion. The jury returns to the courtroom. The foreman tells the judge the jury has reached a verdict of guilty. The judge sets a hearing for sentencing for the next morning. You update your story.

The next day, Jones is sentenced to five years in prison and the sentence is suspended. You think your account of the sentencing will end this story, which has been going on for three months, but it doesn't. Jones appeals. The new evidence his attorney had wanted to present was a doctor's suspicion that Jones had a brain tumor. The appeals court grants Jones a new trial. Your story on this development includes the facts that Jones has undergone surgery, a tumor has been removed and the prosecuting attorney says he will not prosecute again. Jones is free, though he may still face a civil suit for damages for the injury Brown suffered.

This hypothetical case is far from typical, but it does give you some idea of the steps involved in a police investigation and a court case. To be responsible to the public, to the courts and to the accused, a reporter must be commited to following a case from beginning to end.

From the hypothetical example perhaps you have guessed who some of the best sources in court cases might be. Talk to the court clerk about scheduling of court activities, filing of court papers and disposition of routine cases. The judge or the judge's administrative assistant can give you details on such things as court decorum, the length of recesses and the court day, and the time the prosecution or defense is expected to rest. The court reporter may be willing to give you exact words of testimony, or you may need to pay a typing fee to get them. Often the bailiff can tell you where certain people can be found and exactly when to expect court to open. The principals in a case and their attorneys are prime news sources, as are witnesses. Even a member of a grand jury may be a source. The law usually forbids grand jury members from disclosing testimony, but reporters are not forbidden to talk to them or any other persons.

The more you can learn about the law and about the courts in the state or states in which you work, the better job of reporting you can do. Remember that you are neither judge, lawyer nor jury. You are the eyes and ears of those members of the public who want and need to know what happens in the courts.

Covering fires, accidents, crimes and court cases is interesting and rewarding. Every reporter should experience it. However, as a reporter gains maturity through experience, meatier areas of coverage often prove attractive, and news executives seek out mature reporters to cover these areas. Government reporting, taken up in the next chapter, is one such area.

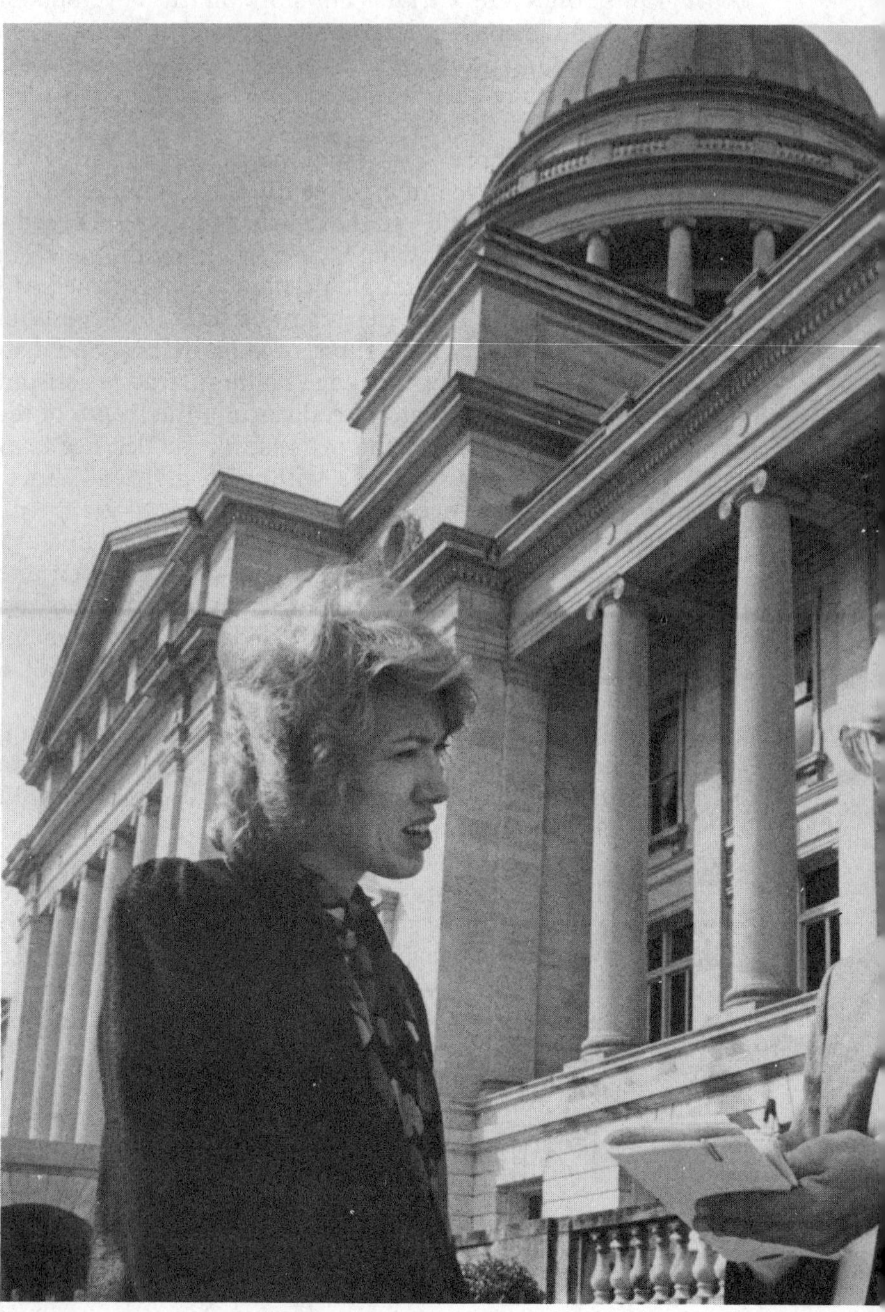

CHAPTER 9

Government Reporting

Local Government
State Government
Excellence in State Government Reporting
National Government
Government Reporting Tips

Courts and law enforcement agencies are a part of government, but only a part. The philosophy of government in the United States holds to a concept called "separation of powers," which works in two ways. First, there is a separation of responsibilities. The legislatures enact the law. The administrations, including the president, governors, mayors and city and county managers, carry out the law and oversee law enforcement agencies. The courts interpret the law.

Separation of powers works in a second way. The U.S. Constitution delegates some responsibilities to the federal government and others to the states. The states leave some things to counties and cities and to independent entities like school districts. Within its legal framework, each governmental body operates independently, although smaller units, such as cities or school districts, often look to larger units, such as the federal and state governments, for financial assistance. Every governmental unit of any size has departments, agencies, commissions and advisory groups, all of which are busy with their own concerns.

Reporters covering government in a democracy have a tremendous responsibility. In every modern society the mass media are a link between government and the governed. In a democracy the importance of the link is magnified because the governed elect the government. Reporters must learn for themselves how the government in their locales operate and then they must keep up with what is going on. They represent the governed in gathering and disseminating the information needed for responsible citizenship.

Incidentally, reporters play another important role—government officials and employees use reporters' stories to keep up with what all the other government people are doing. It has been said that officials and staff members would be paralyzed if they did not have the mass media.

Government and politics are two favorite beats for reporters. They are central to making our society work, and that is probably why reporters find it rewarding to cover them.

Local Government

The basic governmental unit is the municipality. New York City is the nation's largest municipality and sprawls over five counties. Its police force is as large as some nations' armies. New York City provides basic governmental services to almost 10 million persons. Some municipalities serve only a thousand or two. Whether big or small, municipal government involves enacting laws and setting policies and then enforcing the laws and carrying out the policies.

County government is synonymous with rural government to many, a view that falls short of the truth. As municipalities have grown, they have at times joined with counties to combine governmental functions.

Chapter opening photo: Scott Van Laningham of the Arkansas Gazette interviews the governor's press secretary. (Photo by Art Meripol, the Arkansas Gazette)

Furthermore, many counties operate with as modern and efficient governments as do cities. Rural areas depend on county governments for the same kinds of services and governance that cities provide urban dwellers.

Municipal Board, Commission or Council

Cities call their policy-making and law-making agencies the board of aldermen, the city commission or the city council. No matter what the policy-making board is called, its presiding officer usually has the title of mayor. The mayor may also head the executive branch of city government but not always. The members of the city council hear reports from departments, hire and fire department heads, make decisions about the financial budget, decide which companies get franchises for such things as electric service and cable television, enact traffic laws, determine the level of taxation, call bond elections, consider zoning and building code changes and do many other things.

They meet at a regular time and place. The public is eligible to attend and to examine all the pertinent documents. They may also call special meetings. Many states now guarantee the openness of government with freedom of information laws, which include open meetings laws and open records laws. You have already read about these laws in Chapter 6.

The open meetings law may require that an agenda be released prior to a meeting. An agenda gives you material for a brief story on what topics the meeting will cover; more importantly, you can ask questions beforehand of council members, other officials and staff members about the topics on the agenda—and why a particular issue will not be considered. You should know a lot about what will happen at a meeting of the city council or any of its boards before going to cover it.

At the meeting, you should take notes on everything—an inconsequential item may suddenly become controversial. Expect to ask a lot of questions of the council members and others after the meeting to clarify and expand on anything you don't understand. Consult the records when needed. A typical meeting may last several hours and cover a half-dozen diverse topics. You are constantly weighing them for what is most interesting and important to your audience. You may have two or three stories, and you may have to press your editor for enough space to get everything to the public that needs to be told. That is part of your job. Remember, if an action is taken that will cost all or most of your audience some money or that will change the way they live every day, that is news.

Freedom of information laws prevent public bodies from holding secret sessions, except for matters listed in the law, such as discussion of personnel. Do not hesitate to ask one or more persons who attended closed sessions what happened. An informative story may result, you may get background information you can develop into a story later or you may discover that the council was discussing things it was not supposed to discuss in secret. You or your boss can call this to the attention of the council or of the public.

The government beat also provides stories when the city council is not meeting. These originate in the commissions and the various departments.

Other Boards and Commissions

The city council may farm out some of its duties to boards and commissions. The zoning board, for example, considers requests for construction to see if they match the kinds of structures and uses prescribed in the city's zoning ordinance. A person may not build a chicken processing plant next to a residential area, for example, even though society needs both. The planning commission takes a broader view, looking to the future. It considers changes in zoning laws, annexations and upgrading streets and utilities. The parks and recreation commission oversees the property, staff and programs of zoos, playgrounds, beaches, parks and other municipal recreational areas. Some boards may be almost autonomous, as long as they stay within their budgets; others may be advisory only, with the city council accepting, revising or rejecting recommendations. Covering boards and commissions puts more meetings on the government reporter's calendar.

Mayor or City Manager

If the city's chief executive is an elected official, he or she probably has the title of mayor. If the post is appointive, the title is usually city manager. In either case, this person is a vital source of news. He or she has the ultimate responsibility for the smooth operation of city government and often plays a key role in policy making, even if only in an advisory capacity.

The city manager's office usually handles the city government's public relations efforts. The reporter is the conduit to the public for many things the city manager and other officials want to get to the public; the city manager has the answers to many of the questions you have about municipal affairs. The public is the chief beneficiary of this symbiotic relationship.

City Attorney

Every governmental body needs legal advice to determine its powers and boundaries. The city attorney provides legal advice to the city council and city manager. If someone says that the city is doing something it shouldn't be doing or should be doing something it isn't, the city attorney is a good person for the reporter to consult.

Other City Officials

Reporters visit the offices of other city officials, learning how records are kept and what are appropriate times to interview the official. Stories often appear originating from the following offices:

TAX ASSESSOR

Governments raise money to pay for their administration and services by taxing the public and charging fees for services. The tax assessor has a key role in this process as the officer who decides how much each item of taxable property is worth for tax purposes. The assessed evaluation is then multiplied by the tax rate and the property owner gets a bill for the resulting amount. An increase or decrease in a city's property assessments is not only an indication of the revenue the city may expect but also an indicator of its economic growth or the lack of it. A board of equity, or similarly named group, may hear appeals from property owners who think they have been assessed unfairly.

TAX COLLECTOR

This official sends out tax notices, receives tax payments and reports on delinquent taxpayers. The collector's records show who has paid and how much. Interesting stories can often be written about who has not been taxed.

BUDGET DIRECTOR

The budget is the city's plan for receiving and disbursing funds in an orderly manner. The budget director prepares budgets for future years and keeps an eye on how receipts and disbursements are going during the current year.

TREASURER

The treasurer is the city's bookkeeper. He or she makes bank deposits and writes checks. An auditor checks the books from time to time.

DIRECTOR OF PUBLIC WORKS

Potholes have to be filled, water meters have to be read and sidewalks have to be built. The director of public works oversees all such city services. In a big city, these services may be subdivided under such titles as director of sanitation and director of public utilities.

CLERK

City and county clerks record everything from marriage licenses to property transfers and issue a variety of licenses and permits. They oversee elections in their jurisdictions. In some cities, they may keep the minutes of the city council or county commission.

INSPECTORS

Municipalities employ inspectors in several departments to protect the health of citizens and enforce building codes and other regulations. Inspectors often find themselves in the news. Following the 1981 Kansas City hotel sky walk tragedy, the Kansas City Star and Times looked at the record of inspections at the building site of the new hotel and in an editorial were critical of what they found.

Sometime later, the Star looked into how building inspectors used their on-duty time and reported that inspectors were falsifying their work reports, saying they were inspecting buildings when they were taking extended coffee and lunch breaks or while they were at home or in bars. On Jan. 30, 1983, the Star published the following story by Richard Johnson and David Hayes under a banner headline on page 1. Read the following abridged version of their story to learn how innocuous city employees sometimes are part of a major story.

City's Inspectors Lie, Cheat on Jobs

By **Richard M. Johnson** and **David Hayes**
© 1983 The Kansas City Star Company

PULITZER PRIZE WINNER

Many city inspectors responsible for ensuring the safety of buildings in Kansas City regularly lie about their working hours, loaf at home or in bars and restaurants when they are supposed to be on the job and steal tax money by falsifying work and mileage records, a two-month investigation shows.

The inspectors' dawdling and their falsifying of daily mileage and time sheets were documented during a surveillance and records check conducted by the Kansas City Times and the Kansas City Star, which lasted from late November to last week.

During the probe reporters observed 18 of the city's 46 code inspectors from the Public Works Department . . .

None of the inspectors followed was found to be honestly reporting the work he did. Instead, each was found to have falsified his work sheets to inflate the amount of time spent checking construction sites for compliance with city codes. . . .

Kansas City has been the site of two of the worst structual failures in the nation's history—the collapse of the Kemper Arena roof in 1979 and the collapse of the Hyatt sky walks in 1981. . . . The reporters found that all but one of the inspectors observed spent time in restaurants or bars, repaired their cars or simply went home when they were supposed to be working. . . .

Some of the inspectors also were observed running personal errands or strolling through stores at shopping malls. . . .

And many of the inspections, when actually made, took only two to three minutes, even though several inspectors reported to the city that the checks took up to 10 times as long. In some cases the city employees reported conducting inspections when they merely drove by the construction site. . . .

Discrepancies occurred regularly on the time sheets of the eight general inspectors on whom the newspapers' investigation focused—even though each record was signed with an affirmation: "I hereby certify that the information given above is true and correct." Under Missouri law, falsifying a public record can be a misdemeanor. . . .

William Turner, inspection superintendent, said Friday that the drive-by checks were an inadequate way to make inspections. He also said his division does not tolerate early departures from work or falsification of records.

"We feel it is very important for (the time sheets) to be filled out accurately," Mr. Turner said, "and in fact they must be filled out accurately."...

Many inspectors refused to comment or shed light on their observed work habits. A few attempted to explain away the discrepancies on their work records and others acknowledged they often stopped work early or lied on their time sheets. One inspector, for example, called the time record he routinely falsified a "lie sheet."

Myron Calkins, city public works director, said Friday that the newspapers' observation of the inspectors was "a good example of the private sector working with the public sector to see that services that are intended to be provided are provided."

He asked if the city could get reporters "to do this on a regular basis."

When asked whether the reporters weren't doing what his supervisors should have been doing—checking on inspectors—Mr. Calkins became visibly angry and said the city couldn't be expected to supervise its inspectors each hour every day.

Mr. Calkins, who at one point in the interview grabbed a reporter's tape recorder and turned it off, said the city would investigate any specific charges and take disciplinary action if appropriate....

Kansas City's problems in its inspection programs are not new. Neither are the city's promises of action to correct those problems. Eight years ago The Kansas City Star published reports that inspectors from the same city division were loafing on the job. At that time the city vowed to act. Officials took steps they said would improve the inspectors' performance.

Then in 1981 the Hyatt Regency sky walks collapsed, leaving 113 persons dead and hundreds injured. It was called the worst building disaster in U.S. history. The Kansas City Times later found that inspectors had reported spending only 18.5 hours inspecting the project during the 28-month construction period.

The collapse of the sky walks was caused by design flaws that violated the Kansas City Building Code, according to the National Bureau of Standards....

Last year City Hall announced a new effort to guarantee the safety of its structures, including a move to beef up the city's building code and to tighten its inspection program.

The investigation of the last two months has revealed the outcome of the effort.

The report of the investigation occupied three and a half pages of the Star's news section, including the top half of the front page. Photographs showed inspectors going into their homes, restaurants and bars when their time sheets said they were inspecting. Time sheets were pictured with the reporters' logs of where the inspectors actually were at the times they listed.

A banner headline in the next day's Kansas City Times read "City suspends inspectors, removes supervisor." Smaller heads read "Angry officials pledge quick action in scandal" and "City spends less on inspections, despite promises."

This story focused on one city service: building inspection. It spans the spectrum of skills, values and knowledge that a reporter must have. These included news value—the editors and reporters knew that the hotel tragedy would linger long in their readers' minds; persistence—the reporters dug out obscure records and dogged the footsteps of the inspectors day after day; fairness—before the story was published the reporters confronted the high officials concerned and the inspectors and included their statements in the story; public service—the story brought action which could reduce unsafe construction practices. It was an expensive story to cover and took lots of hard work, but, according to the newspaper's publisher, it was a story the Star and Times felt it had to do.

State Government

California's population exceeds 20 million. Alaska and Wyoming have fewer than a million citizens. Whatever the size or population of a state, its government serves a broad area and diverse population. (Rhode Island may be the exception.) Conflicting interests pull and tug at the governor and legislature everyday. The state budget is a good example. Annual or bienniel sessions of the legislature usually begin with the governor presenting a budget and a legislative program, which may include new sources of revenue. The governor's political allies in the legislature support this program (usually with some modifications) and other legislators strongly oppose all or parts of the program. Democratic and Republican affiliation often affects who supports what. Conflict is a reality, and it has to be resolved by the end of the session if the state is to continue to operate.

Add the state agencies and institutions with their differing wants and needs. Add the lobbyists and the socialites and all those in or out of office with political ambitions.

The capitol press corps has to keep tabs on all the action and sort out what was proposed, who favored it, who opposed it and why. Then the reporters have to try to explain what all this means for the state and its citizens, socially, politically and economically. Much of local and county government is conducted face-to-face. The distances—geographic and social—are greater between members of the public and state government. Reporters' stories help bridge this gap.

Reporters cover many individuals and organizations in state government. Here are some of the more common newsmakers.

Governor

Depending on his or her support in the legislature, the governor's proposals determine the direction of the state government and influence the economy and institutions of the state. As chief executive, the governor has a role in determining the efficiency of the state agencies. Governors appoint judges and members of boards and commissions. Their terms of office often extend beyond the governor's, giving the governor influence in the state for years to come. The governor often is the most important political figure in the state, sometimes with aspirations for the presidency. Gubernatorial influence on the party is important. Covering these matters is serious business.

A DAY ON THE STATE CAPITOL BEAT

Scott Van Laningham's beat is an entire state, in a sense. Van Laningham is one of three experienced capitol beat reporters for Little Rock's 130,000 circulation Arkansas Gazette—the oldest newspaper west of the Mississippi River. Van Laningham was a city hall reporter for a small northwest Arkansas daily newspaper for six years before he moved to the Gazette as a general assignment reporter. After a year there, he was transferred to the state capitol beat. In an interview, Van Laningham talks about a day on his beat.

The day begins with a 7 a.m. cup of coffee and the morning paper. "If you're not familiar with yesterday's hot topics in Washington, D.C., or at city hall, you can miss today's news at the capitol. Armed at least with a passing knowledge of what the rest of the world is up to, I'm ready to set out in search of what state government is doing for, or to, our readers.

"A full slate of legislative committee meetings is on tap for the morning, but my first meeting isn't until 10 a.m. Arriving at the capitol about 9 a.m. gives me a chance to stop by the press room and check out what the competition was up to yesterday. We didn't get beat on any big or little stories, so there's time to make 'rounds,'" he explains.

"I start with the governor's office and work my way down from there, just checking to see what's on their schedules for today and listening for any tidbits that might lead to a story. Not much here.

"The agenda for the legislative Insurance and Commerce Committee's meeting looks rather routine. Legislators bemoan the high cost of insurance but can't decide what, if anything, they can do about it. It's worth a short piece, but not much more. About midway through the meeting, I notice a couple of lobbyists for one of the state's major utilities in the audience. Nothing on the agenda would appear to pertain directly to the utility, so I figure I'd better see if they'll tell me why they're here. They aren't going to testify but explain that the utility does have an interest in one aspect of the insurance issue. It's worth another couple of paragraphs to the story. Reporting what legislators say and do is the easy part; the more interesting, but often harder-to-get story, is what wasn't said or done.

"The meeting breaks up about 11 a.m. I chase down a couple of legislators for elaboration on some of their remarks and ask—always ask—if there's anything else going on. One offers a tip that, with two phone calls, results in a little piece about an upcoming legislative hearing.

"Our editors have held their morning news meeting, so I check with the city desk to see if anything has been added or subtracted from the capitol schedule for the day. Nothing's changed.

"The state Public Service Commission is one of the state agencies I cover, and a brief break before my next assignment provides time to check the morning's filings. I have to remind myself constantly that the dry, technical pleadings and orders in the PSC's log may be dull reading but can have a more direct impact on our readers than 99 percent of the gubernatorial dictates or legislative hearings. But again, nothing here.

"Next is a luncheon speech by a former governor who wants his old job back. He complains about a lack of leadership by the current governor and cites problems that have made recent headlines in three state agencies. It's pretty standard political rhetoric. I know that the head of one of the state agencies cited was appointed by the man now criticizing the agencies' operations. It's not big news but adds an element to the story.

"It's now about 1:30 p.m. and my first chance to write up the legislative hearing. I send it to the desk, followed shortly by a piece from the tip about the upcoming legislative hearing. By about 3 o'clock the former governor's speech has been moved to the desk, but an editor has a question about the utility's concern on the insurance issue. A quick call to the lobbyist provides the clarification, and I move a revised piece with the additional information back to the desk.

"Just as I'm thinking I might get out of the office at a reasonable hour—perhaps 5 or 6 p.m.—the desk informs me that a wire service has moved a piece out of Mississippi about a utility issue that could have ramifications for Arkansas ratepayers. Phone calls to the major players in a related Arkansas case are required.

"After writing a note to the editors containing a brief description of my contributions to tomorrow's

> paper, it's now 4:30 and time to head back to the PSC for a final check of the day's filings. Again, no news in the filings.
> "I hunt up a PSC staff lawyer for comments about the Mississippi developments and return to the office about 5:30. Only the local angle to the Mississippi developments remains to be written. By a little after 6 p.m., my stories are all in. The three of us who cover the capitol now divide up tomorrow's schedule, discuss today's highlights and get ready to go at it again."

The governor is also one of the glamorous persons in the state. The governor's wardrobe, hobbies, favorite foods, sports preferences, sense of humor or lack of it, health problems, good or bad fortune, travels and daily schedule are all matters of interest to people in the state. Light stories are there if the reporter looks for them. The governor's press secretary makes announcements and answers—or helps the governor dodge—reporters' questions.

Other reporters also are hard at work on this beat and seeking to match or exceed your coverage. Your news organization will subscribe to a wire service, which will also be covering the governor, legislature and state agencies. If you fall behind the wire services on stories your boss expects you to cover, you will promptly get a phone call asking you why. The spotlight is on the state capitol, and if you are covering it, it's on you too.

Legislature

Imagine more than 100 elected representatives living in the state spotlight, most of whom want to get closer to the center of the spotlight, even to the governor's office. They also want to do things for their own districts and, often, to be good public servants. The legislature is a rough and tumble arena of words and votes. Each legislator starts out with his or her own single vote. Some legislators eventually become more influential than others, though, through alliances, political debts, the necessity for compromise and the advantages of seniority.

All of Nebraska's legislators are organized into a single legislative house. The other 49 states each have a senate and a house of representatives, although the names vary. In most states, the lieutenant governor is the titular presiding officer in the senate; the lower house elects a speaker, usually nominated and supported unanimously by the majority party. The speaker's powers of appointment and of controlling the debate on the floor automatically make this post important. Party delegations, usually the Republican and Democratic legislators, have leaders—majority or minority—who seek compromises and strategies to give their delegations maximum strength, and they have sergeants at arms (sometimes called *whips*) who try to keep the members voting the party line. Chairpersons of the standing and ad hoc committees and subcommittees wield strong influence over legislation, for it is in the committees that the details of bills are hammered out and the votes are taken that usually determine whether the full house will act on a bill. Chairpersons decide which bills will be considered first, for example.

Time is almost as important as persuasion and organization in the legislative process. The end of the legislative day or week or session is often hectic as legislators hurry to kill a bill or get one through. The people who determine when each bill is to be brought up for debate and vote, often the ways and means committee, have time as their ally.

Watching and reporting on the legislature at work is often more fascinating than a close athletic contest. The action on and off the floor has all the elements of conflict and personality that a good sports story contains. What the reporter is writing about is much more important, because the actions don't just go into a dusty record book—they determine how people live.

Attorney General

Next to the governor, the attorney general is perhaps the most interesting elected state official because of the varied responsibilities the office has. Lawyers from the attorney general's office act as defense attorneys when the state or its officials are brought before the courts. They act as prosecutors when the state brings action against a corporation, company or individual. At times—when asked for *opinions* on the constitutionality or legality of acts by state, county, municipal or other bodies—the office acts in an advisory capacity. The attorney general may also have investigatory powers that make the office something of a law enforcement agency.

Some seek the office of attorney general as a stepping-stone to a U.S. Senate seat or a chance at the governorship. Young lawyers see a few years as an assistant attorney general as the road to a distinguished legal or political career. They are good sources for a reporter to know.

Secretary of State

This elective office keeps many of the state's records in good order and oversees statewide elections. Its employees are good sources around election time.

Boards and Commissions

Boards and commissions often affect the daily lives of state citizens. The commission that regulates rates and activities of the public utilities, for example, clearly generates news of interest to every citizen in a state. Examples of the agencies headquartered in a capital city are: the board of regents, which oversees state-supported colleges; the education department, which sets standards and disburses state aid to schools; the department of transportation, which builds and maintains highways; and the health department, which assures clean water and other hygienic standards. Pay closest attention to these agencies when their members come from across the state for meetings. Follow up on the boards' requests for studies or reports, which often contain information that makes good stories.

Lobbyists

Almost every commercial, professional, labor, political and social group wants to influence legislation. These associations have offices in the capital city and are sources of many stories outside the usual government beat. Their representatives, or lobbyists, register with the secretary of state and try to influence the legislature's decisions. They often follow legislation of interest to their groups more closely than reporters can and can be good sources if you keep in mind that they are advocates of a special interest group.

Excellence in State Government Reporting

Fred Anklam's story in the Dec. 20, 1982, Clarion-Ledger of Jackson, Miss., (reprinted below) captures the mad rush toward adjournment of a special session. It has a special drama because 25 years earlier both the newspaper and the Mississippi Legislature were advocating closing the public schools rather than integrating white and black pupils in the same schools. This story describes the victory one group of Mississippians, including the governor and The Clarion-Ledger, won over racial prejudice. This story and the editorials and news stories that preceded it won the 1983 Pulitzer Prize for reporting. The story indicates how reform is tied to finances and how give-and-take is an integral part of the legislative process.

Conferees Reach Tentative Accord on Education

By **Fred Anklam Jr.**
The Clarion-Ledger

PULITZER PRIZE WINNER

Tentative agreement on an education package that includes mandated kindergartens and more than $100 million in tax increases from sales and other taxes was reached Sunday night by a House-Senate conference committee.

The six committee members were tight-lipped about details as they emerged shortly after 8 p.m. from the House Education Committee room, where the conferences have been held since Friday afternoon.

A committee member who asked not to be identified said the bill raises better than $100 million in taxes, enough to take care of teacher and state employee pay raises for next year.

The bill begins the reading aide program that places teaching assistants in the first three grades, but delays kindergarten implementation for three years, the member said.

Final committee agreement should come this morning, once a draft of the bill is completed by the legislative staff and signed by the conferees. Because it includes taxes, the bill must be approved by 60 percent of both houses to pass.

The House convenes at 10 a.m. and the Senate at 4 p.m. It was not certain Sunday night if the bill would be ready for House consideration when that body convenes. If the bill is not ready, the House could recess for a few hours, then take it up.

The tax package included with the bill has a built-in repealer that allows the taxes to cease after a few years when the economy is expected to pick up, according to a committee member.

Among the taxes proposed in the House bill was a surcharge on income tax rates, which would have automatically repealed in three years. Conferees wouldn't say if the surcharge is still in the bill.

Sen. Ellis Bodren of Vicksburg, chairman of the Senate Finance Committee, would only say a sales tax is included in the tax package.

"I hope it will be acceptable to the Senate," Bodren said.

The two houses had differed sharply in the tax section, with the House voting for a $91.5-million package of increases in a variety of taxes, including individual and corporate income taxes. The Senate opted for a 1 percent increase in the 5 percent state sales tax to raise $128 million for the state.

Rep. Robert Clark of Ebenezer, the House Education Committee chairman who chaired the conference committee, said conference members were reluctant to discuss details until the bill is in final form and ready for presentation to the House and Senate.

While the bill gives teachers a $1,000 across-the-board pay raise and increases in the supplements for years of experience, a Senate proposal to place teachers in the state insurance program was left out, a committee member said.

The bill apparently retains a new Senate-proposed AAAA pay scale for teachers who have a doctorate and teach in the academic discipline in which they hold their doctorate.

The big snag all along for the conferees appeared to be whether to allow voluntary kindergartens for some school districts beginning next year, or to delay kindergartens for three years to give all districts a chance to build classrooms and make other preparations for them.

The House had approved a proposal giving school districts the option of starting up kindergartens next year but mandating that all districts would have them by 1986. The Senate voted to delay any kindergartens until 1986.

"I'm positive reasonable people are not going to let that difference keep us from achieving the very constructive result we have sought," Gov. William Winter said at midafternoon while waiting in his Capitol office for the negotiations to end. Winter retired to the Governor's Mansion before the agreement was announced.

Winter, who met with the conferees, said he had "made it clear I'm not stuck on particular details of the bill," although he said "the sooner we can implement kindergartens, the better." House Speaker Buddie Newman of Valley Park and Lt. Gov. Brad Dye, who serves as president of the Senate, met with the conferees Sunday evening, about two hours before the agreement was reached.

The House and Senate met briefly Sunday afternoon, then adjourned until today. Sen. Bill Alexander of Cleveland, president pro tempore of the Senate, took the podium during the brief Senate session to complain about editorials in The Clarion-Ledger and editorial cartoons in the Jackson Daily News.

"The Clarion-Ledger wants to tell us how to do it (the education package); how to cross the t's and dot the i's," Alexander said. He complained that editorial cartoons appearing in Friday's Jackson Daily News and the Sunday Clarion-Ledger/Jackson Daily News attacking Bodron "went way beyond the bounds of propriety" by injecting race into the education debate.

Alexander urged other Capitol press members to have a "heart-to-heart" talk with employees of the two newspapers, which he said are practicing "vicious yellow journalism." Alexander received sustained applause from his Senate colleagues after his comments.

Anklam pulled together complex information from a variety of sources for this story. His liberal use of direct, partial and indirect quotations brings the story to life. Note that Anklam did not give sources for some of the information—something that only an experienced beat reporter who knows the subject intimately should attempt. Note also that the story includes criticism of the newspaper, which is required for completeness, fairness and balance.

National Government

Perhaps you may be one of the lucky few to get an internship or summer job that will take you to the national capital to cover the federal government. The legislative, administrative and judicial processes are much the same as those at the state level, but the competition for news, the magnitude of the decisions made and the brightness of the public spotlight all are greatly intensified. Add three to six zeros to every dollar figure you've been used to dealing with at the state level.

Although the competition is greater in Washington, the lode of news to be mined also is vastly greater. People in every community want to know the effects of major legislation, court decisions and administrative actions, and they want to know about the small acts—by national standards—that may have resounding effects locally. If you are covering Washington for your state or region, the congressional delegation from your area will be a primary beat. Your next most important beat will be the governmental agencies that deal with the problems of your region. For example, if you represent the Mountain States, where public lands under the control of the federal government occupy vast areas, you're going to spend a lot of time at the Department of the Interior. If you are from the Midwest, the Plains or areas of the South, the Department of Agriculture will be more important to you.

Even if you do not make it to Washington, the federal agencies and courts in your community are major beats, as are the offices of your senators and representatives. When the member of Congress goes "out to the district," his or her press secretary will get in touch with you because the purpose of the member's visit is to let the voters know they are listened to, and the way to do that is to get on the evening newscast or in the headlines. Be ready with tough questions.

Take a look in the yellow pages of your phone book under United States Government. The offices of each agency do business with members of your audience every day. News organizations in all major cities assign a reporter to the federal beat. Read the national news for stories about agencies that are active where you are. Follow up those stories to learn of the local ramifications. Soon you will have sources who will keep you as busy as Scott Van Laningham.

Government Reporting Tips

Every reporter who covers government spends time and effort determining what is available to be covered, keeping up with when it can be covered and deciding which stories must be covered and which must be given less treatment or ignored. Regular contacts with all the offices involved is the first step. A good appointment calendar in which all upcoming meetings are recorded is essential. You should ask when important votes will be taken and what issues a committee hearing will cover. Check with more than one source on these matters.

Conversations with participants in a committee hearing or legislative debate beforehand or afterwards may be more important than the official business transacted. Arrive early, wait around after adjournment and check with the important sources before writing the story. If you can't be at a hearing, a debate or a session of a board, telephone officials and clerical people who were present and get an early look at the minutes of the meeting if possible. You *can* get a story that way, but it's not the best way.

You have to "think government" as well as "think reporting." While brushing your teeth, try to predict how the vote in a county commissioner's meeting on a millage increase will go, which commissioners will vote for and which against, and why. Check your prediction and write a reaction piece on why things did not go as expected if your prediction proves wrong.

Talk politics and government with your sources. Almost always they are gregarious. Spend time with them and listen. For example, a lunch may provide the atmosphere in which a source has time to explain things in detail or to drop a hint—as opposed to merely answering a direct question.

Usually reporters are highly competitive. Competing news organizations seek to outdo each other on the same stories. This healthy competition keeps the media honest and energetic. But there are ways in which reporters can work together and still remain competitive. For example, they can resist governmental secrecy. If every newspaper and station carries a story about a governmental body or an official hiding something, action to disclose usually is taken. Reporters can create opportunities for fuller disclosure of news about government. Professional groups, such as local chapters of The Society of Professional Journalists, Sigma Delta Chi, can sponsor debates, breakfast background sessions or panel discussions on important issues. Reporters and editors can swap views with news sources and members of their audiences at these sessions.

Collectively, reporters can also resist manipulation by government agencies or officials by recommending ground rules of their own for press conferences, cameras in the courtroom, accompanying officials on trips or releasing information.

Covering government is important and complicated, but there are a number of things you can do to prepare for a career in public affairs reporting. Absorb all the news stories you can on public affairs. Take political science and history courses, especially those dealing with state and local government. Work for an elected official or a government agency or a news medium as an intern. Cover campus and local government for your campus newspaper or radio station.

Think government and think reporting.

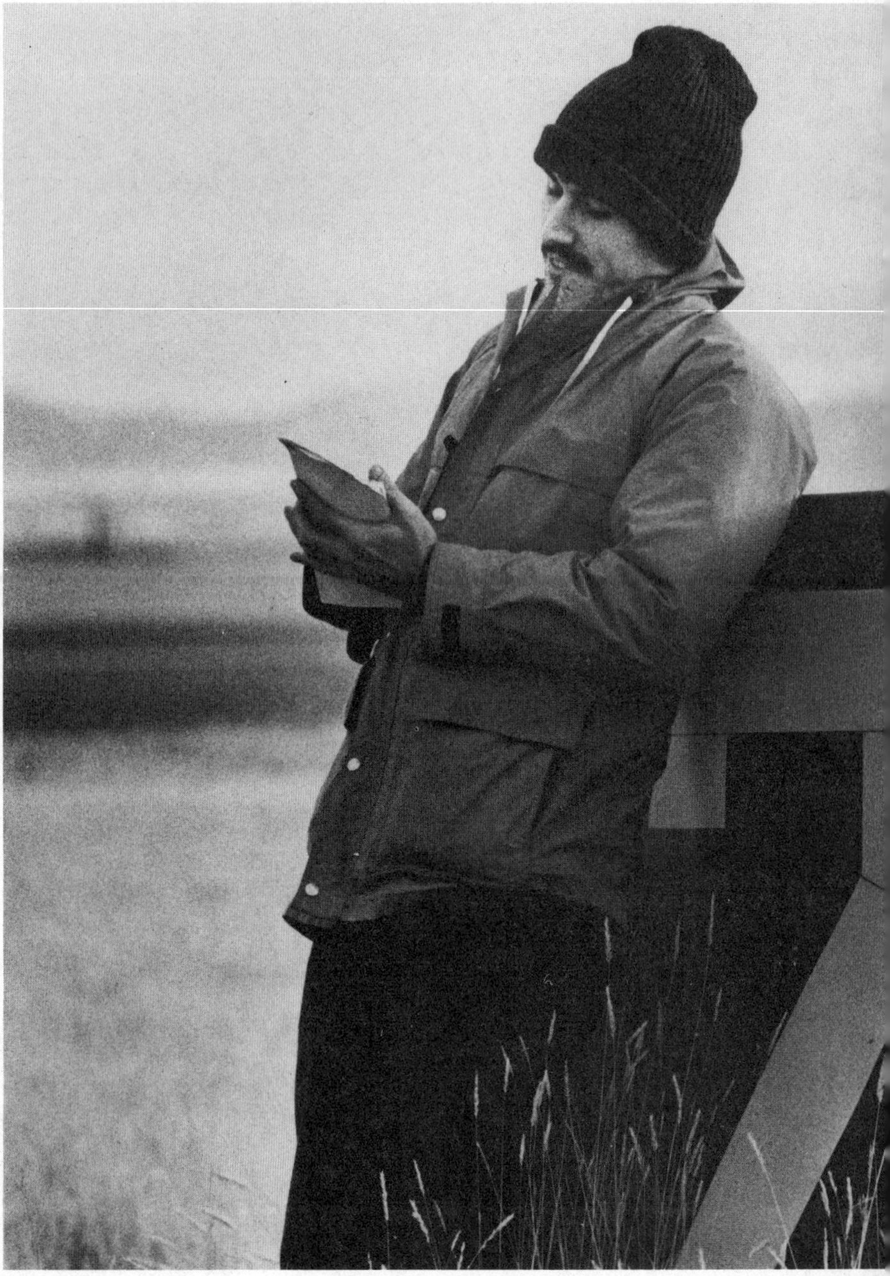

CHAPTER 10

Specialized Reporting

Education Reporting
Business and Economic Reporting
Agricultural Reporting
Consumer Reporting
Science and Medical Reporting
Arts, Entertainment and Sports Reporting
Finding A Specialty

Years ago, in a movie entitled "Thirty," a shy newspaper reporter who specialized in weather and religion asked his boss for the title "Editor of Heaven and Earth." Specialties abound in reporting today. Some of the more common ones include education, science, arts and entertainment, business, agriculture, consumerism and sports. This chapter gives a brief overview of each.

Education Reporting

Education reporting is on an upswing in the media and with the public. Education is a $230 billion a year enterprise in the United States (as expensive as national defense) and it touches the lives of every person for the one or two decades he or she is a student, and then for some more years if that person becomes a parent. Every taxpayer wants to know if tax dollars spent on education are being used efficiently. Covering education means being in the middle of controversy. It also is exciting, filled with the enthusiasm and potential of youth.

For a decade after 1954, education probably was the biggest story in the United States. The federal government became involved in the school systems in 1954 because of the Supreme Court's school desegregation decision. Education had been a local issue, by and large, until that time. In its decision, the court ordered states with separate schools for blacks and whites to end that practice. The order was the catalyst that triggered a peaceful social revolution, the civil rights movement, which ended discriminatory laws in the United States. It resulted in dramatic changes in education as school districts, cities and counties were ordered to adopt desegregation plans that assured blacks and other minorities of being able to go to integrated schools. This process of integration is still underway and is a continuing news story. One of its controversial aspects has been the busing of pupils across cities to achieve integration.

Desegregation had barely gotten underway when, in 1957, the Soviet Union's scientists beat their American counterparts into space with the launching of an unmanned artificial satellite, Sputnik I. Most Americans had considered the Soviets backward in science and technology. Suddenly they were ahead in space research and technology. Sputnik forced a re-evaluation of U.S. education, particularly in the sciences and mathematics. The quality of U.S. education came under fire and under the scrutiny of the public. The newspapers and airways were full of stories about education.

By the 1970s, enthusiasm for education had declined. The baby boom was over. Schools were half empty in the suburbs that mushroomed right after World War II. Busing had changed city schools. They no

---

Chapter opening photo: Reporter Peter Rinearson of The Seattle Times watches crosswind landing tests of a 757 jetliner for his Pulitzer Prize-winning "Making It Fly" series. (Alan Berner/The Seattle Times)

longer were neighborhood social centers. Drugs and crime spilled into the schools. Disorders that accompanied the Vietnam War centered on college campuses. What had been the pride of the nation—its schools and colleges—had lost much of its appeal as a subject of news stories.

In the mid-1980s, publication of a report, "Nation at Risk," by the National Commission on Excellence in Education warned Americans that the educational system was deteriorating at a time of increased competition from abroad and decreased natural resources at home. It warned that the dawning of a technology-based information age made quality education vitally important. The current resurgence of interest in education is based on this new awareness.

Education is a top beat in many newsrooms now. The managing editor of the Louisville Courier Journal said in 1985 that it is the top story in his paper. The Jackson, Miss., Clarion-Ledger won a 1983 Pulitzer Prize for 81 stories it published about inadequacies in Mississippi's educational system. In short, there is a demand for reporters who can cover education.

Covering education usually begins with covering the local school districts. Unlike other countries in which educational policy is set at the national level, in the United States the local school superintendents and school boards still determine the quality of education in a community. The superintendent is the person who is in a position to insure that quality, if he or she has the confidence and support of the district's school board and its voters. The board hires the superintendent and must approve of his or her policies or modify them. School funds come from state aid, property taxes in the district, and federal sources. The

---

HINTS FROM A YOUNG EDUCATION REPORTER

Reporting the goings-on in the local schools is an important but not often glamorous newspaper job.

Feature stories about the district's teachers and children are the most widely read and they're fun to write. Keep an eye out for interesting people on the beat. But other facets of the schools are equally as important.

School board decisions, for example, affect everyone, including those who no longer have children in school. Most people are affected by board budgets.

Learn the budget basics. Federal and state aid pay part of a district's bills, but the remainder is made up by the local taxpayer. A new school year may mean an increase in local taxes. Meet the district's financial officer and review the budget. Then translate its effects to the reader in simple terms. For instance, explain that a 7-mill increase in property tax will cause the tax on a $60,000 home to increase $35 a year. If you are unsure how to calculate such examples, ask the financial officer to help you.

Just as important as the budget lingo is the specialized language of teachers and administrators. Translate "educationese" into English. District officials often speak over the heads of readers, and it's up to you to know and explain that SMH means severely multiple handicapped and that the ESL program stands for English as a second language.

Think through the implications of any decision or discussion by the board. Will an increase in enrollment, coupled with a discussion of real estate mean the district will be building a new school in five years? Where are the newly-purchased maps and globes going? Will the predominantly upper-middle class schools get them and the minority-dominated schools receive hand-me-downs?

Translating the cold facts and "educationese" into real effects for parents, children, taxpayers and teachers is the secret to good education writing.

Katherine Weickert
Lawrence (Kans.) World-Journal

board must go to the voters to increase the tax and to get bond issues for new schools and other capital improvements. Thus, covering the superintendent and the board is at the heart of covering education.

But covering school boards is not easy. The news media have trouble covering the numerous school boards that serve their audiences. Also, school board members tend to be the amateurs among politicians, serving for shorter periods, for no pay and sometimes with the attitude that they are doing the community a favor by serving. Sometimes they expect the media to treat them, as well as the teachers and the students, gently. School boards probably avoid the intent of open meetings laws more than any other public body. Reporters must remember, however, that the boards make public policy and spend tax dollars for the most important enterprise of local government. Covering the school board requires the same thoroughness and determination as any of the other branches of government.

A reporter can build confidence with the board president and the superintendent, who prepare agendas for board meetings, by showing an interest before the meetings and by seeking clarifications of actions taken before writing a story about the meeting. The board usually wants good media relations, because the media offer the quickest and least expensive access to the public.

Covering the school board and the superintendent's office is just the beginning of education reporting. In the classrooms and hallways of the schools the reporter discovers how well the policies are working and uncovers many other stories by drawing upon his or her own experience as a student. Schools provide many kinds of education: We all expect school to prepare us for a career—vocational or professional education. School also provides us with a knowledge of the world we live in—liberal arts education. For children, school is a socializing process—lifestyle education. Schools are centers for cultural, athletic and social life—extracurricular activities. To ignore any of these is to miss a lot of good stories. Let's examine the story possibilities in more detail.

- The education reporter can take advantage of a new concept in news. Traditionally news has been event-oriented or crisis-oriented: what happened *today*. Education, on the other hand, depends on an orderly *process* of building knowledge and competency. A new concept of news concerns the revelation of *how to better understand and live our lives*. For example, the Baltimore Sun won a 1985 Pulitzer Prize for a story about a blind 10-year-old black child who has learned how to live a rewarding life. Recall that The Sun also devoted time and energy to cover the most recent discoveries on how the brain works. (See Chapter 5.) Both stories reflect this new concept.
- The education reporter can look at *vocational and professional education* from two viewpoints: success stories in traditional vocational fields and innovative methods of bringing new vocations into the curriculum. Find successful teachers in vocational fields and interview graduates they have taught. To find innovative

methods, follow your senses and listen to what the students are saying. A new smell, a new humming sound or talk about a new use for school computers may be the clue to a story.
- Let students or principals also lead you to the *extraordinary teachers* who can bring Tennyson, the Black Plague or binary mathematics to life. Tell your audience how they do it.
- *Lifestyles* of the young and active seem surrealistic to adults, yet they become the memories these young people live by when they become mature adults. Making some sense out of, or at least accurately describing, these lifestyles is a public service that may bring the generations into touch with each other.
- Perhaps one of the least covered stories in education involves *integration of ethnic and social groups* in our schools. Its success may be the key to a unified nation in the 21st century. It would be difficult to find a bigger journalistic challenge than reporting about socialization in the schools.
- Securing necessary *financial resources* is a measure of the success and public acceptance of educational institutions. Follow the ways these institutions seek and secure funds and how they spend them. You can approach the school funding story from many angles: Follow the public relations effort of showing the needs for renovated and new buildings that precedes any school bond election. Compare the programs offered by rich and poor school districts. Examine teacher salaries in relation to economic indicators and other professions. Examine school budgets for frills and neglect of important programs. The funding story is never-ending—you will no doubt find other issues as well.
- A continuing trend in education is the growth of *non-public schools*. In many parts of the nation, parochial and public schools have long provided a dual system of schools. Religious groups that never before sponsored schools are doing so now, and more nonsectarian private schools are being established. Affluence, urbanization and busing are cited as causes. Covering this trend is a controversial and important story.

In its series of stories on education in Mississippi that won the Pulitzer Prize in 1983, The Clarion-Ledger of Jackson touched almost every aspect of education coverage that has been mentioned. One story in the series, which explains why financial support of public education had suffered, deals with very sensitive social issues in that state. This comprehensive story leans heavily on facts and figures gleaned from public records. It brings life to these figures by telling what teachers, parents and educators think and feel about the school situation. It is an example of how the evolutionary process of education can be made newsworthy.

Desegregation in Mississippi Leaves Public Schools Wanting
Financing, White Children Often Withdrawn From Schools

By **Nancy Weaver**
Clarion-Ledger Staff Writer

PULITZER PRIZE WINNER

In January 1970 when federal courts ordered the immediate desegregation of schools, the Wilkinson County Board of Supervisors quickly slashed the school millage from 19 to 13.75.

Then-Superintendent Bernard Waites took his children out of public school and enrolled them in a private academy hastily set up in a local church. "There was no way I was going to send her (his second-grade daughter) out to a black school with 2,700 black kids," he said.

Wilkinson County schools are now all black and have the lowest millage assessment in Mississippi. Since 1970 supervisors have rejected five requests to increase local support.

What happened in Wilkinson County was typical of most public school districts in predominately black communities.

Between 40,000 and 50,000 whites left public schools in January 1970 when most schools were desegregated, according to Rims Barber, director of Mississippi's Children's Defense Fund.

The number of students attending private schools more than doubled between 1968 and 1971. About 1,000 teachers, mostly white, resigned from 30 Mississippi school districts in January 1970, according to the National Education Association.

In many school districts whites withdrew support—financial and otherwise—from the public schools. Many white public school officials put their kids in private schools.

The white flight created a new dual system of education in some areas of the state—public schools for blacks and private schools for most whites.

"I don't think a school system can survive being all black or all white," said Joseph Travillion, Claiborne County public schools superintendent.

"If you lose the power structure in the public schools, you ain't got nothing," said Lisso Simmons, dean of education at Delta State University in Cleveland.

Before desegregation black schools had less money, inferior facilities, fewer teachers and didn't offer as many courses as white schools.

During the 1961–62 school year, the state spent an average of $140.41 on each student, white and black. But local districts augmented the state funding disproportionately. In Yazoo County an average of $245.55 in local funds was spent on each white student but only $2.92 on each black. In Coahoma County an average of $139.33 was spent on each white student but only $12.74 on each black student.

In often-dilapidated black schools classes averaged 28 students. The average class in a white school numbered 23. There were 2,473 white teachers with graduate degrees, compared with 553 blacks.

During the 1949–50 school year, black teachers earned an average of $711 annually while white teachers averaged $1,806. By the 1961–62 school year the gap had narrowed with white teachers averaging $3,742 annually and black teachers $3,236.

The Jackson public schools offered typing, stenography and shorthand courses in black schools in 1964 but no courses in the use of business machines or bookkeeping. Junior ROTC wasn't offered in black schools and auto mechanics wasn't offered in white schools.

In 1964 in an attempt to voluntarily desegregate, many of the state's public schools adopted freedom-of-choice plans allowing students to attend the school of their choice.

It didn't work. The first school desegregation suit in Mississippi was filed in 1964, but it wasn't until January 1970 that the U.S. Supreme Court insisted the schools be integrated. Eventually federal court desegregation orders were issued to about 75 percent of the state's school districts.

Many counties reacted like Wilkinson County and the schools are still feeling the effects today.

Wilkinson County's 1970 tax reduction forces the district to use revenues from 16th Section land to operate. School superintendent Charles Johnson said he'd rather use that money for equipment or building repairs.

"They wouldn't have cut it in the first place if all the kids were together," he said. Most white students attend private academies or public schools in other counties, Johnson said, even though state law requires children to attend school in the district where they live.

Waites, the former superintendent who now teaches at the all-white Wilkinson County Christian Academy in Woodville, said whites were paying 95 percent of the property taxes in 1970. "They did not want to continue to pay all these taxes and receive no benefit," he said.

"The controlling money of Woodville is supporting this private school," said Louis Gibbs, a black general contractor in Lessley. His youngest child graduated from public school last spring.

Waites acknowledged he had difficulty accepting desegregation of the public schools. "It's the idea of accepting them (blacks) socially," he said. "At times I didn't feel too good walking the halls of these black schools myself."

Also reeling from desegregation is Noxubee County. In a county that is about 60 percent black, the public school system is 99 percent black.

The county schools have been "cheated" of support from the community and the school board said Superintendent Reecy Dickson. "These institutions are just standing. They're more day-care. It's like nobody's going to school," she said.

At the Noxubee County High School in Macon, ceiling tiles dangle over the heads of students in the vocational building. At Wilson Elementary School in Brooksville, plywood has replaced glass in some windows and broom handles are used to close doors in mobile units.

The school district ranked 146th out of the 153 in the amount of local funds spent on schools during the 1980–81 school year, according to the state Department of Education. Local funds accounted for 11 percent of the district's budget, while state funds made up about 64 percent and federal funds about 25 percent.

School board member James C. Avery of Macon said the mobile units at Wilson Elementary School won't be used any more because declining enrollment means all students can use the school building.

But in areas where whites were determined to preserve quality public education, schools survived.

In Leland, school officials worked to keep whites in the public schools when desegregation was ordered in January 1970. The all-white school board reassured parents that quality would be maintained. School board members kept their children in the public schools.

Maurice Brown, a Leland planter who was on the school board from 1956 to 1981, credited leadership by board members and school administrators for keeping about half the estimated 1,000 white students enrolled in public schools prior to desegregation.

"We thought the number of white students in the public schools was going to determine to a large extent the strength of the public schools," Brown said.

To ease parents' fears, the school board adopted team teaching so that every child would have teachers of both races, Brown said.

Vocational education was emphasized and the practice of awarding three types of diplomas—college preparation, vocational proficiency or simply meeting graduation requirements—was discontinued.

The black population of Leland schools has dropped a little with a declining birthrate, said Brown. "Our percentage of whites has climbed a little since 1970," he said.

The Natchez public schools made a similar effort to keep whites enrolled after desegregation. "When you have white students you have white support. You have to have community support to have a good school system," said Claude Porter, superintendent of the Natchez Separate School District.

To ease parents' fears when desegregation was ordered in December 1969, Porter, then principal at an all-black school, gave white parents tours of the schools their children would attend after integration.

About 2,000 white students left the public schools after integration, but about 3,200 remained in the 8,200 student system. During the 1981–82 school year, about 36 percent of the students were white. Adams County is about 51 percent white.

The Adams County Board of Supervisors has set school taxes at 25 mills plus 3 more mills for bonded indebtedness, the highest allowed by state law. Board of Supervisors President Maxie Wallace's children are in the public schools.

In 1981, the desegregation suit against the Jackson Public Schools was dismissed when school officials argued the system was fully integrated. Black parents, who challenged the dismissal, later dropped their appeal, saying they would closely monitor the state's largest school system to ensure progress continued.

The dismissal of the lawsuit marks the beginning of the end to federal court involvement in the day-to-day operations of Mississippi's public schools, said state Superintendent of Education Charles Holladay.

But a group of black parents in Simpson County successfully sought to reopen the federal court desegregation suit against the county schools to solve what they charge are lingering racial problems.

The Rev. Artis Fletcher of Mendenhall, whose children attend the public schools, complained that there has been an erosion of black authority in the schools since desegregation and he's worried that his children won't have black educators as role models.

U.S. District Judge Dan Russell set a trial for this spring to determine whether the schools have violated his 1970 desegregation order.

Simpson County Public School superintendent Bill Smith would not comment on the allegation.

Fletcher and other parents argue that racial discrimination in today's classrooms is indicated by the high percentage of blacks who are disciplined by suspension, placed in special education classes or excluded from classes for gifted students.

Completeness, fairness and balance were crucial in presenting this story. Ask yourself how those qualities were achieved. Note the interesting integration of statistics into the story and the geographic and historical scope of the article. Note also that the end of the story suggests Mississippians haven't heard the last of the issue.

Covering higher education is almost a different beat. Colleges and universities are not tied closely to neighborhoods and their students are adults. Research plays an important role at most colleges and universities. Each institution has a high public profile and must seek resources based on its own needs, reputation and constituency. Interaction of the campus community (students, faculty and administration) with the social, political and economic communities off-campus extends far beyond the local community. The campus is a major cultural center for the region. All these characteristics of colleges and universities make them a good environment for developing substantive and interesting stories.

Covering education requires training itself. The education profession is institutionalized in schools of education. Scan the course listings for those that would prepare you for covering education.

If you become an education reporter, learn who the respected education faculty members are at your local college or university and use them for sources. In addition, the Education Writers Association offers seminars, workshops and publications. Education Week, the Chronicle of Higher Education and the Phi Delta Kappan report on education nationwide and are sources of trends and background.

Business and Economic Reporting

In recent years economic news has taken on new importance. American production no longer dominates world markets. We now are energy dependent and import far more than we export, making the United States a debtor nation. A high national debt and large federal deficits plague us. Every individual and institution now is concerned with how to meet these changes. Economic policy has become the most important political issue. Business and economics are at the top of the news daily. As a result, the demand for business reporters is growing. It is not a popular specialty, however.

It is a sad fact that too few news-oriented media professionals have taken the trouble to learn how our economy works and how businesses are operated successfully. It is sad for two reasons. First, too few news people develop the business skills and background necessary to become publishers and broadcast executives; as a result management of the news media falls into the hands of those lacking skills and background in news reporting. Second, not enough of the best reporters and editors have the knowledge needed to report on or make news decisions about the vital areas of business and the economy. The public is deprived of insight into the enterprises that finance our society. Let's take a look at economics and business from a news point of view.

In the 18th century, Benjamin Franklin, writing under the pen name of Silence Dogood, gave a simplified explanation of why the private enterprise system works. He described farm women living outside the city of Boston who took wool, spun it, dyed it and knitted it into mittens. One farmer, discovering that his family had a surplus of new mittens, took some to market with him and sold them, giving the proceeds to the women in his household. They went to Boston and bought pretty bonnets. The other farm women in the community asked the bonnet wearers how they could afford the finery. Suffice it to say that a cottage mitten industry soon was thriving in the hinterland, and bonnet sales were up in Boston. There were warmer hands in the city and more charming women in the country. Idle time was turned to good use, and so on.

This philosophy of private enterprise proclaims that all benefit when each uses his or her ingenuity and energy to his or her own benefit. It is a philosophy that the U.S. Constitution supports with its protection of private property. Based on this idea, giant business enterprises and vast networks of financial activity have developed and hundreds of new enterprises spring up every week. It has been truthfully said that the business of America is business. The leading business publication, The Wall Street Journal, advertises that it is "the daily chronicle of the American dream."

However, a majority of Americans are not entrepreneurs. They do not understand how business works and their dreams lie elsewhere. Reporters of business and economic news serve the dual function of providing insight to all those outsiders and of keeping business people up-to-date.

Although laws, regulations and licenses abound, individuals or groups are still free to use the resources they have to start a business and offer goods or services in the marketplace. Within the law, each business may operate as it pleases as long as it pays its bills. This private enterprise system is just that—private. Covering business is more difficult than covering government. A business person is free to answer the questions a reporter asks or to remain silent, to show the company records to the reporter or to keep them secret. There is no freedom of information law requiring privately held businesses to divulge their records. Only if a privately held business goes into bankruptcy or is sued by a creditor are its affairs likely to become part of the court record—and thereby available to reporters. In short, it's difficult to cover business.

Note that the term *privately held* was used. Such businesses are those owned by a single person, a family or a group of partners. When a business offers ownership shares to the public, it is *publicly held* and is obligated by law to report its financial condition to its stockholders and the public. Most of the bigger businesses are publicly owned. The reporter has something on the record to start with when doing a story on a publicly owned company. In fact, the daily reports of the American and New York Stock exchanges often serve as a barometer of the activity, growth or stagnation of a company.

Businesses send a lot of messages to the public through the mass media. By advertising, they offer their goods or services to the public, competing with other businesses in terms of price, quality, availability and service. (In the Silence Dogood story, the bonnet-wearers told the other women where they got the finery; that's word-of-mouth advertising.) Advertising revenue pays the bills for the mass media, allowing them to stay in business and be profitable. A mass media business that is strong financially can also be independent. It can resist pressure from a single advertiser or a group of advertisers. It can courageously get and use stories exposing wrongdoing, since it has the resources to staff investigations and to defend libel suits if any develop. The private enterprise system makes a free press work.

However, there can be unfavorable side effects. Advertisers can try to control news content. Most media outlets, though, have no trouble separating the news function from the advertising function. Reporters play a major role in separating advertising from news. They avoid working as publicists or ad copy writers for advertisers and resist efforts to publicize products and services in their stories.

A related problem is more difficult. Can a reporter aggressively pursue possible wrongdoing involving a big advertiser or the company that owns the medium? New York Times columnist Russell Baker raised this question in 1986 in a column on the takeover of RCA (the parent company of the NBC television network) by General Electric. Baker noted that special tax breaks to defense contractors had allowed GE to make $6.5 billion over a three-year period without paying any income tax. He asked if these tax-free profits had given GE the resources to offer $6 billion for RCA. Baker also asked if NBC News staff members would pursue stories about congressmen or candidates who wanted to make "Pentagon profiteers pay income tax."

On a smaller scale, a movie critic who wrote a whimsical column in a small paper "reviewing" the local fast-food outlets got into trouble when he suggested that one advertiser's hamburger was habit-forming though it had no taste at all. He satirically suggested that the advertiser put marijuana or some other substance in the burgers to bring the customers back for more. He had to face the angry advertiser and was told by his editor to restrict his reviews to movies. Advertisers see very little humor in their products.

Businesses, like other institutions, have aggressive public relations programs. They are enthusiastic about their products and services and about the bright people who work for them. Executives want the public to share this enthusiasm. They want to minimize unfavorable news or at least to make sure that their side of the story gets to the public. A major part of what public relations people do is called media relations; they encourage and assist the media in developing stories that will reflect favorably on the business. They also provide the information that their clients or employers are willing to make public about unfavorable matters. You can work comfortably and effectively if you understand this relationship, recognize the public relations professional as an advocate of an institution and preserve your own status as a professional who acts as a proxy for the public.

Reporters covering business live much of their lives with public relations people, but they also need to know and understand chief executive officers, directors, labor leaders, manufacturing workers and clerical staff people. They particularly need to be able to understand financial executives and analysts. Reporting, with its emphasis on writing, attracts many practitioners who do not like numbers or mathematics. They soon realize that reporting is no refuge. Good reporters have a rule of thumb, "look at the money"—where it came from, who controls it and where it goes. That means numbers, math, charts and graphs.

The best means to understanding how a publicly held business operates financially is its annual or quarterly report. The report always contains a balance sheet, which shows its size and how its assets and liabilities are divided, and a profit and loss statement, which shows the revenue brought in, the expenses incurred and what has happened to the profits, if any. These two tables also include last year's figures in each category. Understanding what these two tables reveal will allow you to understand the financial status of privately held companies also, provided that you can get the figures from the company.

Learning how to use these tables is straightforward. Get a booklet that explains financial reports from a financial broker such as Merrill Lynch Pierce Fenner & Smith. Read it and make sure you comprehend all the details. Become familiar with such exotic jargon as debentures, price-earnings ratio and leverage. The broker who gave you the booklet may have time to explain things you don't understand, particularly if you appear to be a potential client. Then apply your new interpretive abilities to some financial reports from corporations. Ferreting out the status of a company can be as absorbing as working crosswords.

Most brokerage firms also can provide you with booklets on the securities markets, which will explain how stocks and bonds are bought and sold. This will make the market quotations in metropolitan newspapers intelligible. Track the stock of some of the companies you have already learned about. You will begin to think in financial terms. If you develop some expertise, you may be able to pay yourself for the time spent by making some profitable investments. This raises an important point. Business and financial reporters face ethical dilemmas: Should they invest on the basis of information they get as reporters? Most definitely they should never use the news columns to influence a security they might be interested in buying or selling.

Covering business is not merely crunching numbers any more than covering sports is spouting batting averages. Like sports, business is people working as teams and people in competition. The people bring business news to life. Take Sam Walton, for instance. He started a discount business in an old building in remote Bentonville, Ark., years ago. By the mid-1980s he was one of the wealthiest men in the nation. He said he did it by establishing discount stores in smaller communities than his competition chose and then moving into the cities where they were after establishing a ring of successful stores around each city. In addition, he said, he had more distribution centers, so that he could restock any item within 24 hours, providing better service to customers than the competition. Although he didn't say it, the tax breaks provided to those establishing new businesses also helped him to success. All this, along with the fact that he still drives his pickup truck around Bentonville and that his company doesn't have a public relations department, makes his story one worth telling.

The business reporter can find success stories like Sam Walton's everywhere. There are stories of new products and services, the people who conceived them, the people who financed their production and the people who figured out how to market them. There are stories about the companies that have survived for a century and the people who started them and have kept them going. Write failure stories, too. More new businesses fail than succeed. Try to tell people why some businesses fail. When an old, established business dies, you may have a major news story. Business people live and think business. They like to talk about their business lives. Get them started talking, and you will probably learn more than they had planned to tell you.

Everyone in your audience has hopes and anxieties about the future regarding money. They want to know what the economy is going to do and what economists are doing to make it—and them—prosper. Every person going into a mass media profession should take at least one economics course and potential business reporters should take courses in accounting, finance, marketing and management. An economics course will help you understand the economists' analyses of what happens in business as well as their economic forecasts. Indexes (indices, the economists sometimes call them) give clues to what has happened in the economy. The Consumer Price Index measures the change in price for a set of consumer goods and helps measure inflation or deflation. Some labor contract wage clauses and retirement benefits are linked to the CPI. The Gross National Product is a measure of goods manufactured. A highly sophisticated index is the Index of Economic

Indicators, sort of an index of indexes, which is used to estimate broad economic trends. You and some economists in your area might relate the indexes based on nationwide data to your local economy with an index. You could call it the Hometown Index.

Business executives know that information is the key to intelligent decisions, and they are willing to spend money to get it. As a result, an amazing array of information related to business and the economy is available. Business reporters who know how to tap into it are ahead of the competition. Start with the Directory of Directories, which will lead you to an association that relates to almost any business interest. If you looked up newspapers, for instance, it would lead you to the American Newspaper Publishers Association, the American Society of Newspaper Editors, your state press association, and similar groups. For basic information on most American businesses, start with Dun and Bradstreet's Million Dollar Directory or the Standard and Poor directories. The United States Government Manual is a directory and handbook that includes the agencies that regulate businesses and report on economic trends. The MIT Press Dictionary of Modern Economics and Munn's Encyclopedia of Banking and Finance will help you understand technical terms and provide background information. The current business reports, produced by the U.S. Bureau of the Census, is one of a number of statistical sources available. Become a reader of business and financial newspapers and magazines: The Wall Street Journal, Barron's, Business Week and others.

The business beat will put you close to the economic engines that run your community and the nation.

Agricultural Reporting

Everyone eats, wears clothes and wants a roof overhead when it rains and snows. Agriculture provides those things. Most of the time since World War II, agricultural products in the Western world have been in surplus, while malnutrition and starvation have continued in the underdeveloped areas. Agriculture has changed from a solar-powered enterprise, where draft animals ate homegrown grass and grain to provide the energy for tilling the soil, to an industry that depends on manufactured tractors, fertilizers and pesticides. One farmer, with the help of all these processed goods and expensive services, can feed, clothe and provide shelter for far more people than his grandfather could, but to do so requires far more cash or credit to pay the operating expenses. The federal government's agricultural programs have added another factor complicating the agricultural picture.

Agricultural reporting is a neglected area. The health and comfort of everyone and the economic well-being of society are closely related to agriculture. Yet people in cities have little understanding of it, because they take it for granted and coverage is sparse. In rural areas it is hampered by the limited resources available to smaller broadcast stations and newspapers. But exciting things are ahead in agriculture, and the mass media have an important role to play in what happens to agriculture.

Genetics and communications will be two key issues in news about agriculture. Scientists are discovering how to alter the characteristics of plants and animals through the manipulation of genes, the biological matter that combines the traits of parents—plant or animal—into the traits of their offspring. Their goal is to breed more productive plants and animals, capable of resisting diseases and parasites, that will provide more usable food and fiber from less water and nutrients. The hazards of unfavorable side effects are great. This is a science, health and economics story that agricultural reporters will cover in the decades to come.

Satellite telemetry and computer analysis of agricultural information promise to take some of the guesswork out of agriculture. Farmers have always been vulnerable to adverse weather, natural catastrophes such as floods and insect invasions, as well as to vagaries of the market place. Now, satellite surveillance of arable land and productive seas is beginning to provide accurate worldwide crop predictions. Weather satellites have improved our weather forecasting ability. We are looking to agricultural economists to analyze this new data more effectively. A new era of agricultural forecasting and planning could be ahead, and the mass media have a role to play in this process.

Agricultural reporting has many facets. It has a seasonal aspect in that you follow the crops from planting to harvest to market. It has a human interest aspect: the farm family with its closeness and its problems, the agricultural scientist seeking better production methods (that frequently backfire). And it has a business aspect: the farm community and farm-related industries thrive or languish along with the farmer.

More than any other industry, agriculture is dispersed geographically and is an enterprise with independent producers at its base. For this traditional independence to continue, the mass media will need to play an important role in keeping farmers informed. The alternative is a vertically structured agricultural industry controlled at every level by large corporations. The corporations will develop their own information and distribute it exclusively to their own producers. This latter trend is underway. In either case, agricultural reporting promises to be lively and changing in the coming decades.

Consumer Reporting

Consumer reporting is the flip side of business reporting. It looks at goods and services from the point of view of the buyer and user. Competition in business results in choices for the consumer. Consumer reporting gives the audience information it wants on how to use discretionary time and money. Sometimes the consumer reporter is the consumer's advocate when services or products do not live up to their publicized standards. The reporter who follows up on consumer complaints builds an audience and builds goodwill with that audience.

Newspaper research indicates two important groups of people want more consumer reporting: the elderly, a growing proportion of the population; and the young, whom the newspapers want to recruit as regular readers. What kind of consumer news interests them? Information on new products and services, continuous monitoring of the marketplace for bargains and values and trends in consumer behavior head the list.

Two pitfalls of consumer reporting are angering advertisers and providing free advertising of goods and services. Legitimate news relating to consumer affairs should reach the audience regardless of how it affects the supplier of the goods or services, even if the supplier is an advertiser—and even if the supplier is not an advertiser. "Legitimate news" is the key to ethical consumer reporting. Should one do features about a local business, or satirical critiques of goods or services? Test the stories by asking if they are newsworthy: how many of the elements of news do they have?

Columns provide two additional avenues for consumer reporting. First, the consumer service column brings in mail or telephone calls and permits the newspaper to lend its influence in support of its readers. Remember a tip on consumer service columns, though: When grievances between a consumer and an institution are involved, do not report to the public until the grievance is resolved. That way the newspaper is not involved directly in the disagreement. Second, the specialty column—about anything from wines to automobiles—permits the reporter with a special interest to write about it, even if he or she usually covers another area of news.

Science and Medical Reporting

Science and medical reporters face a special problem. Scholars, including scientists and physicians, prefer to get the support of their colleagues before they submit their findings or discoveries to public scrutiny. It is good scientific practice, and it reduces the public criticism they might receive from jealous or skeptical fellow scholars. That's why so many news stories about new practices in medicine are attributed to articles in periodicals such as the New England Journal of Medicine, a respected professional publication for doctors and medical researchers. A science reporter may get wind of a breakthrough and learn from the researcher that the possibility of a story does exist. Often the the reporter will not get the story, though, until the researcher "has published." At that point, the researcher and colleagues probably will be happy to explain and discuss the breakthrough.

Reading the leading journals of the discipline will keep a science and health care reporter abreast of the latest developments. Another source for potential stories on scientific discoveries is grant proposals submitted by researchers in the local community. They outline the research goals, the possible results and establish a tentative timetable. To read journals and grant proposals, and talk with scientists, a science reporter needs to know the jargon and the basics of each discipline.

Two tensions often exist between scientists and reporters: the scientist's fear that the reporter will sensationalize the story and the difference between what the scientist considers news and what the reporter considers news.

Scientists can cite long lists of "cancer cure" and "miracle drug" headlines to support their claim that reporters sensationalize scientific research. Part of the problem is in the modes of writing that the two disciplines use. Scientific reports first describe the research plan, then how it was carried out, then what the results were and then the conclusions (usually tentatively). Journalistic writing looks for the lead—the focus of the news, the most important facts—then proceeds to support these facts and far down into the story, if at all, gets to the details of how the facts were arrived at. A careful science writer tries to give the necessary background—not just to placate the source, but to provide perspective for the reader.

Scientists and reporters do not always agree on the newsworthy aspects of a scientific inquiry. Often a scientist works for years to make a small amount of progress in a relatively obscure scientific discipline. A breakthrough may bring the entire discipline into the public eye for the first time in years. The reporter considers the entire body of knowledge news because it hasn't been widely reported. The scientist may think the reporter has missed the point and is not giving the new development enough emphasis. A good reporter can usually strike a happy medium between giving the public an adequate understanding and providing the scientist with adequate recognition.

(Incidentally, "breakthrough" is a sensational term in the view of many scientists.)

The science reporter must have a basic understanding of science, which can be obtained through course work at any college of university. Only with a foundation in the sciences can the reporter begin to understand and communicate with scientists and doctors.

Almost every scientific and medical discovery today is scrutinized carefully as to its impact on the environment or the harmful side effects it may have on persons who use it. Thus, science and medical writers also report on controversies that involve strong ethical and religious beliefs—issues about abortion, fertility enhancement, prolongation of life versus the quality of life, the use of nuclear power plants and the disposal of hazardous wastes.

Arts, Entertainment and Sports Reporting

We are what we think. The arts, entertainment and sports provide us with models of beauty, cleverness and prowess. A gymnast's performance that receives a score of 10 in the Olympics, a sculpture halfway around the world and a comedian's impression of the current political scene. All these appeal to that part of our nature which is not entirely rational; they appeal to our esthetics. The mass media take these things out of the arena, the museum and the auditorium and bring comments about them and audio, video or print replicas of them into living rooms, taverns and dentists' offices. The media expand our exposure to arts, entertainment and sports far beyond what we could ever experience in person.

Covering arts, entertainment and sports requires a different kind of professionalism. The reporter must have an appreciation of the art, entertainment or sport and at the same time must view it with the skepticism of objectivity. Personalities, economics, conflict and tradition are appropriate topics in this kind of reporting.

The news and picture magazines that developed in the first half of this century, became popular because they presented traditional news in succinct and graphic pictorial or prose form. Look, Life, Time and Newsweek graced most coffee tables. In the back of these magazines were photographs of art works and reviews of books, the theater and the other arts. Stories and pictures about the feats, foibles and personality quirks of movie stars, singers, debutantes and the rich lightened the content. A popularization of art and a contribution to the establishment of American popular culture resulted. Public radio and television fill a similar role for the arts today.

What are "the arts"? Painting, sculpture, orchestral and vocal music, drama, musical comedy, opera, ballet, architecture, fiction, non-fiction prose, poetry, motion pictures, television and industrial design are a few. But what about needlework, sandcastles and tatoos? And what is the difference between art and entertainment? Making distinctions with regard to such matters is the ultimate challenge in reporting on the arts—the challenge of being a critic.

Just liking or even appreciating art is not adequate background for reporting on it. One must be a student of the arts, which is a lifelong pursuit. Many reporters and critics center their formal education, travel, home study and social life on the arts. Eventually one acquires a sophisticated background for reporting. As a reporter covering the arts you get paid for living with beauty.

The rewards can include getting to know personally people who are idolized from afar by most of the public. And surrounding the arts are patrons who sacrifice so that the talents of others may bear fruit, dilettantes who pretend to be artists, fans and hangers-on, and snobs who use art as a way to flaunt power, wealth or social status. The reporter who specializes in the arts lives in and reports on a very interesting environment.

The arts environment blends into a community's entertainment environment, and most news organizations combine the two under the title "arts and entertainment." We can characterize entertainment reporting as telling our audience "what's happening that's enjoyable."

Newspapers in particular serve as an entertainment bulletin board for the public. They publish the television listings, a synopsis of each movie playing in town and calendars of what is happening at the clubs, concert halls and theaters. When you write this material, accuracy and completeness are necessary. Members of your audience are going to depend on what you write to determine how they spend their money and their precious leisure time; they don't want any unpleasant surprises.

Your audience is interested in what happens behind the scenes. How do local impresarios discover new talent or lure in established talent? What are the logistics of a major concert, performance or tour? How do the economics of entertainment work in your community—how much will a local audience pay and for what kind of entertainment? Watch for trends and report them.

One word of caution: you aren't a publicity agent. You want to tell your audience what it wants to know, not what the promoters want to advertise. The promoters should pay for their advertisements.

Sports journalists report on those who strive to excell at physical prowess, an activity that is also entertaining to millions.

Newspapers and magazines made professional baseball and the college games of football and basketball into national sports. The great sports writers such as Grantland Rice and the early radio announcers such as Graham McNamee provided vivid accounts of the action. Television has bypassed the journalists, bringing the games directly to the audience. Journalists now analyze and interview, providing additional insights to those who have already watched the competitions.

The sports reporter must address both the person who has seen a sports event and the interested person who did not witness it. The reporter never assumes that everyone knows the score, or even who won, or where and when the event took place. The basic description must be there, even if the reporter is writing about the Super Bowl. Then the reporter provides the analysis and background: Why did one team win? How did the athlete prepare for the world record performance? Can the losing team maintain its competitive spirit?

The best place to begin covering sports is out of the limelight. Covering a minor sport or covering a minor team and league in a major sport allows a beginning sports reporter to establish a perspective on what is required of athletes, what their expectations are and what playing the game means. The added distractions of big money, high pressure recruiting, pack journalism and superstars can come later. By covering some high school sports for a season or two and a semipro baseball team in the summer, a sports writer lives the sport with the athletes.

What are the attributes of most sports stories? Anticipation, participation and retrospection are the three most common. What resources are being used to assure the best possible performance—athletes, training, facilities, coaching, merchandising? What was the nature of the performance—weather, spectator and facility conditions, the unexpected turn of events, the strategies and tactics actually used. What are conditions after the event? What happened—and why and how? What is the relationship to the next event? Most sports reporting revolves around these kinds of questions.

Some sports attract big crowds every day they are played. Others involve solitary performances until the great international games take place. These latter sports are open territory for the enterprising sports writer (or any writer). David Halberstam, renowned for his reporting on the Vietnam War and other national and international news, wrote "The Amateurs," a book about four sculling champions that few people have heard of, and it became a best-seller.

Sports is an imitation of life—life lived between the goal lines, life lived from the opening whistle to the final gun, life with morality spelled out in a rulebook. Many young people learn about life through sports, and through sports reporting. Sports reporting is great preparation for other kinds of reporting, but many sports writers follow the craft "until the One Great Scorer comes to write against your name."

Finding a Specialty

Somewhere in this survey of the more prominent kinds of specialized reporting you may have discovered a specialty that appeals to you—perhaps more than one. Almost any college or university offers courses that would help prepare you for your specialties and help you decide whether you want to pursue them. Internships in a specialty may also be available. The sooner you pursue a specialty, the more quickly you develop marketable expertise in it.

A reporter with a specialty has three characteristics:

- The ability to gather information by interviewing and digging into records and the writing skill to turn the data into news stories.
- A broad knowledge of the world and the audience being addressed, usually acquired through a liberal arts education and the experience of rubbing shoulders with the public.
- One or more specialized fields of knowledge.

Many would-be specialist reporters have the first two attributes but lack the last. Other experts in a narrow field try to be reporters but lack the first two attributes. Specialty reporting requires all three.

Almost every field of human endeavor is more complicated than it was a generation ago. Specialists are needed today to get beneath the surface of the news and explain the *why*s of our existence.

PART 4
Presenting the News in Special Ways

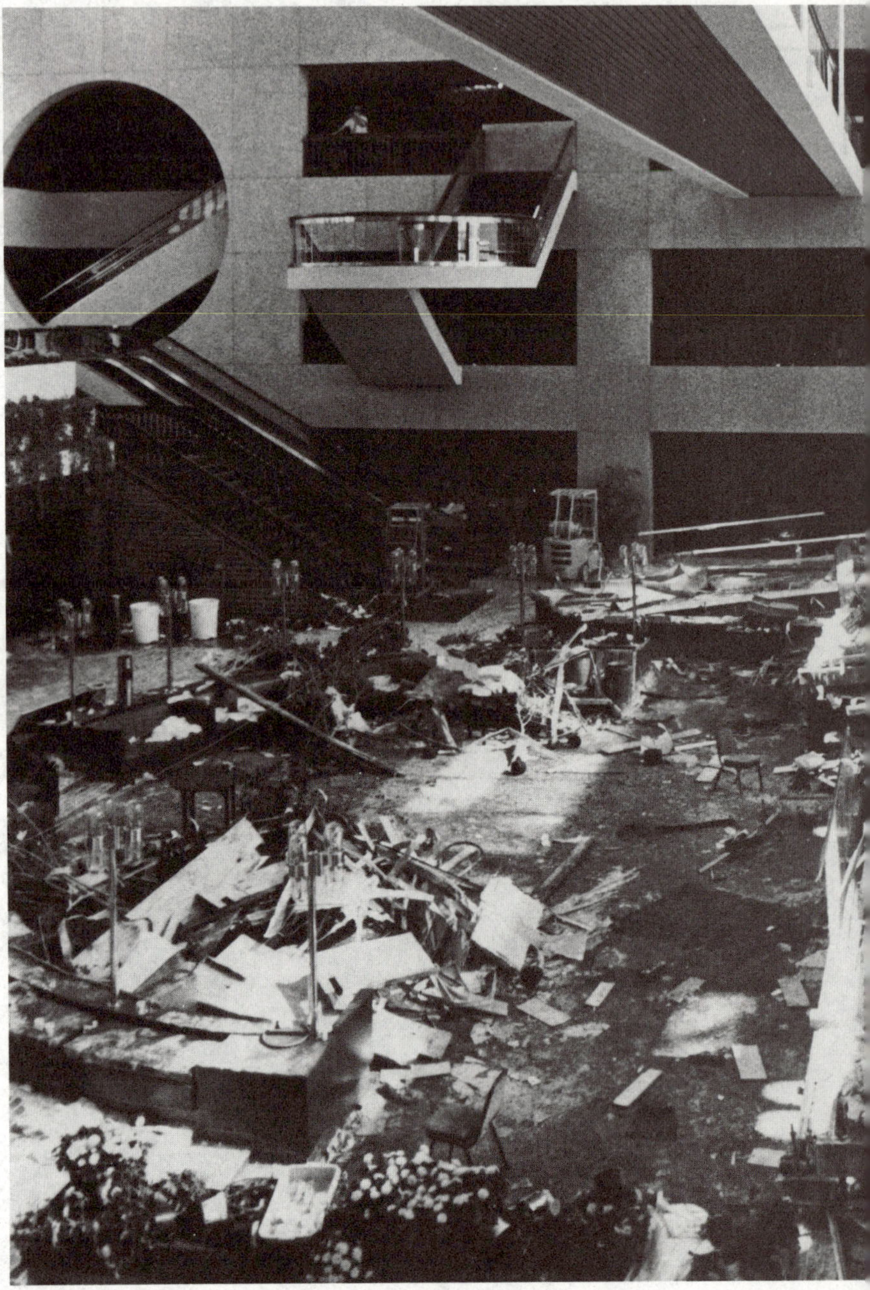

CHAPTER **11**

Interpretive Stories

A New Kind of Reporting
Interpreting the News
In-Depth Interpretive Stories: Interpreting a Disaster
News Analyses
Columns and Editorials
Using Sources
A Pitfall

A New Kind of Reporting

Just after World War II, the report of the Commission on the Freedom of the Press declared that the mass media has the obligation to provide "a truthful, comprehensive, and intelligent account of the day's events in a context which gives them meaning." The Commission was established after the war by a grant from Henry Luce, the publisher of Time and Life magazines, and the Encyclopedia Britannica, to examine the performance of the news media.

The report was roundly criticized by publishers. Presenting news events in "a context which gives them meaning" went against the accepted norms of reporting at that time. In the first half of the 20th century, an editor's refrain was: "Just give me the facts." The idea was that readers would do their own interpreting of the facts. The goal was to be objective, to avoid drawing conclusions from the facts. Editors and publishers did write editorials, which contained the newspaper's official opinions on issues, but that was the only place for interpreting the news.

Reporters had experienced the need to interpret news events before the Commission's report. Many of those covering President Franklin D. Roosevelt's New Deal during the Great Depression of the 1930s were confronted by new programs based on new economic theories. The effort to overcome the ruinous effects of the Depression was the biggest domestic story of the 1930s. Stimulating the economy through government spending went against traditional economic thought. The old technique of quoting economists on both sides of the theoretical fence failed to provide a coherent picture of what was happening.

During this period emerged the public affairs columnist, a bright writer whose essays explain the meaning of the news, particularly political news, under his or her byline. Columns by Walter Lippmann, Roscoe Drummond, Dorothy Thompson, Arthur Krock and others were placed on the editorial page, along with the editorials, letters to the editor and sometimes a political cartoon.

The Commission's recommendation to put the news "in context," however, did not catch on until five years after the Commission issued its report. It took Sen. Joseph McCarthy of Wisconsin to demonstrate to reporters, editors, network news executives and the public the weakness of the "just-give-me-the-facts" school of reporting. McCarthy became the best known senator in the nation by claiming that Communists or Communist sympathizers infested the State Department, the Army and the news media. He would tell reporters at a morning news conference that he would hold a news conference in the afternoon to announce that he had uncovered more Communists. His sensational allegations often fell far short of the truth, but under the existing techniques of reporting, the truth rarely caught up with the allegations.

McCarthy was eventually discredited, and in the process, news people debated the accuracy and fairness of their reporting practices. They

Chapter opening photo: Debris fills the lobby of Kansas City's Hyatt Regency Hotel after a catwalk collapsed, killing and injuring hundreds. (AP/Wide World Photos)

began to realize that experienced reporters had expertise and insight into the topics and issues they specialized in, and that this insight should be shared with the public. The *news commentary* or *news analysis*, written by reporters and often appearing adjacent to the straight news account, came into existence. One of the pioneers of journalism education, Curtis MacDougal of Northwestern University, wrote a textbook, "Interpretative Reporting" (1938), and the term *interpretative*, or *interpretive*, has stuck to the kind of reporting that places the news "in context."

The reporter today uses interpretive techniques in many stories. If a city council proposes a tax increase and it's the third tax increase in five years, the reporter is justified in referring to this sequence of events as a trend. That reference is interpretation. This chapter will cover several kinds of interpretive reporting: the in-depth interpretive story; the news analysis, a straightforward interpretation that usually accompanies major breaking stories; the column, which is usually personalized interpretation; and the editorial, which is the "official" interpretation of issues or events by a publication or broadcasting station and is not really reporting.

Interpreting the News

Suppose tuition at your school is to be raised 20 percent next year, and work-study funds will be cut by 10 percent. What will the effect be on the university and its students? Of course it will mean that some students may not be able to come back to school and that some who had expected to enter the university will enter a less expensive school or drop out.

The story is more complicated than that, though. You cover the student financial aid office regularly and have found that fewer students than in the past seek work-study assistance because they can earn more working part-time at a newly opened industry in town. Your sociology research seminar has recently completed a study which shows that at your school, the students who need financial aid the most have disproportionately higher ACT test scores when they enter school than those who need no aid, and that they maintain higher grade point averages while in school.

You are in a position to write an interpretive article that indicates how serious each of the two changes will be. Work-study cuts may not harm the school. Tuition increases may reduce the academic level of the student body as well as its size.

You have been able to answer the question, What does this mean? Interpretive reporting also frequently tries to answer the question, How did this happen? You might go on in your story to indicate how changing priorities in the expenditure of tax dollars in your state and in the nation relates to tuition and work-study aid.

Interpretive reporting goes beyond many of the traditional news values, such as proximity, timeliness and conflict, that are the basis for deciding what stories to report. The news media need to address the *how* and *why* questions with every major issue. Today, they are criticized for dealing only with the surface questions relating to *who, what, when* and *where*.

Shortly before his death in 1985, Milton S. Eisenhower said the failure of the mass media to answer the questions *how* and *why* was their major shortcoming. Eisenhower spoke from more than 50 years experience in public life, as reporter for his hometown paper and editor of his college paper, as president of three great universities, as head of information for the Agriculture Department and as a troubleshooter who worked directly for six U.S. presidents, including his brother, Dwight D. Eisenhower. As an example, he cited stories given wide play on the networks and in the newspapers about student riots in Mexico City during the 1970s. Because of his interest in Latin America, he searched the media for the students' reason for rioting. Eventually he found the rioting was in reaction to a steep increase in city bus fares, which made commuting to school more expensive. "That should have been up front," said Eisenhower. "What freedom of the press means to me is my right to know why things are happening."

Interpretation is necessary, but it is not easy. It demands extensive knowledge of a field and hard work to stay current. For instance, the previous example of an interpretive story was drawn from an area that you are familiar with—you have had 12 to 15 years to become an expert at going to school. You know about ACTs, SATs, GPAs and work-study programs. You have experience. You know how to approach a story about financial aid. Think about how long it has taken you to become an expert at going to school, the time and effort you would need to develop a beat in the financial aid office and what is involved in a serious research project. Reporters have to do all those things on their beats—government, business, science, agriculture or any other area—before they can expect to write good interpretive stories.

Reporters are nosy people. If they get a hint that something may be important or interesting, they delve into it and they often end up with a news story. Interpretive reporters are even nosier. They wonder why that newsworthy event happened or what a new turn of events means. Interpretive reporters go beyond simply describing the environment; they are curious about how the environment got that way and what will happen to the environment as a result of current changes.

Confronted by a set of facts, an interpretive reporter turns them this way and that way in an attempt to view them from all possible perspectives. The reporter may then go get additional facts—those that other reporters may have missed and those that aren't in the headlines—and background material, what's been reported in scientific or professional literature, what experts think about the issue. The reporter then applies *logic* and *common sense* to the facts at hand.

Let's return to the example of the tuition increase and cut in work-study funds. Assume you're an interpretive reporter. When you hear the school's announcement, like everyone else you think, "Well that's going to make it rough for many students." But as an interpretive reporter, you go on to ask questions about how rough, which students it will hurt worst, which change will have the most effect (tuition or work-study) and, in addition to the obvious reduction in enrollment, what the effects on the university will be.

Work-study students have to work to get through school. If they can't get work-study funds, what other alternatives do they have? you wonder. You begin to form a list inside your head or on a scrap of paper: loans, summer jobs, on-campus jobs not requiring work-study eligibility and off-campus jobs. One by one you tick off the ideas on your list. A couple of phone calls indicate that loan money is pretty hard to get and on-campus jobs are drying up. The financial aid office reports that most work-study students are already depending on summer jobs. You then remember the new factory in town. A check with the Chamber of Commerce indicates that the new plant was attracted to the city because it needed workers with post–high school education, and it has tailored its production techniques to accommodate part-time students. The plant personnel office tells you how many students are already working there and indicates what its hiring patterns may be in the future. Your checklist has paid off. You have half your story.

What will be the effect on the university? The registrar will agree with your prediction that enrollment will drop. But no one can tell you which students will drop out. Students from low-income families? Students with poor grades? Married students? Out-of-state students? Before long you have a long list of possibilities. You can check them out with the registrar, the university's institutional studies department, the counseling center, student financial aid, the married student organization, and so on.

You may approach the issue from another perspective: Given that a certain reduction in enrollment is going to occur, a reduction in what category of students would be most detrimental? Children of alumni? Freshmen and sophomores? Graduate students? Students who make poor grades? Students who make good grades? Wouldn't it be terrible if potential Rhodes and Fulbright scholars dropped out?

Now you have the job of checking out the possibilities. Sometimes a good, efficient reporter is also a lazy reporter. The first question a lazy reporter asks is: Who already knows? That might lead you to the College of Education or the sociology department, where research is being conducted using student subjects. You might seek out the experts and pick their brains. Note that in the first hypothetical case, the campus reporter had been in a course where research had been conducted which the reporter used in the story. The reporter was less lazy than lucky. (In reporting, as in the rest of life, luck counts.)

Now you need to think about what you have learned and interpret the facts using logic and common sense. How does one learn to think logically? Study mathematics. Write essays and get a smart person to criticize them. Take courses in philosophy—an introduction to philosophical problems or formal logic, for instance. Play chess. Figure out why your team lost a game it should have won. Common sense has been described as not making mistakes. What keeps you from making mistakes? Experience. How do you get experience? By making mistakes. Get involved in reporting early. Know you are going to make mistakes. Get others to check your work and criticize you. Most of all analyze your mistakes and figure out how to avoid similar mistakes in the future.

Whether you're a lazy reporter, a lucky reporter or a digging reporter (which is the best kind of all), the ability to apply reason and common sense to a new set of facts is the key to interpretive reporting. There is one other attribute the interpretive reporter must have: self-confidence.

Let's take an inventory of a young reporter who has been covering county government for three years. The reporter has a broad education with a double major in journalism and political science and two years of experience as a staff member on a college daily plus a summer reporting internship on a major metropolitan daily. During three years of covering county government she has gone through the budget-making process three times, has gotten to know practically every employee at the courthouse and on a daily basis has weighed the information coming out of the courthouse as to its potential interest and importance to the public. Who knows more about the county's government? Perhaps one or two long-time county politicians do. These old-timers also have the advantage of knowing the history and background of everything, but our reporter has one advantage the politicians do not have: an objective perspective. The reporter, in making daily judgments on the basis of public interest and importance, has not had her perspective distorted by the necessity of thinking about what will get votes or lose them, for example.

The reporter should be able to interpret county affairs as well or better than almost anyone, particularly if she has the support of a wise city or managing editor who once covered the county beat. Remember, our reporter accepted the responsibility of representing the public in getting information on the county when she took on the beat. That includes interpretation of what is going on. She can do it. She should be proud of her work. She should be confident in interpreting the facts she knows so well.

In-Depth Interpretive Stories: Interpreting a Disaster

An assistant managing editor of the Kansas City Star had finished an early dinner at the Hereford House on a Friday evening and was leaving when she noticed a woman with blood on her blouse tearfully making a call from a pay telephone in the lobby. The editor soon realized that there had been an accident at a tea dance at the nearby Hyatt Regency Hotel. Into the editor's mind came the thought: big story. She returned to the newsroom and began trying to reach other top editors of the paper to alert them. As you know from previous chapters, the story occupied the staffs of the Kansas City Star and Times around the clock for almost a week. With 113 persons killed and 188 injured, the event was called the worst hotel disaster in history.

Almost as soon as the thought "big story" crossed the editor's mind, another thought occurred: How did this happen? She and the other editors and many of the reporters who covered the disaster realized that reporting how it happened might be the most important thing they could do. Their reporting could help ensure the future structural safety of buildings. Interpreting the cause of the disaster became an important part of the Hyatt Regency story, and the newspapers' success in pursuing the cause must have played a major role in the Pulitzer panel's decision to recognize the Star and Times.

One of the first stories the Star and Times published quoted the mayor of Kansas City as saying that the city would conduct a complete investigation of the tragedy to determine the cause. The editors viewed this statement and other plans for investigations with some skepticism.

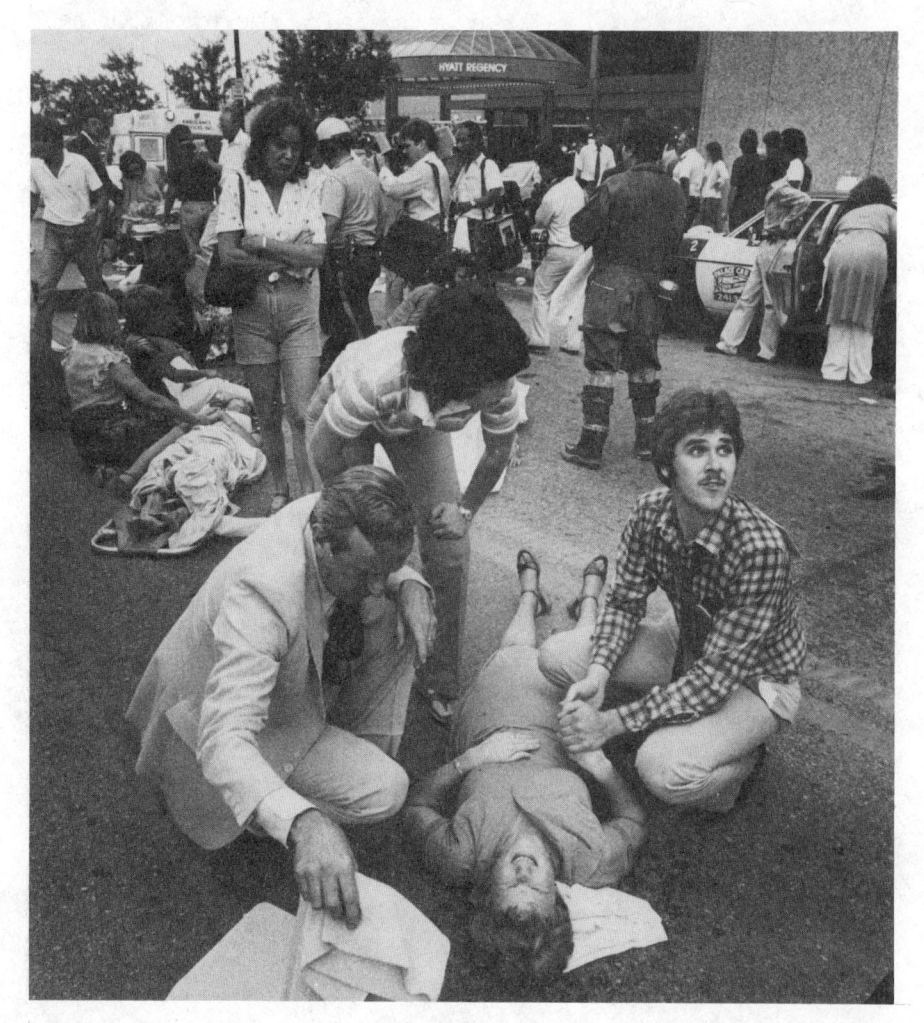

A Hyatt Regency victim is assisted by Kansas City residents. (Photo by Greg Smith/Kansas City Times)

Not many years earlier the roof of a large public building, Kemper Arena, had collapsed. The report of an official investigation into the collapse did not appear for many months, and the editors had no "second opinion" as to the validity or completeness of the official investigation. They had to accept the report at face value, and, they said, that made them feel uncomfortable.

INTERPRETIVE TECHNIQUES

Interpretation involves answering the question, What does this mean? To answer this question, you must take the information at hand and enter it into your brain, as though it were a computer, and think about it in an orderly fashion. Program your brain to analyze issues and occurrences. The programs available to you include some methods of logical thinking.

- Cause and effect. If A is the cause and B the effect, A and B must correlate, directly or inversely: If A increases, then B must always either increase or decrease. A must precede B in time. Even if these two criteria are met, C could be the cause of both A and B.

- Deductive reasoning. In deductive reasoning, one moves from a general premise to a particular case. John Jones has been diagnosed as having cancer of the lung. On the day of his surgery, an X ray shows that the foreign growth in his lung has shrunk. The surgery is canceled. Doctors tell him that when a growth shrinks, it invariably is not malignant. Although the doctors could not be absolutely sure Jones does not they move from a general premise to Jones' particular case and conclude that in all likelihood he does not have cancer. This is deductive reasoning.

- Inductive reasoning. This type of reasoning moves from a specific case to a general conclusion. Although Joe denies being near the scene of Mary's murder, police find under her fingernail a hair from his head and a thread from an unusual sweater he owns. They move from these specifics to the general conclusion that he may have killed her and charge him with murder.

- Analogy. This is a literary and rhetorical device for simplifying complex matters. If two issues are similar in a number of respects, they are likely to be similar in many others. Previous disputes between a union and a company have followed a path of A (presentation of demands), B (rejection), C (fruitless negotiation), D (strike threat), and E (settlement at strike deadline). Then if A and B take place at another time, a reporter begins to see that the two situations are analogous and he or she can suggest that it may be likely the whole sequence will be repeated.

- Relative weights. Explaining the relative importance of the elements of an issue is good interpretation. The snail darter is a rare fish. Environmentalists claimed it was found only in one locale, Stream A, and prevented construction of a dam that would have destroyed its habitat. Subsequently, the snail darter was found in several other streams. The relative importance of Stream A as a snail darter habitat has decreased. Perhaps now the dam can be built.

- Human nature. Behavior and belief is influenced by culture, geography and environment. Often it appears irrational; sometimes it is. Emotion cannot be explained logically, but it is a reality and strongly influences human affairs. Logic is not always the key to interpretation; sometimes the best interpretive approach is to answer the questions: Whose ox is being gored? Where's the money? Who moves up the ladder?

Consider all of these items as a commercial that advertises the programs available to you for developing your brain as an interpretive computer. The programs are available to you through courses in logic, mathematics and the natural sciences to develop analytical skills, and the social sciences and humanities to develop understanding of the human condition. The programs are also available at your nearest bookstore and in the experiences that will confront you throughout life.

Like all computer programs, just having these on the disk does not help you. No matter how "user friendly" they are, unless you use them regularly, you will not become proficient in them. IBM's slogan used to be "Think." It must be yours if you want to write interpretive stories.

To adequately interpret the cause of the sky walk collapse, the editors decided they needed to weigh all the evidence they could get, publish their interpretation and then let it be tested by what the official investigation or investigations reported later. This decision began to look like a good one within a week; the city council denied funding for the mayor's investigation. There didn't seem to be much governmental interest in providing the public with information on the disaster's cause.

The newspapers needed all the data they could get. On the evening of the disaster, photographers were instructed to get pictures of all the debris and remaining structure related to the sky walks at the scene. The day after the collapse the site was closed to the press. On the one occasion when photographers were allowed in the warehouse in which the debris was stored, they were again instructed to get long-lens shots of the key support points.

Were the sky walks planned properly from an engineering standpoint and were the plans properly carried out? This seemed to be a key question to the editors. They sent reporters to city inspection offices to look at the original construction drawings. The editors realized they lacked engineering expertise, so they employed an engineer to interpret the drawings and compare them to the photographs.

The interpretive story that resulted indicated that changes made between the time the sky walks were planned and when they were constructed resulted in added stress that could have caused the collapse. Pictures accompanying the story showed the original plans, photographs of the support points, an artist's renderings of how the support points would have looked if the original plans had been used and how the modified support points probably looked before the collapse.

When the editors saw the story in print, they felt they had done a good job of trying to explain to the public how the tragedy happened. When the official report of the National Bureau of Standards supported their interpretation, they felt even better about their effort. Here is that story.

Critical Design Change Is Linked to Collapse of Hyatt's Sky Walks

By **Rick Alm**
and **Thomas G. Watts**
© staff writers 1981 The Kansas City Star Company

PULITZER PRIZE WINNER

(1) A critical change in the original design of the Hyatt Regency hotel's sky walks doubled the stress on that part of the walks that later pulled apart during the collapse, The Star has learned.

(2) City records—in combination with visual examination by two experts and photographic evidence—reveal that, at some point, a change was made that doubled the stress on three steel "box beams" supporting the fourth-floor sky walk.

(3) It was those beams that tore downward and away from their ceiling-anchored moorings, and both that walkway and a second-story walkway hanging below plummeted to the hotel lobby.

(4) However, one of the experts—a structural engineer hired by The Star—cautioned that it is not yet possible to determine whether that tearing failure was the primary cause of the collapse, or merely one in a chain of structural failures. But it is clearly significant, he said.

(5) The tragic collapse Friday night killed 111 persons and injured 188 others, at least 29 of them critically. At the time of the collapse, about 1,500 people were attending a tea dance in the hotel lobby. Many were standing on the sky walks, most on the second-story bridge, watching the dancing below, some of them either dancing or swaying to the music, according to eyewitnesses.

(6) The original design plans were revealed today when city officials made all Hyatt construction records available for inspection, including the specifications for the project and the construction plans.

(7) Those records and the altered design, as constructed, were studied by Wayne Lischka, a structural engineer retained by the newspaper in the wake of Friday's tragedy. The Star consulted another engineer who had viewed the wreckage after the accident and who later was shown close-up photos of the damaged sky bridges. He independently corroborated Lischka's conclusions.

(8) This second engineer asked that his name not be used for fear he would be ostracized by the local architectural community—that it would affect his business.

(9) Once the design change was made, Lischka explained, the box beams beneath the top walkway were required not only to support its weight but also that of the second-floor sky bridge, 30 feet below. Each sky bridge has been calculated to weigh about 65,000 pounds—almost the weight of a loaded semitruck.

(10) After examining the original design blueprints on file at City Hall and close-up photographs of the collapsed sky walk debris, Lischka determined that the box beams under the top sky bridge tore away from nuts that were on the lower ends of steel suspension rods that still remain anchored in the ceiling.

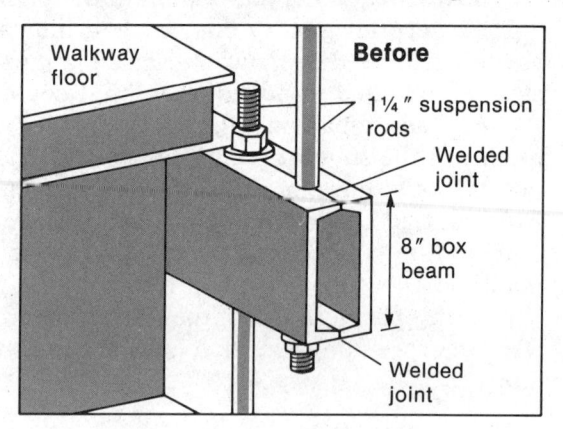

Before
Walkway floor
1¼" suspension rods
Welded joint
8" box beam
Welded joint

After
Nut and washer on threaded end of suspension rod tears through joint in box beam on 4th floor sky walk.

Cross-section view

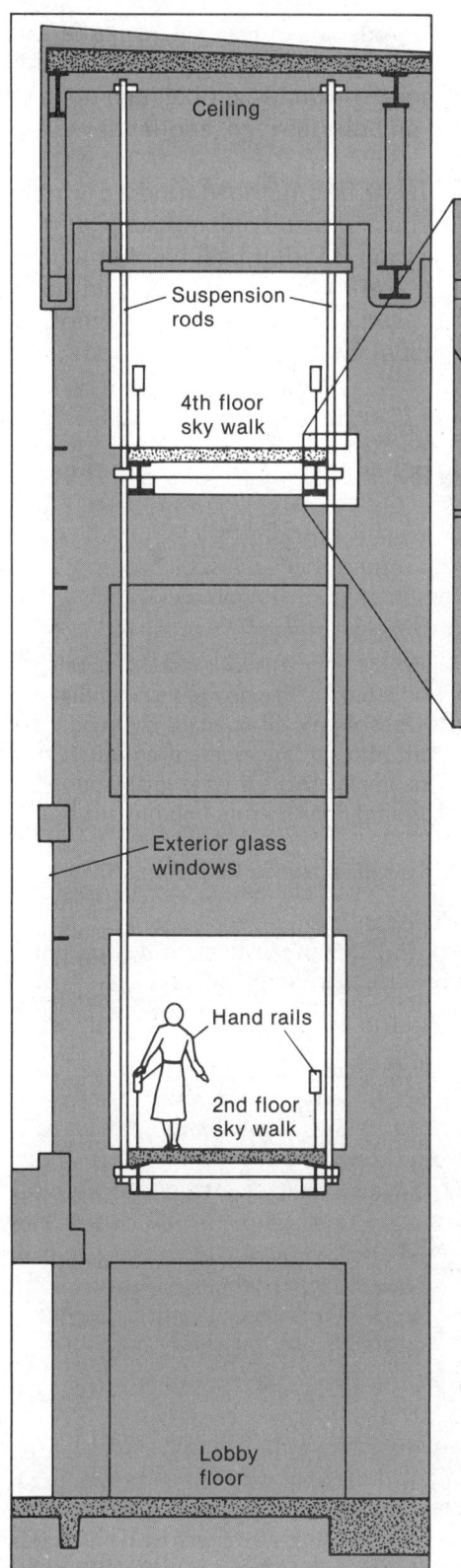

Original concept   **As constructed**

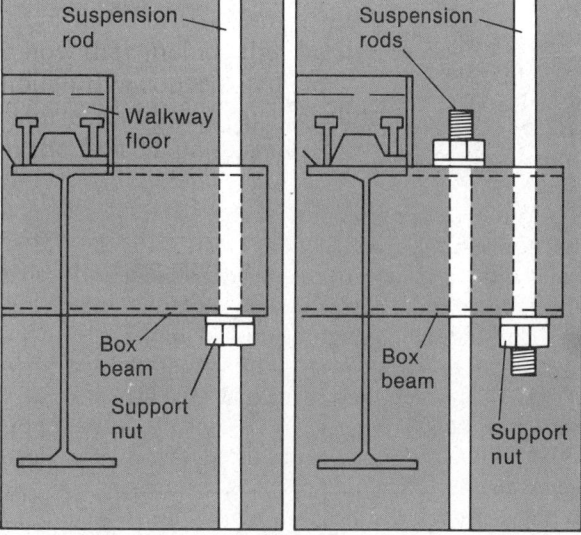

Detailed view

(11) Whether the failure was the result of poor design, faulty construction or flawed materials cannot be determined without access to the site of the accident and the remnants of the disaster, followed by intensive inspection and perhaps laboratory testing.

(12) Hotel authorities have closed off access to the debris for their own intense study, as several investigations are under way by parties involved with the ownership and design of the 40-story hotel.

(13) It was neither clear from the City Hall records made public today who intitiated and approved the sky walk design change, nor when. Although it is common for design changes to be made during construction, those changes apparently are not required to be reported in writing to City Hall.

(14) In fact, one document drafted by the architects instructs contractors to report "discrepancies between actual installation and contract (specifications) documents" only to the owners of the hotel.

(15) Tom Leittem, an attorney for the Hyatt's architects, said today his clients would make no

more comment on the Hyatt tragedy until at least Thursday evening.

(16) Myron Calkins, city public works director, has ordered his employees, including all city building inspectors, to make no comments to anybody about the Hyatt and not to respond to questions from the news media. Calkins was unavailable for comment today.

(17) The original hotel architects' plans—approved by city officials in the fall of 1978—called for six suspension rods, anchored in the ceiling, three to each side, to hold both sky walks aloft.

(18) The base construction of the walkways looks something like a ladder with three rungs—with long steel I-beams making the sides of the ladder and shorter beams making the rungs. The shorter "rung" beams—which ran the width of the walkways—were attached to long steel rods which were in turn affixed to the ceiling of the lobby.

(19) It was at the point where these long rods attached to the "rung" beams that the tearing took place. Under the original plans, the rods would have gone from the ceiling through the fourth-floor walkway and continued to the side beams at the bottom of the second-floor walkway.

(20) That was changed sometime during construction so that one rod connected the top walkway to the ceiling, then another rod connected that walkway to the lower one.

(21) The three box beams were formed from two steel "C-channels" welded together at top and bottom to form a rectangular, hollow beam, much like this: [ ].

(22) Two sets of steel nuts and washers were to be installed on each suspension rod to support the walkways. One set was to be below each walkway to hold the sky walks in place.

(23) Yet when the sky walks were constructed, the critical change was in place. Instead of having each suspension rod extend continuously from the ceiling through box beams supporting both walkways, the six rods dropped from the ceiling and ran through only the box beams underneath the width of the highest walkway. Inches from the first rods, and through those same box beams, six other rods were added, suspending the lower walkway from the higher sky walk, rather than from the ceiling itself.

(24) Such a change meant that two separate support rods were installed inches apart on each of the three critical box beams.

(25) That change, said Lischka and the other structural engineer who has contributed to The Star's inquiry, doubled the stress on the three steel box beams and nuts beneath the higher walkway.

(26) Close-up photographs of the wreckage make it clear that the single-rod concept was abandoned in favor of two separate rods bolted separately but inches apart at the base of the top sky walk.

(27) "Properly constructed, two rods are just as strong as one. But in the two-rod design, with the increased stress, you've left yourself less room for error," Lischka said.

(28) "This is one area that warrants close review by the investigative teams," Lischka added. "It's not unusual to find that changes are made during the course of construction, between the original design and what's practical to build on the construction site. But in this case the change made this connection even more critical."

(29) Normal procedure when such changes are proposed is for an engineer to study any planned change to make sure it doesn't alter the structural stability of the building. There are no city records to show when the change was made or who might have approved it.

(30) Lischka said he had other concerns as well.

(31) The C-channels that formed the three 9-foot box beams running under the width of each walkway were welded at top and bottom. Photographs of the end of one of those box beams indicate the steel was torn like a staple through paper when the box beam pulled away from the washer and nut at the bottom of a ceiling-anchored steel suspension rod.

(32) Lischka said investigators will have to determine if the ripping was the actual cause of the failure. Or was it a result?

(33) One critical question is this, Lischka said, "If the box beams pulling away from the nuts and washers on the end of the ceiling-connected suspension rods were the cause of the collapse, what type of loading would force that to happen?"

(34) Lischka said investigators must pay close attention to the ends of the box beams because that is where the two rods were attached—along the welded seam of the two C-shaped members that formed the box beam.

Many interpretive stories read like an obvious explanation. They are deceptively simple. In fact, the reporter spends hours studying and analyzing before writing the final story. The reporter writes outlines, early drafts and revisions rewritten to make the interpretation easy to understand.

Go back and examine the lead of the story, which is three paragraphs long. Those paragraphs contain 102 words. Of those words, one is five syllables long, three are four syllables, seven are three syllables, 27 are two syllables and 64—almost two-thirds—are one syllable. Reporters Alm and Watts described a complicated and technical matter with everyday conversational words.

Those three paragraphs pinpoint where the failure seemed to have occurred, and describe what had happened. The fourth paragraph cautions that the exact cause of the collapse has not been determined. The story continues in a highly organized manner to add one fact at a time to the interpretation of what may have happened, as follows:

- Paragraphs six through eight describe where the information came from and the competence of those who analyzed it.
- Paragraphs nine through 11 give more details on where the break occurred and a cautionary note as to what failed.
- Paragraphs 12 through 16 explain that the newspaper has not had access to the debris or to several sources and that contractors were not required to report design changes to the city.
- Paragraphs 17 through 24 describe in detail the original plans and how they differed from the actual structure.
- Paragraphs 25 through 29 present the opinions of the engineer the Star retained on the crucial joints.
- Paragraphs 30 through 34 outline other concerns of the engineer.

The clarity of the interpretation is particularly remarkable since it was published on the day that the city released the original plans for public examination.

For their coverage of the tragedy, the editors of the Star and Times used a special technique which emerged from the hours-long meetings they held immediately after the tragedy to plan the coverage. During the meetings they predicted which stories they would have in the next day's paper. By knowing which aspect of the tragedy each story would cover, they could assign a writer to each story and then ask reporters, to pass along information as they got it to the appropriate writer. A team effort developed. Reporters and writers critiqued and supported each other. The technique allowed the staff to create a coherent report on the tragedy that filled a full section of the paper but was not repetitive.

To help interpret the cause of the tragedy, the Star employed an engineer, as you recall. Editors and reporters met with the engineer, turned his explanations into stories, checked the stories with him and with another engineer, and then rewrote to incorporate changes that needed to be made.

The editors' coordination of graphics with the text of the stories allowed readers to see what the reporters were describing. Reproductions of portions of the plans from the city's files were combined with photographs of the sky walk debris and artist's renderings of the joints that failed.

Each step in this process was done with the reader in mind. As they prepared the stories, the reporters and editors must have asked: What does the typical Kansas City reader, the family of one of the victims and the firefighter who spent 12 hours trying to rescue victims want to know about the cause of this tragedy? How can we tell them what they want to know truthfully, tastefully and responsibly?

This kind of painstaking care in explaining complicated matters is a vital part of interpretive reporting. A good reporter can grasp what an expert or a document says about a complicated matter and turn it into a news story. A good editor can back up the reporter, spotting what has not been brought out, smoothing over rough spots in the writing and suggesting improvements to the lead and in the organization of the material. This teamwork takes time and a willingness to communicate with colleagues. There is a lesson here. If you write interpretively, do not sit on a story until deadline; your editor can't help you make it better if he or she has to hurry the story into print.

News Analyses

Experienced reporters frequently write a second type of interpretive story—the news analysis. When something out of the ordinary of universal importance happens—a natural or human-caused disaster, for example—everyone wants to know: What does this mean? The news analysis is the mass media's first attempt to answer that question. While an in-depth interpretive story probes deeply into a story, for example, an explanation of the cause of the sky walk collapse, a news analysis uses background that is immediately available.

If the networks broadcast live coverage of a tragedy, such as the 1986 explosion of the space shuttle Challenger, the broadcast journalists will give all the facts they know and then the anchor will say something like: "Here to tell us whether this is a serious setback to the American space program is a reporter who has been covering space for us since the first American manned flight." The reporter will then tell the audience that he does not think NASA will send up another shuttle until the cause of this disaster is found, that many shuttle customers will turn to the French Arianne launch vehicle to get their satellites up and that the U.S. military will have to rethink its launch plans. The reporter has had time to make a telephone call or two to some of the news sources he has cultivated over the years to check some things he is already pretty confident about, and he is prepared to give an almost instant interpretation of the event.

Newspapers carry stories, usually labeled "analysis" or "news analysis," regularly alongside their factual coverage. News analysis has become popular during the past 25 years. Controversial among journalists when it first was introduced, such stories now are an accepted part of news work with their own slang appellation—"thumbsuckers."

News analysis stories are usually printed in the news columns and are primarily informed speculation based on fact, rather than expositions of opinion like columns or editorials. The stories are often written as needed by the most appropriate staff member, even a relatively inexperienced reporter if he or she has the best background to write it.

The process often goes like this: "Give me a thumbsucker on the governor's race to go along with that story on Jones withdrawing," the editor may say to his top political reporter. The political reporter then runs down the list of remaining candidates in her mind. She compares the political base each has with the one Jones has just vacated. She speculates on whether Jones will endorse another candidate and makes a discreet inquiry or two among Jones' friends. She remembers what happened in a previous race that was influenced by a withdrawal and tries to recall whether there were any hints that Jones would withdraw. From all this she comes up with a story that is somewhat more speculative, gossipy and analytical than the news story that quotes what Jones said at his withdrawal press conference and provides formal quotations from other state political figures. While "sucking her thumb," the reporter did a lot of remembering and quite a bit of comparing, ventured a few guesses which she checked out quickly and then wrote her analysis.

To be able to write incisive news analysis when called on to do so, you need to be making incisive analysis of the news all the time. That is, stay abreast of things that you are covering. Eat, sleep and talk all the time about what is going on in your area. Then when the call comes, your instant interpretation will be at your fingertips or perhaps even on the tip of your tongue.

Columns and Editorials

Traditional reporting has little opinion in it; its goal is objectivity. Columns and editorials, on the other hand, draw conclusions from facts but essentially are statements of opinion. Although this book concentrates on reporting, a discussion of columns and editorials at this point is useful for three reasons. First, reporters need to know that there is a place in the mass media for the expression of opinion, that it has a respected tradition and a useful role. Next, an examination of the techniques used in opinion writing provides a perspective on objective reporting. Finally, the techniques used in writing columns and editorials apply to interpretive reporting.

Let's look at the column first. Everyone reads columns; at least that was the impression given by a funny song in a Broadway musical of the 1950s. According to the song, one of the lines that was supposedly going through the mind of a stripper as she languidly removed her long white gloves was: "Walter Lippmann wasn't very brilliant today."

The line was funny because for 30 years Lippmann was the political columnist most highly respected by intellectuals—so why would an exotic dancer be thinking about him? Furthermore, to say that he "wasn't very brilliant today" indicated that he was somewhat brilliant but not up to his usual standard of superior brilliance. Unlike most columnists, Lippmann was able to simply quit writing columns for a few weeks if he wanted to travel to Europe or elsewhere to do research. Newspapers would run a little box saying he would be back in two weeks and publish guest columns in the space usually occupied by his "Today and Tomorrow" column. A letter to the editor on one such occasion urged him to hurry back and start pontificating again so the letter writer would know what to think about the momentous events then going on.

Lippmann and other columnists began to interpret events for the public in the late 1920s. Radio and television developed their own commentators, such as Bill Moyers and David Brinkley. Many reporters aspire to being syndicated columnists or network commentators, and the few who are successful help millions of people to better understand our complicated world.

The typical political column often maintains a liberal or conservative stance. From this point of view, it examines issues as they take center stage in the public eye. Rarely does it break new ground in providing information. Perhaps its greatest value is in providing perspective on an issue as it relates to the past and to other contemporary issues. An experienced and insightful political reporter can step into this kind of column writing, perhaps beginning with a once-a-week "Around the Statehouse" column and later moving into more analytical interpretation of issues.

Because of their conflicting points of view, columnists provide differing interpretations for readers. One such confrontation took place on the editorial page of the New York Herald Tribune in the mid-1960s. The issue was American involvement in Vietnam. Lippmann's column, appearing each Tuesday and Thursday under the political cartoon, interpreted the issue from the point of view of proper national priorities, the weakness of the South Vietnamese government and the vulnerability of the American position. The Herald Tribune's other star columnist, Joseph Alsop, interpreted the issue from the point of view of America's need to project an image of strength, the idealism and effectiveness of American advisers to the South Vietnamese military and the danger of a Communist takeover in Asia. His columns appeared in the same spot in Monday, Wednesday and Friday editions. The two columnists debated the Hawk and Dove positions before the appellations became common.

The humorous columnist takes a whimsical look at many of the same issues that serious political columnists tackle. Art Buchwald walked into the Paris offices of the European edition of the New York Herald Tribune not long after the end of World War II and told the editor the paper needed a column on Europe by an American. He has been writing funny columns ever since. His column explaining the American tradition of Thanksgiving to the French (complete with Kilometre Standish) was republished each year for a decade. He moved his home and his point of view to Washington in the mid-1960s.

Columnists in a local setting, such as Herb Caen in San Francisco and Mike Royko in Chicago, become institutions, almost landmarks. They are chroniclers of interesting trivia, commentators on the social and political scene, and entertainers.

There are a myriad of other specialized columnists. The opinions of a community's sports columnist often are the reference points for the fanatics who follow the community's teams. Other columns, local and syndicated, aim at every special interest from investments to home gardening. The column is one way a general-interest medium can appeal to a narrow spectrum of its audience. If you have a hobby or an area of expertise, you may be able to supplement your reporter's paycheck by writing a weekly column on that subject.

Almost anyone has an interest that could be turned into a column. Many reporters try to be columnists. Few succeed. Why? Column writing is rigorous. Even a weekly deadline can be trying, since every column must be good—pertinent, incisive and preferably easy to read. The columnist needs to be "very brilliant" every time.

There are other constraints. The column appears at a set time (not when the columnist is inspired or when news happens). It usually occupies a set spot in the publication and each column must be about the same length as the previous column. The column usually has a set style or point of view, which the columnist maintains, addressing specific kinds of issues. (It would be very confusing to the reader, for example, if a publication came out with James Reston giving advice to unhappy spouses and Dear Abby commenting on foreign affairs.) Columnists have to be highly disciplined.

The columnist has some advantages over the reporter. He or she develops local or national name recognition and is assured of a forum in one or many publications. If the column is popular, the columnist is likely to have better access than a reporter to sources of information and advice.

In summary, the columnist must be an expert in a subject area and a careful and effective writer who has the discipline to produce on a schedule. Staying abreast is all important; the columnist is a scholar without tenure who usually must publish with less time for reflection and in less technical language than his or her academic counterpart.

Like columns, editorials are a traditional part of newspapers. They are not as pervasive or entrenched in magazines, radio and television. Even in newspapers, the tradition of formal editorials goes back only about a century. Editorials were invented and became prominent as the concept of objective reporting took hold. As we noted in Chapter 2, for almost 200 years Colonial and early American journalism mixed opinion with fact throughout the newspaper. The newspaper as a whole took a partisan position on economic, political, religious and social issues. As objective reporting became the ideal, the opportunity for newspapers to say which "side" they thought was correct diminished. The editorial, a frank statement of the newspaper's opinion on important issues, emerged.

Editorials are usually set apart typographically by a different column width and type face or type size and appear on an opinion page with columns, political cartoons and letters from readers. This is done to alert readers that the newspaper has stopped being objective and has started giving opinions, although many readers fail to perceive the distinction.

Since the strength or weakness of opinions and a willingness to stand up and express oneself on controversial issues is an expression of personality, editorials may reflect the personalities of those who write them. However, many of today's editorials read or sound as if they had come from corporate public relations offices. They are slick, reasoned and as inoffensive as a stand on a public issue can be. That is understandable, since most media now are owned by big business organizations.

Other editorials, down through the years, have reflected a more personal and vituperative or sentimental stance. For example, during the 1960s, the New York Daily News found the opportunity to state in its editorials at least once a month that "the only good Communist is a dead Communist." This sweeping accusation lacked even the intelligence of originality, being adapted from the mindless claim of frontier bigots that the "only good Indian is a dead Indian." During the 1950s, a resolution passed by the Mississippi House of Representatives—by a vote of 89 to 19 with 32 abstentions—accused editor Hodding Carter Jr. of lying in an article on school desegregation. In a humorous and gutsy editorial, Carter responded in his Delta Democrat-Times: "I hereby resolve by a vote of 1 to 0 that there are 89 liars in the state legislature .... those 89 character mobbers can go to hell, collectively or singly, and wait there until I back down. They needn't plan on returning." In 1879, the New York Sun published an editorial that included the phrase "Yes, Virginia, there is a Santa Claus," and with taste and sentiment described the spirit of giving in a way that has caused the editorial to be reprinted more than any other in history.

These examples indicate how editorials can be colorful and express feelings. Editorials have another strength that bears examination: They offer the writer more literary tools with which to explain and interpret than the traditional objective news approach does.

A good editorial will do many of the following things: state a topic, tell why it is important, present the pertinent facts, describe the stands that have been taken on the topic, evaluate those taking the stands, state other alternatives, make comparisons or draw analogies to other issues and topics, and finally, state conclusions. Perhaps no editorial has ever done all those things, but they represent the stages of logical reasoning that the editorial writer goes through in planning what to say on a topic. These thought processes are quite different from what you have been taught to do in writing a straight news story. Interpretive writing of all kinds depends on them.

Roger Linscott of the Berkshire Eagle in Pittsfield, Mass., received the 1973 Pulitzer Prize for editorial writing for his editorial, "Our $213 Million Gift Horse." The editorial interprets an issue and illustrates many of the points just listed.

The issue is stated obliquely in the title, taken from the ancient adage, "Don't look a gift horse in the mouth." (For the 99 percent of you readers who have never been tempted or even had much opportunity to look a horse in the mouth, the adage comes from the once universal practice of determining the age of a horse by examining its dental condition.) Linscott's editorial takes a long hard look at the "gift horse": $213 million available for improving two roads near Pittsfield.

Our $213 Million Gift Horse

By **Roger B. Linscott**
The Berkshire Eagle

PULITZER PRIZE WINNER

When liberal academic types complain that this nation is suffering from a badly distorted sense of political priorities, the complaint is often cast in such abstract terms that it doesn't really register.

But we now have a concrete locally oriented example of what they're talking about, in the form of the state's proposal to allocate $213 million of interstate highway funds to a revamping of Routes 7 and 8 here in Berkshire County.

Nobody in these parts, of course, is likely to object very strenuously to such an outpouring of federal largesse. It would be nice to have a super-road to hustle transients through the area and to give all parts of the county speedier access to the Massachusetts Turnpike. And there is always the rationalization that if the Berkshires don't get the money some other area will.

Nonetheless, $213 million is a staggering sum of money. And at the risk of seeming to look a gift horse in the mouth, it is tempting to consider some of the other things that such a sum could buy.

For instance, with $213 million you could clean up the Housatonic River from its tributaries in Windsor to the Connecticut border, with probably enough left over to create recreational ponds and parks along its course.

Or you could build and equip enough schools to take care of all of the county's public educational needs for the next decade.

Or, if you wanted to dole out the $213 million to the cities and towns of the Berkshires as a revenue sharing device, it would be sufficient to permit a total moratorium on all local real estate taxes, throughout the county, for a period of about 10 years.

Or, to carry it from the sublime to the ridiculous, as a direct per capita hand-out it would be enough to provide a cash payment of nearly $3,000 apiece to every one of the county's 70,000-odd adult inhabitants.

But none of the purposes, worthy or otherwise, can have any claim on the federal money. The highway lobby has long since seen to that. The $213 million (more precisely, 90 per cent of it) would come from the federal Highway Trust Fund, which is lavishly nourished by the federal gas tax and is earmarked by law exclusively for highway purposes.

Indeed, as things now stand the Highway Trust Fund's multibillion dollar cornucopia can't even be applied to alternative forms of public transportation, despite the fact that a decent mass transit system in this country would serve to lighten the burden on our highways and save our cities from strangulation at the hands of the motor car. Just this week, Transportation Secretary John Volpe asked Congress for permission to spend a portion of the fund on mass transit in the coming fiscal year—and the best bet on Capitol Hill is that the answer will be no.

In the case of the Berkshires, the plan is to make available for Routes 7 and 8 most of the money the federal authorities had allocated to the Boston area but which isn't being spent there because of the governor's moratorium on new highway construction within the Route 128 circle. Because of the lower land-taking costs in the hinterlands, the state highway planners figure they can build 66 miles of super-road in the Berkshires for what a mere 4 miles would cost in the congested Boston area. This, they point out, is quite a bargain.

No doubt it is, if measured solely in miles of concrete. And no doubt, if the money has to be spent somewhere and can be spent on highway construction only we should welcome it. But there's no law against wishing for a system in which urgent social needs might be able to take fiscal priority over the inexhaustible demands of the automobile.

The editorial is interpretive because Linscott goes outside "the facts" of this story to examine alternate uses of the money: cleaning up an entire river or solving school needs. He conveys the monumental scale of the expenditure by relating the highway funds to the entire county tax revenues and to a per capita distribution figure.

Linscott next looks behind the facts to see why this situation exists and finds federal regulations preventing the use of the Highway Trust Fund for anything except highways; not even alternative forms of transportation are allowable. He underscores this point by noting that the state government has imposed a moratorium on road building around Boston, the area for which the money originally had been intended.

He presents the claim of highway proponents that building 66 rural miles of highway is "quite a bargain" as compared to the four urban miles that the money would buy and then makes a strong point: that a distorted sense of political priorities prevents the best use of public funds. Linscott's comparisons and explanations are woven into a logical, persuasive message.

Through the use of authoritative sources in the schools and environmental agencies, a reporter could have produced a similarly effective interpretive story on this subject. The clarity of Linscott's logic and his graceful prose are also appropriate to all forms of interpretive writing.

Using Sources

Interpretive reporting begins with inquisitiveness, depends on logical thinking to establish hypotheses and analyze data, and concludes with the ability to explain lucidly. In the process, a reporter's ability to gain the confidence of expert sources and to elicit necessary information from them comes into play. The ability to cultivate good sources is perhaps the most valuable talent a reporter can have. Certainly it is vital when the reporter gets beyond reporting the surface facts and attempts to interpret their importance.

A source is someone who knows the facts a reporter needs to know. If the reporter cannot observe the facts firsthand, he or she must depend on someone else. The facts may be in a book, in other documents or simply in someone else's mind.

The good source is one who trusts the reporter, who is trusted by the reporter and who knows what the reporter needs to discover. So reporters cultivate sources and are careful to maintain a high level of integrity with them. As you've read, reporters have been willing to go to jail rather than break a promise they made to a source. Reporters believe the public has a right to know what is going on and sources know what is going on. Therefore the reporter-source relationship is vital to the public.

Developing trusted sources takes time and effort. You should always treat the source with sensitivity and respect. A source is always worth listening to at length. A source deserves an explanation for the way in which you use his or her information.

The best possible source is one who is knowledgeable in the appropriate areas and who has the same keen sense of the public's need to know what is going on that the reporter has. This kind of source will telephone you if he or she learns something of importance to the public and will understand your need if you make an inquiry. Thank your lucky stars if you find such a source; talk to that source not only about his or her area of expertise but also about news, reporting and public information in general.

Every source has motives for giving reporters information beyond wanting the public to know what is going on. Every source also has some reservations about giving information to reporters. An understanding of the motives of sources and their reservations will help you to maintain good relations with them. It will also give you some sense about when to press the source for more information and when to back off.

Types of Sources

Scientists have reason to be the most sensitive of all sources to inquiries from persons outside their scientific disciplines. Scientists, like reporters, are in pursuit of the truth. The scientist is seeking new, undiscovered truths and has a vested interest in helping you convey the newly discovered truth carefully and correctly.

Let's look inside the mind of a scientist who has just completed a research project. At long last she is convinced that her hypothesis is correct. She has discovered a truth. After the first exhilaration, two doubts assail her: Is it really true, and will the scientific community understand and accept it? She seeks the answer to both these questions by exposing her research methods and results to the scrutiny of other scientists. If the research is replicated and the findings supported, there is a greater probability that it indeed is a new truth. If her colleagues accept her findings, talk about them and incorporate them into their further research, she can feel the confidence and satisfaction that everyone does when personal enterprises achieve success.

The reporter plays no role in the process just described. Only after her colleagues have accepted her research is the scientist really anxious to publicize it further. (That's why good reporters pay attention to scientific journals.) If the scientist were to have gone to the mass media before publishing in a refereed journal, her work would have been suspect—and she might have been accused of pressuring her colleagues into accepting her views. Furthermore, the public press may have had difficulty accurately reporting her discoveries and any errors would have discredited her. Now that her results have been accepted by her peers, however, she is willing to share them with the world. She believes that public knowledge of scientific achievement leads to progress for humanity, and she is also aware that public acclaim for her work will pave the road to another research grant, a better job, the most modern laboratory, in short, to success and esteem.

As a reporter and a scientist seek to understand each other's points of view with regard to a specific story, a professional love-hate relationship can result. Anything that contributes to the trust between source and reporter diminishes the hate quotient. Anything that damages the trust may end the love affair abruptly. Fortunately for both reporter and scientist, the reporter-scientist relationship depends more on reason and less on emotion than do love affairs. However, a wise reporter would pursue a scientist who shows promise of being a good source with great fervor and at the same time with great care.

The same kind of relationship exists between reporters and any source when truth is the common bond between them. No one likes to have his or her pet ideas scoffed at; on the contrary, people want to share them and be admired for them. That's the trade-off a source makes at the point of going public to a reporter with a "truth."

There are many less abstract bases for reporter-source relationships. A common one is the relationship between the reporter and the *bureaucrat*. From a reporter's perspective, a bureaucrat is anyone who, to carry out his or her duties, must obtain the cooperation of the public and in this case, obtain this cooperation through the media. Into this category fall university registrars who need to let students know how and when to sign up for classes, the Internal Revenue Service which needs public cooperation in getting tax returns filled out correctly and returned on time and county clerks who need public cooperation to run elections. These people are ready and willing to explain procedures to the public. Once the door is open, you can expect a high degree of cooperation from such people in helping with interpretation of the processes. This is a quid pro quo or an I'll-scratch-your-back-if-you'll-scratch-mine relationship.

The bureaucrat wants you to understand exactly what the public needs to know. The bureaucrat also knows that at some time in the future he or she may need you as a quick entree into the media to meet an emergency. Maintaining a close relationship with the reporter is a matter of self-interest. The bureaucrat is quite willing to spend time and effort to assist you in getting information in order to maintain the good relationship. You need the bureaucrat as well and therefore should try to avoid being overly critical of bureaucratic red tape. Were it not for the clerks, secretaries, record-keepers, managers and administrators of the world, civilization would crumble—and they are tremendous resources for all kinds of useful information.

The *politician* has a somewhat different motivation for seeking the attention of the public through the media. A politician, for our purposes here, is anyone seeking to climb up the leadership ladder of a social institution or to change the institution. The politician is seeking to "move" things. (The bureaucrat seeks to carry out an established function.) The politician is trying to make headway against opposition—often very active opposition. To do so, the politician must capture the minds of the public through the media. The politician tries to capture and hold the attention of the reporter. So does the opposing politician. The reporter tries to reconcile what is coming from both politicians and to probe into what both are claiming. It is something like interviewing the opposing coaches during halftime—only it's continuous. You must avoid favoritism; if favoritism shows, the favorite will further manipulate you and the rejected politician will reject you. Not surprisingly, a hard-fought election campaign or the windup of a busy legislative session provide high excitement for reporters—followed by exhaustion.

You can expect some kind of response to almost any question you pose to a politician, but the answer may not fit the question. The politician spends a lot of time trying to orchestrate the information that he or she wants you to receive, through position papers, speeches, visits to this or that constituency and statements at the beginning of press conferences. The give-and-take is intense. A wise reporter in a political situation listens carefully, asks internally, "Why is this politician telling me this?" and thinks about what the politician should be putting on the record but isn't.

The *disgruntled member* of an organization is a source often used in investigative reporting, which is discussed in the next chapter. However, such sources are important in interpretive reporting also, because they provide a look into areas of institutions that may not otherwise be available. In this case, the source is not working in his or her own behalf, as in the case of the politician, but against someone else. Competing politicians sometimes understand and appreciate each other; they are birds of a feather. The disgruntled source, on the other hand, is less likely to remain a useful source if you do a balanced job of reporting both sides of the story.

Some sources are *publicity hounds*. They just like the limelight, or they like the feeling of power that planting a story in the media gives them. They often haunt newsrooms. In small doses, they serve the useful purpose of being an extra pair of eyes and ears for you. They rarely contribute to thoughtful interpretation of an issue.

Of much more importance to the interpretive reporter is the official source, the *public relations professional*. This person spends a great deal of time thinking through the policies, actions and plans of the institution he or she represents. The official spokesperson has a lot of information available and is eager for you to reach authoritative people in the institution if the resulting coverage is likely to reflect favorably on the institution.

The public relations person is a source who can lead you to other sources, who can provide information and who can respond to your interpretation of relevant issues with considerable insight. While the PR representative probably has an academic knowledge of the public's right to know—and all the good ones also have a commitment to informing the public accurately—keep in mind that the official spokesperson is a paid advocate of a specific institution. Your client is the public.

Interpretive Technique

Two major problems face a reporter in dealing with sources when writing an interpretive story. One is understanding the expert source and turning the expert's jargon into ordinary language. The other is paring down the information the expert gives you to a quantity that your audience can absorb.

Spending time and energy with the expert can solve the first problem. Play dumb. Every expert is flattered when someone recognizes his or her expertise and is impressed. Draw the source out and go back to pick up explanations of things that were not clear the first time through. Take copious notes. After writing about particularly technical matters, phone your source and check that portion of what you've written with him or her. If deadlines permit, read that portion of your story to a friend. If both the expert and your friend agree that it sounds all right, it probably succeeds at explaining a complicated subject to the average member of the audience.

Spending time and effort on your writing will solve the second problem. If you have ever tried to run a program through a computer and have faced its "fatal error" message, you may have had the experience of asking a dedicated computer programmer, "What did I do wrong?" You want him to respond, "You put a comma where you should have put a space." Instead he gives you a programmer's 30-minute explanation of why a space is needed instead of a comma. An interpretive story probably falls somewhere between the You-put-a-comma-where-you-should-have-put-a-space answer (that's straight news) and the programmer's long explanation (that's a computer journal article).

Clarity in writing is immediately enhanced by the removal of jargon. *Fatal error* is an example of computer jargon. No living plant or animal died. What the computer term means is: "You made a mistake that prevents the computer from doing what you wanted it to do, and it cannot proceed any further." Every human endeavor has its own jargon, a specialized language that speeds communication among those familiar with it and is largely incomprehensible to outsiders.

Consider some terms that cowboys use: cow, heifer, bull, steer, calf, yearling, dogie, maverick and ox. Each has its own meaning. Cow is a generic term for all cattle as individuals; it also is the term for a mature female cow. A heifer is a female cow that has not been a mother yet. A bull is a male cow. A steer is a castrated male cow. A calf is a young cow. A yearling is a one-year-old cow. A dogie is an orphan cow. An ox is any cow used as a draft animal. (A draft animal is one that pulls a wagon, cart or plow. A cart is a two-wheel wagon. There is no end to jargon.) A maverick is an orphan cow that has drifted from his mother's side before being branded. Back in the days of the open range, when herds belonging to different people shared the same grazing land, ownership of mavericks was determined by who got to them first with a hot branding iron. The exception to this generally accepted rule took place on Texas's Galveston Island where the Maverick family owned most of the cattle grazing on the island's open range. The Mavericks assumed that any unbranded calf unaccompanied by a mother cow belonged to them. That's where the term maverick came from. If you want to know more about cow jargon, read J. Frank Dobie's book "The Longhorns". (A longhorn is a descendant of Spanish cattle abandoned in 16th century North America, characterized by its long horns and ability to survive in the wilderness.)

Learn the jargon of your news sources and you will know a lot about their area of expertise. You will be able to interpret their jargon to the public using simple terms like mother, father, one-year-old and orphan.

If deadlines permit, you should use the following editing approach: Write a first draft of your interpretation. Go back through it looking for jargon and for long, complicated sentences. Most of all look for unimportant detail. Then take the marked-up text and rewrite it. Lay it aside. Go back later and see if it makes sense. Look for things you left out that should be there. Get a good night's sleep. The next morning give it a second rewrite to make it read smoothly. Then you will have an interpretive story worth your reader's time.

One way to keep improving your interpretive ability is by continuing to cultivate new sources. If you have gotten to know all the people in your community who are good sources for you, broaden your base by subscribing to some of the publications they subscribe to and by reading books on the subject. It is as important for you to know what is in the local library as it is for you to know who is a good source in your community. In addition—after a suitable period of respite after you graduate from college—you might find it useful to take some graduate-level courses.

A Pitfall

A reporter takes pride in staying out of a story. One of the highest compliments a reporter can give a story written by another reporter is to say, "The facts tell the story." The reader appreciates understatement and a clear presentation of the facts. When the facts are presented without coloring, the reader's reactions to the story are his or her own.

Interpretation takes a step beyond the facts. The reporter tells the reader what is important about the facts, what the facts mean. Often this is desirable, because the reporter has a better perspective on the facts and can more accurately interpret what the facts mean than can the reader. But the reader is being told what to think about the facts. Often the reader has some reservations about being told what to think.

An interpretive reporter is first and foremost a reporter. The facts still must carry the weight of the story. The interpretation needs to spring directly from the facts and should not overwhelm them. If the interpretation predominates, then the reader feels that the reporter is being condescending, perhaps downright arrogant. There is a tendency for reporters to become arrogant, once they attain the status of interpretive reporters or news analysts. They have exercised their self-confidence in going out on a limb and saying what they think the facts mean. The temptation is to depend less on facts and more on interpretation, to sell the sizzle instead of the steak. As that process continues, a "digging reporter" slides in the estimation of other reporters and often of the readers into the status of "thumbsucker." In that context the term isn't complimentary.

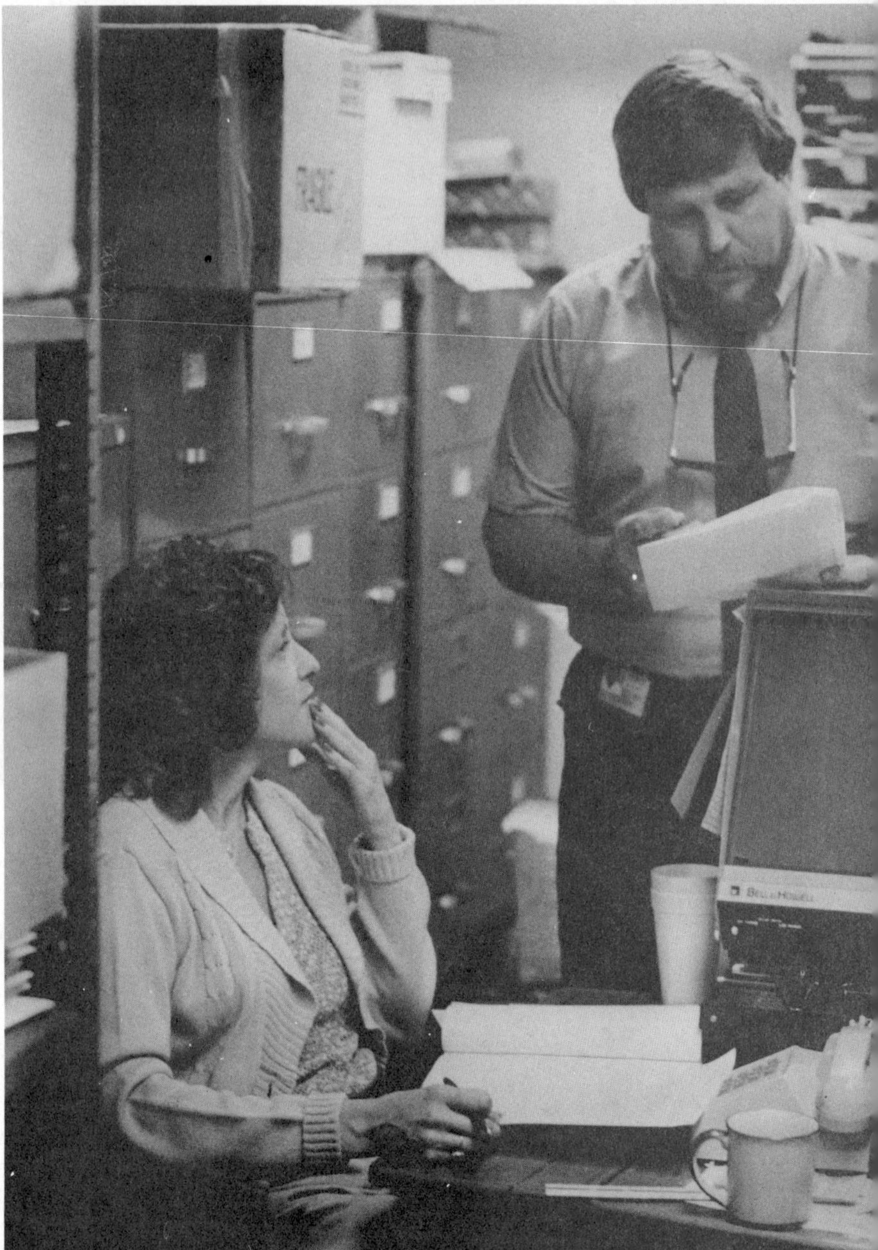

CHAPTER **12**

Investigative Stories

Uncovering the Covered
Practicing First Amendment Journalism
The Investigative Reporter
How to Begin
Interviewing Hostile Sources
Unnamed Sources
Using Records
Blending People and Paper
Anatomy of a Pulitzer Prize Investigative Story

Uncovering the Covered

Tom and Susan have been reporters at the Times for about two years. Tom's beat is the city hall and Susan covers the police station. Thus far, they have both done a respectable job of covering their daily beats, and both have developed numerous sources and a few friends. Then one Tuesday, a press conference brings an unexpected day of reckoning, a comparative test of Tom's and Susan's skills as professional journalists.

At the press conference, the mayor announces the purchase of six new police cars. Tom feverishly scribbles notes at the conference as the mayor talks about how each of the old patrol cars has accumulated well over 100,000 miles.

"They are just plain worn out," Tom quotes the mayor as saying. "These new cars are just what the police department needs." The police chief stands smiling beside the mayor at the press conference and Tom even makes a note of that fact in his story. He sees no need to look deeper into this announcement. It's all pretty routine stuff for a veteran municipal building reporter like him.

In fact, Tom is quite proud of his front page article when it appears the next morning—until Susan stops by his desk.

"Say, Tom," Susan says, "did you bother walking around to the rear of the police station to look at the odometer readings on the old police cars?" Tom says he did not. "Why would the mayor lie?" Tom asks. The mayor has become his valued source and friend.

"Well, I did take a look," says Susan. "None of them had more than 65,000 miles on their odometers. And did you call any of the cops who actually drove those old cars for their opinions?" Susan asks.

"No. The mayor said the cars were in pitiful condition," Tom explains.

Susan shakes her head. "I called and talked with three cops," she says. "They all agreed the older models were comfortable and ran just fine. In fact, they couldn't understand the need for new ones, especially with such huge motors and ugly blue vinyl seats."

Tom begins to make excuses. "Well, I just wrote down what the mayor said," he explains. "The police chief was standing right there. I didn't have much time to do lots of research on the story. Besides, what difference does it make?"

"Well, it will probably make a lot of difference to our readers—and our editors—when they read in my story tomorrow that the six new cars were bought from Felix Larson, an auto dealer who's the mayor's second cousin. And Larson's bid wasn't even the lowest of the five," says Susan, tapping Tom's video display terminal. "When you read a copy of the bid specifications, it's also clear that they were written for one specific type of automobile. Only Larson's cars meet all the technical specifications.

Chapter opening photo: In the investigative file room, Mike Masterson (center), editor of investigative projects for The Arizona Republic, discusses an ongoing investigation with reporter Al Sitter (right) and Huntley Womick, research assistant for the investigative team. (Photo by Earl McCartney, The Arizona Republic)

"Incidentally, I also spent another 10 minutes and checked the mayor's campaign contribution lists for two terms over at the clerk's office," Susan continues. "And guess whose names regularly appear, all giving the mayor a maximum contribution? Why, Felix and Mildred Larson and their 3-year-old son, Homer."

Tom, stunned beyond comment at this point, sits silently as Susan continues.

"And I made another call and found out that Larson's wife's maiden name was Boomerhagen. And six different Boomerhagens contributed $500 to the mayor's last campaign. It's all on the record."

Like a snowball rolling downhill, Susan's story the next day prompts other telephone calls and tips about wrongdoing at city hall. Her effort lays the groundwork for a series on corruption that culminates in the indictment of the mayor and police chief.

Susan has done an admirable job of investigative reporting by peering beneath the glossy veneer that so easily satisfied Tom. There was no cloak-and-dagger espionage or Watergate Deep Throat here, only Susan's persistence, energy and willingness to question. Even putting the investigative approach aside, when you contrast how Susan so vigorously pursued her tips and leads with Tom's acceptance of the mayor's official version, it becomes clear who is the professional journalist.

All reporters should apply Susan's approach to virtually every news story. The object of investigative reporting is really no different than the definition of good, solid reporting anywhere: Ask questions and more questions, focus your energy and creativity toward seeking the full truth in any given issue, and don't take no for an answer.

There are reporters like Tom and Susan working for every newspaper. The Toms of journalism generally manage to get by for awhile, but the Susans excel.

Practicing First Amendment Journalism

A free society offers countless opportunities for success in life. But with that freedom come heavy responsibilities. For example, we elect and appoint our leaders and fund their salaries with our hard-earned tax dollars. Consequently, we expect them to recognize our sacrifices by leading us with honesty and integrity.

The founders of our country believed these responsibilities of government were so vital that they intentionally preserved both freedom of speech and the press in order to ensure they were fulfilled. The First Amendment to the Constitution assured that journalists, in particular, would remain free to aggressively question the leaders and events that shape our lives and destiny as a nation. Our country's founders doubtlessly realized that, unless such questioning is woven within the fabric of a free society, the governing machinery often tends to corrupt itself with power, greed and an eventual willingness to follow the path of least resistance at the expense of moral standards.

In this way, the pursuit of truth and the fear of facing it publicly in print or on radio or television one day has become a powerful deterrent to corruption, even in the smallest communities where the various media perform their responsibilities.

Lately, those journalists who aggressively question the way the community is run have been labeled as investigative reporters or—less politely—typewriter guerrillas.

The latest surge in investigative reporting stems from the Watergate years of the early 1970s when the exploits and achievements of Washington Post reporters Bob Woodward and Carl Bernstein were glamorized in print and in the movie, "All The President's Men." Together, the reporters took what appeared to be a routine burglary in Washington, D.C. and through exhaustive legwork and records searches, created a string of stories that exposed crime and corruption at the highest levels of our government. Following their remarkable series, which culminated with the resignation of President Richard M. Nixon, journalism schools across the country reported record enrollments. The thought that reporters armed only with questions and words could spark such incredible social change appealed to thousands eager to make their own marks.

Dedicated journalists had been fighting and winning similar struggles for truth for decades before the Watergate scandal, though. At the

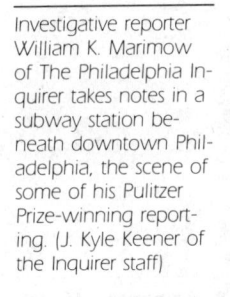

Investigative reporter William K. Marimow of The Philadelphia Inquirer takes notes in a subway station beneath downtown Philadelphia, the scene of some of his Pulitzer Prize-winning reporting. (J. Kyle Keener of the Inquirer staff)

turn of the century, for instance, under the pen name Nellie Bly, New York World reporter Elizabeth Cochrane had herself admitted as a patient to a notorious mental institution. Once inside, she exposed "snake pit" horrors and prompted massive reforms in mental health. In the 1930s—the days of freewheeling, scrambling Chicago journalists whose exploits provided fodder for the play and movie, "The Front Page"—newspapers were filled with exposés of political and social corruption, setting a tradition of aggressive journalism in Chicago that continues today. And many of the Pulitzer Prizes for reporting over the past 70 years have been for investigative journalism.

Those who wind up on the receiving end of investigative stories frequently complain that they are the victims of a newspaper trying to sell more papers. Some are quick to banter about such accusations as sensationalism and yellow journalism. But the truth is that the print and broadcast reporters who hold foremost their responsibility to seek and report truth will often end up with investigative stories. In fact, most daily and weekly newspapers thrive on regular monthly paid subscribers, not on daily street sales from screaming headlines. To be fair, a handful of newspapers today do have a sensational approach to reporting, but most of those are sold in supermarkets, not on street corners.

The Investigative Reporter

Some journalists and educators argue that investigative reporting is not a separate category of reporting. They believe all reporting is by nature investigative in its approach. And we have already said that investigative reporting is just good, solid reporting. There are distinct differences, though, between the way general assignment and beat reporters pursue and report the news and the way investigative, or project, reporters approach the news:

- Investigative reporters are designated as such at many newspapers because they have proven themselves responsible and adept at digging into issues.
- Investigative reporters are generally given more time to develop tips and perfect their stories.
- Investigative reporters generally rely more heavily on documents related to a story. Their searches frequently reveal discrepancies, contradictions and irregularities buried in the public record. General assignment and beat reporters necessarily focus heavily on more easily accessible information and quotations in order to meet the pressures of daily deadlines.
- Investigative reporters are frequently held to higher standards of responsibility since they are given additional freedom and time to perfect their stories.

The basic ingredients of a good journalist—curiosity, aggressiveness, energy, tenacity, integrity and a command of the English language—will inevitably spur reporters to pursue the threads of truth in any story. But the reporters who prove themselves best at this usually wind up as investigative journalists. The most common characteristics of successful investigative reporters, most agree, is their intolerance for deception and injustice and their desire to uncover the covered for as long as it takes to get to the truth of an issue or event. While there are some tips that can help aspiring investigative reporters, the biggest factor is an inherent drive to reveal what is hidden or wrong.

Bob Greene, the Pulitzer Prize-winning editor of the investigative team at Newsday on Long Island, says that whenever he hires a reporter for the Newsday team, he looks for three characteristics: *drive*, a sense of moral outrage at injustices, no matter how seemingly insignificant; *tenacity*, an unwillingness to give up until the truth is uncovered and reported and the issue is resolved; and *capacity*, an ability to synthesize volumes of information and reduce it to clear, meaningful and interesting stories.

Greene says: "Journalists are not paid stenographers. This is a profession of questions and answers. If a reporter is always looking for a handout or a news release to combine with some quick and easy quotes, he or she should be doing something else for a living."

How to Begin

Contrary to movie plots, great newspaper investigations rarely begin with a reporter noticing something amiss. Most often, the investigative story begins with a telephone call or a letter—a tip that something is wrong.

Unfortunately, that is where countless thousands of potentially significant newspaper stories die—on scribbled notes at the bottom of a wastebasket. How a reporter handles a tip is unarguably the most critical point in any piece of investigative reporting. Unless the reporter is willing to devote the time and energy necessary for the next step—called the *sniff*—there will be no investigation. Journalistic investigation is just another name for consulting more people, records and documents than normal.

Susan's story was a mixture of a tip and a sniff. She got the tip from one of the police officers she spoke with. Her sniff was the initial check that proved the tip accurate. Susan received information from a variety of sources and followed that up with information from records. The best investigative stories use just that combination of information.

For example, when Newsday won a Pulitzer Prize in 1974 for Greene's remarkable series that tracked the heroin connection from Turkey through New York to the nation, it was the combination of reliable sources and pertinent records that made it all possible. The sources included law enforcement officers, junkies and the pushers themselves. Police records provided many facts and leads.

Interviewing Hostile Sources

Investigative reporting is not for the timid or the squeamish. The subjects of newspaper investigations frequently find some way to strike back. They use tactics such as organized letter writing campaigns, attacks on a reporter's character or credibility, physical threats, lawsuits and even economic boycotts against the news organization that carried the stories. The investigative reporter who plays hardball should be prepared to dodge a number of foul balls.

Even at the risk of incurring this predictable and understandable hostility, you have an overriding obligation to be fair. For example, it is inexcusable to write a story that accuses or alleges wrongdoing without giving the accused person or agency a full opportunity to explain, deny or otherwise respond. This means personally contacting people who may be openly hostile to you because they know what you are up to or because of the nature of questions that you must ask.

A few techniques can ease your encounter with a hostile source:

- Assure the source that you are interested in obtaining his or her version of the story. Very often, if the source will talk to you, his or her information can add entirely new perspectives to a story, or in extreme cases, nullify the story altogether.
- Let the source know that any preconceptions you may have formed in the course of gathering previous information might well be altered by hearing his or her side.
- Try to meet him or her on neutral territory, preferably in a public place such as a coffee shop or restaurant. This less threatening atmosphere often neutralizes any home field advantage and tends to put both the reporter and the hostile source in a more objective frame of mind. It will also help keep the interview process more civil.
- Begin the interview by collecting background information that tends to put the person at ease. Ask when he or she was born and where. Cover job history and other personal data before leading into key questions. Save your toughest questions for last. That way you already have some information in the event that he or she abruptly ends the interview.
- Always be as creative in securing meaningful responses to accusations as you were in obtaining the original story material. If the hostile source refuses to comment in a telephone interview, send a registered letter with the questions. If that draws no answer, send a telegram seeking a response. Show that you have done everything possible to obtain the source's side of the story.

Remember that every person you interview has a unique side of the story to offer. If you can use social skills and sincerity to hear their version, you'll be surprised how often it will change the way you decide to present the information you have unearthed.

"I can't overemphasize the importance of good sources in any investigative piece," says Greene of Newsday. "Without them, the job becomes extremely difficult and sometimes impossible."

Unnamed Sources

No explanation of investigative reporting would be complete without addressing the issue of using unnamed single source quotations. An unnamed single source quotation is an uncorroborated statement or charge from an unidentified source.

Unless a news organization has a policy on this issue, the decision of whether or not to use an unnamed source rests with each reporter. When unnamed sources are quoted, the reporter must remember that it is his or her credibility hanging in the balance, not that of the source. It is critical for a reporter to buttress the unnamed source with documents and additional sources because it is not unusual for a source—who later feels pressured—to retract earlier revelations, leaving the reporter in the lurch alone.

Remember that it is a cardinal sin in journalism to reveal a source once you have pledged confidentiality. Thus, the unattributed single source who later tells you that you "misunderstood" must nevertheless still be protected. To "burn" a source through public disclosure is to announce to anyone else with thoughts of speaking confidentially that you are not trustworthy. And reporters survive on credibility.

As a rule, get single sources to talk on the record. Many experienced reporters appeal to the source's sense of decency or ethics to convince him or her to speak for the record. If that fails, some reporters try to elicit firm promises from the source at the outset that in the event of legal action against the reporter or the news organization the source will voluntarily reveal himself or herself. That's a good idea, because although many states have passed so-called shield laws to protect reporters from having to reveal their sources to courts or grand juries, such laws do not exist in the federal court system. There reporters are frequently left to defend themselves only on First Amendment grounds.

If you do decide to use information from unnamed sources, be sure to corroborate it either through other sources with firsthand knowledge or with records. Often, a source can remain out of the story altogether by simply steering the reporter to the proper person or documents.

In the end, it is the reporter who writes the information and who must stand responsible for it. The public is understandably more wary of the credibility of any story containing unnamed sources. The bottom line: Try to avoid using unnamed sources.

Using Records

Chapter 6 examined the use of records, or paper trails, but it is important to point out the critical role of records in investigative reporting. For when all is said and done, documents provide the backbone for such journalism.

Many good investigative reporters develop favorite places they can regularly check for both background and ideas. Some glean valuable material from police and arrest reports while others plow the fertile fields of inspection reports. In interviews with dozens of investigative reporters, the following records emerged as the most popular:

- Health, building, fire, audit and other inspection records and reports.
- Police arrest reports, which can give vital insights into everything from crime to court corruption.
- Court transcripts, records, case files and probate records.
- Divorce files, which can provide otherwise difficult-to-get financial information on individuals.
- Motor vehicle department records such as licenses, titles and driving records.
- Local tax assessment and collection records for documentation of real and personal property ownership.
- Public contract documents, including bid offers, which can spotlight potential corruption with taxpayers' money.
- Campaign contribution lists, which must be filed locally and with state offices and which can reveal who has contributed how much to which politicians.
- Grantor and grantee books in the courthouse, which explain who owns or leases property in an area.
- Charters and written regulations, which govern all public agencies, and explain the function and specific responsibilities of each agency. By looking here, you can determine if an agency is living up to its intended purpose.

Just using records to support a story, though, does not make a person an investigative reporter. All good reporters use documents. It's what the reporter does with the records. The investigative reporter continually searches for the discrepancies and disparities with other records or oral statements that document a condition that needs to be reported.

Blending People and Paper

A story based on nothing but sources is likely to be of suspect credibility, while a story based on nothing but dry records may be uninteresting. The mixture of solid sources and pertinent records creates some of the very best investigative journalism.

For example, in 1984, an Arkansas Democrat reporter discovered a 24-year-old autopsy report and blended its findings with the opinions of medical experts and other interviews to produce a series that exposed a forgotten 1960 jail house death as a murder. The stories led to a grand jury which indicted two former policemen for murder. The policemen eventually were exonerated, but the stories performed a valuable public service. The death had been ruled an "accident" from a fall during an "alcoholic stupor." But the autopsy report showed the man had been bludgeoned, probably after his arrest, and that his blood alcohol level at time of autopsy registered zero. That series won the 1985 Heywood Broun Award.

Mary Hargrove of The Tulsa Tribune spent a full year traveling the country collecting documents and conducting more than 300 interviews for a week-long investigative series about evangelist Oral Roberts. That series, the most extensive in the newspaper's history, revealed for the first time all of Robert's vast holdings and his techniques for achieving power and wealth.

Jon Hall of the New Haven Register. (Peter R. Hivzdak/Jackson Newspapers, New Haven)

> **ADVICE FROM A PROFESSIONAL INVESTIGATIVE REPORTER**
>
> Jon Hall, one of the finest investigative reporters on the East Coast, works for the smallish, yet feisty, Register of New Haven, Conn. Hall's exposés have prompted positive reforms in areas ranging from airline security to enforcement of fire and building codes. After nearly 15 years of reporting and editing, Hall, whose official title is investigative editor, offers eight pertinent suggestions for aspiring investigative reporters:
>
> "Remain ever curious about the people and events around you. If something doesn't look quite right, it probably isn't," Hall says.
>
> "Never take no for an answer. If you don't get an answer to your question, keep asking it in every way imaginable until you get an explanation.
>
> "Never be reluctant to question authority or to make people angry in pursuit of the truth.
>
> "Always follow the money trail when you are looking for why something happened. Most actions by human beings revolve around the quest for personal gain.
>
> "First check your facts, then double- and triple-check them. There is no acceptable excuse for getting it wrong because the impact and rippling effect of what you are doing is too enormous to be wrong.
>
> "Find every way possible to obtain the record that proves your point. There is no substitute for a document.
>
> "Strive to be fair in every story," he says.
>
> And, he adds: "Shut up and listen carefully after you've asked the question. Don't try to impress your subject with how much you know and don't talk when they're trying to answer you."

Both series are examples of how reporters skillfully blended sources with documents to produce extraordinary investigative work.

Anatomy of a Pulitzer Prize Investigative Story

Lucy Morgan, a reporter for the St. Petersburg Times, had been hearing the rumors for some time about corruption in the Pasco County, Fla., sheriff's department. But, as is the case with many tips received by reporters, she had placed those on the back burner in order to complete other more pressing projects. Finally, when the rumors began to multiply, Morgan turned her full attention to the issue. Today, she's glad she did.

Morgan, a mother of four who never attended a day of college, shared the 1985 Pulitzer Prize for investigative reporting with fellow reporter Jack Reed because of what they found and reported in Pasco County. Morgan and Reed's six major stories and numerous reaction and sidebar articles published in 1983 and 1984 resulted in reforms within the Pasco County sheriff's department and the indictment of the former sheriff, who was later acquitted but lost the election.

Their special report—entitled "Inside the Pasco County Sheriff's Department"—relied heavily on public records and key interviews. "There was nothing fancy at all," says Morgan. "We just worked long, hard hours, followed tips and double-checked everything. There were no cheap shots."

In the end, the reporters had proved the following:

- The county and the sheriff had failed to perform adequate background examinations of sheriff's department employees. As a result, one of every eight deputies checked by reporters had criminal histories.
- The sheriff had engaged in questionable business dealings with his employees. One wealthy part-time deputy was allowed to help finance and set up a secret investigation into opponents of the sheriff. Another deputy operated a delicatessen in a building owned by the sheriff.
- The crime scenes at murder investigations had been so badly botched that a special consultant retained by the newspaper could not determine what had happened from the investigative files.
- The sheriff deposited his department's public money in the same banks where he had personal accounts. Records showed he had received personal loans and other favorable financial transactions on the same day public money was deposited into those same banks.
- A woman in her early 20s had turned to the life of a prostitute at age 16 after she and a girlfriend had been kept in a mobile home and used as undercover drug informants by some Pasco deputies. Although the girl's mother had reported her missing, the deputies refused to tell the mother they were keeping her daughter and also using her for occasional sex.

Let's examine how Morgan and Reed handled some of those revelations and the sheriff's denials. In a story dated Dec. 7, 1983, Reed began with the following 10 paragraphs. Note how quickly Reed gets to the point in his lead, then follows in the next two paragraphs with specifics. Also notice that the sheriff's denials and those of the bankers are included high in the story. (Some names in the following three story excerpts have been deleted because court decisions involving these individuals were being appealed at the time of this book's publication.)

Anatomy of a Pulitzer Prize Investigative Story **271**

Inside the Pasco County Sheriff's Department

By **Jack Reed**
Staff Writer
St. Petersburg Times

PULITZER PRIZE WINNER

On Sept. 14, Sheriff _____ conducted two transactions with the Bank of Pasco County, one as sheriff, the other as a private businessman.

As sheriff, he opened a new payroll account at the Dade-based bank by depositing $173,965.

As a partner in a new business enterprise, he signed a $320,000 personal mortgage loan from the bank to build a funeral home in Elfers.

More than once, _____'s public and private financial dealings have overlapped, creating a potential conflict of interest that may violate the state's Code of Ethics for elected officials.

A review of the sheriff's investments shows that:

- Six of the financial institutions that have held sheriff's department funds have also made personal loans to _____ since he became sheriff in 1977.

- On three occasions, personal mortgage loans to _____ came at about the same time the sheriff's office made large deposits with the lender (See illustration, this page.) At one of those institutions, _____ and his wife are also small stockholders.

_____ denied Tuesday that his department's large accounts helped him get personal loans from the same financial institutions. "Absolutely not," he declared. "I don't know of any way that would help me get a loan."

Officers at each of the banks involved in _____'s public and private transactions also deny that _____ got the loans because he invested public money with them.

But most also acknowledged that a sheriff, or any influential person in the community, does have an advantage over other loan seekers.

Reed did an admirable job of explaining the point of his story in a concise and interesting manner. The second and third paragraphs play well off each other and the fourth paragraph, which in journalism is frequently called the *nut* or *so what* paragraph, explains why this story is important. The reference to an accompanying illustration within the body of the seventh paragraph helps tie the story to the illustration and makes it easier for the reader to better understand the connection between the two.

Now let's look at the first 10 paragraphs of a story Morgan wrote about the deputies. The article was published Feb. 26, 1984.

Pasco Deputy Did Not Reveal Arrest Record

By **Lucy Morgan**
Staff Writer
St. Petersburg Times

PULITZER PRIZE WINNER

When _____ applied for a job as a Pasco County sheriff's deputy he signed affidavits saying he had never been arrested or convicted of a crime.

The department conducted a background check and paid for his police training at Pasco-Hernando Community College.

Just three months before applying for the job, _____ appeared in a Pasco County courtroom and pleaded guilty to a misdemeanor charge. Five years earlier, he had pleaded guilty to another one.

The two convictions might not make him ineligible to be a law enforcement officer, but not telling the truth about them on his applications could result in the withdrawal of his certification by Florida's Police Standards and Training Commission.

Since joining the Pasco force, _____ has been the subject of several internal investigations. One report detailed his association with a convicted felon who has since been indicted on a racketeering charge with reputed Mafia chieftain _____.

Records on file in the Pasco County Courthouse detail both of _____'s convictions. In 1975, _____ was arrested by the Pasco County Sheriff's Department after he failed to appear in court to answer a petty theft charge.

When he did appear, on Oct. 8, 1975, _____ pleaded guilty and was sentenced by County Judge Dan C. Rasmussen to pay a fine of $173 or spend 10 days in jail.

On Jan. 16, 1980, _____ was back in front of Rasmussen on a charge of failing to register as a person engaged in a building trade. He again pleaded guilty and was assessed $25 in fines and court costs. Rasmussen found him guilty in both cases.

On April 18, 1980, _____ filled out an application for the Pasco County Sheriff's Department. He answered no when asked whether he had ever been convicted of a crime.

A computerized records check and fingerprints submitted to the FBI failed to turn up the two charges.

We discussed the nut paragraph in Reed's story. The equivalent paragraph in Morgan's is the fourth, which explains why this story is important.

Some subtle aspects of Morgan's story serve as a primer for the mechanics of investigative reporting. For example:

- She states her facts simply, directly and clearly.
- She avoids the obvious temptation to begin the third paragraph with the word *but*, indicating a contradiction to the first two paragraphs. She opted instead to let the readers draw their own conclusions by simply stating the facts, which in this instance is an effective approach.
- She makes evident her dependence on public records by direct and indirect attributions in the fifth and sixth paragraphs. The sixth paragraph reference to records on file in the sheriff's department makes the reader wonder how the department could have overlooked their own records in checking the deputy's background.
- The final paragraph provides a good lesson for beginning investigative reporters: Just because information doesn't surface in one set of files doesn't mean a reporter should give up. Morgan found her proof right under the sheriff's department's own nose.

This story was accompanied by reproduced copies of the deputy's sworn affidavit of a clean record and court records showing both misdemeanor convictions. Many newspapers reinforce the credibility of their investigations by reproducing copies of the supporting documents.

A story by both Morgan and Reed in December 1983, documented numerous questionable business activities of the sheriff. Examine how Morgan and Reed lead into the story and how they include the sheriff's reaction high in the story structure. Although this copyrighted story is much longer and part of a package of stories published in the same edition, the highlights are all included in the first 11 paragraphs.

Doing Business With the Boss in Pasco

By **Jack Reed**
and **Lucy Morgan**
Staff Writers
St. Petersburg Times

PULITZER PRIZE WINNER

When Pasco County Sheriff _____ wants to buy or sell a piece of property or find a business partner, he often turns to his employees.

While building his personal wealth, the sheriff has done business with at least eight subordinates and surrounded himself with fellow entrepreneurs.

The sheriff says it's all proper—sheriff's business comes first.

But a closer look at the mixture of public business and private enterprise shows that:

- In becoming a land speculator, mortgage lender, landlord and corporate officer with the help of his employees, _____ may have violated the state Code of Ethics for public officials.
- One of his most profitable transactions was with a deputy who was allowed to help finance and set up a secret investigation (See story, 9–B).
- A jail director who was criticized by a superior for letting outside business interests harm his job performance apparently escaped punishment. One of his outside interests was a delicatessen in a building owned by the sheriff (see illustration, 8–B).
- The sheriff hired a former funeral director to be his department's special projects coordinator. One of their projects, which they discuss during work hours, is a funeral home (See story, 1–B)

_____ says that he has been able to separate his official duties and his private transactions with his employees. "As long as it never interferes with the office that I run, there is no problem with that," he says.

_____ also says that "many sheriffs" and other elected officials do business with subordinates because they are "people they know and trust."

Yet Florida law prohibits a public official from having a work relationship that "will create a continuing or frequently recurring conflict between his private interests and the performance of his public duties."

Two of these stories use bullets, or checks—paragraphs distinguished by small dots or checkmarks that capsulize a significant finding high in the story. While some editors are averse to using bullets, many investigative reporters frequently urge the use of bullets in their stories as a convenient method for quickly and clearly covering a lot of ground.

"I have found the bullets or checks, as we use them at the Times are the best way to disseminate facts and findings high in a story," says Morgan.

Do you feel Morgan and Reed used bullets effectively in these examples? Were those bullets situated properly in the structure of the story?

Do you sense an accusatory tone in any of the sample stories? Are they too softly written in your estimation? Did you notice in the last story a lack of attribution in the first eight paragraphs? Was attribution needed in those paragraphs, or are the newspaper's findings sufficient to stand on their own without having to use widely accepted phrases such as *according to, records show, documents reveal*, or *reliable sources say*?

Morgan says the Pasco County series generated nearly 4,000 phone calls and letters, some from the sheriff's office. When she received the first call on the day their series broke, Morgan expected a torrent of curse words because the sheriff had been extremely popular. "Instead, the lady praised us and said, 'It's about time somebody had the [courage] to do this,'" says Morgan. "Needless to say, it made me feel great."

As they do with most digging reporters, records played a major role in this investigation. Morgan swears by records. Without them, she says, effective investigative reporting probably wouldn't even exist. In preparing their prize-winning series, Morgan and Reed used dozens of public records, including liquor license records, police standards records, criminal indexes and arrest reports, law enforcement personnel records, and finance and driving records.

Morgan offers the following advice for beginners who aspire to be investigative reporters:

- Become a fanatic about accuracy, even little technical points that may seem insignificant at the time.
- Learn the system you are dealing with to gain necessary perspective. How does it work? How is it supposed to work? It is difficult to report on a system you don't understand.
- Depend on records. Politicians and others can tell you something today and take it back tomorrow—and they do. Documents do not lie.
- Make every effort possible to get the other side.

For Jack Reed and Lucy Morgan, persistent tips from concerned citizens evolved into an example of quality journalism and worldwide recognition for their efforts. Simply put, the reporters took facts discovered in a search for truth and molded them into winds of public opinion that swept across Pasco County, leaving reform in its wake. Such are the results and benefits of investigative reporting when it is done properly.

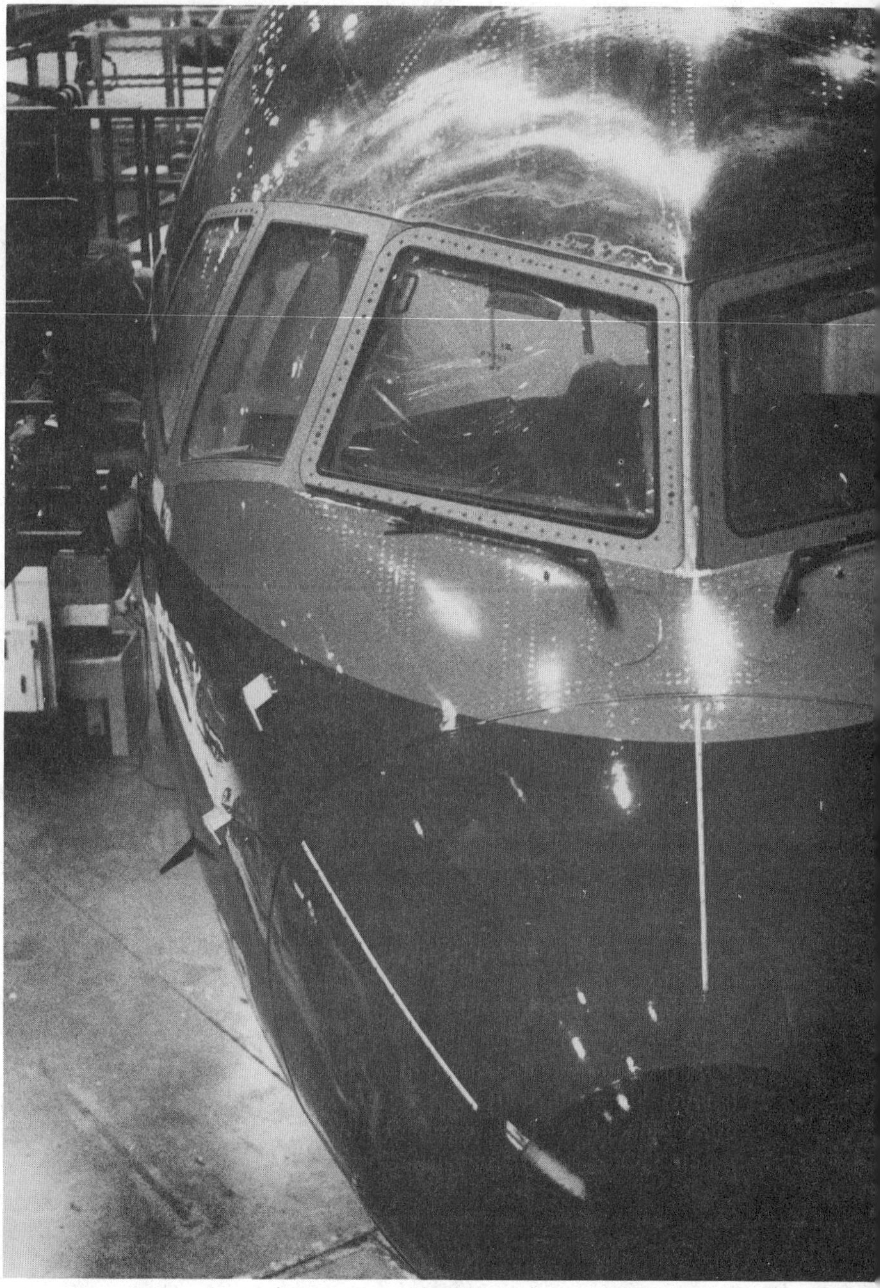

CHAPTER **13**

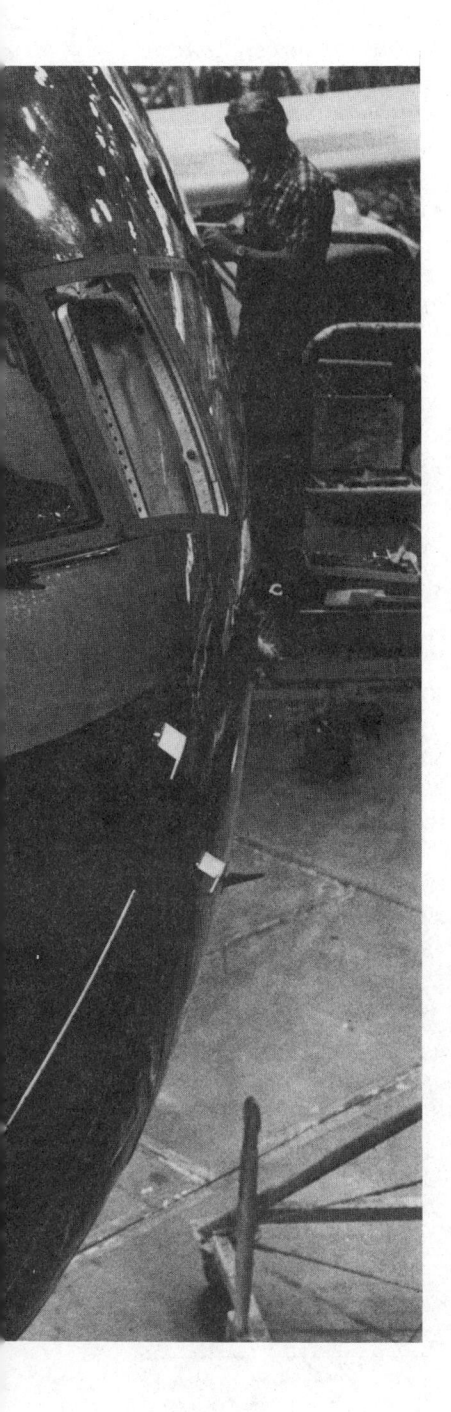

Series

Why the Series
Types of Series
Reprints: Creating a Series After the Fact
Advantages of Series
Disadvantages of Series
Thinking Through the Traditional Series
Organizing and Writing the Series
Tantalizing the Reader
Using Photos in a Series
Examining a Pulitzer Prize-Winning Series

Why the Series?

As newspapers have become increasingly competitive with improved television news, print journalists have played more and more to their primary strength: in-depth reporting in series format. While a television station may more often be first with the breaking stories, the time it can devote to an issue still pales in comparison with the space a newspaper can devote to fully explaining and adding perspective to the same subject.

Newspapers use a series when—in the course of reporting the news—a reporter gathers far more relevant facts than will fit in the space allocated for the story. When this happens, it is only logical to divide the facts into segments or categories of information. Thus, a series presents unique opportunities and challenges to the reporter that he or she would not ordinarily have in the day-to-day course of reporting the news.

There are no restrictions on which types of stories can or should be presented in series format. They can range from features to hard news and investigative pieces. Peter Rinearson of The Seattle Times received a Pulitzer Prize in 1984 for a feature series on building the Boeing 757 airplane, the Los Angeles Times won a Pulitzer for its 27-part series on Southern California Latinos and in that same year, The Boston Globe earned a Pulitzer for a six-part series about problems affecting the city's black community.

A reporter or editor frequently realizes in advance when a particular topic requires a series treatment rather than a single story. That was the case with Jon Franklin, a science and medical writer whose 1985 Pulitzer Prize-winning series was 11 years in the making. The series, also discussed in Chapter 5, grew from numerous brain chemistry developments Franklin covered beginning in 1973. Franklin says the volume of the information and its complexity required a series format.

Franklin, a University of Maryland journalism graduate and an Evening Sun reporter since 1970, first won a Pulitzer in 1979 for a stunning feature account of a brain operation. In 1985, he won his second Pulitzer, this time for explanatory reporting in the nine-day series called "The Mind Fixers." The purpose of the series was to "explain and explore the new science of molecular psychiatry and its impact on mental illness and behavior," Franklin wrote. Quoting one scientist, the series explained that the brain "is an organ; it produces thoughts the same way the kidney produces urine." In addition, chemicals control the brain and chemical imbalances are often the cause of irrational behavior, scientists said in the series. In sum, Franklin wrote in the series, "Ahead lies an era of psychic engineering [with] specialized drugs and therapies to heal sick minds."

Franklin interviewed more than 50 scientists and gathered material from another 50 for the articles. The series began with an overview of

---

Chapter opening photo: A Boeing employee works on the door of a 757 jetliner, from The Seattle Times' Pulitzer Prize-winning "Making It Fly" series, written by Peter Rinearson. (Alan Berner/The Seattle Times)

the chemical workings of the brain and followed with articles about how mental disease and drug addiction afflict the population, how chemicals in the brain control the mind, and how those chemicals cause or can control depression, schizophrenia, and perhaps criminality. The series also looked at how high-technology machines can be used for diagnosis.

The series received national recognition, Franklin says, because he was able to put various parts of a puzzle together. He explains: "What I am selling is coherence. I take things and make them make sense. I look for patterns, not information. There were two pieces of information in that entire series that hadn't been printed somewhere else. Probably most of it had been in The Washington Post and The New York Times. What was new was pattern. I was the first to put it all together. News isn't worth much without pattern."

On the other hand, sometimes a quick decision is made to create a series from an ongoing story. For example, Paul Henderson, a Pulitzer Prize winner for special local reporting at The Seattle Times in 1981, realized after writing one long story that even more information would be needed if he was to show beyond a doubt that an innocent man had been wrongly convicted of rape. After three major stories, published two weeks apart, the court overturned the conviction of Steve Titus and set him free based on the reporter's evidence of mistaken identity. Weeks later, another man confessed to the crime.

"Sometimes I still can't believe it worked out the way it did," says Henderson, now a private investigator in Seattle. "I didn't plan for it to be a series in the beginning. The first story was just a wide-ranging background piece about Titus, which also pointed out numerous inconsistencies in that case. Afterwards, I realized there was more work to do, so I wrote two additional stories. One pointed to the glaring discrepancies in the time elements surrounding the rape. The other story stemmed from my investigation into the common patterns in other similar rapes. That story showed it was the same person doing the raping on each occurrence and that person could not have been Steve Titus."

Types of Series

There are three basic types of series. The first type is the *traditional series*, which is the most prevalent series, consisting of two or more stories that are planned and prepared in advance.

The second type is the *occasional series*, a series which inadvertently becomes one not by preplanning but because stories appear about the same subject over a period of months. For example, a reporter who during six months writes 15 stories about ongoing developments in a local hospital scandal has, in effect, created such a series.

The third type is the *running series*, a series that begins with several preplanned major stories on a topic and expands with time because of new developments or follow-up articles. This type of series is frequently linked for continuity's sake with a common symbol, title or logo accompanying each story. This series is often found in competitive environments where reporters may not have time to develop a full-fledged traditional series for fear of being scooped. By writing an original lead story or two and following those afterwards, the net effect can be the same.

Reprints: Creating a Series After the Fact

Increasing numbers of newspapers have also turned to reprinting stories on the same subject, thus providing a complete package of all stories and editorials previously published on that topic. These can include reprinting an entire series after-the-fact in a single package such as a tabloid. The reprints can be inserted into the daily newspaper. More often, they are produced and distributed separately by direct mail.

Through reprints, newspapers can effectively repackage and redistribute important material. These series reprints are usually available to journalism schools and the public upon request. In some instances, news organizations charge a nominal fee to cover the cost of republication. Reprints allow readers who may have missed some of the stories

Phyllis Gillespie, a reporter for The Arizona Republic's state desk, reviews clips and records in the newspaper's computerized editorial library. (Photo courtesy of The Arizona Republic)

when they were originally published to see the full story from beginning to end in a more dramatic format.

Papers as large as The Philadelphia Inquirer, the Los Angeles Times, The Orange County Register, The Milwaukee Journal, The Arizona Republic, The Seattle Times, The Miami Herald and the San Francisco Examiner frequently reprint their major series each year. But many smaller papers such as The Charlotte Observer, the Portland Oregonian, The Tulsa Tribune, the Arkansas Democrat and the New Haven Register also have published reprints of their important series on public service issues.

Advantages of Series

There are definite pluses to using a series format as opposed to one long story. Here are five major advantages:

- The reporter can use virtually all the significant information he or she has gathered.
- The reporter can explore passing references of important points in one story and develop them into full-blown stories of their own. This would include the crucial development of the human element in a story which tells readers what the story means in their lives.
- By splitting a ponderous story into three articles of around 30 column inches each, the chances that people will read it are greatly enhanced.
- Shorter stories allow more opportunities for additional graphics and photographs and appealing layout.
- In an investigative series, the pressures of anticipation over the revelations yet to come can sometimes prompt positive results far more effectively than a single story with a one-shot message.

All of these advantages came into play in a series Chuck Cook and Maria Cone researched and wrote for the Orange County Register in Santa Ana, Calif., in 1982. "Deadly Smoke" was a 12-part series packaged to run over three days. Complete with handsome graphics and photography, the series gave a humanized and detailed account of the plight of many firemen who endured disease and disability after inhaling the dangerous smoke from burning plastics and other chemical derivatives.

Cook says the key elements in that series, which was recognized by the Edward Meeman Awards for environmental reporting, were the human stories that made the rest of the series seem relevant. "A key to making any series excellent lies in humanizing the effort ... telling your readers why this is important in their lives and what it has done to other people with whom they can relate," he explains.

If necessary, "Deadly Smoke" could have been done in one long article, Cook concedes. "But that would have meant focusing strictly on the hard news, nuts-and-bolts problem with virtually no examples of the human effects," he says. "It would have ended up long and lifeless, without any real perspective."

Cook has written scores of in-depth series in the past 16 years, several of which have won national recognition. They have included investigations into Memphis State University basketball recruiting, questionable cell hangings in Orange County and the poisoning of highway road oil in Texas. Cook says none of those efforts could have been accomplished with only a single story. "In order to bring the full stories to light, it was necessary for all three of those to be in running series," he says.

Another story that took full advantage of the series format was the Oral Roberts investigative story mentioned in Chapter 12. In 1986, Mary Hargrove, the special projects editor at The Tulsa Tribune whose reporting has been nationally honored on several occasions, and two other Tribune reporters published a 16-story series on the empire of the evangelist. The reporters worked off and on for a year on the Roberts' series, which ran on the front page for nine days. Afterwards, the newspaper produced reprints, which were sold to recover production costs.

Hargrove says the response was enormous. "Hundreds and hundreds of people called, wrote and ordered reprints of the series," says Hargrove. "But then again, you've got to realize we were writing about a worldwide institution right here in Tulsa. I'd estimate we had 85 percent readership for the Roberts series, which, granted, ran awfully long."

She says it took every inch to effectively tell the complete story of Robert's vast financial and personal empire while also blending in the human elements that helped readers relate to the overall effects of that empire.

Hargrove knows that a series is almost always a gamble: A newspaper usually commits large quantities of valuable editorial time and space in the hope that the topic will be interesting and meaningful to its readers. If few people read the series, the loss is significantly more serious than a single unread story.

Disadvantages of Series

Every reporter understandably likes to see his or her name in print as often as possible on the splashiest stories in the newspaper. But most stories in daily newspapers just don't warrant a longer exhaustive approach. Many editors select which stories will become series based on the potential for public service. For instance, an editor at a newspaper with limited resources might allow a reporter a month to complete a four-part series on shoddy care and mysterious deaths in a local nursing home while refusing another reporter's request to spend that much time and effort looking at potential mismanagement of funds in the city's summer softball league.

So, along with the positive aspects of series come some inherent restrictions. Here are four disadvantages to the series approach:

- Limited space at most newspapers today often becomes a factor in deciding to opt for a single story rather than a series.
- A series can lose the reader. Some readers may read the first two installments of the series, then be out of town for three days and miss the rest. Some may be interested in the third installment but nothing else.
- In a series, you are most likely fighting a publishing delay that may affect the timeliness of your stories. A traditional series is likely to be several weeks old by the time it sees print. Many things can change in that period of time.
- Most series have limited appeal. A large amount of space is devoted to a very specific subject and you run the risk of losing a large percentage of the readers, who may have no interest whatsoever in that topic.

The Roberts series attracted an astounding number of readers, but in contrast, Hargrove says she has no idea how well received a series on Veteran's Administration hospitals will be when it's published. "How many people around here will be interested in VA hospitals?" she wonders. "It's shaping up as a very powerful series but I don't know if anyone will read it or even care about it in the end. We are doing it primarily as a public service to inform the public of what we have found in these hospitals."

To avoid the disadvantages of a series, the one rule Hargrove most espouses is to "write it so well and so compelling that you're going to *make* them want to read it."

Consider these leads from several of the stories in the Tribune's series on Oral Roberts:

Tiny plastic bags of cement appeared in mailboxes of thousands of Oral Robert's prayer partners last March.

Oral Roberts, a pioneer in television evangelism, has lost more than half of his viewing audience in the past eight years, dropping from first to third in national ratings among preachers.

In 1977, God called Oral Roberts to the California desert.
"You must build a new and different medical center for me," God said, as quoted by Roberts. "You build it exactly as I have given you the vision."

In the mid-1960s, when Oral Roberts dug a hole in south Tulsa farmland and called it a university, some paid no attention, others snickered.

Today, Tulsa evangelist Granville Oral Roberts controls a $500 million international conglomerate which has a major impact on the city's economy.

But a sense of urgency prevails in Robert's ministry as he grapples with a current financial crisis as well as the dilemma of maintaining contributions after he is gone.

The last lead was actually the first in the series. Would you have guessed that? Why? Did these leads make you want to read more of each story? Which was the most interesting lead in your opinion? Why? Which lead contained the most pertinent information? Did you notice the combination of hard news and feature leads? Can you see ways these same leads could have been tightened or improved in any way? Probably not. Most journalists would agree that all of the leads are well researched and presented—they are textbook examples of series leads.

Thinking Through the Traditional Series

The long-term, traditional series requires planning and a sense of timing both inside and outside the newsroom. Here are some practical suggestions to bear in mind when you embark on a typical long-term series.

- Your first step will often be selling the idea to an editor, usually through an internal memo. The memo should clearly and succinctly present the expected parameters of the story, what you hope to accomplish, the estimated time and resources required and at least one solid reason why it is important for you to do the series.
- Recognize at the outset that you will need to stay organized. This means thinking through such things as:

    1. The most effective sequence for conducting your various interviews.
    2. Which questions should be asked first and which are best saved for last, when the subject is already at ease and has already responded to the majority of your questions.
    3. Scheduling time for writing hurried rough drafts of each story as the series progresses rather than waiting until everything is on hand. The rough drafts will serve as skeletal frameworks on which you can more easily build and perfect the body of each story.

- Make certain the person preparing your accompanying artwork is keeping pace with your story developments so he or she can provide the most appropriate and effective visuals for the series.
- Quit when you have enough information. Many reporters don't know when they have gathered enough facts. They continue collecting information until they could literally fill an encyclopedia on the subject. When you finally do have enough to prove the points, or adequately tell the story, stop collecting and begin your story.

Organizing and Writing the Series

How and where do you begin writing a series once the facts are collected and lying in a pile on your desk? What goes first? How can you best group the information to fit in the various stories of your series?

There are some time-tested methods for arranging your material once it is gathered. Although each reporter has different work and organizational habits, these practical suggestions should make your task easier:

- Separate your notes, documents, interviews, photographs and other material into individual file folders according to topic.
- Then go through each folder and place all feature or sidebar material on a given topic inside yet a second folder enveloped by the first.
- Ask yourself why you decided to write the series to begin with. What have you shown or tried to show? In other words, what is the bottom line?
- When you've made that determination, begin with the bottom-line story first. This first story is often a fact-filled overview of the condition or problem accompanied by a sidebar story, which helps to humanize the series.
- The subsequent parts of the series and related sidebars can become more focused explorations of critical points that were skirted in the original overview.
- Experiment with various leads to create variety in your series. One story might carry a feature lead while the next day's could have a harder edge if the facts dictate. Some reporters have started using anecdotal leads in italics to capture the readers' attention. Variety adds interest and texture to a series.

Let's study an example of what we are talking about in the sixth point. Consider this sample opening for part one of a five-part series on nursing home abuses in your city:

Elderly and handicapped patients are suffering from neglect, improper medication and squalid living conditions at the Fairmont Nursing Home, a Times investigation has found.

Among the documented discoveries at the 40-year-old nursing home on Scott Street:

- 79-year-old Beulah Ledbetter died of staph infection five weeks after a massive bedsore formed on her left hip. Medical records show her infection was left untreated for the first two weeks.
- Tom Acel, 87, wandered away from the home last February during a supervised recreation period and was found frozen to death in a nearby field the next morning, according to police reports.
- State Health Department records reveal that, since 1982, the Fairmont has received more than 300 deficiencies, primarily for filthy conditions and improper distribution of medication.

You can see how the major points have been placed right up front and highlighted with bullets in this first story. But suppose you have dozens of such findings to incorporate in the series? You would place your strongest findings up front and follow with the weaker points in descending order.

Each of the bullet items above can become separate, detailed stories in later installments. The story of Beulah Ledbetter might be the lead series story for the second day, followed on day three by the specifics of Tom Acel's tragic death. In this way, you have provided initial insights into the problems you will be writing about in the stories ahead while whetting the reader's appetite for additional specifics and details.

The goal in any series is to offer a logical sequence of stories that tells a story of its own. The series, like an individual story, should offer a beginning, a body and a suitable wrap-up story. In the end, a reader who follows the effort should feel fully informed and satisfied with the entire body of work.

James Polk of NBC News. (Photo courtesy of National Broadcasting Company, Inc.)

THE SERIES: LIKE PUTTING SHOES IN BOXES

"For weeks, maybe months, you've been collecting shoes; all kinds of shoes. Not necessarily pairs, either, and far too many to fit into just one shoe box. Consider these shoes as facts for the series.

"By now, you've got a hodgepodge of at least 25 assorted shoes. There are hunting boots, rattlesnake-skin cowboy boots, galoshes, rubbers, shower sandals, high-heeled pumps, work boots, wing tips, combat boots, cordovans, Hush Puppies, basketball sneakers, dance and ballet slippers, beach thongs, baseball spikes and football cleats.

"While they differ in appearance, they do have one thing in common—they are all shoes. So you go to your editor and convince him to give you four shoe boxes to put them in, with each box large enough to hold a pair of large fishing boots. These boxes are like parts of the series.

"In the first box you toss the hunting boots, the combat boots, the cowboy boots, the galoshes and all the other weighty, heavy-duty shoes you can fit in. This might be the first day's story, loaded with the most substantial facts you've found.

"In the second box, you put the rest of your more substantial shoes: the wing tips, the heels, the cordovans and maybe the dance slippers for a smidgen of entertainment value. The facts that seem to flow better in a separate story can go here.

"Meanwhile, you throw away the shower shoes and the rubbers and any others that are simply too thin to leave much of an impression. These are the facts that really prove irrelevant in the end. You also toss out the baseball spikes that proved too dangerous to fit in anywhere without leaving scratches. Consider these the potentially libelous details that you couldn't prove or found distasteful.

"In the third box, you put all the light-hearted shoes: the sneakers, the beach thongs, the Hush Puppies, the ballet slippers and your bedtime bunny rabbits. You use the football cleats as a kicker. The facts that add perspective and color to your series can be used in this story.

"Now you sort through your pile of leftover shoes to select all that are right-footed and put them in a fourth box; or you might even use left-footed shoes if you have more of them as leftovers. This is the story where you find room for any relevant material that might have been inadvertently left out.

"When the job is finally done, you go back to your editor and persuade him to give you another box. In that one you put a note to the manufacturer, telling him everything he did wrong in styling his shoes and how he can make them a lot better the next time. This is the story that reviews your findings and suggests reforms which may be in order."

James Polk,
NBC News

Tantalizing the Reader

A series of stories offers unique opportunities to tease readers into becoming involved with what you have to say. Editors usually make these decisions, but reporters often assist.

One way to intrigue readers is to design an interesting title and eye-catching art, or a *logo*, that is easily spotted on a page. This encourages readers to go immediately to the series. Think back over some of the series titles we've discussed in this chapter: "The Mind Fixers," "Deadly Smoke" and "Oral Roberts: The Man, The Money and the Religion." Besides their gripping titles, each of these series carried a logo with each story. In 1985, a reporter for the Arkansas Democrat in Little Rock received the Heywood Broun Award for his series about the 1960 jail death of a black Army veteran named Marvin Williams. The Williams series of 25 stories over seven months carried a common logo of a simple graveyard cross bearing the inscription, "What Happened to Marvin Williams?" The logo is shown in Figure 13–1.

Some journalists find it difficult to develop original logos or titles for a series. Problems usually develop when journalists strain to make a point, or try to become cute with the material. The most effective logos and titles are almost always the most simple and direct.

Even more important in developing a daily following in a series are the teaser phrases used at the end of one story to promote the next installment. Basically, a teaser phrase gives an enticing glimpse of what is to come. Give careful thought to these five or six words. They could

Many untruths mar '60 death findings

BY MIKE MASTERSON
Special Writer

© 1984 Arkansas Democrat

"*His party had been drinking and were so intoxicated they didn't know what happened.*"

For 24 years, these vague words falsely branding Marvin Williams as a drunkard have been indelibly scrawled on his death certificate buried deep in the files at the Arkansas Department of Public Health.

Former Faulkner County Coroner Robert A. McNutt, who wrote the sentence, must have known they were untrue at the time he penned them on May 9, 1960. Two separate reports proving "negative alcohol" content in Williams' bloodstream, reports signed by four different doctors at the University of Arkansas Medical Center had been sent to him in the days after Williams' death. Yet the record shows the coroner never moved to correct his statement.

In fact, Marvin Williams' death certificate, prepared by McNutt, is replete with unexplained errors and falsehoods, the *Arkansas Democrat* has learned.

McNutt, now deceased, on Friday, May 6, 1960, sent a letter along with Williams' body to the Arkansas State Medical Examiner's Office in Little Rock. Even the coroner's letter (included here with the death certificate) described Williams as a stuporous drunk on the night he died.

"He was arrested for drunkenness. He had to be supported to walk. The injury on his forehead was caused

See WILLIAMS, Page 8A

Figure 13-1 Example of a logo.

well mean the difference in someone making a mental note to be sure to read the next installment.

For instance, if the account of Tom Acel's death is set to run in tomorrow's newspaper, which of these teasers in today's paper would make you want to grab a paper tomorrow morning?

> Man dies near home
>
> Elderly man dies of cold
>
> Man wanders away, dies
>
> Patient freezes overnight
>
> Tom Acel: Dead in the cold

The last teaser is clearly the real grabber of the five.

Using Photos in a Series

A series is not limited to words. Even ordinary mug shots can add life to what might otherwise be enormous expanses of gray type in a newspaper series. Newspapers such as The Philadelphia Inquirer strive to supplement their series with photographs of the people they are writing about. As a result, the reader can put faces with the names of key players. A good example is one of the Inquirer's latest series about the Philadelphia courts entitled "Disorder In the Courts." The 10-part series contained photographs of 36 lawyers and judges, as well as other pictures taken in and around various courtrooms. The face shots added a human touch to the series.

The Charlotte Observer's "Brown Lung: A Case of Deadly Neglect" series was made even more powerful by graphic photographs of those afflicted with the disease.

In some cases, the major part of the story can be told in pictures. Newspapers have published running photojournalism series on topics ranging from nursing homes to street people.

While most journalists think of a series being only a matter of words, it's wise for a reporter's editor to incorporate a photographer or an artist or both into a series from the beginning so they can either accompany the reporter on interviews or begin to prepare necessary illustrations or graphics well in advance. Like the reporter, a photojournalist requires time to prepare mentally and physically for a series of stories. It is unfair to ask any photographer to produce quality work that tells a story in itself if he or she is given only a short time to prepare.

Examining a Pulitzer Prize-Winning Series

In 1980, the Charlotte Observer undertook an eight-part series that exposed the systematic neglect of *byssinosis*, or brown lung disease, among textile workers in North Carolina.

Fifteen staffers, including reporters Bob Drogin, Marion Ellis, Howard Covington, Robert Conn, Bob Dennis, Robert Hodierne and project editor Laura Stepp, contributed to the series, which received the Pulitzer Prize for public service in 1981. Stepp, now the Maryland desk editor of The Washington Post, shares the story of their massive series:

"The key to any good news story is a good reporter. What got the brown lung series started was a persistent bulldog named Howard Covington. In mid-1978, Howard, a native of North Carolina and the grandson of a former mill owner, started pestering his editors to take a good, hard look at a strange lung disease often called 'Monday Morning Syndrome' that was afflicting textile workers in both Carolinas. At the time, the Observer was in the midst of our series on tobacco—and we told Howard that brown lung would just have to wait.

"Meanwhile, hearings were going on in Washington over the proposed cotton dust standard and the Columbia Journalism Review ran a long article on how newspapers in the South were ignoring one of the major occupational hazards in their region. That wasn't exactly true. We had covered the Washington hearings and had written on brown lung from time to time. What was true was that we hadn't taken an in-depth look at the disease, independent of any news event.

"We did that, starting in September, 1979. I gave Howard and Marion Ellis, another investigative reporter, a couple of weeks to roam around in Raleigh, the state capital, and in some mill towns. They came across some good stuff.

"One of the best tidbits they got—and which let us know early that we were on the right track—was a state report, never made public. The report said as many as 10,000 mill workers in North Carolina could be working in dust levels that could kill.

"Howard was raised in Raleigh and his physical location in the capital helped immensely in getting access to government documents and sources. He talked to midlevel people in government agencies that oversee textile mills.

"He confirmed through them that brown lung was, indeed, a major problem and one that was being neglected by all those supposedly concerned. So after three weeks, I met with Howard and Marion and we went over their information. The story we wanted to do was a big story. It would require money as well as guts. So we had another meeting with Rich Oppel, the editor, and key department heads.

"Getting other departments involved early was a crucial step politically, I think. Doing a series on such a big scale would mean other departments might have to tighten their belts for a little while. That would go a lot smoother if the other departments felt they had some say in the decision—if not whether to do it, at least how to do it.

"The next day, I called together Howard, Marion and two other reporters I felt should be in on the project—our medical writer, Bob Conn, and our labor writer, Bob Dennis. Together with the metro editors, we sketched out what we call a budget—a list of stories we wanted to do and who would do each one. Also at this meeting was our photo chief who assigned one photographer, Phil Drake, to do all our photography.

"As the reporting progressed, it became clear we were moving much faster in North Carolina than we were in South Carolina, so I pulled in another reporter, Bob Drogin, to help Dennis cover South Carolina. Drogin had good writing skills which I knew would be needed down the road. Bob Hodierne, our Washington reporter, got involved toward the end by finding out what, if anything, Carolina's congressmen and senators had done to help brown lung victims.

"Six reporters on one series is probably too many. An editor with that many reporters has six different points of view as to what the series should say, six people who are absolutely sure they know how it should be written—not to mention the headaches caused by the fact that *four* of the six were named Bob.

"Our guys tried to get everything on-the-record and they succeeded. They found state and federal documents especially useful when they could get their hands on them. Many of those documents were supposedly secret—so they talked sweetly to a couple of secretaries and when that didn't work, they enlisted me or Oppel to call the appropriate department head.

"The Brown Lung Association, a worker's advocacy organization, also had studies and research they shared with us. But the reporters had to verify anything in the association's records before they could use it, since they had an obvious point of view.

"When it came time to write, I limited the number of writers to two for any one story. And when it came time to edit, we tried to limit the number of editors—although the reporters will tell you we were less successful on that score.

"Our editing style on a series of this size is [a teamwork approach]. I was the first line editor, then came the metro editor, the managing editor and, finally, the editor. The publisher also got copies of the stories. But he only injected his opinions a couple of times as far as I know. Our lawyer also read all the pieces.

"All that editing is, in one respect, a royal pain. But, on the other hand, no one was so dogmatic that he just had to have his way. And most suggestions were good ones.

"One of the things about the series I'm proudest of is that, out of all 44,000 words, not one fact has been challenged. I attribute that in large part to careful reporting and careful editing. I don't want to overlook the important role that copy editors and layout editors played in the series. And the editorial department played a major role by running a hard-hitting lead editorial every day of the series, coordinated with the news pages. This was crucial in getting the serious attention of industry officials and public policymakers.

"Another important element in a series like this is a good logo—something catchy but not blown out of proportion. Finally, the editor himself came up with it—'A Case of Deadly Neglect.' Promotion is also important to a series like this—too important, in fact, to be left up just to the promotion department. We saw the radio and house ads in advance and took some of the worst hype out. We didn't need hype, because the facts were strong enough."

Among the Observer's findings were:

- Textile companies had kept secret from some workers the fact that they had been diagnosed as having brown lung disease and had kept them living in dusty areas.
- Six years after the government began regulating cotton dust, inspectors had not even checked most of the Carolinas' 614 cotton-processing plants for illegal levels of dust.
- Many industries found to exceed safe standards avoided cleaning for years while officials allowed them to continue operating.
- Although 18,000 Carolinians had been disabled by brown lung, industrial commissions in the Carolinas had approved compensation for only 320 workers.
- Charities, medical groups, labor unions and churches had done little to help the brown lung victims. The United Way had turned down all requests for money from the Brown Lung Association, a non-profit disabled workers organization.

The series eventually resulted in scores of positive reforms for the brown lung victims: 11 new mill inspectors were added to the North Carolina mill inspection staff, the state's industrial commission got $150,000 to add three new deputy commissioners to speed up compensation decisions, the governor alone ordered two dozen changes that streamlined the way the state awarded compensations and ordered previously closed records about the mills to remain permanently open.

Today, nearly a decade later, positive effects are still being felt in the Carolinas as a result of the Observer's powerful and compelling series.

The process that Stepp and her colleagues used to launch, research, write and publish the series embodies the basic steps in doing any series.

There was no magic here, only professionalism and hard work:

- She sent two reporters to sniff out the possibility of a big story. They worked hard, found a secret document that said plenty about the problem and set the stage for a series launch.
- The reporters and editors sat down to discuss the preliminary findings and lay a master plan for proceeding with other departments at the paper, including the photo, editorial page, copy editing and promotion departments.
- The reporting staff was picked, assignments were made and everyone went to work. Stepp served as the clearinghouse for all material and coordinator for everyone involved.

- Once the material was in hand, she assigned no more than two people to write each story in order to maintain some continuity of tone and style.
- In the end, many people at the newspaper had shared in the finished product. "Brown Lung" had proven to be a prime example of what coordination, talent and teamwork could accomplish.

Now let's look at the initial paragraphs of several of the stories in the brown lung series. Carefully examine the early focus of each story and the quality and power of the writing. Decide if you might have approached it differently, remembering what Stepp said about trying to manage six journalists having six different points of view.

Brown Lung: A Case of Deadly Neglect
A Story of Dust, Delays—And Death

By **Bob Drogin**
Observer Staff Writer

PULITZER PRIZE WINNER

Cotton dust is a killer in Carolinas mills.

Already, 18,000 Carolinas workers are disabled by byssinosis, or brown lung, the lung disease cotton dust causes. Only about 320 have received compensation.

Now, six years after officials ordered mills to clean up, about 115,000 of the Carolinas' 391,500 textile workers remain exposed to dust in cotton mills. Health officials say at least 10,000 North Carolinians still work in dust levels that can kill.

It is a case of deadly neglect.

According to last week's Observer series on brown lung in the Carolinas:

- At least five textile companies didn't tell some workers they had been diagnosed with brown lung.
- Companies have contested 80 percent of the 936 N.C. brown lung compensation claims and virtually all of about 200 S.C. claims.
- Both industrial commissions have ignored state laws requiring companies to report on workers diagnosed with occupational diseases such as byssinosis. The N.C. commission has violated its own rules by approving company-written agreements in which workers forfeited all future legal claims.
- The commissions have approved compensation in only about 320 of 1,136 claims filed. Settlements often didn't cover lost wages and medical expenses. Some workers died waiting for compensation.
- Some doctors who advise the commissions on brown lung cases also see patients for textile companies; one former S.C. medical panel member was a consultant for two textile firms.
- In six years—enough time for a worker to develop byssinosis—the 14 state labor inspectors have checked fewer than half the Carolinas' 614 cotton-processing plants. Officials have granted repeated extensions to plants which violate federal cotton dust standards, allowing some companies more than three years to clean up.
- The textile industry has fought tougher federal regulations which would require medical surveillance programs and job transfers for sick workers, and would cut acceptable dust levels in half.
- Most charities, medical groups, state lung organizations, labor unions and churches have done little to help brown lung victims. Even the United Way last year rejected all requests to aid the Brown Lung Association, a nonprofit group of disabled workers.

One brown lung victim is English P. Smith, 53, who worked 34 years at Graniteville Co.'s Granite mill in South Carolina before he collapsed on the job in March 1978. Today, he can't talk without coughing and wheezing and is confined to his home.

Smith, a seventh-grade dropout, filed for workers' compensation after four doctors, including two paid by the company, said he had byssinosis.

Graniteville fought the claim, denying that Smith had byssinosis. Early last year, too sick and too broke to keep fighting, Smith settled his claim for $20,000, half the maximum amount.

Documents filed with the state last summer show a doctor told Graniteville in 1974 that Smith had byssinosis. Yet Graniteville's chief executive, Robert Timmerman, said recently, "I don't believe today that E. P. Smith ever had byssinosis."

Notice how simple and compelling Drogin's eight-word lead is. It condenses the findings of all 44,000 words into one simple declarative sentence. By the end of the second paragraph, you have already gained much insight into the scope of this problem and how it has been neglected—and only 31 words have been written. Do you feel the bullets are positioned properly in this lead story? Does this story seem well edited? Are there many wasted words?

Brown Lung: A Case of Deadly Neglect
A Living Death: A Worker Waits for Company's Help

By **Howard Covington**
and **Marion A. Ellis**
Observer Staff Writers

PULITZER PRIZE WINNER

LOWELL—Landrum Clary, a 68-year-old former millworker, can't live these days without 20 feet of plastic tubing hooked to a liquid oxygen machine.

Clary suffers from chronic byssinosis, caused by breathing cotton dust in the mills for 38 years.

The last company he worked for, A. M. Smyre Manufacturing Co. Inc., discovered Clary's breathing problems in 1968, when it tested him and 440 other workers.

But for three years, until illness forced him to quit, the company kept Clary sweeping up cotton waste in the card room, one of the dustiest places in a mill.

Smyre, a yarn maker in Gaston County, has consistently denied the significance of brown lung, resisted paying Clary and delayed cleaning up its mills despite government fines.

To this day, company President Rick Smyre says he doubts there is a difference between byssinosis and other lung diseases such as emphysema which aren't necessarily job-related.

Smyre, which employs 800 people at three plants, surveyed 441 workers Dec. 9, 1968, at the request of state health officials. Officials wanted to identify workers with byssinosis and probe the effects of job location, age and smoking on the disease.

A team of six medical doctors and three specialists in occupational health, all employed by the state or Gaston County, found at least 25 workers had byssinosis. Company officials, who said they've lost the records, couldn't identify the 25.

But Clary believes he was one and recalls that test vividly.

"They asked us to blow in this little tube as a test," he said. The tube was part of a machine called a spirometer which measures lung capacity and breathing ability.

"They told us if you don't pass (the test), the company will get a letter," Clary continued. "Six or eight weeks went by and I was called out to the office. I was told I had a pretty bad respiratory problem. (Company officials) said, 'The doctors recommended that you get out.' They said they would get me something else, but they never did."

Rick Smyre and Dr. James Merchant, a state physician and leader of the research team, both say Merchant told the workers with serious problems they should seek medical help.

Clary's last job at Smyre—where he worked 17 years—was sweeping the card room floor and cleaning the machines that straightened cotton fibers for spinning.

He decided to leave in 1971 after he passed out three times.

"I just couldn't take it any more," he says. "My doctor said if you want to live you've got to get out of the mill."

Today clear plastic tubing connects Clary to his 84-pound, life-supporting machine, called a Liberator. He can move 20 feet in any direction. When he has to leave his house, he must carry a portable liquid oxygen set.

Notice that this story assumes a more featurelike tone than the lead piece by Drogin. Yet, the initial paragraphs contain some hard facts and a strong message. Remember Polk's comparisons of different types of shoes in the same box? Is this what he was talking about?

The first three paragraphs contain a lot of relevant background material. But it is the fourth paragraph that sets the tone of the article. There we learn that company officials kept Clary sweeping floors in a dusty room for three years after he had been tested.

Notice in paragraph eight how the reporters skillfully phrase the fact that company records are missing. What effect would this story have on a reader?

Brown Lung: A Case of Deadly Neglect
States Let Violators' Cases Gather Dust

By **Howard Covington**
and **Bob Dennis**
Observer Staff Writers

PULITZER PRIZE WINNER

On Jan. 5, 1976, N.C. state inspectors clipped an air filter to Willie Robinson's shirt collar to sample the air he breathed in the dusty No. 1 card room at J. P. Stevens & Co.'s Rosemary Plant in Roanoke Rapids.

Inspectors found more than triple the dust allowed by law. Yet officials fined Stevens, which had $1.8 billion in sales last year, only $600—$400 less than the maximum. They also gave the company a year to clean up.

When Stevens didn't meet the deadline, officials simply extended it—for three years.

Meanwhile, Robinson's breathing became so bad that he had to be moved to a less dusty job area.

Doctors say Robinson, 37, has byssinosis, a lung disease caused by breathing cotton dust which experts say has crippled 18,000 Carolinas textile workers.

Every day, health officials say, thousands of Carolinians—up to 10,000 in North Carolina alone—still work in cotton dust levels the federal government finds dangerous enough to cause serious injury, even death.

Foot-Dragging By Agencies

A key reason: foot-dragging by labor department officials in both states. These agencies have failed to force mills to obey federal regulations and to clean up.

The state labor departments have had six years to make textile plants comply with minimum dust levels established by the federal Occupational Safety and Health Administration (OSHA). That's a year longer than it takes some workers to develop byssinosis, according to British doctors.

Documents in state labor departments and interviews with OSHA and textile officials show:

- State hygienists have failed to inspect most cotton textile plants in the Carolinas. Officials have inspected about 170 of the 461 N.C. plants and 127 of South Carolina's 153 plants.

- N.C. officials have allowed companies that have violated OSHA standards an average of almost two years to clean up—twice the time the federal government says is necessary to do the job. Some companies have taken three years or longer.

- S.C. officials have given companies an average of 2½ years and allowed some to take more than three years.

- In both Carolinas, labor officials have never gone to court to try to close a plant, even when companies ignored cleanup orders.

- Generous officials sometimes give companies even more time to clean up than the companies request. Sometimes they approve plant cleanups without reinspection, based solely on the company's word.

- Officials routinely levy only modest fines, rarely imposing the $1,000 maximum. N.C. officials have never forced a company to pay an overdue fine.

- State officials don't inspect weaving and spinning rooms—where large numbers of people work—despite evidence workers in these areas develop brown lung.

Officials say they do the best job possible, given the limited number of inspectors, their responsibilities for other hazards such as asbestos and the uncertain status of the present dust standards.

Now we see yet another change of tone. The reporters use Willie Robinson to get them into the fact that state laws are toothless when it comes to brown lung. In the second paragraph, the company's total sales figure is neatly incorporated into the paragraph to reflect irony in the situation. The third paragraph contains only 13 words, yet is speaks volumes about the state's attitude toward enforcing penalties against politically powerful mill owners. This is what Stepp meant when she said the facts speak for themselves. The eighth paragraph gives chilling perspective when it compares the length of time for mill compliance with the time it takes to contract byssinosis. Finally, notice the placement of the seven bullets in this story. Despite their number, they are effective because they are short and punchy.

Clearly, in-depth reporting in series format is an important journalistic technique. In fact, when the series approach is used with the right topic at the right time, it becomes perhaps the most powerful weapon in the journalistic arsenal.

PART 5
Responsibility

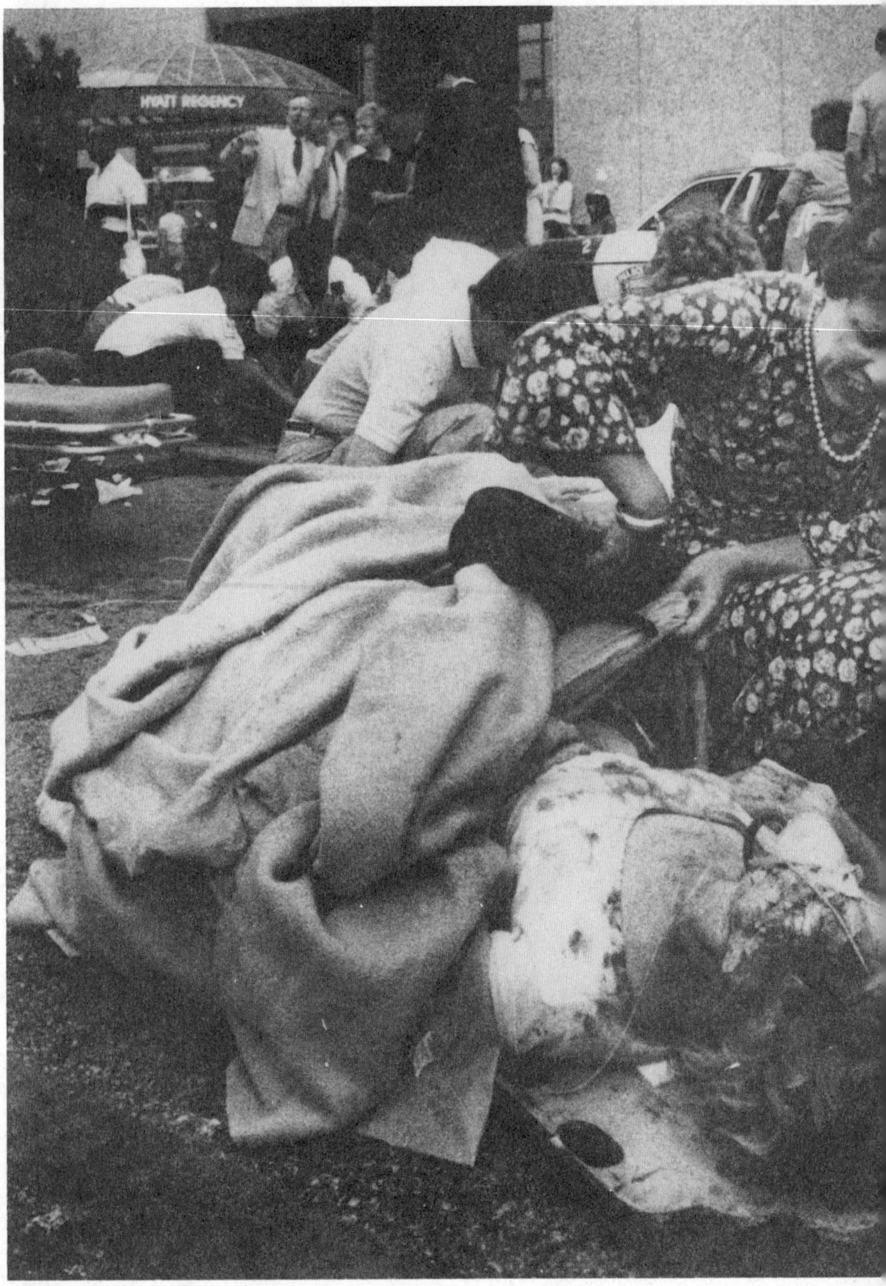
HYATT REGENCY

CHAPTER **14**

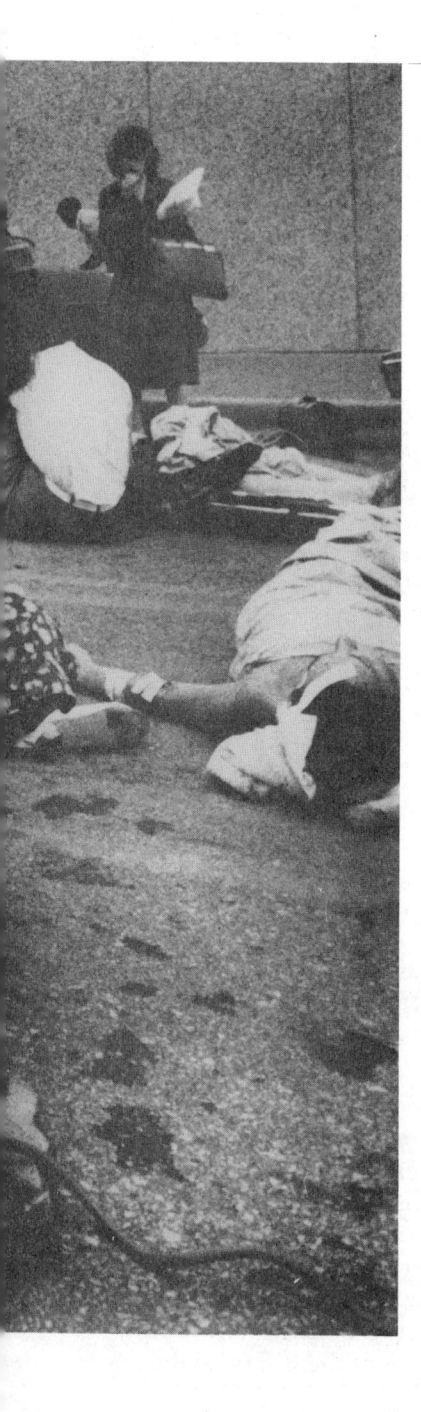

Law, Ethics and Taste

The First Amendment
Libel: A Type of Defamation
An Overview of Defamation Defenses
Public Officials, Public Persons and Private Figures
Invasion of Privacy
An Overview of Invasion of Privacy Defenses
Obscenity
National Security
Fair Trial and Free Press
Reporters' Ethics
Credibility and Good Taste
A Pulitzer Hoax

299

Regardless of how much money you may make as a reporter in the years ahead, your greatest reward will always be helping to tell the story of the world to its inhabitants. Once you are caught up in this endeavor, you will find you have time only for deciding what is worth telling, getting the facts completely and relating them succinctly and fairly to your audience. You will find it difficult to tolerate anything that stands in the way.

Fortunately for our society and its reporters, the law clears the way for free expression, allowing reporters to do their jobs and society to have the benefit of their reporting. By understanding the few laws that do restrict what reporters may report to the public, news professionals can avoid spending time and resources in defending themselves in court and stay at the job of reporting the news.

The laws of our nation allow reporters to perform almost as they wish. They are restricted primarily by their own self-discipline. Self-discipline is necessary if the profession is to keep its freedoms and, more importantly, provide the citizenry with the information it needs in our society. Self-discipline means making your own decisions, or stated another way, it means no one writes down specific rules for every situation you will face. You must think through situations that require you to reconcile conflicting interests and to make decisions as to what is right and fair. The study of ethics deals with these matters. Each reporter needs his or her own framework of ethics.

This chapter takes up the topics of law, ethics and taste. As you continue your education in mass communications and get some experience as a reporter, you will want to take a course in the law of mass communications and another in mass communications ethics. This chapter will get you started on these topics.

The First Amendment

> Congress shall make no law respecting an establishment of religion, or prohibiting the free exercise thereof; or abridging the freedom of speech, or of the press; or the right of the people peaceably to assemble, and to petition the Government for a redress of grievances.

These 45 words of the First Amendment of the U.S. Constitution establish the right of each American to free expression without government or other interference. The First Amendment affirms the right of each individual to voice his or her beliefs and opinions and the right of individuals to differ among themselves. The freedoms guaranteed by the First Amendment are the cornerstone of our democratic process.

The 55 delegates to the Constitutional Convention in Philadelphia in 1787 did not include freedom of expression in the Constitution. Congress adopted it, the first of 10 amendments known as the Bill of Rights,

Chapter opening photo: A woman tries to comfort one of the injured persons removed from the lobby of Kansas City's Hyatt Regency Hotel. (AP/Wide World Photos)

four years later. Freedom of expression, like other human rights, is a very old concept which had to win its way to intellectual and popular acceptance. It still is a minority concept—more than half of the world today lives under governments that restrict the freedom legally, often while paying lip service to it in their constitutions.

What is the thinking behind free expression? Is it really better to let any idiot spout off than to have a responsible, authoritative voice as the sole disseminator of public information? In his treatise "Areopagitica," the Puritan poet John Milton addressed this question in 1644 when he attacked the British law licensing printers. Licensing, or censorship, presumed the censors were infallible, and they cannot be, he said; if they were, he reasoned, all prior public expression would have to be censored, which was an impossibility. Further, he wrote, the best defense against falsehood is to attack it with truth, for whoever heard of truth being defeated in fair competition? The marketplace of competing ideas that Milton envisioned corresponded to the free economic marketplace that Adam Smith espoused. The Age of Reason was dawning. Man was a rational creature, capable of discriminating between truth and falsehood and of discovering new truths. The discoveries of Isaac Newton extended the concept of rationality to the concept of an orderly universe. It was in this philosophical context that the U.S. Constitution was written.

A 19th century social thinker, John Stuart Mill, espoused free expression as a protection of an individual from the dictatorship of the majority. He gave four reasons for permitting unpopular ideas to circulate: The idea may be true; the idea may be false except for a grain of truth, which otherwise would not come to light; even if an accepted idea is totally true, people will hold it as a prejudice rather than on rational grounds unless alternatives challenge it; and finally, unless challenged, commonly held beliefs lose their vitality and people fail to live by them.

Milton and Mill are two of many philosophers who have contributed to the concept of freedom of expression; the artists, poets, preachers, journalists, writers and orators who have practiced it have made it a reality.

Freedom of expression under the First Amendment also protects the expression of ridiculous, sensational and even false information, to which many of the publications sold at supermarket checkout counters testify. It invites abuse. If the marketplace of ideas is to work and the First Amendment is to continue to serve us well, reporters must be responsible and critical of irresponsible expression. Diligent reporters who seek the truth are the best assurance of keeping freedom of expression healthy.

To protect against the abuse of individual rights and the security of the nation, laws have been passed since the Bill of Rights that limit the freedom of expression. Someone said that freedom ends when A's fist meets B's nose. Freedom of expression does not allow an individual to damage someone's reputation without good reason or to violate a person's right to privacy. Obscenity is not protected by the First Amendment either. Finally, revealing information that breaches national se-

Libel: A Type of Defamation

curity at a time of clear and present danger also is illegal. Let's look at defamation first.

You defame someone if you accuse him of a crime, call him a Communist, say he has tuberculosis (particularly if he is in the food business), say he is a sexual deviant, say he beats his wife or say he is a tax dodger. You hold him up to public shame and ridicule. You may damage his ability to make a living. The person has grounds to sue you for *libel*, which is published or broadcast defamation. You can be sued, the news executive you work for can be sued, the news organization can be sued. Being sued is time-consuming and expensive even if you win the case. When you lose, it can cost you your life savings. (Slander is spoken defamation; most suits are brought under the libel laws, which include broadcast defamation.)

Know what libel is and avoid it, but remember there are times when you have to report information that does damage the reputation of people. When the information is true and you can prove it, and when it is important for the public to know it, it is your responsibility to tell the

Teresa Carpenter, a Pulitzer Prize-winning reporter who works for New York City's Village Voice, receives advice from a Voice attorney. (Photo by Nancy Campbell)

public. Even when you can't prove the information to be true in a court of law, it may still be your responsibility to tell the public, after consultation with your editor. In those circumstances, there are justifications—defenses—for publishing the libel. Having a good knowledge of libel is important to anyone even remotely connected to the mass media. Learn as much as you can about it, and stay up-to-date; the courts keep changing the rules.

Defaming someone is easier than you may think. Joe J. Jones makes a speech for the Lung Association telling how he overcame tuberculosis. He is a mechanic. You write a story about the speech, knowing Joe J. Jones really said those words in public and that he cannot give tuberculosis to the cars he works on. But you get sloppy and report Joe's middle initial as G, rather than J. There is a Joe G. Jones in your town who owns and operates a meat market. He didn't make the speech. He doesn't have tuberculosis. If he did, the health department might close him down and if the public knew about him they might buy meat elsewhere. He sues. You are in serious trouble.

Here is another example: Tom Jones goes to trial for driving while drunk. His lawyer, Bill Smith, loses the case. Your story says Bill Smith was convicted in the case. (It's a short item, you were in a hurry and you made a careless mistake.) Bill calls your boss and says, "I think I have a libel case." He probably does. Your boss may be out thousands of dollars. You may be fired. You should be.

First of all, then, defamation involves damaging a person's reputation. If a statement about a person causes others to hate, ridicule, shun, hold up to contempt or lower the individual in the esteem of his fellows, he has been defamed. If a statement injures a person in his ability to make a living, he has been defamed. If a statement causes a person to lose friends or social contacts, he has been defamed. If a statement causes a person to be embarrassed or teased, it may be in poor taste, but it is usually not defamation. Beware, though, that some people take teasing seriously, and all such a person has to do is find a lawyer willing to file a libel suit. Then you will have to get a lawyer to defend you, and that can be expensive.

In addition to showing that the statement is damaging to his reputation, the libeled subject of the statement must prove the following conditions:

- *Identification.* The subject must prove that people who know him would recognize him as being the subject of the statement. If you say a red-haired man hit a woman in a bar but don't give his name and he happens to visit that establishment frequently, other patrons may know immediately who the statement refers to. He may sue successfully. In addition, any other red-haired man who frequents the bar may be able to convince a jury he was identified in the story. However, very large groups, such as the population of the city of Passaic, N.J., cannot sue for libel, because there are too many Passaic residents for any one of them to claim identification.

- *Publication.* The statement must have appeared in a paper that has been distributed or must have been on the air. People other than you and the subject must have had access to the story.
- *Falsity.* The subject must prove that the published material was not true. Until 1986, a person bringing a libel suit did not need to prove that the material published about him was false. In most cases the law said that falsity was presumed. In April of 1986, however, the U.S. Supreme Court changed that rule. The court ruled that when the published material is of public concern the person suing must prove that the material is false. If he cannot prove falsity, he cannot win the libel suit. But remember, the published information must be of public concern. If it is a damaging tidbit of gossip with no relation to public affairs, you still may have to prove truth.
- *Fault.* You and your news organization must be somehow culpable in the publication of the libel. Basically, there are two kinds of fault: negligence and malice. In most states, private persons have to prove *negligence*. That means they have to prove that the publication was due to something other than a simple mistake—that the news organization did something that it should not have done in putting together the story, or that it did not do something it should have done. Only relying on one source or not getting both sides of a controversial story, for example, may be considered negligence. Public officials and public figures must prove actual *malice*. That means they must prove that the news organization knew beforehand that the material to be published was false, or that the organization was so reckless that it did not care whether the information was true or false.
- *Damages.* The person bringing the suit must prove he suffered damages. This is not the same as proving that the published material is damaging. To prove that the material is damaging means proving that the words would tend to damage someone's reputation. To prove damages means the person bringing the suit must prove that he was in fact damaged. If he lost his job because of the publication, he can obviously prove that he was damaged. He does not need to show an actual dollar figure lost. He can call witnesses to show that he suffered humiliation because of the publication. He can show that worry over the publication gave him an ulcer. Any evidence that he actually suffered is evidence that he was damaged.

Once you understand what libel is, make a habit of scanning every story you write to see if it defames anyone. Be particularly careful about routine crime, accident or health-related stories. If you find information that may be defaming, examine the passage to see if it is relevant to the story and important for the public to know. Discuss it with your editor. If it is not important, eliminate it. If it is, make sure you have a good defense and make sure you bring the entire matter to the attention of your editor.

An Overview of Defamation Defenses

Defenses in libel suits include truth, privilege, fair comment and criticism, and consent. If you see a clear reason for publishing something defamatory, be sure it qualifies for one of the defenses listed. As you study the defenses, you will find knowing in your heart that your story is true is not enough.

Truth

If you can prove in a court of law that your statement was true, you will probably not lose the libel suit. It is not sufficient to prove that you accurately passed on information you received—you must prove that the information you passed on was true. If Jones says something libelous about Smith, that does not make it true. Putting Jones' statement in quotation marks and attributing it to him does not protect you in a libel suit; you must prove that what Jones said was true to win using this defense.

Truth must be supported by documents, witnesses or other evidence that can be weighed by a judge and a jury. If you, a red-haired bartender and a woman are alone in the bar, and the bartender hits the woman, you saw it and you know it is true. But if you were the only one who saw the blow being struck and neither the bartender nor the woman will support you with testimony, you cannot prove truth.

Truth may become a more difficult defense to use, because the Supreme Court now requires the plaintiff to prove falsity. That means that by the time you are presenting a defense the plaintiff may have already satisfied the judge that the published material is false. Your evidence of truth must be strong enough to convince the jury that the plaintiff's evidence of falsity was insufficient.

Privilege

What officials say about public business during sessions of courts, legislatures or other official meetings is *privileged*; that is, they cannot be held accountable in a libel suit. You have the same protection if you report an accurate account of what they say. The same is true of official records and your accurate reports of what they say.

Let's go back to the barroom. You call the police. They file a charge of assault and battery against the red-haired bartender. You can report the charge without being in danger of a libel suit. If you want to report details of what took place, be sure to call to the attention of the police the woman's black eye and the bartender's skinned knuckles. But be careful. If no charges are filed and all you have is an investigation report or what a police officer tells you, there may be no privilege. In some jurisdictions, investigation reports are not privileged documents, and what an officer tells you at the scene of a crime is usually not privileged either.

In summary, what public officials say in the official conduct of their business is privileged and you are protected if you report it accurately. Public records are also privileged and you may report their contents as well.

Fair Comment and Criticism

The common law has traditionally protected published or broadcast expressions of opinion, as long as the person expressing the opinion based it on facts and had no ill will against those criticized. Constitutional decisions since 1974 relating to public officials and public figures have broadened this defense. Now this defense gives critics and other experts the right to state their opinions about public matters, period.

In short, there are no false opinions. A sportswriter may criticize a coach, players, owners, the crowd, the condition of the field, the officials and other sportswriters, for example. However, if the sportswriter maligns a player at every opportunity—criticizing him not only for his play but for non-sports matters, such as how he talks to his mother-in-law—then the player may be able to prove the writer had a particular dislike for him or was out to get him, and win a libel suit. If the sportswriter publishes an unsupported statement in the guise of opinion, he may also be subject to suit. For example, the statement "I believe this jock is taking bribes to throw games" is not an opinion, even though the writer began the statement with "I believe." This statement is libelous; it was not supported by the facts. Fair comment and criticism is a defense permitting any person to comment on public issues. Read carefully about actual malice in the upcoming sections to avoid problems regarding statements of opinion.

Consent

If a person gives a reporter permission to publish something defamatory about him, then that person cannot win a libel suit based on the publication. Obviously this defense can rarely be used. If it is used, the reporter must be able to prove the admission.

Public Officials, Public Figures and Private Persons

In 1964 a Supreme Court decision (*New York Times Co. v. Sullivan*) contained these words:

> "Debate on public issues should be uninhibited, robust, and wide open, and it may well include vehement, caustic and sometimes unpleasantly sharp attacks on government or public officials.... erroneous statement is inevitable in free debate, and ... it must be protected if the freedoms of expression are to have the breathing space that they need to survive."

Times v. Sullivan made it a lot harder for public officials to win libel suits. They now have to prove actual malice, that the reporter or news executives knew the defamation was false or that they acted with reckless disregard as to whether it was false or not.

A *public official* is someone who has a "substantial responsibility for or control over the conduct of government affairs," according to a 1966 Supreme Court ruling. Not everyone on a government payroll is a government official.

Later, the thinking in the *Times v. Sullivan* decision was expanded in another Supreme Court case to include *public figures*. A person with "widespread fame or notoriety"—such as Johnny Carson—is an "all purpose" public figure. The courts have said, though, that most public figures are *limited public figures* in that they are private individuals

---

THE COST OF LIBEL

Libel suits are expensive.

Just defending against them can cost a small newspaper $10,000 during a three-year period. The nation's biggest newspapers spent an average of $500 million each on libel defense during a three-year span in the mid-1980s, according to an American Society of Newspaper Editor's survey. About half the cases were described as nuisance suits, without serious legal merit.

The media win about 90 percent of the libel suits filed against them, but the financial cost of defending themselves still is high. Here are some examples of cases the media lost:

- In 1981 Kimerli Jayne Prine, Miss Wyoming 1978, won a $26.5 million award from Hustler magazine. A jury decided that she was identified in a fiction story Hustler published about a sexually active Miss Wyoming.

- In 1985 The El Paso Times was ordered to pay $3.5 million to U.S. Attorney James Kerr. The case involved a column in which Kerr was accused of lying to a grand jury.

- Also in 1985, The Dallas Morning News was ordered to pay former prison official G. Presley Hardy $290,000 for reporting that he had threatened the execution of a prison inmate.

Juries are quite willing to assess a penalty greater than the annual net income of the company involved, though such awards are often reduced or overturned on appeal. The possibility of such a penalty is what makes libel insurance cost so much.

The non-financial costs of libel litigation are also great. In fact, the impact of the increasing number of libel suits on the media's ability to inform the public may be greater than the financial costs.

Eugene Roberts, editor of The Philadelphia Inquirer, has warned that public officials are using the actual malice rule to stifle robust debate of public issues. In a 1985 address, he noted that 15 public officials in the Philadelphia area had brought 19 libel suits against the media.

Other examples abound. Sen. Paul Laxalt brought a $250 million suit against the Sacramento Bee. A county commissioner brought a $19.25 million suit against Potpourri, a Magnolia, Texas, free shopper newspaper, for a letter to the editor (the suit was eventually dropped, as was a court order forbidding Potpourri to criticize the official). The president of the Leflore County, Miss., Board of Supervisors brought a $20 million suit against The Greenwood Commonwealth, a daily with a circulation of 10,000.

The publisher of the Sacramento paper is countersuing, alleging a frivolous suit and urging other threatened newspapers to go on the offensive by countersuing. But John Emmerich, publisher of the Greenwood Commonwealth, notes that small, independent papers don't have the resources to pay for expensive litigation. Emmerich says: "What is good for society? Is it better to have aggressive newspapers that look into wrongdoing of public officials, or is it better to have newspapers that back off of looking into wrongdoing because they possibly might have to spend a lot of money defending themselves in court? How is society better served? I think having aggressive newspapers is the better way."

most of the time. But when they thrust themselves to the forefront of particular public controversies, they are public figures in so far as they attempt a role at influencing the resolution of the issues involved.

Private persons—those who are not public officials or public figures—are another matter. Courts have said journalists are protected if they have not been negligent in reporting about private persons. Thus, you are safe if the court finds that as a reporter you did your job properly—that you reported the facts accurately (including quotations and identifications), contacted the principal parties involved in the story and did all the other things a thorough reporter would do. Your notes, your conversations about stories and any other evidence related to controversies surrounding persons in the news can be sought by attorneys representing libel plaintiffs.

How do reporters treat public officials, public figures and private persons differently? Almost anything that has the remotest relationship to the performance of duties by a public official can be reported. The same is true of public figures (assuming that they meet one of the two definitions of public figure). For private persons, it is not their status but their being a part of the news, a part of public issues, that determines the latitude a reporter has.

The public deserves to be informed about controversies surrounding public issues and the people directly involved in them. What others say about the central figures in such controversies is important to society and can be reported. However, courts and juries continue to modify the circumstances under which people—both those in the public eye and private citizens—may sue for libel. Therefore, you should alert your editor to all such material, take special care that stories which will damage the reputation of someone be provably true and be sure not to maliciously attack people in news stories.

Invasion of Privacy

Suppose you have heard about a plumber who is practicing folk medicine as a sideline. You decide to write a story about him, so you invent some symptoms and, with a fellow reporter who is posing as your spouse, go to the plumber's home. While the plumber is out of the room, your "spouse" takes some photos with a small camera. You tape everything with a mini-tape recorder and hidden microphone. You write a story, complete with photos. It's a truthful account. Can you and your news organization be sued successfully? Yes—you invaded the privacy of someone's home.

The First Amendment protects free expression, but it does not give reporters or anyone else the right to gather information by unlawful means. Invasion of privacy, like libel, is a cause for damages. Actually it is four different torts, all of which protect a person's right to be left alone and protect the depiction of his or her personality and appearance.

The four categories of privacy are unreasonable intrusion, unreasonable publicity, unreasonably placing another in a false light, and appropriating another's name or likeness. Notice that the word *unreasonable* is used in three of the four descriptions. Unreasonable means that the people as a whole in your community would consider the act unreasonable; how highly offended the plaintiff was is not at issue. Of course, the plaintiff's anger over your story is likely to cause him or her to file the suit.

Intrusion

The plumber–folk doctor story is an example of intrusion. Intentionally invading another's solitude, seclusion or private affairs constitutes intrusion. Though the story about the plumber was published, publication is not necessary for an intrusion suit. Intrusion occurs when the privacy is physically invaded, not when something is published. Opening a sealed envelope and reading a personal letter or climbing a tall tree to take a picture over a high fence of a party on someone's patio is intrusion. You invaded someone's privacy and your overt actions in opening the envelope and climbing the tree indicate that you intended to invade the victim's privacy. Both invasion and intent to invade must be shown.

Consent is a defense for intrusion. Identify yourself as a reporter when you enter private property.

Publicity

To be successfully sued for giving publicity to private information, you must report something about an individual's private life that would be highly offensive to a reasonable person and of no legitimate concern to the public. Remember that juries decide these matters. Be careful in reporting the private behavior of public people and do not report the private behavior of private citizens without their explicit permission.

Newsworthiness is a defense for publication of private information. Where a lapse occurs between the time public information is first in the news and when it is used again, the newsworthiness of the information at the time it is used again becomes paramount. Reporting the criminal conviction of a person who has long since been rehabilitated is an example.

If the person gives permission for the use of private information and then after the interview withdraws permission, the newsworthiness of the information again becomes paramount if it is used and a suit is filed.

False Light

If the image of a person portrayed in a news story differs from the truth, that person's feelings may be injured. There may be mental anguish. If the information would be highly offensive to a reasonable person and if the reporter published the material with actual malice—knowledge of falsity or reckless disregard for the truth—a successful suit can result. Damage to reputation is not necessary for a successful suit; it may simply be offensive.

In short, if the information is not true the subject has grounds to sue. A legitmate news photograph with false information in the cutline could result in a false light action, for example. Be careful. Don't gloss over facts. Make sure you can prove they are true.

Appropriation

Both public figures and private citizens are protected by this category of invasion of privacy. The definition according to The Restatement of Torts, section 652C: "One who appropriates to his own use or benefit the name or likeness of another is subject to liability to the other for invasion of privacy."

Public figures in particular lend their names, words and pictures to others, often for a fee, to promote products or services. They also have a right to charge admission for their performances. To use their words or their pictures can constitute appropriation.

You do not appropriate this material when it is news, but when you use or re-use it later in a non-news setting (such as for an advertisement or a general illustration), it may be considered appropriation. Don't use Johnny Carson's picture to promote something without his permission. Don't illustrate a story about auto safety with a wreck picture that has identifiable people or license plates in it. Use brief excerpts of performances. Get a release if a picture is to be used in anyway except as news.

An Overview of Invasion of Privacy Defenses

Newsworthiness is a defense in publicity and appropriation cases, but not in intrusion or false light cases.

Consent to publish or broadcast is a defense in all privacy cases. A person's consent must be as broad as the use of the material by the media. Consent for one use does not permit any other use. For example, a model provided a general release for a photograph of her reading in bed with her "husband." When the publisher added to the picture by putting the title of a known pornographic work on the book she was pictured as reading, and the caption under the picture indicated other than domestic activities were going on, the use exceeded her consent, and she won a judgment.

To avoid invasion of privacy suits, follow these guidelines. Identify yourself as a reporter when you enter private property. If you report private behavior that might be offensive, it must be of legitimate interest to the public and it always should be brought to the attention of your editor. Report accurately. Be careful in resurrecting old pictures or accounts, particularly if there is no legitimate public interest in them. Use brief excerpts of performances. Get a release if a picture is to be used for anything except as news.

A final word: Privacy is a relatively new and developing legal concept, particularly when compared with libel. You will need to follow court decisions regarding it closely.

Obscenity

The courts have ruled that the First Amendment does not protect obscenity. Authors, publishers, moviemakers and others can be fined or jailed for producing obscene material for the public or for purveying it to the public. The government can control such material through postal and customs regulations. Why, then, do movies and videocassettes, magazines and books, and posters and postcards describing and depicting the most bizarre sexual activities abound? The reason is that the courts and the legislatures have had great difficulty in determining what obscenity is and, once a definition is settled upon, in determining whether specific materials meet the test of the definition.

A widely accepted definition of obscenity is: "Whether to the average person, applying community standards, the dominant theme of the material taken as a whole appeals to prurient interests." What are "average person," "community standards," "dominant theme," "taken as a whole" and "prurient interests"? Lawyers can argue, judges can explain and juries can deliberate for hours on these matters. With so many ambiguities in the definition, few obscenity convictions result.

Almost nothing produced by a reporter doing a legitimate job of informing the public could be deemed obscenity. Yet, an understanding of obscenity will benefit reporters because reporters often cover court, police and legislative stories relating to the issue of obscenity. In addition, reporters should have an understanding of obscenity because "community standards" and "prurient interest" relate directly to public taste and what the public will accept into its living rooms for all to see, hear and read. These are matters of ethics and taste rather than legality and will be discussed later.

National Security

Fresh in the minds of the members of Congress when they wrote the First Amendment to the U.S. Constitution was their revolutionary struggle to free themselves from an oppressive government. They had fought a war for independence. They were reluctant to allow the government to restrict the kind of criticism they had recently leveled at the

British Crown. In colonial days, the law of seditious libel had been tested. The law forbade criticism of the government or the king, whether true or not, because such criticism damaged popular confidence in the government.

Yet the members of Congress were soon split on this very topic. Those who became Federalists, such as John Adams, pushed the Alien and Sedition Acts through Congress in 1798 against the opposition of the Anti-Federalists, who included Thomas Jefferson and James Madison. The laws punished those who were critical of the new American government. The laws only stayed on the books until 1801 when Jefferson took office as president, but the issue of how to protect the government from its unscrupulous enemies and preserve free expression has continued to puzzle courts, legislators and journalists to this day.

In this century, courts have ruled that limits on free expression should be considered only when the country faces "a clear and present danger." As an example of clear and present danger, Justice Oliver Wendell Holmes cited the example of shouting "Fire!" in a crowded theater when there is no fire. This irresponsible free expression would cause injury and death as people bolted for the doors, and should be prohibited.

Recent government attempts to limit free expression have met with varying success. For example, during the Vietnam War, the Supreme Court ruled against prepublication censorship when it denied an injunction against The New York Times' publication of stories about the Pentagon Papers—which were contingency plans for conduct of the war. It did not rule out injunctions in more perilous circumstances, however. Later, an injunction forbade a magazine from publishing a story on how to build a hydrogen bomb from information gleaned from publicly available records. The effort was dropped but the story was delayed by seven months.

In 1983, reporters were not allowed to accompany American troops to Grenada. Those who got to the island independently at the time of the landing were taken to Navy ships and denied access to communications they needed to get the story out. This action was a reversal of historic precedent.

As the Grenada action indicates, the Reagan administration took a tough line toward the media where national security is concerned.

In 1986, the director of the Central Intelligence Agency, William Casey, threatened to prosecute The Washington Post and four other newspapers and magazines under a little-used post–World War II law for publishing information on the interception by U.S. intelligence sources of Libyan communications with terrorists.

Writing in Military Media Review, Marine warrant officer Chuck Henry quoted a lieutenant colonel as saying American newswriters from Vietnam onward "are not part of the team so to speak, [and are] oriented to sensationalism, seeking Pulitzer Prizes instead of reporting honestly without bias."

MMR quoted retired Maj. Gen. Winant Sidle, former Army chief of information, as follows: "I don't think an American reporter . . . should be objective to the point where he treats both sides as equals." And a Marine colonel suggested. "If Americans, particularly reporters, used the terms OUR government, OUR public and OUR military, rather than THE government, THE public and THE military, they might better recognize their responsibilities as U.S. citizens."

Interestingly, when war has been declared formally, the news media have practiced voluntary censorship in this nation. In the declared wars—World War I and World War II—every family had one of its members or a close relative in uniform. Public opinion solidly supported a prompt and successful end to the war. The media followed public opinion. But the "informal" wars, "covert actions" and "police actions" that the government now undertakes have put a strain on its relations with the media and the public. The Vietnam War was a prime example. Only a small segment of the population was fighting the war, and public opinion was divided on it. The media presented both sides and in so doing became a part of the controversy.

Two additional complications are global mass communication via satellite and the potential for nuclear holocaust. Stories can move instantaneously, and a global war would be fought in a day. It is now possible to see today's battle in your living room on the evening news via satellite. Theoretically, enemy agents could glean important information from such reports almost as soon they were broadcast. Delivery of nuclear weapons to any point on the globe by rockets can result in complete destruction within moments of the decision to launch. Inflammatory and false information has always been difficult to counteract. Governments and the media face unprecedented time pressures in matters that could precipitate wars now. One solution would be to clamp tight controls on reporters covering national security matters as well as on national security information. This is a possibility the next generation will have to resist.

The public needs accurate information on national defense and violent conflicts in which its government is involved. Journalists free from government control who are committed to accuracy are the most credible people to convey such information to the public. The government and the military have two responsibilities with respect to publishing information where national security is involved: to protect real security information and to be as open as possible about everything else. Reporters have the responsibility to keep the public informed; only in the most extreme national emergency should reporters be a part of governmental secrecy.

Fair Trial and Free Press

The U.S. Constitution protects the right of every citizen to free expression, and the defense of privilege allows what happens in courts to be published with impunity. The U.S. Constitution also guarantees the right of any person accused of a crime to a fair and speedy trial. These two constitutional guarantees sometimes conflict.

An impartial jury of one's peers is one of the ways our system tries to assure a fair trial. The trial is held so that legitimate testimony may be presented to the judge and the jury, with the verdict and possible sentence based solely on the evidence presented and the laws that apply to the case. What if the judge and the jury come to the trial fully aware of the details they have been told about the alleged crime from news reports, and what if they get additional doses of information from the media every day of the trial? Can they render verdicts based solely on the evidence presented in the trial?

Judges, lawyers, reporters and news executives tussle with this dilemma all the time. There are extremists on both sides. Some reporters and news organizations spread rumors and rehash all the sordid details of a case for pure sensationalism. Highly competitive news environments result in excesses. Some lawyers would like to come before juries whose minds are a complete blank; other lawyers sound off in front of reporters outside the courtroom and contribute to the problem.

The trial process includes several ways to safeguard juries from undue influence, without restricting the media. Some of them are:

- *Challenges.* While prosecution and defense attorneys are questioning prospective jurors, they may challenge their suitability. Each side has a limited number of peremptory challenges, whereby a prospective juror may be rejected arbitrarily. In addition, each side may successfully challenge any number of jurors for cause, such as having a preconceived opinion as to guilt or innocence.
- *Warnings.* The judge routinely warns jurors to be influenced only by the evidence and to base their decisions solely on the evidence and not on information received from other sources.
- *Sequestration.* The judge may order the jury to remain in the custody of court officers throughout the trial. Jurors may be housed in hotels overnight and forbidden access to the media or other information until the trial is concluded.
- *Change of venue.* The administrative judge may order the trial moved from the community in which the crime took place. A jury selected at the new locale will presumably be made up of citizens less exposed to pretrial publicity.

The courts cannot assume all the responsibility for assuring defendants of unbiased judges and juries. Reporters must still ask the question, What is in the public interest? The answer usually goes something like this: Information of public interest deserves to be aired with restraint and in a context in which the accused is not guilty until convicted in court.

A further point in favor of reporting about court cases must be made. Our government, including the courts, is based on the rationality and basic fairness of the public. Criminal charges and court cases have always been topics of intense interest in communities, and television, radio and newspaper reports on these matters probably are fairer than the tavern and coffeehouse gossip of the past. Thus, a well-chosen juror can make a fair decision on the evidence despite pretrial publicity.

Another concern of the courts and the public is reporters' harassment of jurors, witnesses and victims. For example, for the criminal justice system to work, victims must come forward to identify suspects and testify against criminals. Lights, cameras, and tape recorders thrust forward by herds of reporters clamoring for attention outside of courthouses comprise a gauntlet few people care to run. When a victim sees his or her trauma detailed before the public, the trauma is increased. As a consequence, reporters often find themselves or their equipment barred from hallways and grounds of courthouses. To mitigate problems, reporters should ask their editors about policies regarding identification of trial participants who may be ridiculed and embarrassed, particularly in cases involving sex crimes.

The judge and the bailiff seek to assure decorum inside the courtroom so that testimony may be heard and the serious nature of the proceedings are assured. They, along with the court clerk, the attorneys and the media reporters, are people at work, doing their jobs. Spectators, defendants, witnesses and jurors also are present. The judge has complete authority over behavior in the courtroom. The judge also decides, within the existing laws and the guidelines provided by the court and bar, what reporters can do. Reporters need to move around to do their jobs. They need to use cameras, tape recorders and perhaps even lights. Abuses by reporters bring more restrictions. Responsible behavior often brings greater flexibility. Reporters should learn from the judge just what is expected of them before a trial begins, particularly if it is a trial that will attract a lot of media coverage. In practice, reporters usually agree among themselves at a trial not to abuse any privileges granted them, such as being able to leave the courtroom and re-enter during testimony.

Agreements between the press and the bar on courtroom behavior have sometimes been established, but what start out as "non-binding codes of conduct" can become the basis for binding decisions by the courts. Reporters may have their interests served best by trial-by-trial agreements on guidelines. The court system is bound by precedent and authority. The mass media system lacks central authority and thrives on innovation rather than precedent. Reporters should encourage judges and lawyers to be flexible in dealing with the media. Both systems are important to society, and they have to co-exist.

Reporters' Ethics

"Decisions on journalism ethics are often made right on deadline in the middle of the newsroom with an angry reader staring at you," Jim Morriss, the editor of a good, small, Arkansas daily, The Springdale News, once told some students. What Jim Morriss said is true because of the nature of reporting. We have said before that disclosure is central to reporting and that what is disclosed and how it is disclosed is extremely important to those directly involved. They are likely to challenge news decisions. Yet no formula for making news decisions exists because no story is exactly the same as any other. This means that making decisions as to what to publish and what to leave out is difficult and it must be done under deadline constraints. Coming to grips with ethical problems requires both logical thinking and sensitivity. Even then, the resulting decisions are compromises that may leave doubt in the reporter's mind.

Philip Meyer, a journalism professor at the University of North Carolina, says that ethics involves dealing properly with those to whom we owe obligations. To whom does the reporter owe obligations? To the public? To those identified in news stories? To the reporter's sources? To other news people? The reporter is obligated to all of these people—perhaps in that order of importance.

The Public

Becoming a reporter means assuming a responsibility to the public, to one's audience. The responsibility goes beyond being truthful. If the public has an interest in an issue or an occurrence, you have an obligation to find out about it and report it. If you are aware of something that the public should know about, you are obligated to report it. Doctors try to heal their patients. Lawyers try to see that their clients are adequately represented under the law. Reporters tell their audience what is going on. That is their reason for being; that is their first responsibility. The first question to ask yourself in making an ethical decision is: Is this important and of high interest to the public?

Those You Identify

Whether dealing with a giant corporation or a criminal in prison, the reporter's second responsibility is to be sensitive to what the story's effect will be on those it names. Be sensitive to the effect on the subject but resist reacting to the subject's personality. Reporters deal with all kinds of people under all kinds of stress; some subjects are obnoxious and some are so nice it's hard to believe they would be involved with anything shady. Letting your personal reaction to the individual color the facts in the story is a disservice to the public and can be unfair to the person identified.

Victims of crime and other persons thrust suddenly and against their will into the public spotlight merit special attention. In most cases, the publicity they receive will either benefit them or cause only minor inconvenience, but in some cases, such as a rape case, the disclosure of a victim's identity can greatly increase the trauma of the victim. Reporting the details of rapes, including the victim's identity, poses an ethical dilemma. It causes trauma for the victim. Yet the public's understanding of the seriousness of the crime and of the innocence of the victim is promoted over the long run by full disclosure. Disclosure of the full details of a case—a rape case, for example—can lead to better understanding. But disclosure often causes a lot of pain. Policies and guidelines will help in making a decision, but finally you and your editors have to decide what to disclose.

Sources

Reporters must get information from many sources. In a few situations reporters are eyewitnesses to facts. Even in such cases, they must depend for background information on documents and on what other people know. Reporters read a lot and talk to many people to stay abreast of what is going on.

Reporting information from anything you read is a crime only if it violates obscenity or national security laws already discussed; how you obtained what you read is another matter. If you stole it, you committed a crime; if you obtained it under false pretenses, you have an ethical problem. You should consider such action only if the information is tremendously important to the public and only if deception is the sole means of obtaining it. Even so, acquiring information under false pretenses should be discussed with executives in your news organization; its reputation is as much on the line as yours.

A different ethical problem faces you if someone else on his or her own initative brings to your attention documents not meant for your eyes. The ethical breach was committed by your source, not you. You condone the breach if you use the information, but you have an obligation to examine the documents since only then can you weigh their importance to the public. Remember that the accuracy and context of such information must be confirmed through additional checking. Again, apprise your news organization of such information. You also owe the original owner of the information an opportunity to comment on it before using it.

The ethical decisions that reporters have to make about using documents are complicated. Some very good reporters and teachers of reporting would encourage you to go much further in securing information; others would forbid you to ever use unauthorized information. First Amendment freedoms give reporters broad latitude as to what they may report; the responsibility to make wise ethical decisions is increased by that broad freedom.

If ethical problems regarding documents are complicated, the problems of dealing with live sources are even more complicated. Reporters and sources, particularly in Washington, D.C., have tried to formalize source-reporter relations in ways you've already read about. Using their jargon (such as direct quotation, not-for-direct-quotation, not-for-attribution, background and off-the-record) is a good way to approach source-reporter relationships.

Sources are like bees: They don't all function the same way but they all contribute and all have to be handled carefully. Sources tell reporters things for many reasons. Some are required to provide you with information by law. Some have the same commitment to informing the public that good reporters have. Others like to talk. Some want to use the mass media to test their views or gain an advantage in political, business or social competition. Still others want to stay in your good graces because they want to have your ear when they need to explain their side of a future issue.

Despite the complexities of dealing with sources, most reporters follow a few basic rules: Be careful about making commitments to news sources. Do not violate the confidence of a news source. Express your displeasure to a news source if a source has favored another news medium at your expense. Be personable, be honest and be skeptical.

Other News People

Competing with other reporters also raises ethical questions. For example, suppose you have a couple of questions you would like to ask the parents of a young man from your town who has been killed in a terrorist attack halfway around the world. You drive to their home and find two dozen newspaper, radio and television newspeople have the place staked out waiting for either parent to appear. Do you rudely shout your questions at one of the grieving parents, in competition with all the others? If a reporter from a television station arrives late and asks what happened, do you share information? (You may need some help tomorrow.)

The advent of broadcasting has increased, by and large, the number of news people covering each major story, the complexity of the equipment used and the kinds of responses expected from news sources. As a reporter, you operate in this environment. How can you protect your sanity, improve the opportunities for thoughtful answers to your questions and, above all, assure that the public learns what it needs to know?

Here are some tips.

Professional organizations such as The Society of Professional Journalists, the Radio-Television News Directors Association, the National Press Photographers Association and others help provide some of the answers, particularly when they have active chapters. Just getting to know the other reporters in your chapter, particularly in different media than your own, helps. A group of experienced professionals who work together in a community can greatly improve reporting opportunities without reducing the competition.

Remember that doing your homework is not unethical and it can give you a competitive edge. Jack James was based in Seoul, Korea, after World War II. He realized that a story transmitted from Seoul before 9 a.m. Sunday would have a chance of being published in Sunday morning editions of U.S. newspapers, because of the time difference, so he made a habit of checking sources each Sunday morning. North Korea invaded South Korea early on the morning of Sunday, June 20, 1950, and James got the story because he went to the U.S. Embassy early that morning.

Stand your ground. Marie Dilg of Topeka television station WIBW was positioned by a telephone the station had installed in the press section in a college auditorium where President Reagan was to speak. Sam Donaldson of ABC sat by her before the speech and reached for the phone. She rapped him on the knuckles with a pencil. "I'm Sam Donaldson from ABC," he said. "I'm Marie Dilg from WIBW and that's my phone," she said.

But be fair. You have the advantage today, but the other person deserves a chance too—and he or she may have the advantage tomorrow. Get the reputation of being someone who always does the best job, but who will also help out the other reporters.

Keep communication open with your news executives. The editor needs to know where you are and what's going on, and also what you think of the story as it is developing. Learn how to have input with your editor as to what stories you will be covering. Be easy to communicate with. Make sure you let your point of view be known. Once decisions are made, act on them with unfailing enthusiasm. News operations have to work smoothly to be good.

Here is a final piece of advice on ethics: Work for an organization that shares your views on reporting. You will learn more about ethics and reporting and be happier with what you do if you begin your career with an organization you can respect.

Credibility and Good Taste

What you report may be true, legal and ethical and still be rejected by your audience. You and the organization you are a part of must be personally and institutionally acceptable to the public as a source of true accounts of important and interesting information—you must be credible. To be accepted, news must also be presented in terms that do not offend people so much that the offensive nature of the message overwhelms the content—the story must be in good taste.

At its core, credibility is an I-don't-know-you, therefore-I-can't-trust-you problem. As you've read, surveys of public attitudes have indicated a growing mistrust of reporters and the media in recent years. The public views reporters as rude, superficial and arrogant, interested only in today's big story. It sees newspapers, magazines and broadcasting stations as being controlled from far away for purely commercial purposes.

In fact, there is a lot of truth in these perceptions. The relation of news media to their communities has changed in recent decades.

For one thing, the communities have changed. The population is more transient; many citizens have little reason to care about the quality of government, business or other social institutions in their city, county or state. The tendency of city dwellers to cluster in ghettos of affluence, youth or old age, and poverty and ignorance has increased. The late editor William Allen White viewed his town, Emporia, Kan., as a microcosm of the nation—that concept is fading. Too few people know what a small town is like for the analogy to have any meaning today, and modern cities and nations are just too complicated for the analogy to be valid. All of these changes make it difficult for the media in a city to speak to its varied audiences with meaning.

In William Allen White's day, everyone in town knew the editor. The editor owned the paper and lived in the town all his or her life. He or

---

CREDIBILITY: TWO EXAMPLES

A few years ago when I heard columnist James J. Kilpatrick tell a group of students about his early days in Richmond, my thoughts went back to 3 a.m. on a Sunday morning on the streets of Greenville, Miss. I had driven all day and all night to get to my new job in a new town. It was my town. I would chronicle its problems, its tragedies and its joys, and thereby share in its life.

My career eventually took me elsewhere and, 30 years later, brought me back to do some research on the newspaper's editorials. As I went through the files, I couldn't help pausing to read my stories from years before. The feeling of belonging to the town returned, along with something of a feeling that I had betrayed it by leaving.

Most of my colleagues at Greenville worked there only a few years—the years during which the legal segregation of blacks and whites in public accommodations and schools was dismantled. Our credibility was questioned constantly. Good reporting of all the community news we could find protected the newspaper's integrity during those times. We had a remarkable editor, Hodding Carter Jr., whose editorials on race relations won a Pulitzer Prize. More importantly, we worked elbow to elbow with two splendid role models, whose example set the tone and the goals for the rest of us.

Charles Scott Kerg, the sports editor, was a reporter in Greenville for 50 years; before that he delivered the Greenville paper as a schoolboy. He had never lived anywhere else, he had only a high school education and his writing was just adequate. But he would attend any meeting, respond to any inquiry from a reader and keep up with any story that came along. He came to work at 7 a.m., took an afternoon break and covered evening stories daily. He is the only person I have ever known who wore out typewriters. While we scurried all over five counties looking for news, he could get more stories than all of us combined with his 250-pound rotund body seated by his telephone. Everyone called him. If they didn't, he knew something was wrong and called them. Because everyone knew his voice, he could cover a beat with two words, "Any fires?"

For 25 years Louise Eskridge Crump was the society editor. She took the job after being a wife, mother, divorcee and novelist. Her "Delta Scene" column ran three days a week and was seemingly filled with light chit-chat. She was charming. She was also instrumental in tying the community to the newspaper through establishment of a debutante ball, a community theater and other social and cultural events. Before the term day-care center was coined, she was the driving force in creating one that served the children of black mothers who worked as maids in the homes of Greenville whites. She knew that Greenville people wanted to project a good image, and on her page she ran lots of pictures of pretty faces and beautiful homes. But she also knew how to get results for better housing and public health by running pictures of shacks and open sewers on the front page. And people in Greenville knew that one way to get something done was to get Louise Crump and the Delta Democrat-Times behind it.

In the years ahead, you may be sent around the world to cover the news, your writing may win national acclaim and you may join the few journalists who become rich. The chances of your doing that are much better than your chances of exceeding Charles Kerg or Louise Crump in your understanding of what reporting is and how to maintain credibility with your audience.

Harry Marsh

she might have been a poor editor or, like White, a very good one. The people in Emporia knew and trusted White. In less-fortunate towns, the citizens knew and mistrusted the editor. They at least had a good sense of what to expect of their newspapers. Today, the newspaper may be owned by a company with headquarters on the West Coast, two of the television stations may be owned by companies with headquarters on the East Coast, and most of the radio stations may have changed ownership twice in the last five years. The cable television company has the same anonymity as the phone company and gas company.

In a medium-sized city, a good editor or station manager gets promoted to a bigger paper or station or finds a better-paying job in four or five years and a poor one gets replaced. Reporters are even more transient, viewing the first years out of journalism school as a time of getting general experience on a small paper or station or of doing menial tasks on a big one and then moving up. The human ties with any community are often a long time in coming. As a result, reporters and media executives have become more aloof.

However, they also have become more professional. They have a better knowledge of how the mass media operate in society than their predecessors did, and they have better training in the skills of communications. Most are college graduates and a majority have an academic background in mass media studies. They are more professional in their outlook. Most scholars agree that the quality of reporting has increased at the same time that ties to the audience have loosened.

William Allen White of the Emporia Kan., Gazette. (Photo courtesy of The Emporia Gazette)

Scholars and professionals in the 1980s view the credibility problem as a major challenge to the mass media. They have proposed a number of solutions: Give the public better news about the news and the news media, and how reporting is improving. Pay closer attention to reader complaints and apprehensions, correct errors and respond to complaints. Ask the public what it wants to know and broaden the concept of news to include information on how to cope with life on a personal and family basis. Re-establish ties with the community through zoned editions aimed at neighborhoods or through talk shows.

Formal programs can improve media credibility, but the individual attitudes of media professionals are even more important. The columnist James J. Kilpatrick regularly tells journalism students the story of his arrival in Richmond, Va., as a cub reporter. He got off the train and walked to the newspaper building through the rain. It was Sunday and the doors were locked, but he walked around it with a feeling of great expectation; it was his newspaper in his town, though he had just gotten there.

That attitude—that it is *your* newspaper in *your* town—helps you to get a sense of your community's definition of taste. Kilpatrick soon learned what was acceptable in his community. Acceptability or taste is a personal matter, but for reporters, taste also is a community matter. Good taste is related to civility and sensitivity. It is subtle. Good taste has practically nothing to do with wealth, and it may completely escape persons with several academic degrees. Etiquette can be improved by reading a book. Good taste is acquired by osmosis. Reporters must be aware of what is acceptable in their community. This awareness helps them in their contacts with news sources and their colleagues, but more importantly, it guides them in presenting news to the public.

For example, if a college teacher stood before his class with no clothes on, no one would hear his lecture, no matter how brilliant it was. The teacher's appearance would be unacceptable. It would be much louder than his words. Communication is difficult at best. One does not have to be offensive to lose an audience, but that is probably the quickest and most enduring way.

Let's look at another example. In 1981, the experienced managing editor of a small Kansas daily was on vacation when a rape hearing was held in his town. A cub reporter attended the hearing and wrote a story that was edited by the publisher, a young Ivy Leaguer with little experience as a news executive. Both were new to the town. The story did not name the two victims. Yet most people knew who the two women were, since both were prominent citizens. The story appeared on the front page, quoting and paraphrasing their testimony, which included explicit language, at length. Both the publisher and the reporter wanted the public to be aware of the vicious nature of the crimes; both felt the clinical language used was the proper way to present a full and complete story. They were protected from legal action by the defense of privilege. The account was accurate. But they had misjudged public taste. Probably the managing editor would not have.

Of the 1,000 words in the story, the portions that used language not regularly used in the newspapers were as follows:

> The woman ... testified that she ... was awakened "by the feel of a hand between my legs." ... During this time, she said, the man unzipped his pants and pulled out his penis.... He then removed his pants and underwear and forced the woman to have sexual intercourse twice.

The second woman's testimony included the following graphic portions:

> She said during this and throughout sexual intercourse she lay there whimpering.... After sexual intercourse the man entered her rectum, she said. She pleaded for him to leave, but he said, "You better make this good, I'm not leaving until you do," and repeated his threat to kill her.

Teachers at the middle school all signed a letter published by the paper. Their letter noted that they used the paper as a classroom tool and they considered the story inappropriate for their students. They charged that the article was "nothing but sensationalism." Eighty-two faculty and staff members at the local college signed a letter stating that publication of the details of the hearing had no public value, was an attack on personal dignity and would deter future rape victims from testifying. The local radio station broadcast an editorial condemning the story for further humiliating the victims and further embarrassing their children.

Of the more than 30 letters published about the story, two were favorable. A former prison guard wrote: "If more blow-by-blow accounts were given, it could make a few more stronger feelings toward crime." The other letter noted that the article "created public awareness" and concluded that "this is good."

Despite the good intentions of the newspaper, the information that the reporter and publisher wished to convey was lost because the language and detail of the story was not in good taste for that community. Several letter writers noted that such graphic details had not appeared in the newspaper before and that they did not want their hometown paper to become a supermarket tabloid. This suggests two points: If new kinds of material suddenly are presented, the audience may be shocked. Also, what is acceptable in a newspaper for sale to adults in a grocery store may not be acceptable in a newspaper delivered at front doors and read in school classrooms. Acceptable good taste is subtle.

As a reporter, you will probably hear from your audience if you describe or picture gory accidents, people falling to their deaths or grieving relatives. Many people, for instance, criticized the media for its coverage of the 1986 Challenger space shuttle explosion. They felt the media payed too much attention to the tragedy and exploited grief.

In striving to be ethical and credible and to write with good taste, a reporter needs a pure and humble heart. Reporting must be done in a hurry and in a competitive setting. The reporter must be accurate and must tell the full story, but he or she should also try to protect the subjects of stories from needless ridicule and to respect the sensibilities of audience members. A reporter cannot make the right decision every time, but that must be the goal.

A Pulitzer Hoax

This chapter and this book end with a sad story. It is the story behind the story of "Jimmy's World," a feature article about an 8-year-old heroin addict written by Janet Cooke and published by The Washington Post on Sept. 28, 1980.

As good a beginning as any for the story is Janet Cooke's application for a job at The Post. Her résumé said she was a Phi Beta Kappa graduate of Vassar College in 1976. She never graduated from Vassar, but her writing at the Toledo, Ohio, Blade was excellent, and the Post hired her as a reporter without checking her credentials carefully.

In a year she had 52 stories in The Post and was recognized as an ambitious, talented reporter who wrote extremely well. She was assigned to write a story on a new kind of heroin being used in Washington. After weeks of research she wrote "Jimmy's World." The story created a sensation when it appeared. It described how a precocious 8-year-old talked his mother's boyfriend into letting him participate in their drug sessions. Cooke quoted the boy directly, described where he lived in detail and narrated an eyewitness account of all three injecting heroin into their veins. Police and social workers tried to find Jimmy. Rewards were offered. Letters and calls came to The Post.

No one had asked Janet Cooke to identify Jimmy. As she was developing the story, she had asked her editors to assure anonymity for him, and the editors had agreed. At the end of the year, they nominated the story for the Pulitzer Prize. On the biographical sheet for the Pulitzer entry, Janet Cooke indicated that she had a master's degree from the University of Toledo and a bachelor's degree from Vassar and that she had studied at the Sorbonne in Paris.

When it was announced on April 13, 1981, that she was among the Pulitzer Prize winners, The Associated Press reported the Toledo, Vassar and Sorbonne information. That did not agree with a story The Blade of Toledo had written based on its knowledge of Janet Cooke. The Blade asked the AP about the discrepency and the AP checked with Vassar College and the Washington Post.

In a long conference with The Post editors, Janet Cooke admitted that she had fabricated the Vassar degree and Sorbonne studies. Her degree from Toledo was a bachelor's, not a master's. She also admitted that Jimmy, his mother and her boyfriend did not exist. She resigned and apologized. The Post returned the Pulitzer Prize, apologized in an editorial and described the entire affair in stories that took up three and a half pages. The headline read, "Janet's World."

Janet Cooke's motives in writing "Jimmy's World" may have been good. She told the Post's editors that her story represented a composite of what she had learned. In failing to inform her readers that it was a composite, though, she committed the cardinal sins of misleading her readers and departing from the truth.

Janet Cooke has been singled out because her hoax won a Pulitzer Prize. Reporters and news executives of vastly more experience have also misled the public. Later in 1981, for example, a New York Daily News columnist, Michael Daly, resigned and admitted that a British soldier he quoted in a story from Belfast did not exist. In late 1985, Darrow (Duke) Tully, the publisher of The Arizona Republic in Phoenix, resigned after admitting that he had never served in the armed forces although his résumé indicated he had been decorated for air combat in the Korean and Vietnam wars, a lie he had maintained and embellished for 30 years.

Excellence in reporting is not measured by whether the reporter's story makes the front page of The Washington Post, the evening network news shows or the Pulitzer Prize list. Excellence in reporting is measured by one's performance in pursuing and presenting the truth.

APPENDIX A
Wire Service Style Guide

Publications should have uniformity in the use of language for several reasons. Uniformity often saves valuable space and editing time. Uniformity also allows readers to comprehend more easily, which contributes to accuracy and overall credibility. Uniformity begins with writers who know the style of their publications.

The Associated Press Stylebook and Libel Manual (or the almost-identical United Press International Stylebook) is the recognized authority in newspaper journalism and is the basis for the individual stylebooks of many publications. It has developed over the decades and is a product of both the accumulated wisdom of news people and arbitrary decisions made to achieve uniformity. It includes entries on abbreviations and acronyms, capitalization, style for names, numerals, titles, punctuation, grammar and word selection. It also defines the jargon of government, weather, weapons, vehicles, organizations and institutions. It has useful conversion tables for temperature, weights and other measurements. Special sections deal with sports, business terms and libel.

The following two lists are gleaned from the AP Stylebook. The first lists the proper spelling and hyphenation of frequently used words and terms. They are included in the Stylebook because they are frequently misspelled or because they have varied spellings. The second lists proper names. Associated Press style is to use the names of people and organizations as they prefer to spell them. The names listed occur often enough to come to the attention of reporters across the country. The list tells when to use Co., Inc. and Ltd. It shows when to use hyphens and when the acronym (initials) of an institution may be used.

Style in writing—like grooming, manners and punctuality—is a habit reporters develop and nurture. Using these two lists and the comprehensive AP Stylebook and Libel Manual is the way to start developing the habit.

Spelling List

able-bodied
aboveboard
absent-minded
acknowledgment
ad-lib
admissible
adviser
advisory
aesthetic
airmail
airtight
a la carte
albino, albinos
allot, allotted
all right
amid
amok
a.m., p.m.
anesthetic
antarctic
ashcan, ashtray
athlete's foot
ax
baby-sit, baby sitter
baccalaureate
back up (v)
backup (n, adj)
ball point pen
barbiturate
barmaid
barroom
bellwether
benefited
best seller
bigwig
blond (adj, masc n)
blonde (fem n)
bloodhound
bona fide
bonbon
boo-boo
bowlegged
bra
broccoli
brussels sprouts
bull's-eye
bylaw
cannot
carefree
caretaker
carmaker

car pool
carry-over
cease-fire
centerfold
cha-cha
changeable
change up (v)
change-up (n, adj)
chauffeur
cigarette
citywide
claptrap
clientele
close-up (n, adj)
coastline
coattails
colorblind
combated
commitment
compatible
consensus
contemptible
corral, corralled
dark horse
deathbed
deep-sea (adj)
defendant
dependent
detente
dialogue
diarrhea
die-hard (n, adj)
dietitian
disc jockey
dispel, dispelled
domino, dominoes
double-faced
doughnut
dressing room
drive-in (n)
drop out (v)
dropout (n)
drought
drunkenness
duffel
dyed-in-the-wool
earmark
easygoing
editor in chief
employee
empty-handed

enroll, enrolled
en route
epidemiology
equitable
Eskimos
espresso
even-steven
every day (adv)
everyday (adj)
Excedrin
exorcise
expel, expelled
extol, extolled
eyed, eyeing
eyestrain
eyewitness
facade
fact-finding
fade out (v)
fade-out (n)
fallout (n)
far-flung (adj)
far-off (adj)
far-ranging (adj)
farsighted
fathers-in-law
fiance (masc)
fiancee (fem)
field house
fiord
first family
first lady
fitful
flagpole
flagship
flimflam, flimflammed
flip-flop
fluorescent
folk singer
follow up (v)
follow-up (n, adj)
foot-and-mouth disease
forbid, forbade, forbidding
forsake, forsook, forsaken
fortuneteller
four-star general
frame up (v)
frame-up (n)
free-for-all

free-lance (v, adj)
free-lancer (n)
freewheeling
freeze-dry
french fries
front line (n)
front-line (adj)
front page (n)
front-page (adj)
front-runner
fulfill, fulfilled
fuselage
fusillade
gaiety
game plan
gamy, gamier
genie
getaway (n)
get-together (n)
glamour
globe-trotter
go-between (n)
goodbye
good will (n)
goodwill (adj)
grammar
grant-in-aid, grants-in-aid
gray
groundskeeper
groundswell
grown-up (n, adj)
G-String
gubernatorial
guerrilla
guru
handmade
hand-picked
hangover
hanky-panky
harass
harebrained
headlong
head-on (adj, adv)
hearsay
heliport
helter-skelter
hemorrhage
hemorrhoid
hideaway
hi-fi
hitchhike
hocus-pocus
hodgepodge

ho-hum
homemade
hometown
hooky
horsepower
hot line
hurly-burly
hush-hush
impel, impelled
impostor
inasmuch as
incur, incurred
index, indexes
indiscriminate, indiscriminately
indispensable
in-law
innocuous
innuendo
inoculate
insofar as
IOU, IOUs
judgment
jukebox
ketchup
kidnap, kidnapped
kindergarten
knickknack
know-how
kosher
kowtow
kudos
lamebrain
lame duck (n)
lame-duck (adj)
lawsuit
left hand (n)
left-handed (adj)
left-hander (n)
left wing (n)
left-wing (adj)
left-winger (n)
legerdemain
legionnaire
letup (n, adj)
liaison
life-size
lifetime
light, lighted
likable
linoleum
lion's share
long-term (adj)
longtime (adj)

make up (v)
makeup (n, adj)
malarkey
manageable
marketbasket
marketplace
marshal, marshaled
meager
medieval
melee
mementos
memos
menage a trois
menswear
merry-go-round
middleman
milquetoast
minuscule
mix up (v)
mix-up (n, adj)
mock-up (n)
moneymaker
monthlong
mop up (v)
mop-up (n, adj)
mosquito, mosquitoes
naive
naphtha
narrow-minded
nationwide
nearsighted
negligee
newsstand
nightclub
nighttime
nitpicking
nitty-gritty
nobody
no man's land
no one
nowadays
occur, occurred
oceangoing
oddsmaker
officeholder
ok, ok'd, ok'ing, oks
old times
old-time
old-timer
one another
one-sided
one-time (adj)
out-of-bounds (adj)
out-of-court (adj)

overall
paddy wagon
pantsuit
pantyhose
pari-mutuel
parishioner
passer-by, passers-by
pasteurize
patrol, patrolled
payload
peacekeeping
peacemaker
peace offering
peacetime
peddler
pell-mell
penny-wise
percent
permissible
piano, pianos
pigeonhole (n, v)
pile up (v)
pileup (n, adj)
pingpong
pipeline
p.m., a.m.
poinsettia
point-blank
pom-pom, pompon
pooh-pooh
potato, potatoes
pothole
predominant
prophecy (n)
prophesy (v)
protester
proviso, provisos
pull back (v)
pullback (n)
pull out (v)
pullout (n)
push-button (n, adj)
push-up (n, adj)
put out (v)
putout (n)
pygmy
questionnaire
quick-witted
raccoon
rank-and-file (adj)
reconnaissance
recur, recurred
red-handed
red-hot

re-elect
referendums
rescission
resistible
restaurateur
riffraff
rights of way
rip off (v)
rip-off (n, adj)
rock 'n' roll
roll call (n)
roll-call (adj)
roly-poly
round up (v)
round-up (n)
rubber stamp (n)
rubber-stamp (v, adj)
runners-up
running mate
rush hour (n)
rush-hour (adj)
saboteur
sacrilegious
salable
salvo, salvos
sanitariums
scuba
scurrilous
second hand (n)
secondhand (adj, adv)
second-rate
semiannual
send off (v)
send-off (n)
sesquicentennial
set up (v)
setup (n, adj)
shake up (v)
shake-up (n, adj)
shape up (v)
shape-up (n, adj)
shoeshine
shoestring
shopworn
shortchange
showcase
showroom
showoff (n)
shut down (v)
shutdown (n)
shut-in
shut off (v)
shut-off (n)
shut out (v)

shutout (n)
side-by-side (adj)
sightseeing
single-handed
sit down (v)
sit-down (n, adj)
sit in (v)
sit-in (n, adj)
sizable
ski, skis, skied, skiing
skillful
sledgehammer
sleight of hand
slowdown
slumlord
slush fund
small-arms fire
small-business man
smash up (v)
smashup (n, adj)
smoke bomb
smoke screen
so-called (adj)
soft-spoken
soliloquy, soliloquies
sons-in-law
spacecraft
speed up (v)
speedup (n, adj)
springtime
standard-bearer
stand in (v)
stand-in (n, adj)
stand off (v)
standoff (n, adj)
stand out (v)
standout (n, adj)
states' rights
statewide
stepbrother
steppingstone
stifling
stockbroker
stool pigeon
stopgap
storyteller
straitjacket
strikebreaker
strong-arm (v, adj)
strong-willed
successor
summertime
supersede
supersonic

swastika
syllabus, syllabuses
tablecloth
tailspin
take-home pay
take off (v)
takeoff (n, adj)
take out (v)
takeout (n, adj)
takeover (n, adj)
take up (v)
takeup (n, adj)
tattletale
teachers college
teammate
tear gas
teaspoon, teaspoonfuls
telltale
temblor
tenderhearted
tenfold
theretofore
threesome
throwaway
tidbit
tie, tied, tying
tie in (v)
tie-in (n, adj)
tie up (v)
tie-up (n, adj)
tiptop
titleholder
tollhouse
toward
trade in (v)
trade-in (n, adj)

trademark
trade off (v)
trade-off (n, adj)
trafficked
trampoline
transsexuals
travel, traveled
travelogue
trigger-happy
try out (v)
tryout (n)
T-shirt
tune up (v)
tuneup (n, adj)
undersecretary
upside down (adv)
upside-down (adj)
upstate
vendor
vie, vied, vying
Vietnam War
voodoo
vote-getter
walk up (v)
walk-up (n, adj)
warhead
warlike
warlord
wartime
washed-up
wastebasket
weak-kneed
weather-beaten
weather vane
weekend
weeklong

well-being
well-to-do
well-wishers
wheelchair
wheeler-dealer
whereabouts
wherever
white-collar (adj)
white paper
whitewash (n, v, adj)
wholehearted
whole-wheat
wigwag
wildlife
wind-swept
wingspan
wintertime
word-of-mouth (n, adj)
workday
workout
workweek
worldwide
worn-out
worship, worshiped
worthwhile
write in (v)
write-in (n, adj)
wrongdoing
year-end (adj)
yearlong
yesteryear
yo-yo
yule, yuletide
zero, zeros
zigzag

Proper Names

Capitalize the following names. Note the specific use of words, punctuation marks and symbols.

Acronyms that are better known than the proper nouns they represent are listed first. These acronyms may be used in first reference (the first time the proper noun is used in the story). An asterisk (*) indicates that the nature of the proper noun should be explained in the text of the story.

In the second part of the list, parentheses indicate that an abbreviation may be used in the second reference in the story. The Stylebook gives other shortened forms as well.

Appendix A

A&P
ABC
ABM*
A.D., B.C.
AFL–CIO
AM, FM
CARE
CBS
CIA
DDT
FBI
ICBM*
KGB*
LSD
MGM
MiG
M–1, M–14
NASA*
NAACP*
NATO
NBC
PTA
ROTC
SALT
SST
TNT
UFO, UFOs
UHF, VHF
UNESCO*
UNICEF
VIP, VIPs
YMCA
YWCA

Academy Awards
Aeroflot
A-frame
Agency for International Development (AID)
Air Force One
Air-India
Al Fatah
All-America
American Airlines
American Automobile Association (AAA)
American Bar Association (ABA)
American Civil Liberties Union (ACLU)
American Legion
American Medical Association (AMA)
American Motors Corp. (AMC)
American Newspaper Publishers Association (ANPA)
American Society for the Prevention of Cruelty to Animals (ASPCA)
American Stock Exchange (Amex)
American Telephone & Telegraph Co. (AT&T)
Amtrak
Arabian American Oil Co. (Aramco)
Asian
Associated Press, The (AP)
Atchison, Topeka & Santa Fe Railway
Atlantic Richfield Co. (Arco)
Band-Aid
Bank of America
Belize
Benzedrine
Berlin Wall
Bible Belt
Bill of Rights
Black Muslims
B'nai B'rith
Boeing Co.
Boy Scouts
Braniff Airways
British Broadcasting Corp. (BBC)
British Petroleum Co. Ltd. (BP)
Bromo Seltzer
Camp Fire
Canadian Broadcasting Corp. (CBC)
Canal Zone
Caterpillar
Center for Disease Control (CDC)
Chile
Citibank
Civil Aeronautics Board (CAB)
Clorox
Coast Guardsman
Coca-Cola, Coke
Cold War
Common Market
Commonwealth, the
Communications Satellite Corp. (Comsat)
Confederacy, the
Congressional Record
Conrail
Consumer Product Safety Commission
Continental Divide
Corn Belt
Cotton Belt
Council of Economic Advisers
Dacron
Dark Ages
Dark Continent
Daughters of the American Revolution (DAR)
D-day
Dead Sea Scrolls
Deepfreeze
Deep South
Democratic Governors' Conference
Democratic National Committee
Dexedrine
Dictaphone
Diners Club
Disposall
Distant Early Warning line (DEW line)
Dixie cup
Dow Jones & Co.
Down Under
Dripolator
Dr Pepper
Du Pont
Eastern Shore
East Germany
Election Day
Electoral College
Emmy, Emmys
Enovid
Equal Rights Amendment (ERA)
Eurasian
Excedrin
Export-Import Bank of the United States
Exxon Corp.
Faeroe Islands
Father's Day

Federal Aviation Administration (FAA)
Federal Communications Commission (FCC)
Federal Crop Insurance Corp.
Federal Deposit Insurance Corp. (FDIC)
Federal Housing Administration (FHA)
Federal Register
Federal Reserve Board
Federal Trade Commission (FTC)
Fiberglas
Filipinos
Food and Agriculture Organization (FAO)
Food and Drug Administration (FDA)
Ford Motor Co.
4-H Club
Fourth of July, July Fourth
French Canadian
Frisbee
Gallup Poll
General Accounting Office (GAO)
General Electric Co. (GE)
General Motors Corp. (GM)
General Services Administration (GSA)
Girl Scouts
Good Conduct Medal
Grand Old Party
Great Plains
Green Revolution
Greenwich Mean Time (GMT)
Groundhog Day
Gulf Oil Corp.
Harris Survey
Hispaniola
Hodgkin's disease
Holy See
Holy Spirit
Holy Week
Independence Day
Index of Leading Economic Indicators

International Court of Justice
Interpol
Japan Current
Jaycees
J. C. Penney Co. Inc.
Jell-O
Johns Hopkins University
Johnson Space Center
Joint Chiefs of Staff
Kennedy Space Center
Keystone Kops
Kleenex
Knights of Columbus (K. of C.)
Kodak
Koran
Kriss Kringle
Ku Klux Klan
Kuomintang
Labor Day
Laetrile
Land-Rover
Lastex
Last Supper
Laundromat
Law Enforcement Assistance Administration (LEAA)
Leaning Tower of Pisa
Lent
Life Savers
Lloyd's of London
Lockheed Aircraft Corp.
Lord's Supper
Lucite
Mafia, Mafiosi
Magna Charta
Mailgram
Mardi Gras
Marines
Maritime Provinces
Mason-Dixon Line
Masonite
McDonnell Douglas Corp.
Medal of Freedom
Medal of Honor
Medicaid, Medicare
Mercurochrome
Middle Ages
Middle Atlantic States

Middle East
Middle West
Montessori method
Moral Majority
Mother's Day
Multigraph
Multilith
Murphy's law
Mutual Radio
National Council of Churches
National Education Association (NEA)
National Governors' Association
National Guardsman
National Institutes of Health
National Labor Relations Board (NLRB)
National Organization for Women (NOW)
National Rifle Association (NRA)
National Weather Service
Naugahyde
Nazi, Nazism
NCR Corp.
New World
New York Stock Exchange
Nobel Prize
North Slope
Northwest Territories
Nuclear Regulatory Commission
Occidental Petroleum, Corp.
Occupational Safety and Health Administration (OSHA)
Old West
Old World
Oreo
Organization of American States (OAS)
Organization of Petroleum Exporting Countries (OPEC)
Orient, Oriental
Ouija
Oval Office
Pablum

Palestine Liberation Organization (PLO)
Panama Canal Zone
Pan American World Airways (Pan Am)
Pennsylvania Dutch
Pepsi, Pepsi-Cola
Peter Principle
Ph.D., Ph.D.s
Philippines
Photostat
Pikes Peak
Plexiglas
Polaroid
Politburo
Popsicle
Prince Edward Island
Procter & Gamble Co. (P&G)
Prohibition
Public Broadcasting Service (PBS)
Puerto Rico
Pulitzer Prizes
Pyrex
Q-Tips
Quaalude
RCA Corp. (RCA)
Reconstruction
Republican National Committee
Reuters
Rh factor
Richter scale
Ringling Bros. and Barnum & Bailey Circus
Rio Grande
Rolls-Royce
Roquefort cheese
R.S.V.P.
Sabbath
Safeway Stores Inc.
Sanforized
Saturday Night Special
Sault Ste. Marie
Scotch whisky
Sears, Roebuck & Co.
Secret Service
Securities and Exchange Commission (SEC)
Seeing Eye dog
Seven Seas
Seven Sisters
Seven-Up, 7-Up
Sheetrock
Shell Oil Co.
Sierra Nevada, the
Simoniz
Sinai
Skid Road, Skid Row
Smithsonian Institution
Smokey Bear
Social Security
Society for the Prevention of Cruelty to Animals (SPCA)
Southeast Asia
Spanish-American War
Sri Lanka
S. S. Kresge Co.
Standard Oil Co. (Indiana)
Standard Oil Co. of California
Standard Oil Co. (Ohio) (Sohio)
"The Star-Spangled Banner"
State of the Union
Stone Age
Strategic Air Command (SAC)
Styrofoam
Sucaryl
Super Bowl
Supreme Court of the United States
Supreme Soviet
Taiwan
Teamsters union
Technicolor
Teflon
TelePrompTer
Teletype
Tennessee Valley Authority (TVA)
Texaco Inc.
Thai
Third World
Tommy gun
Tory, Tories
Trans World Airlines (TWA)
Trinidad and Tobago
TriStar
Truman, Harry S.
Twelve Apostles
20th Century-Fox
Twentieth Century Fund
U-boat
Uncle Sam
Uncle Tom
Uniform Code of Military Justice
United Airlines
United Arab Emirates
United Kingdom
United Mine Workers of America (UMW)
United Nations
U.N. General Assembly
U.N. Security Council
United Press International (UPI)
United Steelworkers of America
U.S. Air Force
U.S. Army
U.S. Coast Guard
U.S. Court of Appeals
U.S. Court of Claims
U.S. Court of Military Appeals
U.S. Customs Court
U.S. District Courts
U.S. Information Agency
U.S. Military Academy
U.S. Navy
U.S. Postal Service
U.S. Tax Court
U-turn
Valium
Vaseline
Vatican City
V-E Day
V–8
Veterans Administration (VA)
Veterans Day
Veterans of Foreign Wars (VFW)
Victrola
Viet Cong
Vietnam
V-J Day
V-neck
Voice of America (VOA)

Volunteers in Service to America (VISTA)
Wall Street
Warner Communications Inc.
Washington's Birthday
Western Hemisphere
Windbreaker
Woman's Christian Temperance Union (WCTU)
Woolworth's
World Bank
World Council of Churches
World Court
World Health Organization (WHO)
World Series
World War I, World War II
Xerox
X-ray
Zionism
ZIP codes

APPENDIX B

America's Open Records Laws

In 1984, The Society of Professional Journalists, Sigma Delta Chi, released a massive compilation and analysis of the America's open meetings and open records laws. The work was done by Rick Dent of the University of Alabama School of Law and David Freedman of Columbia University's law school, as SPJ/SDX interns in Washington D.C. Editorial and publication assistance was provided by the Gannett Company. Society attorney Ben Ginsberg helped guide the project. What follows is an excerpt of the state-by-state findings. Be aware, however, that by the time you read this, the laws in your state may have changed. More detailed information about whether specific records are open is available from the Society, and from the attorney general and the press association of your state.

ALABAMA

Alabama's Open Records law is contained in Alabama Code Sec. 36–12–40, 41 (1982).

Every citizen may see them.

What is covered: Any public writing of the state.

Exemptions: Records expressly exempted from inspection by statute.

Other statutory exemptions: Other state code provisions governing access to records are listed in the index to the code under "Records." These include restrictions on access to (1) income tax returns; (2) records of youthful offenders; (3) records of child care facilities; (4) proprietary information acquired by the Alabama Department of Energy under the Alabama Energy Management and Conservation Act; (5) criminal history and other information held by the Alabama Criminal Justice Information Center on convicted offenders confined to jails, prisons or other penal institutions.

Other restrictions include: (1) attorney disciplinary hearings; (2) certain conservation and natural resource information; (3) probation officers' records; and (4) circulation records and information at public libraries. However, parents of a minor child have the right to inspect such library records that pertain to his or her child. Some public welfare records are open to inspection.

ALASKA

Alaska's Open Records law is contained in Alaska Statute Sec. 09.25.110 to 09.25.125.

Any person may see them.

Who is covered: All agencies and departments.

What is covered: All books, records, papers, files, official writings and transactions.

Exemptions: (1) Records of vital statistics and adoption proceedings; (2) juvenile records; (3) medical records; (4) records required to be kept confidential by federal or state law or regulation.

Other statutory exemptions: Among the statutes declaring certain types of information confidential are: (1) those restricting access to state personnel records; (2) geological, geophysical and other information submitted for persons applying to lease or buy land; (3) reports, logs, surveys and other information held by the Department of Natural Resources relating to oil wells for which a permit to drill was issued by the department; (4) documents in the possession or control of the Alaska Royalty Oil and Gas Development Advisory Board that contain confidential business or marketing information the protection of which is essential to the best interests of the state; (5) information contained in audit reports or tax returns; (6) statements of potential prosecution witnesses; (7) information contained in preparation of parole reports; and (8) criminal history data. Attorney general memoranda have been held to be confidential written material under consideration in closed grievance proceedings involving state employees (July 19, 1976), investigative files of professional licensing boards until the investigation is concluded and all relevant facts are presented at a public hearing (April 6, 1977), and the names and addresses of applicants for the senior citizen tax exemption (April 17, 1979).

ARIZONA

Arizona's Open Records law is contained in Arizona Revised Statutes Sec. 39–121, 41–135.

Any person may see them.

Who is covered: State, any county, city, town, school district, political subdivision, or tax-supported district in the state; any agency supported by state or local funds.

What is covered: All books, papers, maps, photographs or other documentary materials made or received by any governmental agency in transaction of public business.

Statutory exemptions: A number of statutes elsewhere in the state code provide that certain records are confidential. These include: (1) arrest records; (2) consumer fraud records; (3) corrections department records; (4) racketeering investigations; (5) criminal intelligence information; (6) criminal history record information; (7) minutes of executive sessions of public bodies; (8) information obtained by the state fire marshall from an insurer concerning a fire loss; (9) vital statistics; and (10) certain health care facility records.

Certain records have been held to be confidential by attorney general opinions. These include: (1) preliminary draft audit reports of the auditor general; (2) financial statements filed by contractors; (3) investigative reports where disclosure would be detrimental to the interests of the state; (4) classified National Guard operational data if release would seriously and adversely affect the guard's ability to meet its duties; and (5) payroll voucher information concerning payroll deductions. If only a poriton of a record meets the test for confidentiality, then only that portion should be deleted and the remainder released for public inspection.

ARKANSAS

Arkansas' Open Records law is contained in Arkansas Statutes Annotated Sec. 12–2801 to 2807.

Any citizen of Arkansas may see them.

Who is covered: Governmental agencies, or any other agency wholly or partially supported by public funds.

What is covered: Writings, recovered sounds, films, tapes or data in any form required by law to be kept or which constitutes a record of the performance of official functions.

Exemptions: (1) State income tax records; (2) medical, scholastic and adoption records; (3) grand jury minutes; (4) unpublished drafts of judicial or quasi-judicial opinions and decisions; (5) undisclosed investigations of suspected criminal activity; (6) working papers and correspondence of the governor, legislature, Supreme Court justices and the attorney general; (7) information of a personal nature which would constitute an unwarranted invasion of personal privacy; (8) documents protected by order or rule of court.

Certain records are not open to public inspection and copying under court decisions and attorney general opinions. Among these are minutes of executive sessions; health reports of state employees; and investigative and complaint files maintained by law enforcement agencies. Other statutes expressly declare certain records to be confidential. Among these are accident reports; records obtained in investigating medicaid fraud; complaints filed with the Judicial Ethics Committee.

Arkansas Statute Annotated Section 45–443 prohibits publication of information by the news media that would identify a juvenile who is the subject of a juvenile court proceeding without written order of the juvenile court.

CALIFORNIA

California's Open Records law is contained in California Government Code Sec. 6250 to 6265 (Deering).

Every citizen may see them.

Who is covered: Every state office, officer, department, division, bureau, board, and commission or other state body or agency; a county, city, whether general law or chartered; city and county school district, municipal corporation, district, political subdivision, or any board, commission or agency thereof, or other public agency.

What is covered: Any writing containing information relating to the conduct of the public's business prepared, owned, used, or retained by any state or local agency regardless of physical form or characteristics.

Exemptions: (1) Requests for bilingual election materials; (2) preliminary drafts, notes or memos which are not retained by the public agency in the ordinary course of business; (3) pending litigation records; (4) personnel, medical or similar personal files; (5) records of regulation of financial institution and information received in confidence by any state agency; (6) records of utility systems development or market or crop reports; (7) investigative records of law enforcement agencies; (8) exam data; (9) real estate appraisals; (10) personal tax information; (11) library circulation records; (12) records confidential by federal or state law; (13) correspondence of and to the governor or employees of his office; (14) records in the custody of the Legislative Counsel; (15) statements of finances required by licensing agency; (16) financial data in application under the Health and Safety Code; (17) records of a state agency's impressions, opinions, research work product and the like; (18) records of native American graves and sacred places maintained by the Native American Heritage Commission; (19) final accreditation reports of the Joint Commission of Accreditation of Hospitals.

COLORADO

Colorado's Open Records statute is contained in Colorado Revised Statutes Sec. 24–72–201 through 206.

Any person may see them.

Who is covered: State, or any agency, institution or political subdivision. Political subdivision means every county, city, town, school, or special district.

What is covered: All writings made or kept by covered agencies for use in official activities of the agency.

Exemptions: Records made confidential by any other rule, regulation or law.

Access may be denied for: (1) information pertaining to licensing; (2) employment or academic exams; (3) specific details of state research projects; (4) real estate appraisals by the state before any purchase.

Access must be denied for: (1) medical, psychological, and academic data on individuals; (2) personnel files except applications and performance records; (3) letters of reference; (4) trade secrets and confidential commercial, financial or geological data furnished by or obtained from any person; (5) addresses and phone numbers of elementary and secondary public school students.

Other restricted records include: adoption records (19-4-104); records of law enforcement officers concerning children taken into temporary custody (19-2-102); reports and records on child abuse cases (19-10-109); and registration and other records of alcohol treatment facilities (25-1-312). Information assistance in general is confidential, according to 26-1-115.

DELAWARE

Delaware's Open Records law is contained in Delaware Code Annotated Title 29, Sec. 10001-10005.

Any citizen of the state may see them.

Who is covered: Same bodies as covered by the Open Meetings section.

What is covered: Written or recorded information made or received by a public body relating to public business.

Exemptions: (1) Personnel, medical or pupil files; (2) commercial and financial information of a confidential nature; (3) civil or criminal law enforcement files, child custody and adoption files; (4) criminal files and records that would invade privacy; (5) law enforcement intelligence files; (6) records exempted by statute or common law; (7) labor negotiations; (8) anonymous contributors to charity; (9) pending or potential litigation records; (10) records of executive sessions; (11) records of permits for concealed weapons; (12) public library records containing identity of user and materials used.

Other statutory exemptions: Certain records are declared confidential by other state statutes. These include: (1) adoption records (Title 13, 913-924); (2) records of the Preliminary Investigatory Committee and the Board of Examining Officers of the Court on the Judiciary, except for a final order of removal or retirement (Judiciary Court Rule 10); (3) public assistance records (Title 31, 1101); (4) records of the State Personnel Commission concerning character, personal history or health of employees or applicants for employment, except where the majority of the commission finds it to be in public interest that the records be open to public inspection (Title 29, 5948); (5) records of proceedings before the Family Court, except the name of a child arrested for a felony and the names of his parents (Family Court Rule 972); (6) and records and files of the Bureau of Vital Statistics (Title 16, 3110).

DISTRICT OF COLUMBIA

The District of Columbia's Open Records law is contained in D.C. Code Annotated Sec. 1-1521 to 1-1528.

Any person may see them.

Who is covered: Mayor, officer, employee, office, department or other agency of the District government required to administer the law or regulations.

What is covered: All books, papers, maps, photos, cards, tapes, recordings, or other documentary materials used by, in the possession of, or retained by the mayor and other agencies.

Exemptions: (1) Commercial or financial secrets; (2) personal information amounting to an invasion of privacy; (3) law enforcement investigatory records; (4) interagency or intra-agency memos or letters not available by law; (5) test questions and answers used in employment and academic exams; (6) information exempted by other statutes; (7) information authorized by federal law to be kept secret; (8) information related to civil antitrust investigations; (9) fire loss information furnished by insurer to fire marshal and vital statistics records.

Section 1–1524(d) provides that the Freedom of Information Act does not apply to the Vital Records Act of 1981. Under 6220(a) of that act, birth, death, marriage, divorce and adoption records are confidential, except to those having a "direct and tangible interest in them." Other records declared by statute to be confidential include: personnel records (1–632–1); information regarding abused and neglected children (6–2101); information concerning applicants for or recipients of public assistance (3–212); juvenile case and social records and law enforcement records regarding a child (16–2331); registration and other records of detoxification centers (24–524(c)); and income tax (47–1805–4), inheritance tax (47–1936), and gross sales tax returns (47–2018).

CONNECTICUT

Connecticut's Open Records law is contained in Connecticut General Statutes Annotated Sec. 1–15 to 1–21k.

Any person may see them.

Who is covered: Same bodies as the Open Meetings law.

What is covered: Any recorded data or information relating to the conduct of the public's business prepared, owned, used, received or retained by a public agency, whether such data be handwritten, typed, tape-recorded, printed, photostated, photographed or recorded by any other method.

Exemptions: (1) Confidential records by federal or state law; (2) preliminary drafts or notes whose nondisclosure is in the public's interest; (3) personnel and medical files; (4) law enforcement records; (5) trade secrets; (6) exam data; (7) real estate appraisal and other data relating to the acquisition of property; (8) personal financial data required by a licensing agency; (9) collective bargaining; (10) records, tax returns, and other exempted material in state and federal law or communications privileged by the attorney-client relationship; (11) names and addresses of public school students; (12) information obtained by illegal means; (13) adoption records.

Other statutory exemptions: (1) Child abuse records; (2) adoption records; (3) anti-trust investigations; (4) certain labor and employment arrest records; (5) public assistance information; (6) investigations concerning judges; (7) juvenile records; (8) mental records; (9) old age assistance information; (10) paternity records; (11) state sales and use tax.

FLORIDA

Florida's Open Records law is contained in Florida Statutes Annotated Sec. 119.01 to 119.12.

Any person may see them.

Who is covered: Any state, county, district, authority, or municipal officer, department, division, board, bureau, commission, or other separate unit of government created or established by law and any other public or private agency, person, partnership, corporation, or business entity acting on behalf of any public agency.

What is covered: All documents, papers, letters, maps, books, tapes, photos, films, sound recordings, or other materials, regardless of physical form or characteristics, made or received pursuant to law or ordinance or in connection with the transaction of official business by an agency.

Exemptions: (1) Records confidential by other law; (2) all public records referred to specifically by this statute; (3) exam data; (4) active criminal investigation information; (5) information revealing the identity of an informant; (6) information revealing surveillance techniques or personnel; (7) information revealing undercover personnel; (8) criminal intelligence information revealing victims of any sexual battery; (9) criminal intelligence information revealing personal assets of victims; (10) all criminal intelligence information received by an agency prior to January 25, 1979; (11) home addresses, phones, and photos of law enforcement personnel; (12) information provided to an agency for the purpose of ride-sharing arrangements; (13) information revealing the substance of a confession; (14) patient records obtained by the Hospital Cost Containment Board.

Records held closed by interpretation include: (1) abortion records; (2) certain unemployment compensation records; (3) juvenile records; (4) grand jury records.

GEORGIA

Georgia's Open Records law is contained in Georgia Code Annotated Sec. 50-18-70 to 50-18-74.

Any person may see them.

Who is covered: State, counties and municipalities.

What is covered: Documents, papers and records prepared and maintained in the course of the operation of a public office.

Exemptions: (1) Records required by federal law to be confidential; (2) medical records; (3) records that amount to an invasion of personal privacy; (4) identity of person who has furnished medical information used in medical investigation by the Department of Human Services; (5) licenses and records relating to carrying of pistols and revolvers; (6) records declared by state court or law to be confidential.

Other statutory exemptions: (1) Public assistance information; (2) adoption records; (3) vital statistics, except records of marriages, divorces and annulments; (4) probation system records; (5) intangible personal property tax records; (6) tax returns; (7) medical peer review group records; (8) information submitted by references on applications.

Records declared to be confidential by court decision or attorney general's opinions include: (1) records prepared and maintained in a current and continuing investigation of possible criminal activity; (2) the names of informants to law enforcement agencies and, in exceptional and necessarily limited cases, the names of complainants; (3) personnel records of local boards of education; (4) salary information of county employees contained only in personnel files and not included as part of another public record; (5) records of a type traditionally found in personnel files; (6) daily records, diaries and computation sheets of the state Department of Transportation; (7) trade secrets and other confidential business information received by the state energy office from the federal government and private business.

HAWAII

Hawaii's Open Records law is contained in Hawaii Revised Statutes Sec. 92–21 to 92–71.

Any person may see them.

Who is covered: State; political subdivisions of the state.

What is covered: Any written or printed report, book or paper, map or plan of the state or county and their respective subdivisions and boards, but not including records which invade individual privacy.

Exemptions: Records not open if in violation of other state or federal law; attorney general and responsible county attorneys may withhold records in their offices that pertain to the preparation of any action to which the state or county is a party; attorneys may withhold records that do not relate to a matter in violation of the law where nondisclosure is deemed necessary for the protection of the character or reputation of any person.

Other statutory exemptions: (1) Fire investigation records of county fire chiefs may be withheld; (2) public assistance records; (3) applications for licenses to manufacture or sell motor vehicles.

Access to "personal records" is in general prohibited under a separate statute, section 92E–1. In it, a "personal record" is defined as "any item, collection, or grouping of information about an individual that is maintained by an agency," with agency defined as offices, departments, boards, commissions, etc., of the executive branch of the state or of each county. Not covered: the state legislature; council of each county, their offices and employees; the judiciary and courts, their offices and employees.

Other personal records containing criminal history record information, criminal intelligence or investigation records, and reports prepared or compiled at any stage of the criminal law enforcement process; records the disclosure of which would reveal the identity of a source who furnished information to the agency under an expressed or implied understanding of confidentiality.

IDAHO

Idaho's Open Records law is contained in Idaho Code Sec. 9-301 to 9-302.

Any citizen of the state may see them.

What is covered: Every citizen has a right to inspect and copy any public writing of the state except as otherwise expressly provided by statute. Covers same records as above.

Exemptions: Among the records expressly declared confidential by other state statutes are: (1) papers filed with the judicial council or masters appointed by the Idaho Supreme Court concerning removal, discipline, or retirement of judges or justices (1-2103); (2) public assistance records (56-221); and (3) court records concerning child protective proceedings (16-1621).

ILLINOIS

Illinois' Open Records law is contained in Illinois Annotated Statutes Chapter 116, Sec. 201 to 211 (Smith-Hurd).

Any person may see them.

The Open Meeting law also contains no provisions for sanctions against violators.

Who is covered: Any legislative, executive, administrative, or advisory bodies of the state, state universities and colleges, counties, townships, cities, villages, incorporated towns, school districts and all other municipal corporations, boards, bureaus, committees, or commissions of the state, and any subsidiary bodies of any of the foregoing including committees and subcommittees which are supported in whole or in part by tax revenue, or which expend revenue.

What is covered: All records, reports, forms, writings, letters, memos, books, papers, maps, photos, microfilms, cards, tapes, recordings, electronic data processing records, recorded information and all other documentary materials regardless of physical form or characteristics, having been prepared, or having been or being used, received, possessed or under the control of any public body.

Exemptions: (1) Information exempted by state or federal law; (2) information constituting an unwarranted invasion of privacy; (3) files of clients, patients, residents, students or others receiving services for federal agencies or public bodies; (4) personal files or others receiving services for federal agencies or public bodies; (5) personal files maintained with respect to employees, appointees or elected officials; (6) files of bodies engaged in professional or occupational registration; (7) taxpayer information; (8) identities of persons filing complaints with agencies; (9) investigatory records; (10) certain criminal history information; (11) records related to the detection and investigation of crimes or security; (12) preliminary drafts, notes, memos and other records in which opinions are expressed; (13) trade secrets and commercial information; (14) proposals and bids for contracts, grants or agreements; (15) research data; (16) exam data; (17) architects' and engineers' plans; (18) library circulation records; (19) minutes of closed meetings; (20) communications between a public body and an attorney; (21) evaluation information of faculty members by their peers; (22) automated data processing operations information; (23) collective bargaining materials; (24) drafts, notes, and memos pertaining to financial transactions of bodies; (25) real estate purchase documents during negotiations; (26) records related to the operation of an intergovernmental risk management association; (27) student discipline information.

INDIANA

Indiana's Open Records law is contained in Indiana Code Annotated Sec. 5-14-3-1 to 5-14-3-9.

Any person may see them.

Who is covered: Same bodies as covered in Open Meetings law, plus any law enforcement agency. Branch offices operated by managers not covered by statute.

What is covered: Any writing, paper, report, study, map, photograph, book, card, tape recording or other material that is created, received, retained, maintained, used or filed by or with a public agency, and is generated on paper or any other material.

Exemptions: Records that may not be disclosed: (1) those declared confidential by state statute; (2) those declared confidential by rule adopted by public agency with specific authority to do so; (3) those required to be kept confidential by federal law; (4) trade secrets; (5) confidential financial information obtained upon request for a person, not including information filed with or received by agency pursuant to state statute; (6) information concerning research conducted under auspices of institution of higher education.

Records that may be withheld at agency's discretion: (1) law enforcement agency investigatory records; (2) work product of attorney employed or appointed by public agency; (3) examination data used in licensing, employment, or academic examination before exam is given; (4) test or license examination scores where person is identified by name and has not consented to release; (5) negotiations in progress with industrial, research or commercial prospects; (6) interagency and intra-agency advisory or deliberative material; (7) diaries and journals; (8) certain public employees records; (9) patient medical records and charts and minutes or records of hospital medical staff meetings.

IOWA

Iowa's Open Records law is contained in Iowa Code Annotated Sec. 68A.1 to 68A.9. Any person may see them.

What is covered: All records or documents of or belonging to the state or any county, city, town, township, school corporation, tax-supported district or any branch, department, board, bureau, commission, council or committee of such bodies. Adds taped information to definition of documents.

Exemptions: Records that may be withheld: (1) personal educational information; (2) hospital or medical records; (3) trade secrets; (4)

work product of attorney related to claim made by or against the body; (5) peace officers' investigative reports; (6) reports to agencies that would give unfair advantage to competition; (7) appraisal information for possible public land purchase; (8) Iowa Development Commission information on industrial prospect in negotiation; (9) criminal identification files of law enforcement agencies; (10) confidential information in personnel records of state military department; (11) confidential personnel records of public bodies; (12) financial statements submitted to state Commerce Commission; (13) certain library records; (14) information on riot control procedures at adult correctional facilities; (15) health agency records identifying persons with reportable disease; (16) school records; (17) records of professional counselors.

Other statutory exemptions: Criminal history and intelligence data in the possession of the Department of Public Safety are confidential, 692.18. The records of the Merit Employment Department, except personal information in an employee's file if publication of such information would serve no proper public service, are open to inspection, 19A.15. All records of the Department of Banking are public records subject to the provisions of Chapter 68A, except for all papers, documents, reports, reports of examinations and other writings relating to the supervision and regulation of any state bank or other person by the banking superintendent, 524.215.

A smaller group of records has been held to be confidential. Among these are: minutes of testimony attached to and filed with county attorneys' information; fire rescue reports; decision of neutral adjudicators rendered in teacher termination hearings; and prenegotiations materials relative to collective bargaining, as well as working papers and studies.

KANSAS

Kansas' Open Records law is contained in Kansas Statutes Annotated Sec. 45–205 to 45–213.

Any person may see them.

Who is covered: State or any political or tax subdivision of the state, or any office, officer, agency, or instrumentality thereof, or any other entity receiving or expending and supported in whole or in part by public funds appropriated by the state or by public funds of any political subdivision of the state.

What is covered: Any recorded information, regardless of form or characteristics, which is made, maintained or kept by or in the possession of a public agency.

Exemptions: (1) Records the disclosure of which is prohibited by state or federal law; (2) records privileged under the rules of evidence; (3) medical, psychiatric, psychological or drug treatment records; (4) personnel records; (5) identities of informants and undercover agents; (6) letters of reference library, archive and museum material contributed with limitations; (7) information on private donors; (8) exam data; (9) criminal investigation records; (10) civil litigation and administrative adjudication records; (11) security records; (12) appraisals of property, feasibility estimates; (13) correspondence between agency and private parties; (14) employer-employee negotiations; (15) software prepared by private person; (16) well samples, logs and surveys; (17) preliminary materials in which opinions are expressed; (18) certain legislative proposals; (19) legislative research records; (20) library circulation records; (21) census and research records; (22) attorney work product; (23) records of utility customers; (24) competitive bids; (25) sealed bids; (26) correctional records pertaining to individual inmates; (27) records constituting an invasion of privacy; (28) prospective business records; (29) bidder's list of contractors; (30) engineering and architectural estimates related to public improvements; financial information submitted by contractors.

KENTUCKY

Kentucky's Open Records law is contained in Kentucky Revised Statutes Annotated Sec. 61.870 to 61.884.

Any person may see them.

Who is covered: State and local officers; state departments; legislative boards; county and city governing bodies; school and special districts; subunits of the above bodies.

What is covered: All books, papers, maps, photos, tapes, discs, recordings, or other documentary materials owned, used by, or in possession of the body.

Exemptions: Records that may be withheld: (1) personal information that violates privacy; (2) confidential research and business records; (3) prospective locations of unannounced business; (4) details of possible real estate acquisition; (5) licensing, employment, or academic exams; (6) law enforcement investigation data; (7) notes and correspondence with individuals; (8) preliminary data containing opinions on policy recommended or formulated; (9) records confidential by federal or state law.

Other statutory exemptions: Other records are expressly made confidential by Kentucky statutes. These include papers filed with the Judicial Retirement and Removal Commission (Supreme Court Rule 4.1301) and public assistance records (205.177).

Specific records held closed under the law include: Public library registration and circulation records and policy-procedure manuals of a jail.

LOUISIANA

Louisiana's Open Records law is contained in Louisiana Revised Statutes Annotated Sec. 44:1 to 44:37.

Any person of the age of majority may see them.

Who is covered: Any instrumentality of state, parish or municipal government, including committees and advisory boards and public or quasi-public nonprofit corporations.

What is covered: All documentary materials used in the conduct of any business performed under the authority of the constitution, state law or ordinance.

Exemptions: (1) Tax return information; (2) public assistance records; (3) confidential business information in the hands of state officer; (4) financial institution records; (5) reports filed by insurance companies with the state Casualty and Surety Rating Commission; (6) records in control of Supervisor of Public Funds; (7) records in control of State Board of Medical Examiners; (8) confidential mineral reports received by Department of Conservation; (9) records concerning fitness of any person to hold nursing license.

Other statutory exemptions: Other sections of the chapter also provide for exemptions. These are: (1) records involved in legislative investigations (44.2); (2) certain law enforcement records (44.3); (3) records in the custody of the governor (44.5); (4) medical records prepared by public hospitals and other public institutions (44.7); (5) documents filed with the Judiciary Commission (44.12); and (6) records covering public disease investigation (43.3(7)).

Access to law enforcement records is governed by Sect. 44:3. Records of which disclosure is not required are: (1) records pertaining to pending or reasonably anticipated criminal litigation until the litigation is over or has been settled; (2) records containing or which would tend to reveal the identity of a confidential source of information; (3) records containing security procedures or internal security information; (4) arrest records of a person until a final judgement of conviction or the acceptance of a guilty plea, except for booking records, records of the issuance of a summons or citation, and records of the filing of a bill of information; (5) records containing or that would tend to reveal the identity of an undercover police officer; and (6) records concerning status defenders.

MAINE

Maine's Open Records law is contained in Maine Revised Statutes Annotated Title I, Sec. 401–410.

Every person may see them.

What is covered: Any written, printed or graphic matter from which information can be obtained, in the possession of an agency or public official of the state or any political subdivision used in the transaction of public business.

Exemptions: (1) Records confidential by law; (2) privileged records in court proceedings; (3) legislative papers and records used to prepare reports for consideration during the biennium in which they are prepared; (4) materials prepared exclusively for labor negotiations; (5) records and papers used and prepared for faculty and administrative committees of the University of Maine and Maine Maritime Academy not covered by the Open Meeting law.

Other statutory exemptions: (1) Non-conviction data; (2) intelligence and investigative information in certain circumstances: (3) certain criminal and administrative records of the State Police and Bureau of Identification; (4) evaluations and exams of public employee applicants; (5) personnel records of public employees; and (6) information concerning hazardous waste.

MARYLAND

Maryland's Open Records law is contained in Maryland Annotated Code, Article 76A, Sec. 1–6.

Any person may see them.

What is covered: All written documents prepared by any branch of the state government, by any branch of a political subdivision, and by any agency or instrumentality.

Exemptions: Records that may be withheld: (1) certain law enforcement investigation records; (2) exam data; (3) details of state research projects; (4) real estate appraisals made for the state; (5) interagency and intra-agency memos or letters not available to a private property in litigation with the agency.

Records that must be withheld: (1) medical, psychological, and sociological data on individuals; (2) adoption and welfare records of individuals; (3) personnel files; (4) letters of reference; (5) confidential financial, geological, or geophysical data; (6) library, archive, and museum materials on which restrictions have been placed by donor; (7) hospital records related to medical information; (8) school district records; (9) library circulation records; (10) address and phone of public employee, without permission; (11) financial records and non-salary incomes of public employees; (12) professional licensing records of individuals; (13) retirement files and information security manuals.

Section 3(a) mandates the withholding of public records where inspection would be contrary to any state statute, contrary to any federal statute or regulation issued thereunder having the force and effect of law, where inspection is prohibited by rules promulgated by the Court of Appeals or by the order of any court of record, or where the records are privileged or confidential by law. Such records include: court and police records of juveniles (Court Article Section 3–828); information contained in records of birth, death, fetal death, marriage, divorce, adoption, and adjudication of paternity that are kept on file by the State Board of Health and Mental Hygiene (Article 43, Section 14(a)(1)); and hospital records of mental patients (Article 59, Section 19). A mental patient's name is part of his or her hospital records, and therefore information that an individual is a patient in a hospital is not disclosable.

MASSACHUSETTS

Massachusetts' Open Records law is contained in Massachusetts General Laws Annotated C.66 Sec. 10–18.

Any person may see them.

What is covered: All books, papers, maps, photos, tapes, financial statements, or other documentary data made or received by any officer or employee of any agency, executive office, department, board, commission, bureau, division or authority of the commonwealth.

Exemptions: Material exempt by statute: (1) materials related solely to personnel rules and practices; (2) personnel files, medical files and other information that is an invasion of privacy; (3) memos relating to policy positions being developed by agency; (4) notebooks and other materials prepared by employee; (5) investigatory materials of law enforcement; (6) trade secrets and confidential commercial or financial information; (7) proposals and bids until they are opened publicly; (8) appraisals of real estate; (9) the names and addresses of any person contained in an application to carry firearms.

Under Section 18, the chapter does not apply to the records of the general court, to declarations, affidavits and other papers filed by claimants in the office of the commissioner of veterans' services, or records kept by him for reference by the officials of his office.

Under Section 17A, the records of the Department of Public Welfare concerning public assistance and the records of the Commission for the Blind concerning aid to the blind are not open for public inspection. The records of the Department of Environmental Management known as the Massachusetts Natural Heritage Program Data Base are not public records, under Section 17D.

The courts and the attorney general have issued a number of decisions and opinions on whether specific records are open for public inspection and copying. Records that may be withheld include: (1) police reports and citizens' letters to police concerning possible criminal activity; (2) reports held by the commissioner of banks concerning the removal of a bank officer; (3) detailed sheets of long-distance telephone calls made by the Legislature; (4) and information relating to alcohol abuse and treatment to be contained in forms for the Management Information System of the Division of Alcoholism.

MICHIGAN

Michigan's Open Records law is contained in Michigan Statutes Annotated Subsec. 4.1801(1) to Subsec. 4.1801(13a).

All persons may see them.

Who is covered: A state officer, employee, agency, department, division, bureau, board, commission, council, authority, or other body in the executive branch of the state government, but does not include the governor or lieutenant governor, or employees thereof; an agency, board, commission, or council in the legislative branch; a county, city, township, village, intercounty, intercity or regional governing body, council, school district, special district, or municipal corporation, or a board, department, commission, council or agency thereof; any other body which is created by state or local authority or which is primarily funded by public funds.

What is covered: A writing prepared, owned, used, in the possession of, or retained by a public body in the performance of an official function, from the time it is created.

Exemptions: (1) Information of a personal nature; (2) investigation records; (3) security records; (4) records exempt by statute; (5) public records exempted by this law given to another public body in connection with the performance of its duties; (6) trade secrets; (7) information subject to the attorney-client privilege; (8) records subject to physician-patient, psychologist-patient, minister or other privilege recognized by law; (9) public bids; (10) appraisal of real property; (11) exam data; (12) medical and counseling records; (13) communication of an advisory nature with a public body or between public bodies; (14) law enforcement plans and codes; (15) archaeological site information; (16) testing data of bidder's products; (17) academic transcripts; (18) records of any campaign committee; (19) police and sheriff's records.

Other statutory exemptions: (1) Foster care records; (2) income tax information; (3) medical research data; (4) sales tax information; (5) social worker's reports.

MINNESOTA

Minnesota's Open Records law is contained in Minnesota Statutes Annotated Sec. 13.01 to 13.87.

Any person may see them.

Who is covered: A state agency, political subdivision or statewide system; the University of Minnesota and any office, officer, department, division, bureau, board, commission, authority, district or agency of the state; any county, statutory or home rule charter city, school district, special district and any board, commission, district or authority created pursuant to law, local ordinance or charter provision.

What is covered: All data collected, created, received, maintained or disseminated.

Exemptions: (1) Data collected by attorneys in their professional capacity; (2) certain data on individuals seeking or receiving benefits or services; (3) records of instructional personnel; (4) law enforcement records of educational institutions; (5) student records relating to employment by an educational institution; (6) student health data; (7) correspondence between individuals and elected officials; (8) exam data; (9) federal contractors' data; (10) firearms data; (11) security information; (12) trade secrets; (13) labor relations information; (14) Department of Health data; (15) investigative data; (16) library data; (17) licensing data; (18) medical data; (19) certain public hospital data; (20) personnel data; (21) certain public employment data; (22) property complaint data; (23) salary benefit survey data; (24) welfare data; (25) real estate appraisals; (26) certain assessor's data; (27) foster care data; (28) certain housing agency data; (29) certain data of the St. Paul Civic Center Authority; (30) sexual assault data; (31) social recreation data; (32) certain attorney general records; (33) corrections ombudsman data; (34) employee relations data; (35) energy and financial data and statistics; (36) public safety data; (37) certain Revenue Department data; (38) worker's compensation self-insurance data; (39) domestic abuse data; (40) certain Transportation Department data; (41) surplus line insurance data; (42) certain law enforcement data; (43) certain medical examiner's data; (44) court services data; (45) certain corrections and detention data; (46) investigative detention data; (47) criminal history data.

MISSISSIPPI

Mississippi's Open Records law is contained in Mississippi Code Annotated Sec. 25–61–1 to 25–61–17.

Any person may see them.

Who is covered: Any department, agency or other entity of the state or a political subdivision thereof, and any other entity created by constitution, order or resolution. All documentary materials having been used, being in use, or prepared, possessed or retained for use in the conduct of any business of any public body.

Exemptions: All other records declared closed by statute.

Other statutory exemptions: (1) Personnel records; (2) attorney work product; (3) confidential information from third parties; (4) certain judicial records; (5) certain jury records; (6) individual tax records; (7) certain appraisal records; (8) academic records; (9) archeological records; (10) certain hospital records; (11) restrictions on access to Bureau of Vital Statistics; (12) certain information concerning ambulatory surgical facilities; (13) investigative and criminal justice records; (14) licensure application and exam records; (15) and commercial and financial records.

MISSOURI

Missouri's Open Records law is contained in Missouri Revised Statutes Sec. 610.010 to 610.120.

Any person may see them.

Who is covered: Any legislative or administrative entity created by the constitution or statutes of the state, including any body, agency, board, bureau, council, commission, committee department or division of the state, or any county or municipal government, school district or special district; any other legislative or administrative government deliberative body under the direction of three or more elected or appointed members having rulemaking authority.

What is covered: Any record retained by or of any public governmental body including any report, survey, memo, or other document or study prepared and presented to the public governmental body by a consultant or other professional service paid for in whole or in part by public funds.

Exemptions: (1) Any record concerning litigation, legal action; (2) leasing, purchase or sale of real estate records; (3) records of the state militia; (4) records of the National Guard; (5) records of non-judicial mental health proceedings; (6) records of personnel or scholastic meetings; (7) records of labor negotiations; (8) records of work product of body preparing for labor discussions.

Records that are closed to the public include: (1) certain coroner reports; (2) certain records of the Commission of Finance; (3) abortion records; (4) arson investigation and insurance records; (5) prisoner conduct records; (6) pre-parole and supervision records of prisoners; (7) certain records of the Department of Corrections and Human Resources; (8) internal reports regarding institutional security; (9) vital statistics and information concerning illegitimacy; and (10) details of all investigations by the Campaign Finance Review Board. The name and address of a victim of crime who can identify an assailant not yet in custody is not a public record.

MONTANA

Montana's Open Records law is contained in Montana Code Annotated Sec. 2–6–103; Article 2, Section 9 of the Montana Constitution.

Every citizen may see them.

What is covered: The written acts and records of the acts of the sovereign authority of official bodies and tribunals and of public officers, legislative, judicial records and other official documents.

Exemptions: (1) Records of university students; (2) unfair trade practices investigations; (3) artificial insemination information; (4) paternity records; (5) certain birth certificates; (6) adoption records; (7) youth court records; (8) parole boards; (9) certain employee records; (10) certain vehicle accident reports; (11) reports of financial institutions to the Department of Commerce; (12) records of aid to dependent children; (13) consumer protection investigation records; (14) certain records of executive branch officers; (15) health records; (16) tax records; (17) certain unemployment insurance records; (18) certain restrictions on vital statistics.

Other statutory exemptions: Agencies are prohibited from distributing a list of persons only if the intended use of the list is for unsolicited mass mailing. Publication of delinquent taxpayer list by county officers is prohibited. Investigations records of the Department of Revenue concerning banks are not open to inspection.

Cities and towns are covered under Montana Code Annotated Section 7–1–4144 and 7–5–4123. Cities may close records, under that section, when privacy concerns exceed merits of disclosure.

NEBRASKA

Nebraska's Open Records law is contained in Nebraska Revised Statutes Sec. 84–712 to 84–712–09.

Any person may see them.

What is covered: All records and documents of or belonging to the state, any county, city, village, political subdivision, or tax-supported district in the state, or any agency, branch, department, board, bureau, commission, council, subunit, or committee of any of the foregoing. This Open Records law is to be liberally construed whenever fiscal records, audit, voucher, invoice, purchase order, payroll, check or any other record of receipt, cash or expenditure involving public funds is involved.

Exemptions: (1) Student records; (2) medical records other than records of births or deaths; (3) records of elections filed under this section; (4) trade secrets, academic and scientific research work in progress and unpublished; (5) work product of attorney in preparation of litigation for body; (6) investigative records; (7) appraisal and negotiation records concerning purchase or sale of real property; (8) personnel information of public bodies other than salaries and directory information; (9) security information; (10) private citizen account payment information held by public utilities; (11) credit information and other information supplied in confidence and customer lists; (12) library records of patrons; and (13) correspondence, memos, and telephone records related to the performance of the duties of a legislator.

Other statutory exemptions: (1) Records of the Commission of Judicial Qualifications or masters appointed by the Supreme Court; (2) records of any medical staff committees; (3) sales and use tax records; (4) income tax records; (5) juvenile records; (6) adoption records; (7) certain records of the pardons and paroles board; (8) certain public assistance information.

NEVADA

Nevada's Open Records law is contained in Nevada Revised Statutes Sec. 239.005 to 239.330.

Any person may see them.

What is covered: All public books and records of the state, county, city, district, governmental subdivision and quasi-municipal corporation officers and offices of the state, the contents of which are not already declared by law to be confidential.

Exemptions: Any records of a public library or other library which contain the identity of a user and the books, documents, films, recordings or other property of the library he used. Such records may be disclosed only in response to an order issued by a court upon finding that the disclosure of such records is necessary to protect the public or to prosecute a crime.

Other statutory exemptions: (1) Adoption records; (2) certain prison commission records; (3) juvenile court records; (4) certain vital statistics; (5) medical records; (6) certain criminal records; (7) certain divorce records.

NEW HAMPSHIRE

New Hampshire Open Records law is contained in New Hampshire Revised Statutes Annotated Sec. 91–A:1 to 91–A:8.

Every citizen may see them. The right to inspect does not depend upon a need for information.

What is covered: There is no definition of "public record." Every citizen has the right to inspect all public records. After completion of a meeting of covered bodies, every citizen has the right to inspect all notes, materials, tapes or other sources used for compiling the minutes of such meetings and to make copies of the information.

Exemptions: (1) Grand and petit juries; (2) parole and pardon boards; (3) personal school records; (4) records pertaining to internal personnel practices, confidential, commercial or financial information, personnel, medical, welfare and other files whose disclosure would constitute an invasion of privacy.

Other statutory exemptions: (1) Certain unemployment compensation records; (2) child abuse records; (3) support of dependent children records; (4) adoption records; (5) alcohol and drug abuse records; (6) certain bank records; (7) Cancer Commission records; (8) child placement records; (9) records of dangerous sex offenders; (10) certain Insurance Department records; (11) records of malpractice claims; (12) meat inspection records; (13) National Guard reports; (14) certain records of rest homes and certain tax information.

NEW JERSEY

New Jersey's Open Records law is contained in New Jersey Statutes Annotated Sec. 47:1A–1 to 47:1A–4.

Every citizen of the state may see them.

Who is covered: Any board, body, agency, department, commission or official of the state or of any subdivision thereof, or any public board, body, commission or authority created pursuant to law by the state or any of its political subdivisions.

What is covered: All records which are required by law to be made, maintained or kept on file.

Exemptions: Records that are confidential by other state, local or federal law, statute, resolution, executive order, rule of court or regulation. Records of investigations in progress shall be confidential if in the public interest.

Other statutory exemptions: (1) Trade secrets; (2) child abuse records; (3) alcoholism treatment records; (4) resident records of those living in boarding facilities; (5) cancer incidence reports; (6) certain records of the Casino Control Commission; (7) child custody records; (8) discriminatory practices investigation records; (9) records concerning domestic violence; (10) family court records; (11) fire investigation and insurer's reports; (12) Health Department research studies; (13) audits of life insurance companies; and (14) certain labor records.

NEW MEXICO

New Mexico's Open Records law is contained in New Mexico Statutes Annotated Sec. 14–2–1 to 14–2–3.

Every citizen of the state may see them.

Who is covered: Bodies of state, county, school, city, or town.

What is covered: All public records of the state.

Exemptions: (1) Records pertaining to physical or mental exams and medical treatments of persons confined to an institution; (2) letters of reference concerning employment, licensing or permits; (3) letters or memos which are matters of opinion in personnel files or student files; (4) records declared confidential by other law; (5) records under the Confidential Materials Action Section 14–3A–1.

Other statutory exemptions: (1) Certain historical or educational material; (2) arrest record information; (3) attorney disciplinary records; (4) certain health information; (5) children's records; (6) crime victim reparation records; (7) mental illness records; (8) certain public assistance records; and (9) certain vital statistics.

NEW YORK

New York's Open Records law is contained in New York (Public Officers) Sec. 84 to 90 (McKinney).

The public may see them.

Who is covered: Any state or municipal department, board, bureau, division, commission, committee, public authority, public corporation, council, office or other governmental entity performing a governmental or proprietary function for the state or any one or more municipalities thereof, except the judiciary or the state legislature.

What is covered: Any information kept, held, filed, produced or reproduced by, with or for an agency or the state legislature, in any physical form whatsoever including reports, statements, exams, memos, opinions, folder, files, books, manuals, pamphlets, forms, papers, designs, drawings, maps, photos, letters, microfilms, computer tapes or discs, rules, regulations and codes.

Exemptions: (1) Records exempted by state and federal law; (2) records if disclosed would constitute an unwarranted invasion of privacy; (3) records if disclosed would impair contract awards and collective bargaining; (4) trade secrets; (5) certain law enforcement records; (6) exam data.

NORTH CAROLINA

North Carolina's Open Records law is contained in North Carolina General Statutes Sec. 132–1 to 132–9.

Any person may see them.

Who is covered: Every public office, commission, bureau, council, department, authority or other unit of government of the state or of any county, unit, special district or other political subdivision of government.

What is covered: All documents, papers, letters, maps, books, photos, films, sound recordings, electronic data-processing records, artifacts or other documentary material made or received pursuant to law or ordinance in connection with the transaction of public business. Also includes records that are kept in carrying out lawful duties.

Exemptions: Confidential communications by legal counsel to a public board or agency.

Other statutory exemptions: (1) State personnel files; (2) adoption records; (3) attorney discipline records; (4) certain bank records; (5) child support records; (6) commercial feed information; (7) unemployment claims; (8) grand jury records; (9) communicable disease records;

(10) records of mental patients; (11) juvenile court records; (12) certain insurance examinations; (13) National Guard records; (14) probation records; (15) social services records; (16) tax records; (17) records of students with special needs; (18) high school competency exams; (19) certain student test scores.

Records held closed by interpretation include sheriff's investigative material and memos and forms maintained by law enforcement officers.

NORTH DAKOTA

North Dakota's Open Records law is contained in North Dakota Century Code Sec. 44-04-18 and Article XI, Sec. 6, of the North Dakota Constitution.

What is covered: All records of public or governmental bodies, boards, bureaus, commissions or agencies of the state or any political subdivision of the state or organizations or agencies supported in whole or in part of public funds or expending public funds.

Exemptions: (1) Vital statistics; (2) abortion records; (3) aid to dependent children records; (4) air pollution records; (5) pardon reports and records; (6) child abuse reports; (7) predisposition records and reports to judges; (8) crippled children's birth records; (9) certain labor records; (10) family court counselor files; (11) foster home records; (12) health department studies; (13) medical review records; (14) mental patient records; (15) legislative investigation records; (16) maternity home records; (17) motor vehicle accident reports; (18) certain public assistance records; (19) records of school counselors; (20) student records; (21) veterans' records; (22) certain workmen's compensation records; (23) investigation files of fire marshal.

The right of access to police information does not include matters of purported confessions, speculations of guilt, officer views, informants and their statements, and certain test results. Further, personal history and arrest records should not be open.

OHIO

Ohio's Open Records law is contained in Ohio Revised Code Annotated Sec. 149.43; 149.43.1.

Covers: Any governmental unit including, but not limited to, state, county, city, village, township or school district units. Any record that is required to be kept by any government unit.

Exemptions: (1) Medical records, (2) adoption records, (3) parole records, (4) trial preparation records, (5) confidential law enforcement investigatory records and (6) confidential records as defined by state or federal law. "Confidential law enforcement investigatory record" means any record that pertains to a law enforcement matter of a criminal, quasi-criminal, civil or administrative nature, but only to the extent that the release of the record would create a high probability of disclosure of any of the following: identity of a suspect or of an information source or witness; information provided by a source; specific confidential investigatory techniques; information that would endanger the life or safety of law personnel, a victim, witness or source.

Other statutory exemptions: (1) Information submitted to the Bureau of Employment Service; (2) adult abuse records; (3) statistics re veterans' exposure to caustic agents; (4) victim impact statements; (5) juvenile court records; (6) tax information and sealed records of convictions.

OKLAHOMA

Oklahoma's Open Records law is contained in Oklahoma Statutes Annotated Title 51, Sec. 24 (West 1982).

The citizens and taxpayers of the state may see them.

Who is covered: Every public official of the state and its subdivisions who are required by law to keep public records pertaining to their offices.

Exemptions: Income tax returns filed with the Oklahoma Tax Commission; other records required by law to be kept secret.

Other statutory exemptions: (1) Abortion records; (2) adoption records; (3) alcohol rehabilitation records; (4) certain bank records and reports; (5) child abuse reports; (6) certain information of dangerous substances research; (7) complaints filed with correctional institutions; (8) records of the deferred prosecution program; (9) grand jury evidence; (10) mental patient case records; (11) certain hospital records; (12) income tax records; (13) records of judicial complaints; (14) certain legislative records; (15) motor vehicle accident reports; (16) certain student records; (17) unemployment compensation records; (18) certain vital statistics.

Records held closed by interpretation include: (1) records used for internal detection and investigation of crimes; (2) warrant register checks issued on workmen's compensation claims by the State Insurance Fund; (3) criminal histories; (4) state criminal records of Oklahoma State Bureau of Narcotics and Dangerous Drugs.

OREGON

Oregon's Open Records law is contained in Oregon Revised Statutes Sec. 192–410.

Every person may see them.

Who is covered: Every state officer, agency, department, division, bureau, board, commission; every county and city governing body, school district, municipal corporation, and any board, department, commission, council or agency thereof; and any other public agency of this state.

What is covered: Any writing containing information relating to the conduct of the public's business, prepared, owned, used, retained by public body regardless of physical form or characteristics.

Exemptions: Public records exempt from disclosure because of age include: records less than 75 years old which contain information about mental or physical health of a living individual; records less than

75 years old which were sealed in compliance with statute or court order; records of people in custody or supervised by a state agency, court or unit of government for a period of 25 years after termination of custody; student records required by law to be exempt from disclosure.

The following records are exempt from disclosure unless the public interest requires disclosure: (1) litigation records of public bodies; (2) trade secrets; (3) investigatory information; (4) test questions, scoring key and other data used to administer a licensing, employment or academic exam; (5) product, sale or purchase business records; (6) appraisal of real estate before acquisition; (7) names and signatures of employees who sign authorization cards or petitions requesting representation; (8) unfair labor practices charges; (9) circulation records of public libraries.

The following records are exempt from disclosure: (1) communication with a public body or between bodies of an advisory nature; (2) information constituting an invasion of privacy; (3) information submitted to a public body in confidence; (4) information records of the Corrections Division, including the State Board of Parole; (5) records received or compiled by the Superintendent of Banks; (6) certain records made or filed with the courts; (7) public records the disclosure of which is prohibited by federal law or regulation; (8) performance records; (9) records of the Energy Facility Siting Council concerning security.

Other statutory exemptions: (1) Records of the Commission of Judicial Fitness; (2) expulsion records of students; (3) child abuse records; (4) juvenile records; (5) mortality studies; (6) birth and death certificates; (7) certain state fire marshal records; (8) motor vehicle accident reports; (9) employer account records; (10) unemployment insurance records; (11) bank examinations; (12) adoption records; (13) paternity records; (14) corporate tax information; (15) prison inmate medical records; (16) personal property tax returns; (17) community college student and facility records; (18) vocation rehabilitation records; (19) teacher evaluations and personnel files; (20) medical records; (21) private financial records.

PENNSYLVANIA

Pennsylvania's Open Records law is contained in Pennsylvania Consolidated Statutes Annotated Title 65, Sec. 66.1 to 66.4.

Any citizen of the commonwealth may see them.

Who is covered: Any department, board, commission of the executive branch of the commonwealth, the Pennsylvania Turnpike Commission, or any state or municipal authority or similar organization created by or pursuant to a statute which declares in substance that such organization performs an essential governmental function.

What is covered: Any account, voucher or contract dealing with the receipt or disbursement of funds by an agency or its acquisition, use or disposal of services or of supplies, materials, equipment or other property and any minute, order or decision by an agency fixing the personal or property right, privileges, immunities, duties or obligations of any person or group of persons.

Exemptions: "Public records" does not include any report, communication or other paper, the publication of which would disclose the institution, progress or result of an investigation undertaken by the agency in the performance of its official duties or record, document, material, exhibit, pleading, report, memo or other paper, access to or the publication of which is prohibited, restricted or forbidden by statute, law or order or decree of court, or which would operate to the prejudice or impairment of a person's reputation or personal security, or which would result in the loss to the commonwealth or any of its subdivisions of federal funds, "excepting therefrom however the record of any conviction for any criminal act."

Other statutory exemptions: (1) Criminal history records; (2) records of the Judicial Inquiry and Review Board; (3) records of the Pennsylvania Crime Commission; (4) records of the State Ethics Commission; (5) certain public assistance records.

RHODE ISLAND

Rhode Island's Open Records law is contained in Rhode Island General Laws Sec. 38-2-1 to 38-2-12.

Every person may see them.

Who is covered: Any executive, legislative, judicial, regulatory, administrative body of the state or any political subdivision thereof; including, but not limited to any department, division, agency, commission, board, office, bureau, authority, any school, fire or water district, or other agency of Rhode Island state or local government which exercise governmental functions, or any other public or private agency, person, partnership or business entity acting on behalf of any public agency.

What is covered: All documents, papers, letters, maps, books, tapes, photos, films, sound recordings, or other materials regardless of physical form or characteristics made or received pursuant to law or ordinance or in connection with the transaction of official business by any agency.

Exemptions: The following are not public records: (1) all records which identify an individual applicant for benefits, clients, patient, student, or employee; (2) including personnel, medical, welfare, pupil records; (3) trade secrets and commercial and financial information; (4) child custody and adoption records maintained by law enforcement agencies; (5) any records not available by law or rule of court to an opposing party in litigation; (6) charitable contributions requesting anonymity; (7) collective bargaining; (8) any records of a discussion allowed to be held in executive session; (9) preliminary drafts, notes, impressions, memos, working papers and work products; (10) test questions and other examination data; (11) correspondence to elected officials in their official capacities; (12) real estate appraisals and engineering feasibility estimates; (13) all tax returns.

Other statutory exemptions: Health care information and Elderly Affairs Department records.

SOUTH CAROLINA

South Carolina's Open Records law is contained in South Carolina Code Annotated Sec. 30–4–10 to 30–4–110.

Any person may see them.

Who is covered: The same bodies as South Carolina's Open Meetings.

What is covered: All books, papers, maps, photos, cards, tapes, recordings, or other documentary materials regardless of physical form or characteristics prepared, owned, used, in the possession of or retained by a public body.

Exemptions: (1) Income tax returns; (2) medical records; (3) hospital medical staff reports; (4) adoption records; (5) other records required by law to be confidential.

Other exemptions include: (1) certain records of the Board of Financial Institutions; (2) trade secrets; (3) personal information amounting to an invasion of privacy; (4) law enforcement action; (5) investigatory techniques; (6) matters endangering the life, health or property of a person; (7) documents incidental to contracts and proposed sale or lease of property; (8) salaries of employees below the level of department head; (9) correspondence or work product of a legal counsel for a public body, memos, correspondence and working papers of members of the General Assembly and their immediate staffs.

Bodies may also close records by a three-fourths vote of the membership when the public interest is better served by nondisclosure.

Other statutory exemptions: (1) Certain criminal information; (2) Board of Dentistry records; (3) certain labor records; (4) contagious disease records; (5) probation reports; (6) certain information given to the Securities Commission; (7) State Development Board records; (8) TB records; (9) vocational rehabilitation records; (10) workmen's compensation records.

SOUTH DAKOTA

South Dakota's Open Records law is contained in South Dakota Codified Law Annotated Sec. 1–27–1 to 1–27–19.

Any person may see them.

What is covered: "If the keeping of a record or the preservation of a document or other instrument is required of an officer or public servant under any statute of this state, the officer or public servant shall keep the record, document or other instrument available and open to inspection."

Exemptions: Employment examination or performance appraisal record maintained by the Bureau of Personnel.

Other statutory exemptions: (1) Adoption records; (2) birth records; (3) child welfare reports; (4) commercial fertilizer reports; (5) derogatory information; (6) employment information under unemployment compensation law; (7) taxpayer information; (8) hospital inspection information; (9) juvenile records; (10) medical research information; (11) certain payroll information; (12) public assistance records; (13) savings and loan associations; (14) termination of parental relations reports; (15) veterans' files; (16) library records; (17) mineral exploration permit filings.

The following records have been held closed by interpretation; portions of public employee's personnel records; school records; written communication between a city's legal counsel and city officials.

TENNESSEE

Tennessee's Open Records law is contained in Tennessee Code Annotated Sec. 10-7-501 to 10-7-509.

Any citizen of Tennessee may see them.

What is covered: All state, county and municipal records and all records maintained by the Tennessee Performing Arts Center Management Corporation.

Exemptions: (1) Medical records; (2) investigative records; (3) records in the possession of the military department which involve security; (4) student records; (5) records designated confidential; (6) materials confidential by state law; (7) investigative materials of federal agencies; (8) work product of attorneys and journalists; (9) attorney-client communications; (10) appraisal of real and personal property.

Other statutory exemptions: (1) Certain executive records in possession of the secretary of state; (2) abortion records; (3) certain attorney general records; (4) bank examinations; (5) mental illness records; (6) records of the Medical Review Committee; (7) certain savings and loan information; (8) tax records.

Those records held closed by interpretation include criminal reports and certain law enforcement records.

TEXAS

Texas' Open Records law is contained in Texas Revised Civil Statutes Annotated Article 6252-17a.

All persons may see them.

Who is covered: Any board, commission, department, committee, institution, agency, or office within the executive or legislative branch of the state government; the commissioners court of each county and the city council or governing body of each city in the state; every deliberative body having rulemaking or quasi-judicial power and classified as a department, agency, or political subdivision of a county or city; the board of trustees of every county board of school trustees and county board of education; the governing board of every special district; the part, section, or portion of every organization, corporation, commission, committee, institution, or agency which is supported in whole or in part by public funds, or which expends public funds.

What is covered: The portion of all documents, writings, letters, memos, or other written, printed, typed, copied or developed materials which contain public information.

Exemptions: (1) Information confidential by law; (2) information in personnel files; (3) litigation information involving a public body; (4) information that would give an advantage to bidders; (5) real and personal property appraisals and purchase price; (6) drafts and working papers in the preparation of legislation; (7) matters in which an attorney of a public body may not ethically disclose; (8) law enforcement investigation records; (9) private communications of an elected officer which would constitute an invasion of privacy; (10) trade secrets; (11) certain interagency and intra-agency memos and letters; (12) agency reports concerning the supervision of financial institutions; (13) geological information concerning wells; (14) student records; (15) birth and death records; (16) audit working papers of the state auditor.

Other statutory exemptions: (1) Child abuse records; (2) protective service records; (3) certain Banking Department records; (4) delinquent commitment records; (5) Dental Examiners Board records; (6) criminal history information; (7) paternity suit records; (8) personal property tax records; (9) sales use tax records; (10) workmen's compensation claims; (11) venereal disease records.

UTAH

Utah's Open Records law is contained in Utah Code Annotated Sec. 63-2-66.

Any person may see them.

Who is covered: "Public office" means the offices and officers of any court, department, boards, commission, bureau, council, authority, institution or other agency of the state or of its political subdivisions.

What is covered: "Public records" means all written or printed books, papers, letters, documents, maps, plans, photos, sound recordings, and other record made or received in pursuance of state law or in connection with the transaction of public business by the public office, agencies and institutions of the state and its counties, municipalities and other subdivisions of government.

Exemptions: (1) Audit protective services records; (2) child abuse records; (3) income tax returns; (4) certain Insurance Commission records; (5) certain Judicial Retirement Act records; (6) certain Liquor Control Commission records; (7) medical examiner records; (8) motor vehicle accident reports; (9) premarital counseling records; (10) public employee personnel files; (11) sales tax returns; (12) savings and loans association records; (13) state hospital records; (14) Tax Commission records; (15) state Retirement System records.

VERMONT

Vermont's Open Records law is contained in Vermont Statutes Annotated title 1, Sec. 315 to 320.

Any person may see them.

Who is covered: Any agency, board, department, commission, committee, branch or authority of the state or any agency, board committee, department, branch, commission or authority of any political subdivision of the state.

What is covered: All papers, staff reports, individual salaries, salary schedules or any other written or recorded matters produced or acquired in the course of agency business.

Exemptions: (1) Records confidential by law; (2) records which by law can only be disclosed to specific individuals; (3) records which released would violate professional standards and ethics; (4) records which released would violate statutory or common law privileges; (5) criminal investigation records; (6) tax return records; (7) personal documents in personnel files; (8) examination data; (9) trade secrets; (10) lists of names compiled by agencies that if disclosed, would amount to an invasion of privacy; (11) student records; (12) records concerning formulation of policy which would constitute an invasion of privacy if released; (13) appraisal of real estate; (14) litigation records; (15) contract negotiation records; (16) voluntary information gathered before enactment of this chapter; (17) records of interdepartmental and intradepartmental communications; (18) records of the office of internal investigation of the Department of Public Safety.

Other statutory exemptions: (1) Adoption records; (2) consumer fraud investigation records; (3) employer reports; (4) juvenile records; (5) mental illness records; (6) Personnel Department records; (7) welfare records; (8) Vermont Criminal Information Center records; (9) hospital licensing records; (10) inquest records; (11) Judicial Nominating Board records; (12) probation reports.

VIRGINIA

Virginia's Open Records law is contained in Virginia Code Sec. 2.1-341 to 2.1-346.1.

Any citizen of the commonwealth may see them.

Who is covered: Any legislative body, authority, board, bureau, commission, district, or agency of the commonwealth or of any political subdivision, including cities, towns, and counties; municipal councils, governing bodies of counties, school boards, and planning commissions; boards of visitors of state institutions of higher education; and other organizations, corporations or agencies supported wholly or principally by public funds.

What is covered: All written or printed books, papers, letters, documents, maps and tapes, photos, films, sound recordings, reports or other material, regardless of physical form, prepared, owned, or in the possession of a public body or any employee or officer of a public body in the transaction of public business.

Exemptions: (1) Law enforcement data and prisoner records; (2) investigation records of the Alcoholic Beverage Control Commission; (3) state income tax returns, scholastic, medical and personnel records; (4) memos, working papers and correspondence of members of the legislature, governor, lieutenant governor or attorney general or other chief executive officer of any political subdivision; (5) written opinions of city and county attorneys; (6) data for use in litigation or administrative investigations; (7) certain confidential letters and statements placed in educational records; (8) library records; (9) tests and exam data; (10) certain records of the Department of Health Regulatory Boards; (11) active investigation records conducted by any health regulatory board; (12) data recorded and compiled for closed sessions; (13) records of the Department of Aging; (14) coal shipment records of the Virginia Port Authority; (15) contract cost estimates of the software; (16) data compiled by or for faculty or staff of state institutions of learning; (17) financial statements with applications for industrial development financing; (18) lists of registered owners of bonds issued by political subdivision; (19) certain tourism records; (20) confidential information under the Toxic Substances Information Act.

Other statutory exemptions: (1) Abortion records; (2) certain agricultural records; (3) Drug Control Act records; (4) certain medical information; (5) certain insurance information; (6) social services records; (7) vital statistics; (8) local law enforcement records; (9) certain records of the State Board of Elections.

WASHINGTON

Washington's Open Records law is contained in Washington Revised Code Annotated Sec. 42.17.250 to 42.17.340.

Any person may see them.

Who is covered: Each agency

What is covered: Final opinions, policy statements, administrative staff manuals, planning policies and goals, factual staff reports, studies, correspondence and materials relating to responsibilities of agencies, and all public records. "Public record" is not defined.

Exemptions: (1) Personal information of students, patients, clients of public institutions, welfare recipients, prisoner, probationers and parolees; (2) personal information maintained by employers amounting to an invasion of privacy; (3) taxpayer information; (4) investigative records; (5) information revealing the identity of a person who files a complaint with law enforcement if it would endanger the health or property of any person; (6) exam data; (7) real estate appraisals; (8) research data; (9) preliminary drafts, notes and intra-agency memos in which opinions are expressed; (10) records relating to a controversy to which an agency is a party; (11) information identifying an archaeological site; (12) library records.

Other statutory exemptions: (1) Accounting records of special inquiry judge; (2) certain criminal records; (3) bank exams; (4) Judicial Qualifications Commission records; (5) Medical Disciplinary Board records; (6) salary and fringe information survey; (7) sales reports of commercial fertilizers.

WEST VIRGINIA

West Virginia's Open Record law is contained in West Virginia Code Sec. 29B-1-1 to 29B-1-6.

Who is covered: Every state officer, agency, department, including the executive, legislative and judicial departments, division, bureau, board and commission; every county and city governing board, school district, special district, municipal corporation, and any body which is created by state or local authority which is primarily funded by the state or local authority.

What is covered: Any writing containing information relating to the conduct of the public's business, prepared, owned, and retained by a public body. This includes any books, papers, maps, photos, cards, tapes, recordings or other documentary materials.

Exemptions: (1) Trade secrets; (2) personal information that if disclosed would be an invasion of privacy; (3) exam data; (4) investigation records; (5) records exempted by statute; (6) records of undeveloped historical or archaeological sites; (7) certain information of an agency responsible for overseeing financial institutions; (8) internal memos and letters of a public body.

Other statutory exemptions: (1) Motor vehicle accident reports; (2) certain vital statistics; (3) labor dispute records; (4) tax returns; (5) adoption records; (6) Bar disciplinary records; (7) child welfare records; (8) certain medical information; (9) certain hospital information; (10) nursing home patient records.

WISCONSIN

Wisconsin's Open Records law is contained in Wisconsin Statutes Sec. 19.31 to 19.39.

Any requester may see them.

Who is covered: A state or local office, elected official, agency, board, commission, committee, council, department, or public corporate and politic created by constitution, law, rule or order; a governmental or quasi-governmental corporation; any court of law; the assembly or senate; a non-profit corporation which receives more than 50 percent of its funds from a county or a municipality; or a formally constituted subunit of any of the foregoing.

What is covered: Any materials written, drawn, printed, spoken, visual, or electromagnetic information which is recorded or preserved, regardless of physical form or characteristics, which has been created or is being kept by an authority. "Records" does not include drafts, notes, preliminary computations and like materials prepared for the originator's personal use or prepared by the originator in the name of a person for whom the originator is working; materials which are purely the personal property of the custodian and have no relation to his or her office; materials to which access is limited by copyright, patent or bequest.

Exemptions: (1) Records exempt by state or federal law; (2) law enforcement records; (3) computer programs and data; (4) trade secrets.

Other statutory exemptions: (1) Accident reports; (2) adoption records; (3) air pollution control records; (4) child welfare service records; (5) grand juries; (6) family court; (7) health and social service records; (8) illegitimate children information; (9) juvenile records; (10) savings bank exams; (11) TB reports; (12) venereal disease reports; (13) personal property tax returns; (14) public utility accident reports.

WYOMING

Wyoming's Open Records law is contained in Wyoming Statutes Annotated Sec. 16–4–201 to 16–4–205.

Any person may see them.

What is covered: "Public records" includes the original and copies of any paper, correspondence, form, book, photo, photostat, film, microfilm, sound recording, map or other document, regardless of physical form that have been made by the state and any counties, municipalities and political subdivisions and by any agencies of the state, counties municipalities and political subdivisions, or received by them in the transaction of public business.

Exemptions: Inspection contrary to any state statute; inspection contrary to federal law or regulation; inspection prohibited by rules of the Supreme Court or by the order of any court of record. The custodian may deny the right of inspection of the following: (1) investigative records; (2) exam data; (3) details of research projects; (4) real estate appraisals; (5) certain agency memos and records.

The custodian shall deny inspection of the following records: (1) medical, psychological and sociological data on individuals, exclusive of coroner's autopsy reports; (2) adoption and welfare records; (3) personnel files; (4) letters of reference; (5) trade secrets; (6) certain hospital records; (7) school district records of students.

Other statutory exemptions: (1) Motor vehicle accident reports; (2) Judicial Supervisory Commission records; (3) adult protective services records; (4) child endangering records; (5) hospital inspection records; (6) incest records; (7) probation and parole records; (8) certain unemployment compensation records; and (9) use tax records.

INDEX

Accuracy, 13–15, 21, 32, 109, 291
   insuring, 103–4
   in interviews, 101
   and invasion of privacy, 310–11
   in libel suits, 305
   and taste, 322–24
Adams, John, 312
Advertising
   and arts, entertainment reporting, 226
Agenda, 82
   for municipal meetings, 193
Agricultural reporting, 221
Alabama
   Open records laws, 337
Alaska
   Open records laws, 338
Alien and Sedition Acts, 312
"All the President's Men" (Woodward and Bernstein), 262
Alm, Rick
   Pulitzer Prize, 240
American Newspaper Publishers Association, 137
American Press Institute, 20, 21
American Society of Newspaper Editors, 20, 21, 307
   award 1984, 113
Anklam, Fred
   Pulitzer Prize 1983 (reporting), 201–3

Annual reports, 219
"Areopagitica" (Milton), 301
Arizona
   Open records laws, 338–39
Arizona Daily Star, 135
Arkansas
   Open records laws, 339
Arraignment, covering, 186
Arts, entertainment and sports reporting, 225–27
Assignment, the general, 72–73
Associated Press, 8, 154
Associated Press Managing Editors Association, 40, 101
Associated Press Stylebook and Libel Manual, 327
Attribution, 14, 52, 62, 101–3
   hierarchy of, 102–3
   interviewing rules for, 110
   in an investigative story, example, 273–74
   and press releases, 59
   of quotations, 79
Audio story, 67

Bad-news syndrome, 22
Bailiff, 188
Baltimore Evening Sun, 104, 278
   Pulitzer Prize 1985, 212
Barlett, Donald
   "Empire," 120
   Pulitzer Prize, 119

Bayard, Herbert
   Pulitzer Prize, 89
Beats, 144–45
   aerospace, 157–64
   fire, 170–74
   geographic, 144
   jargon used on, 152
   police, 175–82
   press release sources for, 148
   subject area, 144
Belleville (Ill.) News-Democrat, 102
Berkshire Eagle, 249
Bernstein, Carl, 262
Bill of Rights, 300
Bly, Nellie (Elizabeth Cochrane), 263
Bolles, Don, 17
Boston Globe, 19, 278
Brinkley, David, 246
Broadcasting
   as competition, 41
   listener responses, 20–21
   and news analysis, 244–45
   newsroom, organization of, 43
   radio news stories, 65–68
   sensationalism in, 22
The Brookings Institution, 118
"Brown Lung: A Case of Deadly Neglect"
   Pulitzer Prize 1981, 289–96
Brown Lung Association, 291

369

Buchwald, Art, 247
Bullets, 105, 285–86
  to capsulize material, example, 273
  use in series, 294
Bureaucrats, 252–53
Business and economic reporting, 216–21
  sources of information for, 221
Byssinosis (brown lung disease), 290

Caen, Herb, 247
California
  Open records laws, 339–40
"The Camera Never Blinks" (Rather), 22
Carnegie, Dale, 147
Carpenter, Teresa, 92, 302
  Pulitzer Prize 1981 (feature writing), 90–93
Carter, Hodding Jr., 248, 320
Casey, William, 312
Censorship
  Achille Lauro incident, 8
  Chernobyl disaster, 6
  and defining news, 4–5
  John Milton on, 301
  voluntary, 313
Central Intelligence Agency, 312
Charlotte (N.C.) Observer, 289–96
Chicago Tribune, 40
Chronicle of Higher Education, 216
Circulation, 39
Civil suit, 189
Clarity, 65
Cochrane, Elizabeth (Nellie Bly), 263
Codes of conduct, 315
Colorado
  Open records laws, 340–41
Columbia Journalism Review, 290
Columnists. See Opinion writing
Columns and editorials, 245–50
Communication
  importance of presentation, 41
  satellite delivery, 40
  with sources, 38
Competition and ethics, 318
Complaints, 21–24
Completeness
  presentation of conflicting views, 246
Composing techniques, 38
CompuServe, 124

Computers
  circulation lists on, 40
  and copy preparation, 52–54
  databases on, 121, 124–125
  library services, 37
  in newsroom, 33–35
  and tailored newspapers, 40
  writing news stories at, 88
Conciseness, 65
Cone, Maria
  Edward Meeman Award (environmental reporting), 281
Confidentiality, 103, 266
Conn, Robert
  Pulitzer Prize 1981 (public service), 290–91
Consequences of stories, 17–18
Consumer reporting, 222–23
Cook, Chuck, 131–35
  Edward Meeman Award (environmental reporting), 281–82
  IRE awards, 131
  Pulitzer Prize, 119
Cooke, Janet, 324
Cook, Stanton, 40
Connecticut
  Open records laws, 342
Copy desk, 32–33
Copy editing, 64–65
  radio news stories, 67
  symbols for, 53–54
Copy flow, 31
Copy preparation
  alternating paragraph approach, 64
  blending people and paper, 268
  electronic, 52–54
  for interpretive story, 243, 254–55
  for interview story, 111
  for investigative story, 272
  news analysis, 245
  press conference, 85–87
  quotations, 112
  for science stories, 224
  for series, 285–87
  simple news stories, 60–62
  speech stories, 77–79
  team writing, 243
  traditional, 52–54
  traditional, example, 54
County government, 192–93
Court
  of record, 185
  records, 183
  reporting, 184
  systems, 183–86
  U.S. Court of Appeal, 185

U.S. District Court, 185
U.S. Supreme Court, 185
Courts martial, 185
Coverage
  accident, example, 48–52
  advanced meeting story, 79–80
  courts, 182–89
  disaster, 170
  obituaries, 54–57
  press conference, 83–87
  radio news stories, 67
  speech stories, 74–77
  See also Beats
Covington, Howard
  Pulitzer Prize 1981 (public service), 290
Credibility, 85
  and good taste, 319
  improving, 322
  and readers, 319–25
  Two examples (Harry Marsh), 320
  and unnamed sources, 266
Crimes, types of, 185
Crump, Louise Eskridge, 320

Daily (Fairfield, Calif.) Republic, 177
Dallas Morning News, 307
Data bases, 123–26
  Investigative Reporters and Editors (IRE), 124
  kinds of, 124
  wire service, 124
"The Day the Music Stopped" (Hacker), 179–81
Deadlines, 87–93
  deadline writing example, 113
  and organizing a story, 111
"Deadly Smoke" (Cook and Cone), 281
Defamation. See Libel, Slander
Delaware
  Open records laws, 341
Delta (Miss.) Democrat-Times, 248
Dennis, Bob
  Pulitzer Prize 1981 (public service), 290
Dent, Rick, 138, 337
Dilg, Marie, 319
"Disorder In the Courts", 289
District of Columbia
  Open records laws, 341–42
Dobie, J. Frank
  "The Longhorns," 255
Document searches, 119–20
Document sources, 120–24
  annual reports, 129

Index **371**

business competitors, 130
business licenses, 127
city directory, 129
corporation records, 127
court records, 120, 121, 122, 127, 128, 130
driver's licenses, 122
education records, 121
government agencies, 121
inspection reports, 127
investigative reports, 130–31
police records, using, 136
property records, 127
real estate, 121
records, list of types, 267
tax records, 121, 128
travel records, 121
vital statistics, 123, 129
zoning and planning records, 127
See also Reference works, Sources of information
Doughnut (audio story), 67
Dow Jones Newspaper Fund, 28, 42
Drogin, Bob
  Pulitzer Prize 1981 (public service), 290–91
Drummond, Roscoe, 232

Editor and Publisher, 40
Editorializing, 24
Editorials, 247–50
  characteristics of, 248–49
  coordinating with news coverage, 291
  example, 249
Editors
  in broadcast media, 43–44
  city, 30, 31
  copy, 30, 31, 32–33
  investigative, 269
  managing, 30, 31
  news, 30, 31
  newswire, 30
  role of, 4, 23, 29–32, 236
  role as coordinators, 244
  role in series presentation, 291
  and tailored newspapers, 40
Education
  changes in, 210–11
  kinds of, 212–13
Education reporting, 210–16
  example, 214–16
  local school districts, 211–16
Education Writers Association, 216
Edward Meeman Awards (environmental reporting), 281

"8-Year-Old Heroin Addict Lives for a Fix", 33
Eisenhower, Milton S., 234
El Diario-La Prensa, 8
Elements of news, 5–10
  in broadcast media, 43
Ellis, Marion
  Pulitzer Prize 1981 (public service), 290
El Paso Times, 307
Emmerich, John, 307
"Empire" (Barlett and Steele), 120
Ethical considerations, 266
  accuracy, 101
  and advertising revenue, 218–19
  bias, 23, 82, 316
  in business reporting, 220
  confidentiality, 103
  confidential records, 344
  in consumer reporting, 223
  credibility, 20–21
  fairness, 155–56, 265
  honesty, 33, 324–25
  honesty with sources, 109
  identifying crime participants, 177
  in interviewing, 110
  invasion of privacy, 308–10
  libel, 176
  misleading stories, 325
  off-the-record agreements, 103
  organizational compatibility, 319
  protecting sources, 102, 109, 251
  in recording interviews, 104
  in reporting trials, 313–15
  in science and medical reporting, 224
  seeking the truth, 153
  The Society of Professional Journalists, code and taste, 323

Fact sheet, 84
Fairfield (Calif.) Daily Republic, 177
Fairness, 16–17, 110, 182, 291
  and competition, 319
  and the courts, 314–15
  and disgruntled sources, 253
  in education reporting, 216
  improving credibility, 21
  in investigative reporting, 265–66
  in political reporting, 253
Fair trial and free press, 313–15

Farris, Trueman, 40
Feature stories, 83, 157–59, 182
  interviewing, 101
  news, 164
  news, example, 179–81
  timeless, 164
Fire stories, 170–74
  the beat, 170
  content of, 171
First Amendment, 126, 261, 266, 300–302, 308, 311
  and ethics, 317
  limitations on, 176
Flack, 154–56
Florida
  Open records laws, 343
Franklin, Jon
  Pulitzer Prize 1979, 104–7
  Pulitzer Prize 1985 (explanatory journalism), 104–7, 278–79
Freedman, David, 337
Freedom of expression, 300
  and jury information, 314
  limiting, 301–2
  and national security, 311–13
  and obscenity, 311
Freedom of information acts, 81
  Alaska, 137
  in business reporting, 218
  closed door court proceedings, 186
  exceptions, 137–38, 193
  Indiana, 137
  municipal meetings, 193
  Nebraska, 137
  New Mexico, 137
  Open records laws (Appendix B), 337–68
  and police records, 177–78
  recording telephone conversations, 104
  request letter, example, 138–139
  Texas, 137
  using, 136–38
  See also Open records laws
Freedom of the press, 234
  Commission on, 232

Gannett Company, 337
General assignment reporting, 93
General lead, 61, 83
  in radio news stories, 66
Georgia
  Open records laws, 343–44
Ginsberg, Ben, 337
Government, local, 192–98
Government, national, 204

Government reporting
  examples, 196–97, 202–3, 271–72
  tips, 205–6
Government, state, 198–202
  attorney general, 201
  boards and commissions, 201
  budget, 198–99
  governor, 198, 200
  legislature, 200
  Nebraska, 200
  secretary of state, 201
Grand jury, 187, 189
Graves, Richard, 102
Greene, Bob, 266
  Pulitzer Prize 1974, 264
Greenwood (Miss.) Commonwealth, 307

Habeas corpus, 186
Hacker, David, 30
  Pulitzer Prize, 178–82
Hallas, Clark
  Pulitzer Prize 1981, 137
Hall, Jon, 58, 268–69
Hard-copy photography, 40
Hardy, G. Presley, 307
Hargrove, Mary, 128–31, 135, 268, 282
  Pulitzer Prize, 119
Harris Newspaper Group, 22
Harris Survey, 20
Hawaii
  Open records laws, 344
Hayes, David, 108, 153, 196–97
Headlines
  from lead, 49
Henderson, Paul
  Pulitzer Prize 1981 (local reporting), 18, 137, 279
Henry, Chuck, 312
Henry, William A. III
  Pulitzer Prize 1980, 19
Hess, Steven, 118–19
Heywood Broun Award, 287
Hillsboro (Kan.) Star-Journal, 22
Hodierne, Robert
  Pulitzer Prize 1981 (public service), 290–91
Holmes, Oliver Wendell (Supreme Court Justice), 312
Howe, Arthur
  Pulitzer Prize 1985, 18
"How to Win Friends and Influence People" (Carnegie), 147
Hoyt, Clark, 40
Humor in opinion writing, 247
Hustler (magazine), 307

Idaho
  Open records laws, 345
Illinois
  Open records laws, 345
Indiana
  Open records laws, 138, 346
Indictment, 187
Information, public
  newspapers as source of, 41
"Inside the Pasco County Sheriff's Department", 269–74
"Interpretative Reporting" (MacDougal), 233
Interpretive reporting
  compared to editorializing, 249
  in the Kansas City hotel disaster, 236–39
  example of, 240–42
  reservations, 255–56
  techniques, 238, 254
Interviewing, 99–100
  accuracy, 109
  completeness, 111
  examples, 104–8, 113, 178–81
  face-to-face, 96
  group, 96
  guidelines for, 98–99
  organizing, 110–14
  in police stories, 178
  preparation for, 108
  question types, 99
  recording, 108
  techniques for, 100–101, 108–10
  telephone, 96
  using recording devices, 103–4
Inverted pyramid, 50–52, 86
  in multiple incident story, 64
  for obituaries, 56
Investigative reporters, 263–64, 274
Investigative Reporters and Editors (IRE), 108, 118–20, 153
  award, 131
Investigative reporting
  examples, 196–97, 269–274
  the reporter, 263–64
  See also Reference works, Sources of information
Iowa
  Open records laws, 346

Jackson (Miss.) Clarion-Ledger, 202–3, 213–16
James, Jack, 318
"Janet's World", 324
Jargon, 254–55, 317
  when to use, 152

Jefferson, Thomas, 312
"Jimmy's World" (Pulitzer Prize hoax), 324
Johnson, Richard, 196
Journalism Quarterly, 28
Judges, 184
Judgment
  about news worthiness, 12
  and assumptions, 13
  and interpretive reporting, 234
  leads requiring, 49–52
  and objectivity, 15
  and sensitivity, 316
  and truth, 153
  and use of unnamed sources, 266
Jury, 188
  safeguards for fair trial, 314

"The K–9 Cases", 112
Kansas
  Open records laws, 347
Kansas City Star and Times, 108, 153, 170, 172, 178, 196
Kentucky
  Open records laws, 348
Kerg, Charles Scott, 320
Kerr, James, 307
Kidder, Tracy
  "Soul of a New Machine," 165
Kilgore, Barney, 138
Kilpatrick, James J., 320
Krock, Arthur, 232

Law enforcement 176
Lawrence (Kan.) World-Journal, 211
Laxalt, Paul (Senator, Nevada), 307
Layout, 31
Lead, 48, 60–61
  for advance meeting stories, 79, 83
  for disaster story, 174
  feature story, 150–52
  and general assignments, 72
  in interpretive reporting, 243
  for obituaries, 56–57
  quotation in, 150
  for series, 284, 294
  for speech story, 78
  subleads for multiple incident stories, 63
Lexington (Ky.) Herald-Leader, 17
Lexis, 121, 124
Libel, 176, 302–4
  conditions for claiming, 303–4
  costs of suits, 307

defenses, 305-6
justifying, 303
New York Times Co. v. Sullivan, 306
and private persons, 308
Libraries, 123-26
Linotype, 34
Linscott, Roger
   Pulitzer Prize 1973 (editorial writing), 249
Lippmann, Walter, 232, 246
Little Rock (Ark.) Democrat, 17, 268, 287
Little Rock (Ark.) Gazette, 199
Lobbyists, 204
Logo, 292
   Little Rock (Ark.) Democrat, 287
"The Longhorns" (Dobie), 255
Longview (Wash.) Daily News, 90-93
Los Angeles Herald Examiner, 119, 131
Los Angeles Times, 278, 281
Louisiana
   Open records laws, 348
Lowe, Robert B.
   Pulitzer Prize 1981, 137
Luce, Henry, 232

McCarthy, Joseph (Senator, Wisconsin), 232
MacDougal, Curtis
   "Interpretative Reporting," 233
McNamee, Graham, 226
Madison, James, 312
Magnolia (Texas) Potpourri, 307
Maine
   Open records laws, 349
"Making It Fly" (Rinearson), 112-13, 157-67
Manuals, style, 57-58
Marimow, William K.
   Pulitzer Prize 1985 (investigative reporting), 17, 107-8, 112, 262
Marsh, Harry, 320
Maryland
   Open records laws, 350
Massachusetts
   Open records laws, 350
Masterson, Mike, 260, 288
Mayor, 193
"Megatrends" (Naisbitt), 40
Mergenthaler, Otto, 34
Messerschmidt, Al, 184
Meyer, Philip, 316
Miami Herald, 8, 184, 281

Michigan
   Open records laws, 351
Military Media Review, 312
Mill, John Stuart, 301
Milton, John, 301
Milwaukee Journal, 281
Milwaukee Sentinel, 40
"The Mind Fixers" (Jon Franklin), 105-6
Minneapolis Star and Tribune, 119
Minnesota
   Open records laws, 352
Mississippi
   Open records laws, 353
Missouri
   Open records laws, 353
Modem, 124
Montana
   Open records laws, 354
Montgomery, Dennis, 34, 154-57
Moore, Mike, 23
Morgan, Lucy
   Pulitzer Prize 1985 (investigative reporting), 135, 269-74
Morgue (newspaper library), 37, 73
Morriss, Jim, 315
Moyers, Bill, 246
Multiple source story, 79
Municipalities, 192
   attorney, 194
   boards and commissions, 194
   budgeting, 195
   executive, 194
   freedom of information, 193
   management, 194-96
   policy-making bodies, 193
   taxing, 195

Naisbitt, John
   "Megatrends", 40
National Bureau of Standards, 239
National Press Photographers Association, 318
National security
   freedom of expression and, 311-13
Natt, Ted, 90
NBC News, 108, 153, 287
Nebraska, 200
   Open records laws, 138, 354
Nevada
   Open records laws, 355
New Hampshire
   Open records laws, 355
New Haven (Conn.) Register, 269

New Jersey
   Open records laws, 356
New Mexico
   Open records laws, 137, 356
News
   cultural, defined, 4
   defined, 4
   geographic, defined, 5
   role of editors, 11, 23
   role of exclusion in defining, 10-13
News analysis, 244-45
Newsday, 264, 266
News hole, 31, 51
News media
   independence of, 218
   management of, 217
Newspaper Advertising Bureau, 20
Newsroom organization, 29-32, 33
   in broadcasting media, 42-43
   electronic newsroom, 33-35
   traditional newsroom, 35-36
   in transition, 36
News stories
   multiple incident, 63-64
   simple, 60-62
Newsworthiness, 73
   in interpretive reporting, 234
   of municipal actions, 193
   new concepts of, 212
   as defense in invasion of privacy, 310
   and patterns of information, 279
   and press releases, 59
New York
   Open records laws, 357
New York Daily News, 36, 248
New York Herald Tribune, 246, 247
New York Sun, 175, 248
New York Times, 8, 36, 106, 312
New York Times Co. v. Sullivan, 306
New York Times Index, 125
New York Tribune, 89
New York Village Voice, 93, 302
New York World, 88, 89, 263
Nexis, 124
Noise in communication, 18
North Carolina
   Open records laws, 357
North Dakota
   Open records laws, 358
Notes
   backup for recorded material, 103

future file, 114
recorders to supplement, 75
techniques for taking, 75–77
at time of criminal arraignment, 187
Nut (so what) paragraph
in an investigative story, 271–72

Obituaries, 54–57
Objectivity, 15–16, 232, 245, 248, 312–13
Obscenity, 311
Ohio
Open records laws, 358
Oklahoma
Open records laws, 359
Omnibus Crime Control and Safe Streets, 104
Open records laws (Appendix B), 337–68
covering educational institutions, 132–34
Alabama, 337
Alaska, 338
Arizona, 338–39
Arkansas, 339
California, 339–40
Colorado, 340–41
Connecticut, 342
Delaware, 341
District of Columbia, 341–42
Florida, 343
Georgia, 343–44
Hawaii, 344
Idaho, 345
Illinois, 345
Indiana, 346
Iowa, 346
Kansas, 347
Kentucky, 348
Louisiana, 348
Maine, 349
Maryland, 350
Massachusetts, 350
Michigan, 351
Minnesota, 352
Mississippi, 353
Missouri, 353
Montana, 354
Nebraska, 354
Nevada, 355
New Hampshire, 355
New Jersey, 356
New Mexico, 356
New York, 357
North Carolina, 357
North Dakota, 358
Ohio, 358

Oklahoma, 359
Oregon, 359
Pennsylvania, 360
Rhode Island, 361
South Carolina, 362
South Dakota, 362
Tennessee, 132, 135, 363
Texas, 363
Utah, 364
Vermont, 364
Virginia, 365
Washington, 366
West Virginia, 366
Wisconsin, 367
Wyoming, 368
See also Freedom of information acts
Opinion and libel, 306
Opinion writing, 245
conflicting news, 246–47
constraints on, 247
political stance, 246
Orange County (Calif.) Register, 131, 281
Oregon
Open records laws, 359
"Our $213 Million Gift Horse" (Linscott), 249
Ownership of newspapers, 30

Package (audio story), 67
Pagination, 40
Paulu, Tom
Pulitzer Prize 1981 (feature writing), 90–92
Pennsylvania
Open records laws, 360
Pentagon Papers, 312
Phi Delta Kappan, 216
Philadelphia Inquirer, 17, 18, 108, 112, 113, 119, 120, 281, 289, 307
Phoenix, Arizona Republic, 17, 119, 123, 177, 260, 281
Photographers
role in series, 289
Plugs, 148
Police stories, 175–82
criminal coverage, step by step, 186–89
in human terms, 181–82
traffic, 176
Political reporting, 253
Polk, James (NBC News), 108, 286, 287
Pulitzer Prize, 153
Prepared text, 76
Preparing copy. *See* Copy preparation

Press conference, 260
Press kit, 84
Press release, 84
rewriting, 59–60
transforming the, 148–52
Printing Impressions (magazine), 40
Privacy, invasion of, 308–10
categories, 309
defenses, 310–11
Privileged communication
and libel suits, 305
Protecting sources, 317
Public affairs writers, 232
Public Agenda Foundation, 13, 16
Public figures and libel, 306–8
Public officials and libel, 306–8
Public, the, 18–21
Pulitzer, Joseph, 13, 88
Pulitzer Prize, 11
hoax, 33, 324–25
nominations for, 89
Pulitzer Prize winners
Alm, Rick, 240–42
Anklam, Fred (1983, reporting), 201–3
Barlett, Donald, 119
Bayard, Herbert, 89
Carpenter, Teresa (1981, feature writing), 93
Conn, Robert (1981, public service), 290–91
Cook, Chuck, 119
Covington, Howard (1981), 290
Dennis, Bob (1981), 290
Drogin, Bob (1981), 290–91
Ellis, Marion (1981), 290
Franklin, Jon (1985, explanatory journalism), 104–7
Greene, Bob (1974), 264
Hacker, David, 178–82
Hallas, Clark (1981), 135
Hargrove, Mary, 119
Henderson, Paul (1981, special local reporting), 18, 135, 279
Henry, William A. III (1980), 19
Hodierne, Robert (1981), 290–91
Howe, Arthur (1985), 18
Linscott, Roger (1973, editorial writing), 249
Lowe, Robert B., 135
Marimow, William K. (1985, investigative reporting), 107–8, 112

Morgan, Lucy (1985, investigative reporting), 135, 269–74
Paulu, Tom (1981, feature writing), 90–92
Polk, James (NBC News), 153
Reed, Jack (1985, investigative reporting), 135, 269–74
Rinearson, Peter (1984), 112–13, 157–67, 278
Robertson, Nan (1983), 106–7
Robertson, Rich, 119
Steele, James, 119
Tofani, Loretta (1983), 107
Trussell, Robert, 173
Watts, Thomas G., 240
Weaver, Nancy (1983), 214–16
Wilson, Linda (1981), 90
Pulitzer Prize-winning examples
 of beat reporting, aerospace, 157–64
 of beat reporting, fire, 172–74
 of beat reporting, police, 179–81
 of an editorial, 249
 of education reporting, 214–16
 of government reporting, 202–3, 271–73
 of interpretive reporting, 240–42
 of interviewing techniques, 104–8, 178–81
 of investigative reporting, 269–74
 Kansas City hotel disaster, 173–74, 240–42
 Mississippi public education story, 202–3, 214–16

Quality
 in broadcast media, 44
 errors in news stories, 32
 role of copy editor in assuring, 31–33
Quarterly reports, 219
Questions
 for interpretive reporting, 238
 types used in interviewing, 99–100
Questions, six traditional, 48–49, 61, 63–64, 72, 77, 79, 83, 86–87
 and interpretive reporting, 234
The Quill (magazine), 23
Quotation, 62, 76–79, 86, 91
 direct, 101
 in feature stories, 150–52, 164
 in government reporting, example, 202–4
 interview story, 112
 in leads, 150

minimal, example, 113–14
and misquotation, 103
partial, example, 112–13

Radio-Television News Directors Association, 42, 318
Ranney, Dave, 22, 23
Raspberry, William, 22
Rather, Dan, 22
Readers, 244
 as clients, 254
 complaints of, four major, 21
 and credibility, 156–57, 319
 number of, 39
 preferences of, 20
 response of, 19
 role in defining news, 10
 time spent on papers, 19
Reader story (radio), 67
Reed, Jack
 Pulitzer Prize 1985 (investigative reporting), 137, 269–74
Reference works, 124–126
 Biographical References (list), 125–26
 Business References (list), 126
 Chronicle of Higher Education, 216
 Consumer Price Index, 220
 Dictionary of American Biography, 125
 Dictionary of Modern Economics, 221
 Directory of Directories, 221
 Dun and Bradstreet, 221
 Education Writers Association, 216
 Encyclopedia of Banking and Finance, 221
 Gross National Product, 220
 Index of Economic Indicators, 220–21
 Miscellaneous (list), 126
 National Directory of Addresses and Telephone Numbers, (business and government), 37, 126
 The New York Times Index, 125
 Official Washington Post Index, 125
 Phi Delta Kappan, 216
 Standard and Poor directories, 221
 U.S. Government Manual, 221
 Who's Who in America, 121
Reporters, 28–29, 88, 93, 170, 182, 234–36
 in broadcast media, 41–44

characteristics for art reporting, 225
characteristics for interviewing, 96, 109
characteristics for news analysis, 245
competition and cooperation, 205
composing skills, 38
court, 189
developing taste as, 322
educational background for specialized reporting, 217, 219, 235
and ethics, 315–19
investigative, 260–69
job security, 32–33
open mindedness, 114–15
and police reporting, 182
responsibility to public, 316
role of, 4
rules for dealing with sources, 318
writing style and tone, 294–96
Reporting
 educational background for, 220, 224
 interpreting public affairs, 232–36
 specialty, 227
 sport stories, 226
Restatement of Torts, 310
Rhode Island
 Open records laws, 361
Rice, Grantland, 226
Rinearson, Peter, 11, 13–15, 152–53, 210
 Pulitzer Prize 1984, 112–13, 157–67, 278
Roberts, Eugene, 307
Robertson, Nan
 Pulitzer Prize 1983, 106–7
Robertson, Rich, 123
 Pulitzer Prize, 119
Rolling Stone (magazine), 40
Roper Organization, 20
Royko, Mike, 247
Ruch, Tonda, 137

Sacramento (Calif.) Bee, 307
Saint Louis Globe-Democrat, 102
Saint Louis Post-Dispatch, 88
Saint Petersburg (Fla.) Times, 135, 269
San Francisco Examiner, 281
Science and medical reporting, 223–24
 Jon Franklin, 278

scientists as sources, 251
Seattle Times, 18, 112, 137, 152, 210, 278, 281
Seper, Jerry, 123
Series
  advantages of, 281–82
  disadvantages of, 282–84
  organizing material, 287
  reprints as, 280–81
  tantalizing the reader, 287–89
  types of, 279–80
  using photos, 289
  why use?, 278–79
Shield laws, 102
Sidebar, 83, 97–98
Sidle, Winant (Major General), 312
Sigma Delta Chi. *See* The Society of Professional Journalists
Single source story, 79
Slander, 302
Slug, 35, 52
  in radio news writing, 67
Sniff, 264
  example, series, 292
Society of Professional Journalists, 23, 29, 102, 137, 318
  code of ethics, 84
  open meetings and open records laws, 337
"Soul of a New Machine" (Kidder), 165
Sound bite, 67
Sources of information
  about national government, 203
  agenda, 82
  biographical data, 108
  bureaucrats as, 252–53
  business quarterly, annual reports, 219
  Chamber of Commerce, 235
  court records, 183
  dispatcher's log, 174
  and ethics, 317–18
  experts, 235, 239
  experts as, 254
  fire department, 172
  hostile, 265–66
  for interpretive reporting, 250–55
  for interviews, 97
  for investigative reporting, 274
  leak, 152
  morgue, 82, 97
  organizational chart, 152
  the paper trail, 118–19
  people as, 108, 152, 155–57, 251–55

police records, 186
police spokesperson, 175
politicians as, 253
press conference, 260
press release, 79
private interview, 85
public information, exceptions to open access, 120
public information office, 81, 85
public records, 132–35, 269
public relations departments, 219, 253–54
reporters' files, 184
scientific journals, 252
scientists as, 251
secondary, 121–22
speech transcripts, 76
tips, 264
unnamed, 266–67
using effectively, 137
See also Reference works
The Source, 124
South Carolina
  Open records laws, 362
South Dakota
  Open records laws, 362
Springdale (Ark.) News, 315
Steele, James, 120
  Pulitzer Prize, 119
Stone, Vernon, 42
Structure of news stories
  clarity, 65
  conciseness, 65
  inverted pyramid, 50–52
  lead, 48–50
  primary theme, 78
Style
  manuals, 57–58
  and mood setting, 91
  proper names (Appendix A), 331–35
  in radio news writing, 66–68
  spelling list of selected words (Appendix A), 328–35
  and verb usage, 66
  wire service, 57–58
  wire service guide (Appendix A), 327–35
Summary lead, 48–49, 61
  for feature story, 150–52
Sunshine laws. *See* Freedom of information acts
Supreme Court case, libel
  New York Times Co. v. Sullivan, 306

Tailored newspapers, 40
Taste as criterion in reporting, 322–24
Tennessee
  Open records laws, 363
Texas
  Open records laws, 137, 363
Thompson, Dorothy, 232
Throwaways, 151
Thumbsucker (analysis), 245
Timing
  deadlines, 14, 87–93
  deadlines, dealing with, 36–39
  and inverted pyramid structure, 51
  in the legislature, 201
  and radio news stories, 66
  for series, 284
Tips, 264
Titus, Steve, 279
"Today and Tomorrow" (Lippmann), 246
Tofani, Loretta
  Pulitzer Prize 1983 (investigative reporting), 107
Traditional newsroom
  copy preparation, 52–54
Transcripts of speeches, 76
Transition
  among subjects, 77, 79
  in news stories, 111
Trussell, Robert
  Pulitzer Prize, 173
Tulsa (Okla.) Tribune, 119, 128–31, 268, 282
Types of news stories
  advance meeting, 79–83
  advance speech story, 74
  feature, 101, 150–52, 157–59, 164
  fires, 170–74
  general assignment, 93
  hard news, 107
  interview, 96–115
  investigative, 260–61
  news feature, 179
  police, 175–82
  press conference, 83–87
  of radio news stories, 67
  sidebar, 97–98
  speech story, 72–79
Typewriter guerillas (investigative reporters), 262

Ullmann, John, 119
Uniform Code of Military Justice, 176
United Press International, 8

United Press International
  Stylebook, 327
University of Missouri School of
  Journalism, 41
USA Today, 36
Utah
  Open records laws, 364

Van Laningham, Scott, 192, 199
Vermont
  Open records laws, 364
Virginia
  Open records laws, 365
Vital statistics
  as information sources, 123

The Wall Street Journal, 36
Washington (state)
  Open records laws, 366
Washington Journalism Review,
  135

Washington Post, 8, 22, 33, 36,
  107, 262, 312, 324
Washington Post Index, 125
"The Washington Reporters"
  (Brookings Institution study),
  118
Watts, Thomas G.
  Pulitzer Prize, 240–42
Weaver, Nancy
  Pulitzer Prize 1983, 214–16
Weickert, Katherine, 211
Weinberg, Steve (executive director, IRE), 108, 118, 119, 120, 135, 153
Westlaw, 120, 124
West Virginia
  Open records laws, 366
White, William Allen, 320–21
Who's Who in America, 97
WIBW (Topeka, Kan.), 319
Wichita (Kan.) Eagle-Beacon, 40

Williams, Marvin, 287
Wilson, Jean Gaddy, 41
Wilson, Linda
  Pulitzer Prize 1981, 90
Wire service, 124
  style, 57–58
Wisconsin
  Open records laws, 367
Woodward, Bob, 262
Wrap, 67
Wyoming
  Open records laws, 368

"Yassir Arafat Tries to Dodge
  the Bullet" (Zucchino), 113
Yozwiak, Steve, 177

Zucchino, David
  American Society of Newspaper Editors Award, 113

PN 4781 .F73

DATE DUE			
MAR 3 '89			
JUN 16			